Psychology and Medical Care

G. Kent
Department of Psychiatry
University of Sheffield

M. Dalgleish
Department of Psychiatry
University of Sheffield

 Van Nostrand Reinhold (UK) Co. Ltd.

Published by Van Nostrand Reinhold (UK) Co. Ltd.
Molly Millars Lane, Wokingham, Berkshire, England

Library of Congress Cataloging in Publication Data

Kent, G. (Gerald)
  Psychology and medical care.

  Includes bibliographies and index.
  1. Medicine and psychology.   2. Psychology.
3. Medical care — Psychological aspects.   I. Dalgleish, M.
(Mary)   II. Title.   [DNLM: 1. Behavior.   2. Psychology,
Social.   3. Memory.   4. Intelligence.   HM 251 K37p]
R726.5.K35   150   82-6895
ISBN 0-442-30516-8   AACR2
ISBN 0-442-30517-6 (pbk.)

Typeset by Colset Pte Ltd, Singapore
Printed in Great Britain by
The Thetford Press Ltd, Thetford, Norfolk

Psychology and Medical Care

Department of Social and Administrative Studies,
Barnett House,
Wellington Square,
Oxford.

**This book is to be returned on or before
the last date stamped below.**

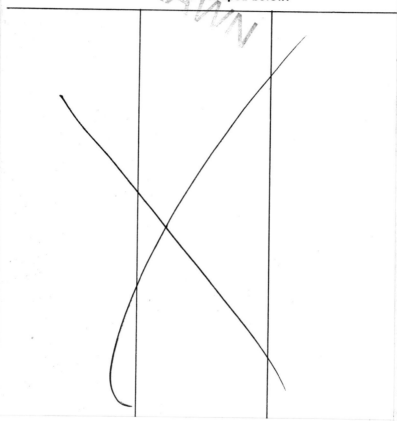

About This Book

This book is an attempt to provide a basic grounding in psychology, presented in such a way as to draw out the relevance of the subject to medicine. Where possible, medical examples are used to illustrate psychological principles and particular attention is given to aspects of medical care, such as the doctor – patient interview and compliance with medical advice. We have tried to present research critically; for example, discussing how a result might be interpreted in more than one way. Our view is that the ability to evaluate 'facts' is as important as the 'facts' themselves. It has been said that medical knowledge has a half-life of about 5 years. The rate of change in psychology may be similar, and we hope the book will provide the reader with some of the skills required to appraise research work in the future. We have attempted to include sufficient source references to enable the reader to pursue aspects of particular interest, either simply for further detail or for research purposes (some medical schools include a small research project as part of their behavioural sciences course).

Ideally, the book would be most usefully read from beginning to end as concepts and methods are introduced and developed as the text progresses. To this end, the book is divided into three sections: psychological processes, human development and doctor – patient communication, the first laying foundations for the second, and both of these adding to an understanding of the third. Inevitably, the boundaries between the sections are to some extent arbitrary and there are also overlaps between chapters. To draw together topics that appear more than once, there is an extensive *subject index* to allow easy cross-reference. We have tried to make the substance of the chapters clear by a *contents* list at the beginning and a brief *summary* at the end of each. Further *suggested readings* are given at the end of the chapters to enable more detailed study of particular areas. We have been selective in the choice of topics, covering those areas that seem, to us, most relevant to the social aspects of medical care. There are many areas of psychology that are not covered. There is, for example, little discussion of physiological psychology, and sleep and dreaming is not mentioned. So that the reader has access to such topics, a short *appendix* on how such information might be obtained from the library is included.

There are many possible ways to understand people. This book concentrates on the contributions of psychology. Although the word 'psychology' literally means the study of the mind, psychologists usually define it as the study of behaviour. The ways in which people behave provide clues about the way the mind works. The viewpoints provided by anatomy, physiology and bio-chemistry are traditionally important in medical care. Others, such as those provided by psychology, sociology and anthropology, also provide useful insights. At different times, one viewpoint may be more relevant than another: the support a patient has from his or her family might be relatively unimportant in the operating theatre but crucial for recovery. These different ways of seeing people are not independent of each other; in concert they provide a more comprehensive picture of what is going on than can be obtained from a single point of view.

We are grateful to the many publishers and authors who have allowed us to quote from their publications.

We would also like to thank the following people who have read and commented on parts of the manuscript: Clare Bradley, Chris Brewin, Peter Clarke, Faye Cooper, Peter James, Alec Jenner, Rod Nicolson, Glenys Parry, Tony Roth, Phil Seager, Peter Smith and Chris Spencer. We would also like to thank David Miller for his help with the appendix. Responsibility for the final version lies with us.

Contents

PART 1
Psychological Processes

1
Making Sense of the Environment

1.1 Introduction

The information a scientist can collect about the environment depends on the instruments available. The arrival of the telescope in Europe, for example, meant that the moons of the planet Jupiter became readily discernible, leading to the downfall of the Ptolemaic (i.e. earth-centred) view of the solar system. The development of instruments sensitive to small variations in the speed of light made the Michelson – Morley experiment possible, calling the Newtonian view of physics into question and opening the way for Einstein. But the analysis and interpretation of the information provided by even the most sophisticated scientific equipment depends on how this information is processed by man himself; in the first example, an individual who believed that the earth was the centre of the universe would look for an alternative explanation for the data collected by the instruments.

The way in which people process information has been studied extensively in psychology and the field is characterized by many and varied theories. One way of viewing the manner in which we process information is in terms of three interdependent phases[1]. This chapter includes a brief description of the first, or sensory, phase but is largely devoted to the second, or interpretive, phase. Some aspects of memory, the third phase, are covered here, others in Chapter 4.

3

Emphasis has been placed on the interpretive phase because this ties in most readily with aspects of medical care considered in the second part of this chapter. Interpretation provides a way in which people can organize and understand incoming information and thus reduce their uncertainty about their environment. The way in which people interpret their world depends on, for instance, past experience and the context in which the event occurs.

1.2 Sensing the Environment

The sensory phase has been studied in several ways. One approach has involved the tracing of neural connections between the sensory receptors (visual, auditory, etc.) and the brain. Here, the concern has been with the ways that the anatomy, physiology and biochemistry of receptors (such as the rods and cones in the eye) affect how the environment is encoded and how the messages are passed along pathways to the cortex. Researchers in this area would be interested in, for example, the anatomy of the retina. A simple demonstration of the presence of the blind spot (where the optic nerve leaves the retina) is illustrated in Fig. 1.1.

Related to this approach is a concern with patterns of neural firing in the brain. Some of this work has involved the recording of single cells in the cortex, exploring the ways in which lines and angles are coded in the brain. Perhaps the best known workers in this field are Hubel and Weisel, who studied the recordings from micro-electrodes inserted into the visual cortex of cats while showing them horizontal or vertical lines. They found that some neurons fired only when a vertical slit of light was presented in the cats' visual fields, others fired when the line of light was horizontal and yet others when the line moved[2]. The patterns of firing were found in specific neurons, suggesting that they had a defined and limited function.

Various techniques have been used to investigate how neural pathways develop, generally involving the study of animals reared in controlled environments. Early researchers reared animals in the dark and found that light deprivation resulted in irreversible damage to the visual pathways. Retinal ganglion cells atrophied, for example. It seems from work of this kind that although the pathways are 'wired-up' from birth, exposure to stimuli is necessary if they are to develop fully. When cats were shown only vertical stripes from birth, they

Fig. 1.1   An illustration of the presence of the 'blind spot'. Cover your left eye, hold the book in front of you and focus on the dot. The X can be seen with peripheral vision. At a certain distance (about 9 inches), which can be found by moving the book closer and further away, the X will disappear. At this point, the light reflected by the X is reaching your 'blind spot'.

were apparently blind to horizontal stripes: both behavioural and electrophysiological measures of these animals indicated little response to horizontal lines. Using Hubel and Weisel's technique of single-cell recording, no neurons could be found that fired to lines oriented at right-angles to the cats' early visual environment. Further, simple exposure to light and patterns alone is not adequate for full development — self-produced movement is also necessary. Held and Hein[3] yoked kittens in pairs, as shown in Fig. 1.2. One kitten was able to move actively, gaining experience about its environment as it moved, while the other, reared in identical conditions in every other way, was a passive recipient

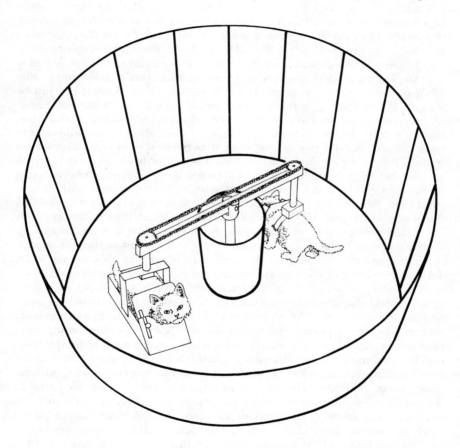

Fig. 1.2 The apparatus used by Held and Hein. The main difference between the kittens' experience was that one kitten could move actively whereas the other was a passive recipient of visual information. (Reproduced from R. Held, 'Plasticity in Sensory-Motor Systems, © (1965) by Scientific American, Inc. All rights reserved.)

5

of visual information. While in the gondola, the kittens moved around a drum patterned by vertical lines; at all other times they were kept in the dark. The tests of development included paw placement (a normally reared kitten will extend its paws as it is held towards a surface) and blinking to an approaching object. The active kittens were able to perform the tests adequately, whereas the passive kittens were not able to do so, suggesting that activity is necessary for the learning of such behaviour. When the passive kittens were allowed to move their limbs in the apparatus, they were soon able to react appropriately, a result that indicated that their neural pathways had not atrophied.

Yet another approach to the study of people's senses has become known as signal-detection theory. One concern has been with the question of sensory thresholds. The intensity of a stimulus can be said to have reached an observer's threshold when he can detect it 50% of the time, but there is no simple relation-ship between detection and intensity. A short experiment can be conducted to test this. Place a clock on one side of a quiet room and walk away from it: stop when it can no longer be heard and then walk back to where it can just be noticed. While standing in this position, the ticking will fade in and out. Some-times it will be necessary to walk closer to the clock in order to hear it and some-times it will be possible to walk further away. The fading in and out is due to spontaneous neural firing in the central nervous system, which generates 'noise'. Whenever a stimulus is detected, it is seen or heard against this back-ground activity. Sometimes a signal will be heard when none is present, some-times a signal will not be heard when it is quite loud. This means that there is no simple on – off threshold in the detection of a light or tone, only a probability that a certain intensity will be identified. The clock experiment illustrates one important conclusion from this kind of research — that it is not possible to specify a person's experience from knowledge of the event or stimulus alone.

These approaches to the study of sensation are not independent of each other. An understanding of the reasons for changes in threshold is enhanced by an understanding of spontaneous neuronal firing, for instance. Nor can these approaches be considered in isolation from higher-level processes such as inter-pretation and memory. An example of their interdependence can be easily arranged by simply putting this book down and listening to the sounds being produced around you. The first notable feature will probably be the large number of sounds, sounds that you probably didn't hear when you read the above paragraphs. You were attending to the reading and not noticing this irre-levant noise. A similar phenomenon can be experienced at a noisy party: in spite of the music and loud voices, it is possible to attend to one conversation out of many. Your attention may be changed if someone calls your name, a partic-ularly meaningful stimulus. A second notable feature of the noises around you is that you will find yourself labelling or interpreting each one. As you listened to each sound, you made sense of it by explaining its source. A series of low-frequency sounds outside the room was translated into someone's footsteps; a high-frequency sound outside, a car's brakes. It is very difficult to hear the sound alone without making some kind of interpretation about it. The sounds are processed to become integrated into a meaningful environment. It is this feature that characterizes the second phase of information processing, in which the data provided by the sensory systems are given meaning.

1.3 Interpreting the Environment

It is often difficult to appreciate that the environment is not only sensed but also interpreted. Most of the objects we see are unambiguously one thing or another, and we have no apparent difficulty in making sense of them. A chair is obviously a chair after all. However, the ease with which interpretations are made is an indication of the familiarity of most objects we encounter in our daily lives, rather than evidence for a simple and direct link between sensation and understanding.

The process of interpretation can be illustrated in several ways; one way is to provide only a portion of the information which is usually present about some object and ask people to try and make sense of it. Fig. 1.3a may appear to be a random jumble of fragments with no obvious meaning. It is instructive to spend some time in trying to make sense of the figure.

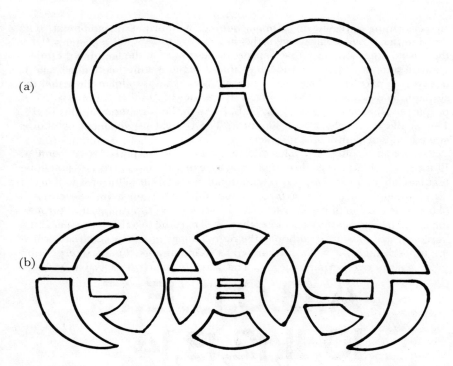

(a)

(b)

Fig. 1.3   It is difficult to see what (a) represents without the additional information given in (b).

However, when the information shown in Fig. 1.3b is superimposed on these fragments (for instance by tracing Fig. 1.3b on thin paper and moving it up the page until the gaps in Fig. 1.3a are occluded) their organisation becomes apparent. This process of fitting together apparently unconnected pieces of information to make a meaningful picture is one which is constantly being performed in daily life. For example, an individual might be concerned with piecing together the reactions of other people in order to develop an idea of how he or she is seen by others. The process of diagnosis is another example. Initially, a number of seemingly unconnected complaints may be presented by a patient. These symptoms are explored, additional information is gathered and past experience consulted. Some kind of overall link which connects the previously unrelated symptoms together is sought. These links are hypotheses which are tested through further questioning and physical examination. In a difficult case — i.e. where the link is difficult to find — others' views of the condition might be sought in order to make the interpretation. The aim of the following sections is to consider the importance of context, past experience and selective attention during this interpretative process.

Context

In performing a dissection a major source of information is context. The decision that a particular nerve is the one you are looking for is made easier if there is no other structure that appears more similar to the textbook example. Context provides a pattern into which the ambiguous stimulus can be fitted. It does this in part by arousing expectations about what is to follow, whether the situation is dissection or, as in Fig. 1.4, a series of numbers or letters. Most people read the top line as A, B, C, D, E, F and the bottom line as 10, 11, 12, 13, 14, yet the B and the 13 are identical. The context in which the symbol is embedded determines how it is 'seen'.

Psychologists often use illusions to explore the importance of context. Illusions are objects or pictures that encourage the viewer to perceive something that is really non-existent. Representational paintings are illusions, in that the artist attempts to portray a three-dimensional space on a two-dimensional plane. The illusion of depth is achieved in several ways, but primarily through the use of perspective (parallel lines that seem to come together and meet at the horizon), size constancy (although the retinal image of an object varies according to its distance, it is not interpreted as changing in size) and interposition (near objects overlap far objects). The ways in which perspective and size

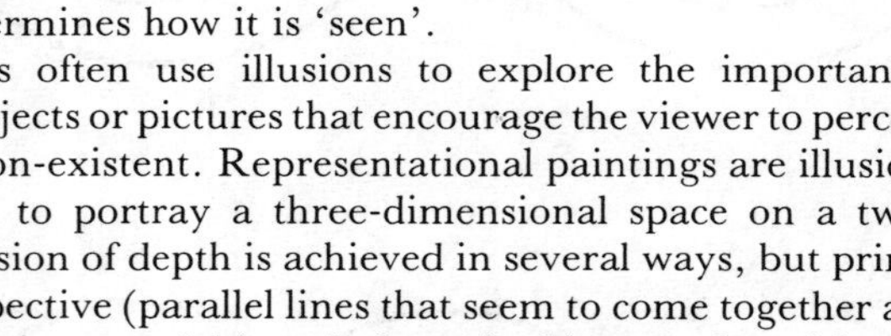

A, B, C, D, E, F
10, 11, 12, 13, 14

Fig. 1.4   The effect of context on recognition. The same symbol is identified as 'B' or '13' depending on its context.

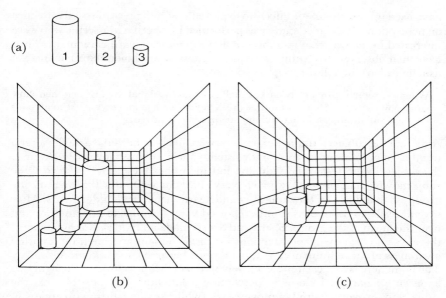

(a)

(b)   (c)

Fig. 1.5   The perceived volumes of the cylinders vary according to the lines of perspective. (Reproduced from P.H. Lindsay and D.A. Norman, *Human Information Processing***, 1972, by permission of Academic Press, Inc.)**

interact are shown in Fig. 1.5. Fig. 1.5a indicates the relative size of three cylinders. But the same two-dimensional drawings take on different meanings when context is added. In Fig.1.5b cylinder 1 looks very much bigger than cylinder 3, whereas in Fig. 1.5c cylinders 1 and 3 appear to be about the same size. Perspective indicates that cylinder 3 is further away, so that the volume of both appears to be equal. The context has changed the perception.

Context is not limited to visual features. The likelihood of interpreting a patient's complaint as psychological or organic may depend on his social class, part of the context of diagnosis. Fielding and Evered[4] taped interviews between a doctor and an actor playing a patient. In one condition, the actor used a middle-class accent during the interview, and in the second condition he used a working-class accent. These versions of the same interview were presented to different groups of listeners who were asked to indicate the probable cause of the complaint (a possible heart disorder). The same symptoms were seen as being more likely to be psychosomatic in origin when they were presented in a middle-class accent than when they were presented in a working-class accent. Speech cues apparently provided a context that led the listeners to expect different aetiologies.

Other people can also influence the way an object is interpreted, particularly if the stimulus is at all ambiguous. A dim light in a dark room will appear to move erratically if it is looked at steadily for a period of time. Some researchers

9

have used this 'auto-kinetic effect' to explore the significance of social influence on perception. The classic study was performed by Sherif and Sherif[5], who were interested in the way that members of a group move toward agreement. They gave their observers (or 'subjects' as participants in psychology experiments are usually called) the following instructions:

> When the room is completely dark, I shall give you the signal 'Ready' and then show you a point of light. After a short time the light will begin to move. A few seconds later the light will disappear. Then tell me the distance it moved.

Although the subjects' initial judgements were likely to be very variable, after a number of occasions (or 'trials') consistent values were usually given. At first, the subjects were tested individually, but then Sherif and Sherif placed three subjects who had previously given very different estimates together in one group, so that they saw the same light and heard each other's judgements. After several trials all three consistently reported values similar to one another and near the mean of the group. Sherif and Sherif made no requests for agreement, there was no argument, no sanctions for disagreement and often no reported awareness of social influence. Yet, the reports became more and more similar. The point here is that each subject's perception of the movement of the light was apparently changed by others' perceptions. Although it is possible that the subjects only *reported* similar movements (while keeping their perception to themselves), this is unlikely given that they were generally unaware of how the guesses of the other people in the experiment influenced their estimates.

In this study, Sherif and Sherif placed three people together to see what occurred. As it happened, everyone had an influence on each other. However, it was not possible to control these influences in any systematic way, so Sherif and Sherif could not specify the nature of any effects. When they wanted to explore the influence of someone who consistently estimated differently from those in the study, they had to have someone working with them who could be instructed how to behave. A 'confederate' of the experimenter was introduced in the next study, a person who was instructed to make his estimates consistently higher or lower than those of the other person in the experiment. On any one trial, the subject gave his estimate and then the confederate gave a higher (or lower) 'guess'. After several trials, the subjects gave estimates that were more and more similar to those of the confederate than they were in the beginning. By the end of the series of trials, the subjects' estimates were very similar to the confederate's. The unfortunate aspect of this procedure is that it involves deception by pretending that the confederate is also a naive subject. The experimenter manipulates the subject's environment in ways the subject cannot recognize. Psychologists who use this procedure emphasize that they tell their subjects about the deception after the experiment and explain why it was necessary. In this last experiment, the subject was presented with both an ambiguous stimulus and someone who was very sure of himself, even though he appeared to have the same information. As a result, the subject's reports tended to conform to those of the confederate.

Another way in which context plays a role in perception has been termed the

10

'halo effect' — the tendency to generalize from one attribute to a number of others. Physical appearance seems to be a particularly important characteristic. Dion[6] asked university students to judge the misbehaviour of young children, some being physically attractive, others less so. The attractive children were judged less harshly than the unattractive children, with more lenient punishments recommended for the same behaviour. It seemed that physical attractiveness modified the students' perceptions of why the children misbehaved. Several other assumptions are also made about attractive people, including the expectation that they will obtain more prestigious occupations and have happier marriages. There is also evidence that this 'beautiful is good' stereotype affects the first impressions of health professionals. Many medical staff were asked to indicate their impressions of patients shown in a series of photos. In some cases the photos depicted a physically attractive man or woman, in other cases the individual shown was unattractive. On 12 of the 15 scales used, the medical and paramedical staff indicated more positive impressions of the attractive people than the unattractive ones. For example, they were taken to be more responsible, more motivated and more likely to improve. There were no differences between the professionals, doctors being just as likely to make these assumptions as were the paramedical staff[7].

Generalizations about people on the basis of those they associate with is another example of the halo effect. In one experiment, subjects were shown a silent film of a couple talking. The man was said to be the boyfriend of the woman in the film. In some films, she was made-up to look attractive, in others unattractive. The subjects' task was to rate the man's characteristics on a checklist. On virtually every scale, the woman's appearance had an effect: the man was rated as more friendly, intelligent, energetic and physically attractive, for example, when the woman was attractive. The favourable characteristics of one person were attributed to both members of the couple. These experimenters also manipulated the woman's perceived intelligence by telling the subjects that she was either a waitress or a medical student. This condition had much less effect on the subjects' ratings, although the man was said to be more intelligent, self-confident and talented when the actress was said to be a medical student[8].

There are some instances in which the use of context can not only change perceptions but also have a detrimental effect. Maguire and Granville-Grossman[9] found that 33% of patients suffered from a physical illness in a sample of 200 admissions to a psychiatric unit, yet it had been diagnosed in only half these patients. Conversely, 23% of a sample of in-patients in medical wards were found to have psychiatric disorders, but few cases were recognized by the medical staff[10]. It seems as though each unit provided expectations about patients that made diagnosis of particular complaints less likely. Another study of psychiatric units illustrates this point in a slightly different way. Rosenhan[11] reported a study in which eight experimenters had themselves committed to various psychiatric hospitals, claiming that they were hearing voices (a symptom often associated with schizophrenia). After admission, these 'pseudopatients' acted in their usual, normal way and the research question was how long it would take before the staff (who were unaware of the study) realized that

11

there was nothing abnormal about these patients and discharged them. In fact, staff recognized none of the pseudopatients (although some patients did) and some experimenters had difficulty in obtaining their release. Part of the difficulty here seemed to be that although people in psychiatric hospitals are expected to be unusual in some way, they often act normally, making it difficult for the staff to distinguish between the real and the feigning patients. Given this ambiguity, the safe course of action in this context was to assume that the experimenters were schizophrenic and should not be discharged.

In these studies, the context of a psychiatric unit or a medical ward appears to have led the staff to expect certain conditions but not others, making some interpretations more plausible than others. Context in everyday situations is similarly based on past experience (either directly or through reports by others) and can be modified by future experiences. This second aspect of the interpretive process is considered in the next section.

Experience

Much of the research on the importance of past experience has been concerned with visual phenomena. One line of evidence is cross-cultural. One researcher lived with the Bambuti pygmies — forest dwellers whose vistas extend to 30 metres at most. On one occasion he took a tribesman onto a broad plain with a herd of buffalo some miles away:

> He asked me what kind of insects they were, and I told him they were buffalo, twice as big as the forest buffalo known to him. He laughed loudly and told me not to tell such stupid stories, and asked me again what kind of insects they were. He then talked to himself, for want of more intelligent company, and tried to liken the buffalo to the various beetles and ants with which he was familiar.
>
> He was still doing this when we got into the car and drove down to where the animals were grazing. He watched them getting larger and larger, and though he was as courageous as any Pygmy, he moved over and sat close to me and muttered that it was witchcraft. Finally when he realised that they were real buffalo he was no longer afraid, but what puzzled him was why they had been so small, and whether they had *really* been so small and had suddenly grown larger, or whether it had been some kind of trickery. (Ref. 12, p. 305)

Unfamiliarity with large distances made interpretation of the buffalo problematic for the pygmy. With experience, there is a tendency for the perceptual system to compensate for changes in the retinal image with viewing distance — called *size constancy*. The pygmy had little experience with large distances and therefore did not use size constancy.

Conversely, past experience can mislead an observer about objects. The Ponzo illusion (Fig. 1.6) is an example of how the application of perspective and size constancy can lead to an illusion of length. Because cues for perspective are present (the vertical lines are converging as if they were parallel lines receding into the distance), the top horizontal line appears to be farther away than the lower one. Since they have the same retinal size, the top line 'must' represent a longer one, and this is how it is interpreted. Similarly, several 'impossible

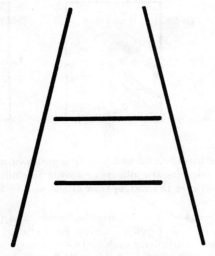

Fig. 1.6 The Ponzo illusion. The vertical lines are interpreted as lines of perspective, so that size constancy is applied to the horizontal lines. The top line appears to be longer than the bottom one, although they are both the same length.

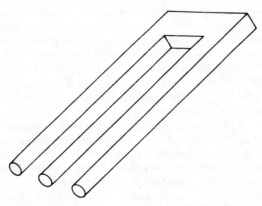

Fig. 1.7 An 'impossible object'. The depth cues in this picture are conflicting, making it difficult to interpret in an integrated way. People unfamiliar with graphic representation have littl difficulty in reproducing this figure from memory. (Reproduced from G Kimble, M. Garmeny and E. Kigler, *General Psychology*, *4th edn.*, 1974, by permission of John Wiley & Sons, Inc.)

(a) (b) (c)

Fig. 1.8 **(a) can be interpreted as a young woman or an old woman, but seeing (b) first predisposes the observer to see the old woman, whereas seeing (c) first encourages the perception of the young woman.**

objects' have been designed that confuse the viewer and make an integrated interpretation difficult. The Devil's Tuning Fork (Fig. 1.7) is an example. Although the object will be difficult to draw from memory for the reader, some Africans with no formal education have little difficulty in reproducing this figure.

A classic example of the role of experience in perception is the young – old woman demonstration. This illustration does not depend on cross-cultural differences and provides an opportunity to perform a simple experiment. Fig. 1.8a can be seen as a young attractive woman or an old unattractive one, depending on how her features are interpreted. Looking at Fig. 1.8b and 1.8c may make these two possibilities clearer. A simple experiment would involve showing Fig. 1.8b to one group of subjects, Fig. 1.8c to another group. In a good experiment the subjects in each group, or condition, would be randomly assigned. This could be accomplished by, for instance, placing all their names in a hat, and as the names are picked out assigning individuals to one condition or another by flipping a coin. Fig. 1.8a would then be shown to all subjects. Those who saw Fig. 1.8b will tend to see the composite drawing as an old woman, while those who saw Fig. 1.8c tend to see the composite as a young woman, showing past experience is important in perception.

In a similar way, a physician's past experience with a patient or with a set of symptoms may lead him to interpret what a patient says in certain ways. One of the first decisions a physician generally makes is to diagnose a complaint as physical or psychiatric, and most doctors tend to exclude the possibility of physical disorders before considering social or psychological problems. In some of the consultations that Shepherd *et al.*[13] examined, it was only when patients failed to respond to medication and continued to complain that doctors began to consider psychological difficulties. Such a course of action on the doctors' part is understandable: since in their past experience most patients have presented them with physical symptoms they are more likely to perceive organic difficulties than social ones, a situation not dissimilar from the old – young woman demonstration. Many difficulties are composite — it has been estimated that

14

40% of consultations between doctor and patient are initiated by patients who present physical symptoms as a way of gaining the doctor's attention in order to talk of more personal matters. If a physician decides that a condition is primarily biochemical in origin, a different treatment will be recommended than if he decides it is psychosomatic. The initial decision determines to some extent the nature of subsequent questions and interpretation of further information. It is this feature of the interpretive process that is considered next.

Selective Attention

The data an observer notices will be influenced by his purposes. Yarbus[14] asked the subjects in his study to look at a photograph, shown in Fig. 1.9a. Eye-movement patterns were recorded and two patterns, from the same subject, are also shown. When the subject was asked to estimate the wealth of the people in the photograph, a pattern such as that shown in Fig. 1.9b was found, but when their ages were to be noted, Fig. 1.9c formed a typical pattern. The subject's eye movements can be seen to be concentrated on the faces or scattered around the room, reflecting Yarbus' instructions.

In a similar fashion, once a tentative interpretation is made — and this generally happens early on in an encounter with an object or a person — there is a tendency to attend to information selectively, to look for data that will confirm the initial interpretation. Much research has been conducted on the notion that people often bring perceptual biases to a situation (a bias generally determined by past experience of some kind) that limits the range of perceptions they make. One example of perceptual bias is called mental set, the tendency to use a solution that has worked well in the past, on problems where this solution is not the best one. The jar problem is a good example of this tendency. Table 1.1

Table 1.1   The Jar Problem

Use the jars to obtain the amount of water indicated in the right-hand column. (Reproduced from Luchins, *Mechanisation in Problem Solving, The Effect of Einstellung*, Psychological Monographs, 1942, 54, by permission of the American Psychological Association.)

Problem	Jar capacities			Amount to be obtained
	A	B	C	
1	21	127	3	100
2	14	163	25	99
3	18	43	10	5
4	9	42	6	21
5	20	59	4	31
6	23	49	3	20

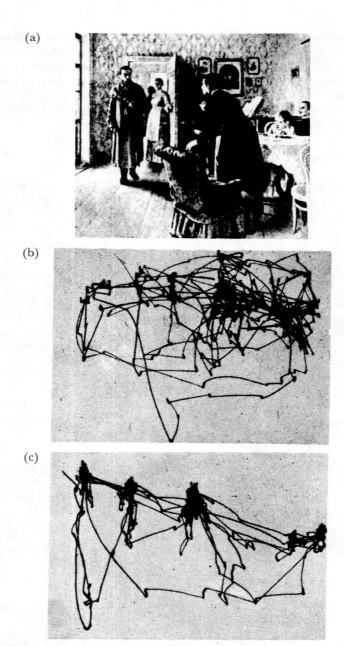

Fig. 1.9   Subjects were asked to look at the photograph (a) in order to estimate either the wealth or the age of the people portrayed. When asked about their wealth, the pattern of eye movement shown in (b) emerged, but when asked about their ages the subjects showed the (c) pattern. (Reproduced from Yarbus, *Eye Movement and Vision*, 1967, by permission of Plenum Publishing Corporation.)

presents six problems, the task being to use jars A, B and C to obtain the amount of water indicated in the right-hand column. After a little thought, a way of obtaining these amounts becomes apparent. Before reading further, it is instructive to perform all the tasks.

All of these problems can be solved in the same way (B – A – 2C), but looking at problem 6 again, it is possible to see how a routine has built up which led to a failure to use the simplest solution (A – C).

This example illustrates how one way of looking at objects can hamper future efforts. The same principle holds true in social situations. A classic study of this phenomenon involved showing a film of a team sports event to supporters of each side. Tempers flared both during and after the game. When asked to estimate the number of fouls committed by each side, the supporters varied significantly in the number they perceived, consistently attributing more blame for injuries to the other side. The experimenters concluded that:

> The data here indicate that there is no such thing as a game existing out there in its own right which people merely observe. The game exists for a person and is experienced by him only in so far as certain happenings have more significance in terms of his purpose. (Ref. 15, p. 133)

Although the supporters' biases in this study are obvious, it is also the case that everyone has biases that 'distort' their perceptions. Toch and Schulte[16] were interested in the effects of police training on awareness of violent scenes. Their study provides another example of the effect of selective attention in perception, but also provides an opportunity to describe the importance of comparison or 'control' groups in psychology experiments. In their study they used a tachistoscope, a piece of apparatus that flashes pictures or letters on a screen for very short periods of time. Pairs of drawings were presented for 0.5 s, one depicting a scene of violence, the other a neutral scene. An example of each is shown in Fig. 1.10. The subjects were asked to identify the drawings, a difficult task at such short exposure times. The number of times a violent figure was recognized was taken as an indication of awareness of violence. Toch and Schulte could have assessed the effects of training in various ways. Whatever their choice, they would have required some sort of comparison: if they had simply studied the

Fig. 1.10 An example of the violent and non-violent drawings used by Toch and Schulte. (Reproduced from Toch and Schulte, *British Journal of Psychology*, 1961, 52, 389–393, by permission.)

policemen after their training, their results would have been difficult to interpret. They would have no standard against which to compare the results. One method could have been to test the policemen before and after their training, and their recognition scores compared. Perhaps the subjects would recognize more violent scenes, compared to neutral ones, after training than before. Another method — the one they used — was to include other groups of individuals in their study. These are called 'control' groups because they are designed to rule out, or control for, the possibility that other factors, besides the one thought to be important, are responsible for the results. There could be several reasons why trained policemen are more aware of violent scenes than other groups of people. One possibility is the hypothesized variable — the training itself. Another possibility is that the kind of person who enters the police force is much more aware of violence than those who choose another profession. Further, although training may increase awareness, it may be *relatively* unimportant compared to the self-selection of police cadets. In order to test these possible alternative explanations, Toch and Schulte included two control groups in their study. One group consisted of psychology students, the other of police cadets who had not yet received training. When the results from the three groups were compared, those policemen who had completed their training recognized about twice as many of the violent figures than either control group. They also found little difference between the control groups themselves, so Toch and Schulte could conclude that training is the important variable and that the effect of self-selection into the police force is minimal.

The importance of control groups in research will arise throughout the book. The results from studies that do not use controls are often open to several interpretations, and sometimes the control groups are not adequate. The aim is to use subjects who are as alike as possible to the experimental group subjects, differing only on the crucial variable. Perhaps the best way to do this is to randomly assign subjects to different groups. In some instances, this procedure would not be practical or ethical, however, and other strategies would be used. Say a researcher was interested in the effects of breathing techniques on the experience of pain during childbirth. He could approach a course organizer and, hopefully, receive permission from the organizer and the prospective parents to do the study. But in order to have confidence in any results he might find, he would have to be careful about choosing the control group. Parents who attend these classes differ in more ways than one from parents who do not elect to attend. They are more likely to be middle-class and to do more reading about childbirth than most parents-to-be, for example. If the researcher found differences in the experience of birth in this sample as compared with another group of parents, the differences might not be due to the breathing exercises but to a better diet or to greater knowledge about birth. If the researcher were lucky, the classes would be over-subscribed and he could use the parents who were unable to enter the course as his control group. If no such group of parents were available, he might resort to matching — trying to find parents who are similar to those in his experimental group on relevant variables. In general, age, sex and social class are the variables most commonly used, along with any other aspects that are relevant to the particular study (perhaps income and the number of books parents have read on childbirth, in this case).

To return to our discussion of the role of selective attention in perception: increased awareness of certain stimuli and mental set may go some way towards explaining physicians' tendency to interpret their patients' symptoms most often in an organic way. Since medical training is primarily concerned with physical illness, doctors may be much more aware of physical aetiologies and treatments than social or psychological ones. They may also attend more closely to symptoms of physical distress than those of psychological distress. Some evidence for this possibility is provided by Maguire and Rutter[17] who found that medical students in their final year obtained less social and psychological information while taking case histories than first year students. This is not to say that their training makes them neglectful, only that medical education may bias physicians in certain ways. The evidence that mental set can be problematic in medical care comes from several descriptive studies. For example, Stimson[18] outlines the experience of one woman who had a history of respiratory problems that frequently required prescribed antibiotics. It seemed to her that the doctor was too willing to diagnose all her problems as connected with the respiratory condition:

> No matter what I have got wrong with me, if I go over to the doctor with a terrific headache that I'm getting — 'Oh, it's all to do with your chest' — anything, no matter, if I'm worried about something now, and I want to go to the doctor's, see, perhaps I'm getting these headaches or something and I'm getting a bit concerned about them now, no matter what, I can guarantee when I come out of that doctor's, it's to do with my chest. No matter what I get, you're missing a period and he says — 'It's to do with your chest'. (Ref. 18, p. 102)

Apparently, the physician had solved her problem in one way in the past, and this prevented him from entertaining alternative possibilities.

The tendency to perceive only certain kinds of information is not, of course, limited to the medical profession. Chapters 2 and 3 include discussion of psychological methods of treatment, about which there are several schools of thought, each with its own theories and practices. The ways in which psychologists make sense of their patients' difficulties determine to a large extent the kinds of information they gather and the treatments they recommend. For instance, a psychologist who believes that someone's fear of open spaces is an expression of poor relationships with others will take very different action from one who believes that the patient has in the past been rewarded in some way for such a fear.

Self-Fulfilling Prophecy

Some perceptual biases are remedied by further experiences, but this is not always the case. An observer may selectively attend to those features of a situation or characteristics of a person that are consistent with his or her expectations and ignore those that are not. A person who believes that everyone is unfriendly and hurtful is likely to be defensive and suspicious, selectively attending to instances of rejection. This may, in turn, make him difficult to get along with, perhaps resulting in the very behaviour he expects — rejection. Here, an inaccurate perception evokes behaviour that makes the originally false perception come true. This kind of circularity in social situations has been termed the self-fulfilling prophecy.

Interest in this phenomenon began as psychologists realized that they often achieved results in their experiments which were in accord with their own predictions but which could not be replicated by other psychologists who did not share their theories. Robert Rosenthal has been an active researcher in this area. In one study, six experimenters were told that their rats had been specially bred for 'maze brightness': that is, their rats would learn to find their way through a short maze in order to reach some food very quickly. Another six experimenters were told that their rats were dull, and would take a long time to learn their way through the maze. The allegedly brighter rats really did learn to run the maze faster (or, in another study, more quickly learn to push levers in order to obtain food) even though they had been randomly assigned to the groups of experimenters. The rats' performance was influenced by the experimenters' expectations.

This idea has also been tested in classrooms. Educational theorists suggested that some pupils failed to learn because they had a history of failure, a background that teachers used in deciding how intelligent they were and how worthwhile it was to pay careful attention to their work. Meichenbaum et al.[19] studied a group of young women who had been sent by the courts to a training centre. They administered a series of tests that purported to predict intellectual 'blooming', and the teachers were told that certain girls could be expected to show remarkable gains in intellectual competence in the coming months. In fact, there was no such test, so that the only differences between these girls and those in the control group were in the expectations of the teachers. Soon, the teachers began to note and comment upon relatively insignificant instances that confirmed their expectations. When Meichenbaum et al. checked the school records of exam results, they found that those who were supposedly predicted to do better did so on objective tests in mathematics and science (but not in literature and history). These girls were also more likely to show 'appropriate' behaviour in the classroom (e.g. paying attention to lessons rather than looking distracted or whispering together).

Although some researchers have failed to replicate such findings, many other studies have supported the notion of expectancy effects[20]. It appears that the person with the expectations changes his behaviour to conform with his predictions. Teachers with favourable expectations gave more information to supposedly bright students, which may explain why they actually learned more. Similarly, more statements were requested of 'gifted' pupils and they were praised more frequently by their teachers. Teachers who had been led to believe that some of their students were very bright leaned forward more when they were addressing them, looked them in the eye, nodded and smiled more frequently. It may be that the experimenters with the 'maze-bright' rats held,

20

stroked and played with them more than the experimenters with the 'maze-dull' rats, providing them with more stimulation.

An interesting study on the effects of expectations on behaviour is provided by Jahoda[21]. The Ashanti of West Africa believed that infants born on different days of the week have different personalities. Those born on Mondays are supposed to be quiet and even-tempered, those born on Wednesdays aggressive and quarrelsome. Jahoda consulted the police records for the district, trouble with the authorities being his dependent measure of aggression. He found that the Monday-borns had a low rate of criminal offences, Wednesday-borns a high rate. It seems possible that the parents reacted to their children in ways consistent with their expectations, and that these expectations were incorporated into the children's personalities, thus fulfilling the prophecy. There has been much discussion of the possibility that many of the differences in behaviour shown by males and females is due to such expectations, a topic considered in Chapter 8.

Expectations play an important role in the medical setting as well. Placebo effects (discussed in Chapter 11) are based partly on the patient's perceptions of the efficacy of drugs, and several studies have shown that physicians who are enthusiastic about a particular course of treatment achieve better results than those who are sceptical. Beecher[22] traced the literature on a particular surgical procedure that was eventually discarded as a result of a properly controlled experiment. Before this experiment, several surgeons indicated that the procedure was useful, whereas others found it ineffective. Beecher showed that surgeons who were sceptical about the operation and who told their patients they did not expect any change in their condition had low success rates, but that surgeons who were enthusiastic achieved good results. The reasons for findings such as these are not altogether clear (and it is possible that some patients might have pretended they were improving), but there is adequate evidence to conclude that for some patients objective changes in physiology occur due to expectations.

The way the environment is understood, then, is only partly determined by the sensory data impinging on the person. Not only is the data sensed by a nervous system that is constantly active and that introduces 'noise', it is also interpreted. Interpretation is dependent on context, past experience and selective attention. But the process of interpretation does not end here: the way the environment is perceived can sometimes affect the way it works, resulting in a self-fulfilling prophecy. These influences on perception are significant, but perhaps the most important point is that interpretation always takes place. In a sense, people can be regarded as scientists who have developed theories in order to interpret their environment. These theories generate hypotheses and are modified when new information is inconsistent with old ways of seeing things. In a further test of his hypothesis that diagnosis of mental illness is influenced by what staff expects to see, Rosenhan[11] led the staff of a teaching hospital to believe that within the next 3 months one or more pseudopatients would attempt to have themselves admitted to the psychiatric unit. Of the 193 patients admitted during this time, 41 were alleged to be pseudopatients by at least one member of staff, 19 by a psychiatrist and one other staff member. In fact, there were no pseudopatients: the faulty theory led to incorrect expectations and thus to misperceptions.

Some way of organizing events is necessary because an environment that appears to be random does not allow us to predict the future or to understand the present. When it is in fact random, special efforts will be made to fit events into some kind of pattern. An illustration of this tendency is given by a study in which subjects were invited to ask questions concerning problems in their personal lives. The only restriction on these questions was that they had to be answered by a simple 'yes' or 'no' — such as 'Should I continue with my present course of studies?' After some 20 questions, the subjects were asked what they thought of the advice they had been given. Most of them agreed that the advice was sound, but some found it unhelpful. But none of them reported that they thought the answers were random (which they were), preferring to find ways of explaining those answers that did not make obvious sense.

In the next part of the chapter the situation of people who enter hospital for treatment or observation is considered, extending the principles of interpretation to their circumstances. There are two aspects to this extension. First, hospitalization is an unfamiliar event to most people, making it possible to conduct research on the process of interpretation. Principles learned in this setting may apply to other situations. Second, and no less important, are the practical implications of work on hospitalization. If research can show how patients can be made more comfortable in hospital through helping them to make sense of their new environment, this could result in better care and earlier recovery.

1.4   Uncertainty and Medical Care

The research discussed in the previous section indicates that people have a strong tendency to make interpretations about their environment. They will attempt to find patterns even when none exist. An explanation for this tendency is that interpretations simplify the complexity of incoming information, thereby leaving room (or capacity) to deal with unexpected or unfamiliar events. Interpretation also allows the perceiver to select data, attending to features that appear to be relevant and ignoring those that are not. A common strategy in diagnosis is for the doctor to make a tentative interpretation and then follow it up, asking specific questions in order to test the hypothesis[23]. Interpretations provide a short-hand, a way of 'chunking' information to make it easier either to assimilate or remember. It is much more difficult to remember the letters SCLOGPHYOY than PSYCHOLOGY because the word 'psychology' has a meaning, a meaning that can be remembered more efficiently than a random series of letters. In the same way, a patient may remember advice more accurately if the doctor provides some explanation of the treatment (see Chapter 13). Because people have a limited capacity for information, interpretation provides a way of organizing and simplifying data.

When an interpretation cannot be made easily, people often search for possibilities that would reduce the uncertainty. The experience of having symptoms of illness is a good example of this tendency. Symptoms are often ambiguous and carry implications of threat to health and life-style, making them a focus for hypothesis-testing for the patient, family and physician. The threat implied by symptoms cannot be realistically appraised until their cause and potential consequences have been determined. Ambiguity is high because symptoms are often novel, difficult to localize and of varying severity[24]. A person who experiences cardiac arrhythmia, for example, may believe that he is suffering from a serious cardiac disease or a temporary disturbance due to over-exertion. Since heart-attack symptoms overlap with symptoms of gastro-intestinal disturbance, competing interpretations may be plausible. A person who has had frequent stomach upsets is more likely to attribute the pain to the stomach than the heart, whereas a person whose father died of a heart attack may be more likely to make the infarction interpretation. Evidence suggests that the difficulty in interpreting symptoms is an important cause of delay in seeking help in the critical minutes and hours following a myocardial infarction[25, 26]. Thus, the factors involved in the interpretation of external events (i.e. past experience, selective attention, context) often apply equally well to the perception of internal physiological events.

The anxiety and stress that people experience when anticipating or experiencing pain has been documented by several researchers. There appears to be a relationship between uncertainty and distress, as Johnson[27] has illustrated. She asked her subjects to rate the degree of distress they experienced while a tourniquet was applied to an arm, ratings being taken every 30 s. She experimentally manipulated the subjects' uncertainty about how they would experience the tourniquet by giving one group of subjects relevant information (e.g. how it would feel) and the other group irrelevant information (e.g. a technical description of the tourniquet). Her results are shown in Fig. 1.11. Although the distress of the group who knew what to expect rose during the 5-min experiment, subjects who had not been told what the tourniquet would feel like reported a consistently higher level of distress. Apparently, reducing the uncertainty about what could be expected made the experience less distressing.

A real-life example of uncertainty is experienced by patients on admission to hospital. That patients do feel anxious is not surprising, given the disruption to their life-style represented by a stay in hospital. Emotional support between family members is affected, there is a reduction in independence and a lack of privacy in hospitals. Most germane to the present discussion, patients are troubled by the difficulty of interpreting what is happening to them. Cartwright[28] asked patients to outline their complaints about the hospital they entered. The most frequently expressed complaint was 'They didn't tell me what I wanted to know', reflecting the importance of being able to make sense of surroundings. Another survey found that patients' anxieties centred around the operation (31%) and 'Not knowing what to expect' (34%). Events associated with hospitalization have been rated for their stressful qualities (see Chapter

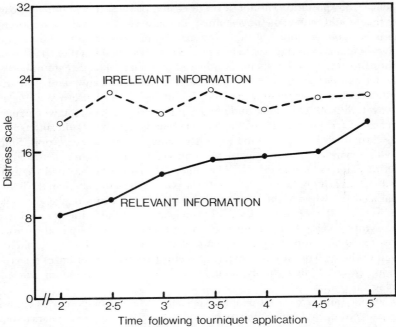

Fig. 1.11 Mean distress ratings (16 = moderately distressing) when subjects were given relevant or irrelevant information about the application of a tourniquet. Those given irrelevant information reported lower levels of distress. (Reproduced from Johnson, *Journal of Personality and Social Psychology*, 1973, 27, 261–275. © 1973 by the American Psychological Association. Reprinted by permission of the author.)

10), a scale that indicates that unfamiliarity of surroundings and disruption to routines present considerable problems to patients.

Preparing the Patient

If these aspects of hospitalization are so important, then helping patients to interpret this unfamiliar environment and to predict what is going to happen to them should make their stay more satisfying and less stressful. A large body of evidence indicates that this is the case. Some of the evidence is based on cor-relational research. Correlation is a way of measuring the strength of an asso-ciation between two variables, having a value between zero (no relationship at all) and 1 (one variable predicts scores on the other precisely). A correlation may be positive or negative, a negative correlation indicating that higher values of one variable occur with lower values of the other, such as the more visits to an antenatal clinic, the fewer the obstetric complications. The variables of height and weight are positively correlated, in that taller people tend to be heavier than

24

shorter people. Knowing the height of a person allows a better prediction of his or her weight than not knowing height. Wriglesworth and Williams[29] provide an example of this kind of research. They measured patients' satisfaction with the amount of information they had been given and the degree of their confidence in the medical staff. They found a significant positive correlation, indicating that as satisfaction with information increased, so did confidence in staff. The problem with correlational studies is with interpretation of the results. It is tempting to conclude from this study that information given to patients was responsible for their confidence. Such a conclusion is consistent with other research, but this study by itself does not necessarily lead to it. Other interpretations can be made. It is equally possible that cause and effect works the other way around — that staff members are more likely to give information if the patient has confidence in them. Alternatively, it may be that confidence and information are related to each other only indirectly, through a third variable. The correlations could be due to the patients' personalities. Perhaps some patients would report that they were satisfied with their treatment no matter what it was like (and would therefore say that they were satisfied with both the information they were given and the competence of the staff), whereas others would complain regardless of the quality of their care (and would therefore report that they were dissatisfied with both staff and information). This possibility may be made clearer if the example of height and weight is used once more. Although these two variables are correlated, it would not be reasonable to say that height causes weight or vice versa — they are both expressions of a third process, growth.

Despite these drawbacks with the interpretation of correlational studies, they do have advantages. First, they serve as an impetus for experimental work, which is more suited to deal with competing interpretations. Second, correlational studies can be performed when experimental manipulations are ethically or practically difficult. For example, a researcher might be interested in testing the hypothesis that children's language develops more quickly when their mothers talk with them more frequently. Rather than asking one group of mothers to talk with their children more than another group, the investigator might observe the mothers and correlate their behaviour with the children's development. Although a significant correlation would be suggestive, it would not be conclusive, since it could be argued that mothers talk with their babies more when they are developing quickly.

Fortunately, the area of preparing patients for hospitalization is one that is open to experimental research. Since preparation is not given in many hospitals, it would not be unethical to give some patients more attention than is routinely provided. For example, Leigh et al.[30] used a self-report questionnaire to measure patients' anxiety before and after they were given information about the anaesthetic procedures they were to undergo. One group of patients was given a booklet outlining the information, a second group was given the information personally by an anaesthetist and questions were answered. A third group, the control group, was given no extra information. Although the anxiety of the control-group patients decreased only slightly over time, the anxiety of

25

the informed patients decreased significantly, particularly in the group who were given the information personally and who were invited to ask questions about the procedure.

These studies were concerned with patients' anxieties and their satisfaction with care. Although these aspects are important, other measures could also be taken, such as days required in hospital after the operation or the amount of pain-killer requested by the patients. If preparatory information was shown to affect measures such as these, this would provide convincing evidence that information is important for patients' well-being.

Much of the impetus for research in this area was given by Janis[31]. He conducted interviews with patients about to undergo surgery and noted that they fell into three groups. One group of patients showed high anxiety about the impending operation: they felt very vulnerable, sometimes being unable to sleep and sometimes trying to postpone the operation. A second group of patients showed moderate fear: they asked for information about the operation and worried about specific features of the surgical procedure, such as anaesthesia. The third group of patients showed little fear, sleeping well and tending to deny that they felt worried. These patients seemed to feel almost completely invulnerable.

Janis then went back after the operation to see how these patients had fared. The first group (high fear) was found to be the most anxiety-ridden and most concerned with the future. The third group (low fear) was more likely than other groups to show anger and resentment towards the staff and often complained about the treatment. For these two groups the stay in hospital was distinctly unhappy. In the case of the second group — the group that showed a moderate degree of anxiety — the reactions to the operation were very different. They were less likely than the other groups to display emotional disturbance and showed high morale and co-operation with the medical staff. It seemed that a moderate amount of fear about the realistic threat of the operation was associated with good recovery. These patients could cope with the pain and distress of the after-effects of the operation adequately. One patient volunteered that he knew 'there might be some bad pains, so when my side began to ache I told myself that this didn't mean that anything had gone wrong'.

The reasons why the patients in the moderately fearful group were able to cope with the operation more successfully were not altogether clear, but Janis suggested that it was because they asked for information about their treatment and were thus able to prepare for its consequences. The kind of patient who was in the moderately fearful group is illustrated by the following extract:

A young housewife, for example, had been somewhat worried before a lung operation and then, like most others in the moderately fearful group, showed excellent cooperation and little emotional disturbance throughout the post operative period—except for one brief crisis she had not expected. She knew in advance about the acute incision pains and other unpleasant aspects of the postoperative recovery treatments, since she had undergone a similar operation once before and had asked her physician many pertinent questions about the impending second operation. But on the first postoperative day a physician entered her room and told her she would have to swallow a drainage tube, which she had never heard about before. She became extremely upset, could not relax sufficiently to cooperate, and finally begged the physician to take the tube away and let her alone. During an interview the following day she reported that she began to have extremely unfavorable thoughts about the physician at the time he made the unexpected demand; she suspected that he was withholding information about the seriousness of her condition, that he was unnecessarily imposing a hideous form of treatment on her, and that he was carrying out the treatment 'so badly it was practically killing me'. At no other time during the long and painful convalescence following the removal of her lung did she have any such doubts about this physician or any other member of the hospital staff; nor did she at any other time display any form of overt resistance. Evidently this was the one stressful event she had not anticipated . . . .(Ref. 31, p. 102)

Janis came to believe that it is important for people to worry about future events so that they can mentally prepare themselves. This appears to be in direct opposition to the view that patients should not be 'worried' by information lest they become upset by it. Another case study is illustrative:

. . . let us consider the reactions of a 21-year-old woman who had earlier undergone an appendectomy. At that time she had been given realistic information by her physician. Before the operation she had been moderately worried and occasionally asked the nurses for something to calm her nerves, but she showed excellent emotional adjustment throughout her convalescence. About two years later she came to the same hospital for another abdominal operation, the removal of her gall bladder. In the preoperative interview with the investigator she reported that her physician had assured her that 'there's really nothing to it; it's a less serious operation than the previous one'. This time she remained wholly unconcerned about the operation beforehand, apparently anticipating very little or no suffering. Afterwards, experiencing the usual pains and deprivations following a gall bladder operation, she became markedly upset, negativistic, and resentful toward the nursing staff.

Chronic personality predispositions do not seem to account fully for this patient's reactions, since she was capable of showing an entirely different pattern of emotional response, as she had on a previous occasion. The patient's adjustment to the fear-producing situation appeared to be influenced mainly by the insufficient and misleading preparatory communications she was given before the second operation. Since nothing distressing was supposed to happen, she assumed that the hospital staff must be to blame for her postoperative suffering. (Ref. 31, p. 98)

If the information received by a patient before surgery helped him in coping with pain, then a short experiment could be performed to test this hypothesis. One group of patients would be given only basic information — the time and duration of the operation and that the patient would awaken in the recovery room. These patients would form the control group. A second group of patients — the experimental group — would be given much more information about the operation. This experiment was actually performed by Egbert et al.[32]. In addition to the standard information given to a control group, the experimental group received:

1. a description of the post-operative pain, including where it would be localized, how much could be expected and how long it would continue;
2. reassurance that post-operative pain was normal and could be expected;

3. advice on how to relax abdominal muscles and how to move without tensing them (all patients had abdominal operations);
4. assurance that they would be given pain-killing medication should they require it.

The results were striking. The experimental group required only half as much sedation during the first 5 post-operative days (see Fig. 1.12) and had an average of 2.7 fewer days of hospitalization. One patient from the control group complained, 'Why didn't you tell me it was going to be like this?'

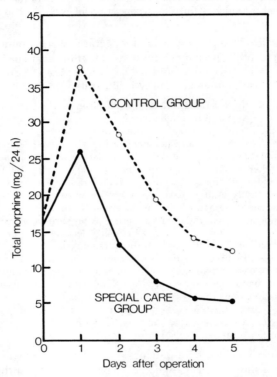

Fig. 1.12 **Post-operative narcotic treatment of patients given routine and extra preparation for surgery. (Reproduced from L. Egbert, G. Battit, C. Welch and M. Bartlett,** *New England Journal of Medicine*, **1964, 270, 825–827, by permission.)**

Since this pioneering work, many researchers have explored the importance of preparatory information. Several issues have arisen during the course of this research. Not everyone seems to benefit from this information, so that psychologists have attempted to develop ways of identifying these patients. There is some indication that those who avoid gathering information about the operation can be distressed if it is presented without their request and show somewhat worse adjustment thereafter[33]. Investigators have also attempted to develop measuring tools as ways of identifying how anxious someone is (e.g. the Fear of Surgery Scale)[34]. One problem with work in this area is that researchers have often included several preparatory techniques in their experimental designs, so that it is often difficult to ascertain which kinds of preparation are the most effective. There is general agreement, however, that for patients who request information it should be specific rather than vague and aimed at the individual patient's concerns and anxieties rather than simply giving the same information to all patients. In the research mentioned earlier concerning the anaesthetist's visit[30], the opportunity to ask questions resulted in a greater reduction of anxiety than simply giving the patient a booklet to read. There is also evidence that encouraging accurate expectations about sensations form an important component of preparation: in one study, subjects who were told what sensations would follow from the procedure showed less distress than subjects who were merely informed about the mechanics of the procedure. Another issue involves the relationship between pre-operative anxiety and post-operative recovery. Although Janis contended that moderate anxiety is the preferred state (both high and low anxiety being less desirable), many others have provided evidence that the relationship is more simply linear, with higher anxiety associated with poorer outcome, lower anxiety with better outcome. This latter viewpoint is also more consistent with laboratory studies of pain: anxious subjects estimate the magnitude of electric shocks to be greater than non-anxious subjects.

In general, there has been support for Janis' original recommendations:

1. to give realistic information, so that patients are able to prepare themselves and to correct unrealistic fears;
2. to provide reassurance that others (particularly the medical staff) can be counted on to give assistance (reassurance counteracts fears of helplessness);
3. to encourage plans for coping with future difficulties, such as the pain and social consequences of treatment.

Investigators have also examined treatments besides surgery. For example, Wilson-Barnett[35] explored the effectiveness of explanatory information on patients who were to have a barium enema. None of the patients had experienced this before, so that they were all unfamiliar with the procedure and the sensations it produces. The experimental group received a written and verbal explanation of the investigation, an explanation based on both observation and previous patients' comments. The verbal explanation took about 5 min, the written information was given to the patients to keep, and any questions were answered. The control group were visited for the same amount of time and asked how they were getting on in hospital. (Giving the control group an equal amount of attention makes this a particularly convincing study. One criticism of research in this area is that many experimenters have neglected to talk with their control-group patients, so that it is possible that patients in experimental groups find their stay in hospital less stressful simply because someone took the time to talk with them and was interested in their worries, rather than because they gained more information. This criticism does not apply to this experiment because Wilson-Barnett arranged for all patients to have a chat. She also took her measures 'blind', so that the investigator who measured anxiety did not know which condition a particular patient was in. As was shown earlier in the chapter, researchers may often find the results they expect to find, not because they 'cook' the data but rather because they are more likely to perceive what they expect to perceive.)

Measures of the patients' anxieties were taken on several occasions, as shown in Fig. 1.13. Before the interaction between nurse and patient, there was no difference in anxiety between the experimental and control group subjects (Score 1). Since there was also no difference between the groups after the preparatory information was given, it seems that this knowledge did not adversely affect the patients in the experimental group (Score 2). But 30 min before the

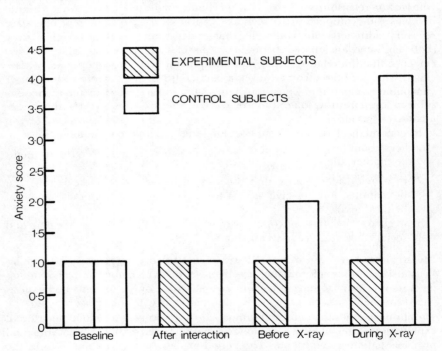

Fig. 1.13 Average anxiety scores of patients having a barium enema. The experimental subjects had the procedure explained to them, but the control group subjects did not. The control subjects' anxiety began to rise just before the X-ray and continued to rise during it; this was not the case for the experimental subjects. (Reproduced from J. Wilson-Barnett, *Journal of Advanced Nursing*, 1978, **3**, 37–40, by permission.)

X-ray, differences between the groups appeared (Score 3) and were stronger during the X-ray (Score 4). Although anxiety in the control-group patients increased, the experimental subjects showed no such increase.

Research has also been conducted on timing. Johnson[36] concluded that anxiety about operations begins well before entering the hospital, indicating that preparation and support could profitably be given before admission. Ferguson[37] arranged a pre-admission home-visit by a nurse for children about to have a tonsillectomy. The nurse completed the admission documents with the mother and gave her information about general hospital rules, such as what to bring to the hospital, what tests to expect, the fasting requirements on the morning of surgery and what the operating room looked like. They were also told that the child would have a very sore throat after surgery and might vomit. The mothers were given the opportunity to ask questions and express concerns. A group of mothers who received no home-visit comprised the control group. Ferguson measured both mothers' and children's anxieties at admission and 10 days after release from hospital. For children of 6 – 7 years of age (but not younger) the pre-admission visit resulted in fewer indications of poor post-hospital adjustment (e.g. difficulty in sleeping, eating, general anxiety) and mothers were less anxious during and after hospitalization.

The difficulties that children experience on entering hospital are particularly distressing for both parents and hospital staff. Some research (see Chapter 7) has indicated that the child's family background is an important variable, in that children from secure homes are less likely to be disturbed by the experience. Research has also indicated several ways in which their difficulties could be lessened by medical and nursing staff. Ferguson took care to inform the children's mothers about hospital procedures, because there is evidence that anxiety felt by the mother affects the level of anxiety in her child. Skipper and Leonard[38] asked a nurse to attend some mothers when they arrived at the hospital with their children. As in the Ferguson study, the mothers were encouraged to ask questions and express their concerns. The control group mothers received the regular introduction to the hospital with little personal contact. Behavioural and physiological measures indicated a lower level of anxiety in the *children* of the experimental group mothers, and they made a more rapid recovery and experienced fewer after-effects of their stay. The reduction of the mothers' level of anxiety was reflected in their children's recovery. Apparently, one way to help children in hospital is to help their parents make sense of the hospital routine and treatment.

The difficulties that young children experience may also be due in part to the anxiety they feel when confronted with an unfamiliar situation or unfamiliar adults. Unknown people and novel environments have been shown in several studies to increase children's need to be close to their mothers, particularly at ages between about 8 months to 2 years. Yet it appears this anxiety is strongest when an adult approaches a child, rather than allowing the child freedom to approach the adult in his own time. Horner[39] reviews the literature in this area, pointing out that when infants are allowed to control the encounter, anxiety about strangers is much less noticeable. Thus, it may be possible to reduce

31

children's distress in hospital by allowing them some control over their encounters with medical and nursing staff. The anxiety about unfamiliar environments may be alleviated if the child's mother is encouraged to accompany him to hospital and to the ward: children are more willing to explore their environment if there is a 'safe base' to which they can return if necessary.

A third possibility for reducing anxiety in hospital is providing the children themselves with preparatory information. However, the information needed by children may often be different from that needed by adults. Children often think of illness as a punishment for bad behaviour and their conceptions of the content and functions of the human body are often vague or false. A young child's lack of experience with large institutions could make a verbal explanation unsatisfactory, so that preparatory information may well need to be modified to take their individual interpretations and expectations into account. One way of giving information to children is by providing films about the hospital and about treatment. This approach, which has been used with children from about 4 years of age, has typically included pictures of the admission of a child into hospital, aspects of the operation and post-operative recovery. This has met with considerable success. Known as 'peer-modelling', the technique will be discussed in more detail in Chapter 3, but one example is illustrative. Vernon[40] studied children about to have an injection, dividing them into three groups. One group saw a realistic film of a child having an injection, the second group an unrealistic film (in which there was no indication that the injection might be distressing) and the third group saw no film. The children who saw the realistic film appeared to experience the least pain from the injection, whereas the children who saw the unrealistic film were the most upset. It would seem that many of the principles that apply to the preparation of adults may also apply to children, except that the preparatory information may need to be presented in different ways.

Summary

The way in which people make sense of their environment can be considered in three phases — the sensory, the interpretive and the memory phases — but they are interdependent. For example, the way in which a situation is interpreted depends on the memory of past experiences in similar situations. Research on both the sensory and interpretive phases has indicated that it is not possible to specify a person's experience completely from knowledge of a stimulus alone. Spontaneous neuronal firing, for example, affects the sensory phase by introducing noise into the nervous system, making detection of signals probabilistic rather than absolute. During the interpretive phase, the context in which a stimulus occurs and the past experience and purposes of the observer affect both how events are perceived and which events will be selected for attention. People tend to see what they hope and expect to see. These perceptions can result in a self-fulfilling prophecy when an observer acts on the basis of his interpretations.

It appears that people seek to give meaning to their world by making interpretations. When meaning is difficult to find, special efforts will be made to discover patterns, even when no such patterns exist. These principles of interpretation are illustrated by the situation of patients in hospital, who find themselves striving to make sense of an environment which is both novel and threatening. Research has indicated that providing patients with realistic information about their treatment and hospital procedure can reduce their anxiety and recovery time. Their individual perceptions and concerns about hospitalization should be taken into account, reassurance being given to counteract unrealistic fears. Children also benefit from such preparatory information, but their perceptions about hospitals and their own bodies are likely to be different from adults'. Their anxieties about separation from the family may also be stronger. Methods for making their stay in hospital less alarming, for instance by providing films depicting other children undergoing similar treatment, have proved helpful.

Suggested Reading

There are many books that elaborate on the principles of perception discussed in this chapter. Lindsay and Norman[1] provide a good introduction, as do S. Coren, C. Porac and L. Ward, *Sensation and perception*, Academic Press, London, 1978.

R.L. Gregory's *The intelligent eye*, Weidenfeld and Nicolson, London, 1970, discusses the psychology of illusions.

J. Wilson-Barnett, *Stress in hospital*, Churchill Livingstone, London, 1979, provides an introduction and a review of the research on preparing patients for hospital care.

References

1. Lindsay, P.H. and Norman, D.A., *Human information processing* (2nd edn.), Academic Press, London, 1977.
2. Hubel, D.H., The visual cortex of the brain, *Scientific American*, November 1963.
3. Held, R. and Hein, A., Movement-produced stimulation in the development of visually-guided behaviour, *Journal of Comparative and Physiological Psychology*, 1963, **56**, 607 – 613.
4. Fielding, G. and Evered, C., An exploratory experimental study of the influence of patients' social background upon diagnostic process and outcome, *Psychiatrica Clinica*, 1978, **11**, 61 – 86.
5. Sherif, M. and Sherif, C.W., *Groups in harmony and tension*, Harper, New York, 1953.
6. Dion, K.K., Physical attractiveness and evaluations of children's transgressions *Journal of Personality and Social Psychology*, 1972, **24**, 207 – 213.
7. Nordholm, L.A., Beautiful patients are good patients: Evidence for the physical attractiveness stereotype in first impressions of patients, *Social Science and Medicine*, 1980, **14A**, 81 – 83.
8. Meiners, M.L. and Sheposh, J.P., Beauty or brains: which image for your mate? *Personality and Social Psychology Bulletin*, 1977, **3**, 262 – 265.

9. Maguire, G.P. and Granville-Grossman, K.L., Physical illness in psychiatric patients, *British Journal of Psychiatry*, 1968, **114**, 1365 - 1369.

10. Maguire, G.P., Julier, D.L., Hawton, K.E. and Bancroft, J.H.J., Psychiatric morbidity and referral on two general medical wards, *British Medical Journal*, 1974, *1*, 268 - 270.

11. Rosenhan, D.L., On being sane in insane places, *Science*, 1973, **179**, 250 - 258.

12. Turnbull, C., Some observations regarding the experience and behaviour of the Bambuti pygmies, *American Journal of Psychology*, 1961, **74**, 304 - 308.

13. Shepherd, M., Cooper, B., Brown, A. and Kalton, G., *Psychiatric illness in general practice*, Oxford University Press, London, 1966.

14. Yarbus, A.L., *Eye movements and vision*, Plenum, New York, 1967.

15. Hastorf, A.H. and Cantril, H., They saw a game: a case study, *Journal of Abnormal and Social Psychology*, 1954, **49**, 129 - 134.

16. Toch, H.H. and Schulte, R., Readiness to perceive violence as a result of police training, *British Journal of Psychology*, 1961, **52**, 389 - 393.

17. Maguire, G.P. and Rutter, D.R., History taking for medical students: 1. deficiencies in performance, *Lancet*, 1976, **2**, 556 - 558.

18. Stimson, G.V., Obeying doctors' orders: a view from the other side, *Social Science and Medicine*, 1974, **8**, 97 - 104.

19. Meichenbaum, D.H., Bowers, K.S. and Ross, R.R., A behavioural analysis of teacher expectancy effects, *Journal of Personality and Social Psychology*, 1969, **13**, 306 - 316.

20. Darley, J.M. and Fazio, R.H., Expectancy confirmation processes arising in the social interaction sequence, *American Psychologist*, 1980, **35**, 867 - 881.

21. Jahoda, G., A note on Ashanti names and their relation to personality, *British Journal of Psychology*, 1954, **45**, 192 - 195.

22. Beecher, K.K., Surgery as placebo: a quantitative study of bias, *Journal of the American Medical Association*, 1961, **176**, 1102 - 1107.

23. Byrne, P.S. and Long, B.E.L., *Doctors talking to patients*, HMSO, London, 1976.

24. Leventhal, H., The consequences of depersonalisation during illness and treatment, *In* Howard, J. and Strauss, A. (eds.), *Humanising health care*, Wiley, New York, 1975.

25. Croog, S.H. and Levine, S., Social status and subjective perceptions of 250 men after myocardial infarction, *Public Health Reports*, 1969, **84**, 984 - 997.

26. Hackett, T.P. and Cassem, N.H., Factors contributing to delay in responding to the signs and symptoms of acute myocardial infarction, *American Journal of Cardiology*, 1969, **24**, 651 - 658.

27. Johnson, J.E., Effects of accurate expectations about sensations, *Journal of Personality and Social Psychology*, 1973, **27**, 261 - 275.

28. Cartwright, A., *Human relations and hospital care*, Routledge & Kegan Paul, London, 1964.

29. Wriglesworth, J.M. and Williams, J.T., The construction of an objective test to measure patient satisfaction, *International Journal of Nursing Studies*, 1975, **12**, 123 - 132.

30. Leigh, J.M., Walker, J. and Janaganathan, P., Effects of preoperative anaesthetic visit on anxiety, *British Medical Journal*, 1977, **2**, 987 - 989.

31. Janis, I.L., *Stress and frustration*, Harcourt Brace Jovanovich, New York, 1971.

32. Egbert, L., Battit, G., Welch, C. and Bartlett, M., Reduction of postoperative pain by encouragement and instruction of patients, *New England Journal of Medicine*, 1964, **270**, 825 - 827.

33. Auerbach, S.M. and Kilman, P.R., Crisis intervention: a review of outcome research *Psychological Bulletin*, 1977, **84**, 1189 – 1217.
34. Martinez-Urrutia, A., Anxiety and pain in surgical patients, *Journal of Consulting and Clinical Psychology*, 1965, **43**, 437 – 442.
35. Wilson-Barnett, J., Patients' emotional responses to barium X-rays, *Journal of Advanced Nursing*, 1978, **3**, 37 – 40.
36. Johnson, M., Anxiety in surgical patients, *Psychological Medicine*, 1980, **10**, 145 – 152.
37. Ferguson, B.F., Preparing young children for hospitalisation, *Pediatrics*, 1979, **64**, 656 – 664.
38. Skipper, J.K. and Leonard, R.C., Children, stress and hospitalisation: a field experiment, *Journal of Health and Social Behaviour*, 1968, **9**, 275 – 287.
39. Horner, T.M., Two methods of studying stranger reactivity in infants: a review, *Journal of Child Psychology and Psychiatry*. 1980, **21**, 203 – 219.
40. Vernon, D.T.A., Modelling and birth order in response to painful stimuli, *Journal of Personality and Social Psychology*, 1974, **24**, 794 – 799.

2
Personality and Psychopathology

2.1 Introduction

There are many ways of predicting how people will act in a particular situation. One source of information is the role or place in society that a person holds. If an individual is a teacher, for example, it is possible to predict that he or she will talk in front of a class of students occasionally. A doctor is likely to take medical histories, perform physical examinations and to prescribe drugs. Knowing an individual's role thus provides a measure of predictability. However, all teachers have their own individual manner of teaching, although they may impart the same facts to their students; equally, two doctors may have very different styles of consultation although they may recommend the same course of treatment. These differences between people, which make each individual unique, are usually put down to the person's personality. Just as some

36

researchers have been interested in studying the similarities between people, employing concepts such as roles and socialization to account for the consistencies (see Chapter 6 and Part II of this book), others have developed concepts and theories to account for these individual differences in personality. It is this latter work with which the current chapter is concerned.

Individual differences are due to both genetic and environmental factors. Since each person's genetic code predisposes him or her to behave in certain ways and genetic factors interact with the environment (see also Chapter 5), each person's behaviour is the result of both kinds of influence. Although most personality theorists would agree that the factors interact, some place more emphasis on one than the other. Freud, for example, considered people to be primarily biological machines: in his early work the influence of the environment was thought to be secondary. For other theorists, people are seen to be motivated by a search for personal meaning arising largely from environmental factors, and little attention is given to biology.

There are many personality theories and it is beyond the scope of this book to consider them all. Three kinds of approach that reflect important trends in personality research have been selected: first, psychodynamic theories based on Freudian thinking but changed and developed considerably since Freud's early work by the neo-Freudians who place greater emphasis on the importance of interpersonal relationships; second, cognitive approaches, which concentrate on how people interpret their environment, attempting to understand individual differences by exploring the ways in which people order and make sense of their experience; and third, descriptive approaches, which seek not so much to explain why people act as they do but to discover ways in which people can be grouped according to similarities in their personalities. The psychodynamic and cognitive theories have been developed by therapists through their experiences with patients, and each contains implications about how psychotherapy might be conducted.

Before discussing these theories, it may be useful to distinguish the psychiatrists and psychologists who work in the area. Psychiatry is a speciality, like surgery or paediatrics, which is followed after training in general medicine. Unlike psychologists, psychiatrists are qualified to prescribe drugs. Some psychiatrists consider personality disturbances to be due to chemical imbalances and that the difficulties can be remedied through the use of medication. This area of research falls outside the domain of this book. Other psychiatrists consider personal problems to be due to disturbances in relationships with other people, so that personal psychotherapy is seen to be the answer. In practice, both methods are often used: a patient who is depressed may be given a tranquillizer while undergoing personal therapy. Psychologists will have completed an undergraduate course in psychology, covering in depth many of the topics discussed in the first two parts of this book, and usually a postgraduate course in a specialist discipline. Educational psychologists, who are also qualified and experienced teachers, are concerned mainly with school-age children, helping those who, for instance, are disruptive or have difficulties in learning. Clinical psychologists attempt to assist people who seek help for a wide range of psychological problems, which could include fears of specific objects (e.g. of spiders or open spaces) or more generalized anxieties. Like psychiatrists, clinical psychologists could use psychotherapy in their treatment, or, as discussed in the next chapter, behavioural techniques. Psychiatrists and psychologists often share the same theoretical positions and use the same methods, medication being the exception. Experimental or academic psychologists often have no therapeutic commitment, but concentrate on research, and are responsible for much of the work discussed in this book. Usually, their concern is theoretical rather than practical, aiming to discover general principles about how people operate. These principles are usually developed within the artificial confines of the laboratory and their applicability to 'real-life' situations is tested afterwards.

2.2   Psychodynamic Approaches

Freud

Sigmund Freud is considered to be the father of the psychodynamic approach to personality. Although many aspects of his original theory have been modified by later therapists, his contribution to psychiatry and psychology is enormous and it is important to give at least a brief outline of his thinking. His perspective grew out of experiences with patients whom he treated in Vienna at the turn of the century, and his theory is much easier to understand in the context of this cultural background.

It was shown in the previous chapter that people interpret situations in ways that are consistent with their past experience and expectations. Freud was no exception. Trained as a neurologist, he was steeped in the medical model. One tenet of medical training is that complaints are symptoms of an underlying cause and important only insofar as they point to an underlying pathology of some kind: if this pathology is treated then the symptoms will disappear of their own accord. Freud would have been less interested in his patients' symptoms themselves than in discovering what those symptoms indicated.

Freud was born in 1856, and his training and thinking originated in the nineteenth century. Many contemporary ideas were included in his theory, such as the unconscious. Although Freud is sometimes credited with discovering the unconscious, the idea seems to have been present in Victorian culture. Stevenson's *Dr. Jekyl and Mr. Hyde* provides an example: by drinking a potion, a hidden side of the doctor's personality was expressed. Further, this unknown personality was destructive and uncontrolled. Freud's contribution was to apply this concept to everyone, arguing that the unconscious formed the greater proportion of a person's personality, with consciousness being like the tip of an iceberg. The unconscious contained feelings and experiences of which, under ordinary circumstances, the person was unaware but which motivated actions or desires. Freud's theory was also consistent with an important trend in Western thinking — biological determinism, the idea that what people do and think is determined by their biology. Harvey's contention that the heart was not a 'vital' organ (i.e. not the seat of life) but simply a pump, was one example; Darwin's theory of evolution was another. Freud saw no reason to believe that thinking and perceiving were any different from breathing or walking. Both kinds of process were seen to be manifestations of the same underlying biological machine.

Machines need energy to work, however, so Freud required an explanation of where the energy came from on the one hand and how it was used on the other. The first problem was easily solved: he reasoned that the energy came from the food we eat. The answer to the second problem was more complex, and he seems to have borrowed a model from another great influence on 19th Century science — Newtonian physics. Like physical energy, he contended that psychic energy (which he called libidinal energy) was present in finite amounts and could be neither created nor destroyed. Since intake of food resulted in the production of energy, if the personality were to be kept in some kind of equilibrium, then this energy must find expression. Again, classical physics provided a way of describing this process. If for some reason the expression of energy was blocked, then, like a hydraulic system, the energy found expression elsewhere: for example, if expression of anger towards a parent were not acceptable, then the individual might kick the cat. If someone had the compulsion to wash his hands repeatedly, then Freud might suggest that he was using up the energy from a blocked impulse. There would be little point in treating the hand-washing alone since the energy would simply find expression elsewhere — called *symptom substitution*.

Thus, Freud was able to construct a theory that was consistent with his own medical training and the cultural perceptions of the time. Symptoms were seen to be an expression of an underlying problem, appearing when energy could not be expressed in an unfettered way. This was a very tidy theory in many ways, but was incomplete. The problem now facing Freud was to explain how and why the energy was blocked. He accomplished this by postulating three systems within the personality. The most basic was the *id*. The id was like a reservoir, supplying the energy required for human behaviour. When the reservoir became too full, the id attempted to reduce the excess energy through forming images, such as in dreaming. Images were obviously not satisfactory in themselves, however, in that some way of relating to reality was needed. Freud argued that the *ego* developed as a system that was responsible for mediating between the id's demands for tension release and the demands of external reality. The ego did not have energy of its own, but only borrowed it from the id in return for satisfying the id whenever possible. Although the id plus ego system provided a way of explaining how impulses were translated into behaviour, Freud saw that personality based on these two systems alone was inadequate, since the ego was amoral: if only the id and ego were present in the personality, people would simply take whatever they wanted whenever they could. Society as a co-ordinated venture could not exist. Thus, he postulated the existence of a third system, the *superego*, as a means of incorporating society's values into the individual. The superego developed in two ways, through rewards and through punishment. Punishments given by others, parents in the first instance, resulted in the conscience which inhibited transgression of rules. Rewards resulted in the development of the positive side of the superego, the ego-ideal. This was responsible for endeavours to please parents, friends and self. When the superego was fully developed, parental and societal values were internalized so a person no longer needed direct control from others, but was self-controlled.

These three systems, the id, ego and superego interacted with and counter-balanced each other in Freud's theory. The ego was a kind of executive, trying to satisfy the often conflicting demands of the id and the superego. Problems were said to arise when one or two systems contained an undue share of libidinal energy, so that someone who had too much energy in the conscience may be over-inhibited and fearful lest he or she be punished for allowing the id to express itself. Many of the patients that Freud originally treated seemed to have an undue amount of energy invested in the superego. They showed hysterical symptoms, such as paralysis, for which no physical cause could be discovered. Freud found that by 'working through' these patients' emotions about their parents and helping them gain insight about themselves, these symptoms would disappear. 'Working through' involved an exploration of childhood experiences, particularly those that were emotionally painful. This was considered to be difficult because many of these childhood memories were no longer conscious, but could only be re-discovered through the use of psychotherapeutic techniques. At first Freud used hypnosis to facilitate recall, but later advocated dream analysis (dreams being regarded as examples of the id's wishes) and free association. The latter procedure involved encouraging the patients to say, without hesitation, whatever came to mind. When hesitation occurred, this was taken as an indication that something of importance was about to come into consciousness.

Freud argued that memories became unconscious because the ego, in its attempts to satisfy the demands of both the id and the superego, used *defence mechanisms*. All of these mechanisms involved distortion of some kind, either of reality or of one's own impulses. For example, *repression* might be an ego-response to a painful memory: the memory might be of being hurt by a parent as a child, but this would be unacceptable to a superego, which demanded that parents should always be loved and respected in an unambivalent way. *Denial* was a refusal to accept the existence of a situation that was too painful to tolerate, such as inscribing 'Only Sleeping' on a gravestone. *Rationalization* was the attempt to find socially and personally acceptable reasons for behaviour that would otherwise be threatening in some way. If, for instance, the reader has ever cheated in an exam (behaviour that might be unacceptable to the superego), the rationalization 'Well, it's alright to cheat if they make the examinations so ridiculously difficult' might be used. An important defense mechanism was *displacement*, which occurred when the original id impulse was diverted from direct expression. The most important impulses for Freud were sex and aggression, but since unfettered expression of these impulses would be unacceptable to the superego they were displaced towards more acceptable channels. Aggression might be diverted to competitive sports, sexual drives to artistic endeavours. Freud believed that these and the other defence mechanisms had two properties in common. First, they were present in everyone, not only those with psychological difficulties. Everyone used them to some extent. Second, the individual was not aware that he or she was using them. These mechanisms were usually unconscious, but could be explored during psychoanalysis.

Freud understood his patients' difficulties in terms of different kinds of conflict between the id, ego and superego. For some patients, the problem was seen as being due to a damming up of libidinal energy: failure to discharge the energy adequately left a residue that could result in a state of anxiety. The problem could be quite transitory and deep psychoanalysis was not needed. For other patients, however, a detailed analysis of personality development was needed. The growing individual was said to pass through oral, anal, phallic and genital stages, each of which marked a particular kind of libidinal expression. During the oral phase, for example, libidinal energy was expressed through the mouth: this is exemplified by the first months of an infant's life, where sucking is the main activity. Gradually, libidinal energy was transferred to the anal zone, and so on. When patients consulted Freud, he saw their difficulties as manifestations of incomplete or inadequate transfer of energy from one bodily zone to the next and the kinds of problems they presented as being partly a result of regression to their earlier phase. This model of psychological growth is analogous to the development of the foetus *in utero*. If an infant is born with some physical handicap, it is possible to specify the time when something went wrong in its development. For example, the limb defects caused by Thalidomide were due to prescription of the drug during the critical weeks of limb growth in the foetus. Similarly, Freud attempted to discover what 'went wrong' in a patient's psychological development by exploring the relevant phase. Someone who presented with a hysterical complaint (such as paralysis of a limb with no physical cause), for example, was said to have regressed to the phallic phase.

Developments in Psychodynamic Theory

It would be a mistake to consider psychodynamic therapy as currently practised to be the same as Freud originally outlined. Although many of his concepts are still in common use, their meaning has been modified in the light of further clinical experience. Many of his students broke with Freud early on, particularly over his emphasis on sex and aggression as motivators of behaviour, and there is now a wide range of psychodynamic theories. Instead of considering the ego as simply an outgrowth of the id, the ego is now commonly considered to have some energy or existence in its own right and to have more positive attributes than Freud assigned to it. Rather than being simply an executive, the ego is often considered to have needs of its own, such as integrity and growth. Perhaps most important, there is increasing emphasis on the interpersonal aspects of personality and personality growth. The infant's first and intense relationship with a mother or mother-figure became all important. The quality of mothering was seen to be crucial, providing the context in which the child first begins to form ideas about the self and the world. If the world (i.e. the mother) were frustrating and inconsistent, then the infant was thought to internalize these experiences and use them as a basis for all later relationships. Libidinal energy changed from being a quantitative force residing in the id to a life drive, responsible for forming relationships with others. Rather than satisfaction-seeking, the human psyche was seen to be relationship-seeking, so that adaptation was replaced by the idea of meaningful encounters with other people. One result of the increased emphasis on the mother – infant relationship is the concern with attachment and maternal deprivation, a topic raised in Chapter 7.

Some psychiatrists and psychologists have gone so far as to question the validity and usefulness of the idea of personality residing solely within the person, arguing that it is a meaningful concept only when seen in relation to other people. The American psychiatrist Sullivan, for example, contended that 'personality is the relatively enduring pattern of recurrent inter-personal situations which characterize a human life' (Ref. 1, p. 110 – 111). According to this position, personality has to do with the individual's relationship to his or her world, particularly with other people, and psychological difficulties are mainly disturbances of communication in inter-personal relationships.

Freud's theory of psychological development has also been altered, most notably by Erickson[2]. He argued that although the idea of stages is a good one, the original Freudian outline was oriented too narrowly within the individual and again not sufficiently concerned with the importance of social relationships. As with Freud's stages, Erickson believed there is a 'proper rate' of 'normal development', but his stages are ecological, taking the totality of the child's experience into account. Siblings, peers and cultural influences are included as well as parental ones. He also uses a biological analogy in describing his theory, but his focus of concern is with ego development and the growth of self-identity. Erickson outlines eight stages of identity development, but perhaps the most important is the first, Basic Trust versus Mistrust. This stage is primarily centred on the first year of life. The infant, when born, has no way of knowing that he will receive continuity of care from his parents. His problem is whether or not to trust that the mother (who is for Erickson the important figure at this stage) will return when she is not physically present and the child's first social achievement is to let her out of sight without distress. She needs to become an inner certainty if basic trust is to develop. To the extent that this certainty is not developed, growth in all later stages will be adversely affected.

The shift in emphasis shown by these later personality theorists — away from the individual in isolation and towards relationships — has several implications for psychotherapeutic treatment. Whereas Freud considered insight the important ingredient (and he had considerable success with this approach) many modern therapists would contend that personality change can best be brought about through a consideration of relationships, beginning with the therapeutic one. Despite the great diversity of approaches, there are some broad areas of agreement about therapeutic principles. One important principle concerns acceptance of the patient's statements, wishes and concerns without condemnation or castigation. In order for people to change, it is argued, it is first necessary to develop an open and trusting relationship with another person. The aim is not to change the person in ways that the therapist thinks are correct, but to allow the patient an opportunity to develop in ways that are personally helpful. Acceptance is regarded as a crucial aspect of psychotherapy, because as soon as someone is penalized for their feelings, these feelings cannot be explored satisfactorily. This does not usually mean that patients are simply allowed to talk while the therapist listens passively. Psychotherapy often involves a degree of confrontation and challenge, except that these challenges may be termed 'interpretations'. A therapist might challenge his patient with the observation that, while the patient is professing relaxation, he is moving or sitting uncomfortably. Or that he is talking about the death of a parent intellectually, without depth of feeling. Most psychotherapists would also agree that giving advice is inappropriate, since this implies taking responsibility away from the patient. One aim of therapy is to help patients cope with their 'problems of living' in ways of their own choosing, and this is impeded if the therapist advises or makes value judgements.

Psychotherapists often place strong emphasis on the need for therapy for themselves as well as their patients. Just like everyone else, psychotherapists have problems in their relationships with others — parents, friends and spouses. They, too, have 'problems of living' and these will affect their relationships with patients. Psychotherapy can involve strong emotional reactions, both positive and negative, from patients. It is not uncommon for a patient to become very dependent on the therapist during treatment, for example, and the ways such dependency is dealt with may well affect the course of treatment. A therapist who fosters inordinate dependency may make it difficult for the patient to progress or end therapy. Anger is another commonly aroused feeling in therapy: a therapist who finds anger particularly distressing may not be able to help the patient explore his or her feelings of hostility.

There seems little doubt that the way the therapist approaches his patient has an effect on the course of treatment. Whitehorn and Betz[3] examined the importance of the therapist's approach in a psychiatric hospital by comparing seven doctors whose patients showed good improvement with seven doctors whose patients showed least improvement. Several differences were found between the two groups of physicians. The first group tended to see their patients' behaviour in terms of personal meanings, rather than a way of arriving at a descriptive diagnosis. When case histories were taken, the personal relevance of past experiences was considered and discussed. They worked towards goals that were orientated towards the perceptions of the patients, rather than curing symptoms, and they were more likely to build trusting relationships with their patients. It seemed that the quality of the therapeutic relationship affected the improvement of the patients, all of whom were originally diagnosed as schizophrenic. The attitudes and personality of the physician appear to be important in non-psychiatric doctor – patient consultations as well (see Chapters 12 and 13).

It is sometimes difficult to see how psychotherapy differs from a close friendship and, indeed, there are many similarities. Caring, attention and commitment are common to both, but they are different in psychotherapy than in a friendship. Contact between therapist and patient is usually limited to hourly sessions (often once per week) and there is an inevitable difference in power. A degree of objectivity is important lest the therapist become so involved that he or she is unable to see where the relationship is floundering. The people involved in a friendship also have vested interests in keeping the relationship fairly constant, whereas the essence of psychotherapy is change. Although few people in their everyday lives set out to end a relationship, an important aim in psychotherapy is to help the patient eventually cope with his or her difficulties without the assistance of the therapist.

Although these broad areas of agreement exist between therapists, there are many differences in how they encourage patients to express and come to terms with their feelings and relationships with others. Many therapists trained in the Freudian and neo-Freudian models emphasize the importance of *transference*. The argument is that, if our first relationship (especially with parents) forms the pattern for all later ones, then a patient coming for therapy could be expected to bring these patterns to his relationship with the therapist, reacting to him or to her as if to the parent. The therapist's job is to help the patient understand these reactions, thus assisting in the understanding of difficulties experienced in relationships outside the consultation. Therapists who use transference tend to be rather unforthcoming in talking about themselves, preferring to present a kind of 'mirror' that reflects the patient's personality.

This method has been rejected by many therapists who believe that mirroring is impossible to achieve. Inevitably, they contend, the therapist's personality is an important aspect of the treatment and can be a helpful addition to psychotherapy. The use of the therapist's own experiences and views is closely associated with humanistic and existential forms of psychotherapy. In order to help people in their search, therapists from these schools place strong emphasis on self-disclosure, genuineness and warmth. Only if the patient comes to understand the reactions his behaviour engenders in others, it is felt, can he be helped to grow. A quotation from Carl Rogers, an important humanistic writer, illustrates the viewpoint:

> The relationship which I have found helpful is characterised by a sort of transparency on my part, in which my real feelings are evident. . . . I become a companion for my client, accompanying him in the frightening search for himself (Ref. 4, p. 34).

Another quotation illustrates the approach:

> . . . so if I sense that I am feeling bored by my contact with this client and this feeling persists, I think I owe it to him and to our relationship to share this feeling with him. The same would hold if my feeling is one of being afraid of this client, or if my attention is so focused on my own problems that I can scarcely listen to him. But as I attempt to share these feelings I also want to be constantly in touch with what is going on in me. . . . I also feel a new sensitivity to him now that I have shared this feeling which has been a barrier between us. I am very much more able to hear the surprise or perhaps the hurt in his voice because I have dared be real to him. I have let myself be a person — real, imperfect — in my relationship to him. (Ref. 5, p. 57).

44

A complex, but fundamental, point in psychotherapy concerns the problem of defining a successful outcome. For many physical illnesses, a patient is said to be cured when the presenting symptom is successfully treated. Similarly, some psychologists have taken removal of the presenting complaint as an indication that psychotherapy has been successful. If this criterion is used, then many patients improve without psychological care, and it has been argued that much of the improvement in patients who have received psychotherapy is due to this spontaneous remission.

Others, guided by psychodynamic theories, contend that an emphasis on the disappearance of symptoms misses the point of psychotherapy. They are less interested in symptoms than in underlying difficulties and consider the quality of the therapist-patient relationship to be the important criterion of success. Rogers puts the problem in this way:

> . . . in my early professional years I was asking the question How can I treat, or cure, this person? Now I would phrase the question in this way: How can I provide a relationship which this person may use for his own personal growth? (Ref. 4, p. 32)

Storr, a therapist who is more closely identified with a traditional psychodynamic approach, makes a similar point:

> Some time ago I had a letter from a man whom I had treated some 25 years previously asking whether I would see, or at any rate advise treatment for, his daughter. He assumed, wrongly, that I would not remember him, and in the course of his letter, wrote as follows: 'I can quite truthfully say that six months of your patient listening to my woes made a most important contribution to my life style. Although my transvestism was not cured my approach to life and to other people was re-oriented and for that I am most grateful. It is part of my life that I have never forgotten.'
>
> Looked at from one point of view, my treatment of this man was a failure. His major symptom, the complaint which drove him to seek my help, was not abolished. And yet I think it is clear that he did get something from his short period of psychotherapy which was of considerable value to him. A man does not write to a psychotherapist asking him to see his daughter, 25 years after his own treatment was over, using the terms employed in this letter, unless he believes that what happened during his period of treatment was important. (Ref. 6, p. 146).

Such a state of affairs may appear to be unsatisfactory to some readers, as it is to some psychologists, and the problem will receive further consideration in the next chapter. For the time being, it is important to note that psychotherapists are critical of themselves and their methods. Freud himself was a great admirer of Darwin, and considered his 'golden rule' of carefully recording observations that seemed unfavourable to his theory, laudable and important. Rather than using experiments to test the validity of their theories or the effectiveness of their approaches (although some experiments have been conducted on the unconscious, e.g. Silverman[7]), psychodynamic therapists have traditionally preferred to report case studies and to rely on their own criteria for success.

There are, however, some more objective ways of measuring the progress of therapy. One method, content analysis, categorizes the patient's statements according to certain criteria. For example, Raimy[8] divided patients' comments into three categories: (1) positive or approving self-references, (2) negative or disapproving self-references and (3) ambivalent self-references. At the beginning of therapy, most of the statements were of the second kind, indicating that the patients had negative views about themselves. As therapy progressed, there was a greater frequency of ambivalent statements. At the end of therapy, those patients who were considered to have improved gave comments mostly of the first kind, suggesting a greater acceptance of themselves, whereas those who were considered not to have improved continued to present ambivalent or negative statements about themselves. It seemed from this study that improvement in psychotherapy was reflected in an increase in positive feelings about oneself. Thus, although it may be difficult to define what a 'cure' may be for many patients in psychotherapy, there are measures, such as that described above, that allow the progress of therapy to be monitored.

The Problem of Classification

Freud classified psychological difficulties in terms of their aetiology. According to his regression theory, patients whose difficulties stemmed from the anal phase would be different from those whose problems originated in the oral stage, and their treatment would vary accordingly. However, his scheme was soon overtaken by one suggested by Kraepelin. This new classification emphasized symptomatology rather than aetiology, so that all those people who showed a particular symptom or set of symptoms were considered to have the same disorder. The three main categories commonly used are neurosis, psychosis and personality disorders. The following is a simplified and brief account of these categories.

Neurosis.   Neurotic people have problems that do not necessarily prevent them from leading a relatively stable life outside a hospital. People who are classified as neurotic are characterized as engaging in self-defeating patterns of behaviour, such as persistent hand-washing, and as having high levels of anxiety. There are several sub-classifications, including phobic neurosis, hypochondriacal neurosis and neurotic depression. When someone has an unrealistic fear of a situation, so intense that the situation is avoided for no apparently reasonable cause, a phobia is said to be present. Some phobias are fear of heights (acrophobia), open or crowded spaces (agoraphobia) and snakes (ophidiophobia). Hypochondriasis is the term given to the condition in which the person is over-concerned with his/her own physical health, perhaps visiting the doctor frequently with complaints of illness, although no physical cause for the complaints can be found. A person is said to be neurotically depressed when dejection and feelings of hopelessness out of proportion to events is shown.

Psychosis.   This term is applied to people whose psychological difficulties tend to be incapacitating and who thus often require hospitalization. They are characterized as being out of touch with reality in some way and social relation-ships are seriously impaired. Hallucinations and bizarre behaviour — both verbal and non-verbal — may be present. Types of psychosis include schizo-phrenia and the affective disorders. There are various types of schizophrenia: paranoid schizophrenia, typified by delusions of some kind (e.g. a certainty that the patient is being followed and spied upon); hebephrenic schizophrenia, characterized by disorganized and childish speech; and catatonic schizophrenia, which sometimes involves a lack of movement. All of these con-ditions have in common peculiar behaviour patterns that are difficult to under-stand. Schizophrenia is not necessarily so very obvious, partly because the symptomatology can be intermittent — patients often have lucid periods when they talk and act in an understandable way. Among the affective disorders are mania (extreme excitability) and psychotic depression (which includes extreme feelings of worthlessness and lack of motivation).

Personality disorders.   Originally, difficulties such as alcoholism and drug addic-tion were classified under personality disorders, since these problems were seen to be primarily due to personality factors. With the awareness that these condi-tions are strongly influenced by social factors (see Chapter 11), the classification of personality disorder is now often limited to those people whose behaviour is antisocial — known as sociopaths or psychopaths. These individuals seem to have little sense of shame or, in Freudian terms, an undeveloped superego. Their motivations for behaviour appear to be directed towards their own needs without regard for others.

This classification of psychological difficulties has proved useful and is com-monly applied. There are, however, several problems with it, and it is becoming increasingly controversial. First, there is reason to doubt whether different diagnosticians use the scheme in the same way. Although therapists tend to agree on broad categories (e.g. neurosis or psychosis), there is much less agree-ment within a category. Among psychoses, for instance, many symptoms overlap, and since patients show different symptoms at different times, one therapist might diagnose hebephrenic schizophrenia, whereas another suggests paranoid schizophrenia. Schizophrenia is diagnosed more frequently in the United States than in Britain, where affective disorders are more commonly found. There is evidence that at least part of this difference is due to the diag-nostic procedures used by the doctors involved.

A second difficulty of the classification scheme is that it is primarily descrip-tive, so that the presenting complaints of patients are often used not to discover the aetiological basis of the symptoms, but rather to classify the patient accord-ing to Kraepelin's system. This is not a problem for those psychologists and psy-chiatrists who believe that each disorder has a biochemical cause, but for those who consider social relationships crucial, such a classification is incomplete on its own. For them, a satisfactory system would involve an explanation of how the condition arose during the patient's psychological development.

A third and related problem is that, by considering all the people who show a set of symptoms as a homogeneous group, there has been a tendency to search for a single cause. To take schizophrenia as an example, some researchers have presented evidence that vulnerability to schizophrenia has a genetic base (e.g. if one twin is diagnosed as schizophrenic the other twin is more likely to be schizophrenic if they are monozygotic than dizygotic[9]), whereas others have argued that it results from family difficulties and disturbances in communication. Evidence for both positions can be found, yet neither can account fully for the onset of schizophrenia. This has led some researchers to consider the interaction between genetic predisposition and environment. The contention is that although schizophrenia has a genetic component, it only becomes evident when the family does not provide a sound and secure environment.

There is a further difficulty with the classification, one that is common to all such schemes. It implies that there are basic differences between people who are neurotic or psychotic, and people who are normal. However, normality is a difficult concept to define. A statistical definition is a possibility: behaviour that is unusual could be defined as abnormal. The problem with this criterion is that the meaning of the behaviour is not taken into account. Playing a violin is statistically infrequent, for example, yet it would be absurd to consider a violinist to be in need of help simply because the behaviour is unusual. Further, since most people will ask for some kind of psychological assistance sometime in their lives, the statistical definition is not an adequate one in any case. Another possible definition of normality concerns the violation of social norms: people who do not conform to the rules and customs of society might be considered abnormal. The difficulty with this criterion is that social norms change, so that behaviour that was considered to require psychiatric assistance in our society at one time (such as homosexuality) is no longer considered a symptom of psychopathology. Social norms also vary between cultures, so that, for example, although experiencing visions is the norm among Australian aborigines, Western psychiatrists might diagnose schizophrenia.

The criterion that is actually used seems to be one of the meaning of behaviour rather than the behaviour itself. It is the meaning given to actions by the individual and the group of people around him that is significant. A person may seek help when, to others, the difficulty may seem a minor one or, alternatively, refuse assistance when the problem seems a major one to friends, family and professionals. This principle applies not only to psychological difficulties but physical problems as well, a topic given further consideration in Chapter 6. Many prefer to consider the problems that require the assistance of a therapist to be only a magnification of the kinds of difficulties that everyone faces, rather than a qualitative difference. The contention is that everyone is neurotic to some extent, for example having unrealistic fears of some kind, and it is only when these fears have a disabling effect that assistance is sought. According to this approach, there is a continuum between normality and neurosis and between normality and psychosis, rather than sharp distinctions between them.

One final difficulty with the classification approach merits attention. This involves the tendency for people to define themselves according to the reactions they receive from others. The reader, if he or she has recently entered medical school, may have noticed a change in self-evaluation. Since one of the criteria for selection into medicine involves academic performance, most students about to enter the medical course evaluate their performance and academic competence highly. However, with experience of low grades and sometimes failure in exams, self-evaluations tend to decrease in the first years, rising again later in training[10]. A similar process could be expected to occur in mental health. Psychological difficulties are not well accepted in the community, often resulting in rejection and distrust[11]. Behaviour that has been previously interpreted as eccentric is often re-interpreted when the person is classified as disturbed. Once a person has had therapeutic assistance in hospital, acceptance back into the community can be hindered[12]. It is not just attitudes that change, but behaviour as well. In one experiment[13] subjects were asked to engage in a co-operative task with a stranger, who was actually a confederate of the experimenter. One group of subjects was led to believe that the stranger was psychologically disturbed, whereas a second group was not given this (inaccurate) information. Although those in the first group did not admit to any prejudices against the 'disturbed' stranger, they were less willing to work with him again and there were several behavioural differences between the groups. Insofar as self-evaluations are dependent on the reactions of others[14], classification may well affect the well-being and the behaviour of patients.

2.3   Cognitive Theories

There are many similarities between the psychodynamic and cognitive approaches to personality. In both, past experience plays an important role; in addition, a goal of the therapies that arise from both approaches is to give the patient the means to solve his difficulties in the future. Therapists of both schools would agree that feelings about oneself and one's relationships are crucial. However, the emphasis in cognitive therapy is on the conscious workings of the mind rather than the unconscious. Whereas the psychodynamic theorist might argue that many of the motivations and impulses that result in symptoms can only be made clear to the individual with therapeutic assistance, a cognitive therapist would contend that the person's consciousness holds the key and that people already have the tools available to solve problems if they were used effectively. For these psychologists, the way the person interprets the world is his personality. The assumptions and expectations that he makes about the environment determine his behaviour and his reactions. Two examples of therapists who take this position are George Kelly and Aaron Beck.

George Kelly

Just as a scientist makes observations, has expectations about what will be found and modifies his theories in the light of new results, Kelly suggested that people use the scientific method in their everyday lives. Personal theories about how the world works help the individual to make sense of the environment and lead to certain predictions about future events. For example, someone might have

49

the theory that the world is a kind place and that everyone can be trusted. This theory could lead to the prediction that if money is left on a table in a public place, it would still be there when the owner returns. If the money is not there, the person might predict that someone found it and turned it in to a Lost Property Office — a way of fitting the event into the theory. If the money could not be traced, the person may decide his theory is not a good one and change it. Not only do people have theories about the actions of others, they also have theories about themselves. To say 'I'm not the sort of person who does that kind of thing' indicates a theory about oneself that will determine to some extent how events are perceived and which behaviour will be shown.

Existence is said to be like a series of experiments and each person holds his own theories about how life works, selectively attending to some phenomena and ignoring others. A scientist works first by inductive reasoning, looking for a general rule that explains or accounts for his observations. An infant initially perceives his world with no theory, but gradually builds up a view that can be used to explain why people react to him in the way they do. If adults react negatively towards a child, he might conclude that 'I am worthless' or 'The world is essentially a hurtful place'. These conclusions eventually become premises upon which behaviour and interpretations of others' behaviour are based.

Different people have different ways of understanding their world (their theories) and place emphasis on different aspects of it. For one person, generosity may be important, for another, happiness. When asked to describe someone, the first person might be more likely to use a generosity – miserliness dimension, whereas the second would tend to select happiness – sadness. These descriptions are known as *constructs*. In order to make a person's constructs explicit, Kelly devised a technique that involved the individual naming three objects: three cars for example, or three people. The person is then asked to say how two of the objects are similar to each other but different from the third. Through questioning, the terms in which the world is viewed can be discovered. Rowe[15] provides an illustration, in which a student is asked to name three cars:

> Let us suppose the student names a Rolls-Royce, a Lamborghini and a Ford Popular. Then the psychologist asks the student to tell him one way in which two of these are the same and the other different. The student could reply in a number of ways. He could say that two are fast and one is slow or two are elegant and one ordinary, or two are expensive and one cheap. . . .
>
> Suppose the student replies that two are fast and one slow. Then the psychologist asks, 'Which would you prefer, the fast or the slow?'
>
> Suppose the student replies 'The fast'. Then the psychologist asks, 'Why is it important for you to have the fast one?'
>
> 'Because', the student might reply, 'I like driving fast. I'm really feeling alive when I'm driving fast'.
>
> 'Why', the psychologist will then ask, 'is it important to feel really alive?'
>
> 'Because I want to make the most of my life while I'm here to enjoy it', says the student, thereby defining an aspect of his philosophy of life. (Ref. 15, p. 14)

The last statement made by the student seems to be an important rule for him and could be expected to influence his approach to many situation.

When applied to patients in therapy, the objects (or *elements* as they are termed) are often people (mother, father, self, for example) and the terms the patient chooses to distinguish between them are taken as important constructs. Additional elements can then be added — usually individuals important in the patient's life — and each categorized in terms of the previously elicited constructs, to provide a grid (a 'repertory grid').

Fig. 2.1 illustrates how this information can be presented, being the result of a statistical analysis of information obtained from a repertory grid. In this particular grid, five elements were elicited — mother, father, sister, self and ideal self (how the patient wishes to be). There were also several constructs, including depressed, happy, careful with money. The distance between elements and constructs is taken as a measure of their similarity. Thus, the self is similar to the mother and both are careful about money. By contrast, the sister is quite different, being happy rather than depressed and perceived as being more similar to the patient's ideal self than is the patient. The repertory grid thus provides a way of portraying for both patient and therapist how the patient views the world.

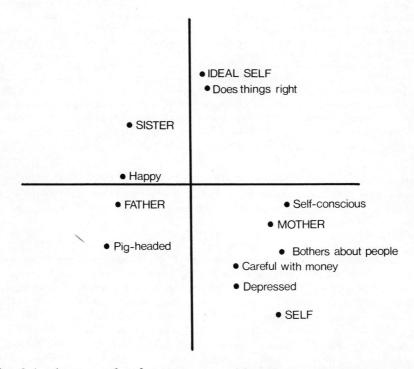

Fig. 2.1 An example of a repertory grid analysis. (Reproduced from D. Rowe, *The Experience of Depression*, 1978, by permission of John Wiley & Sons Ltd.)

This first step then leads to a consideration of how the patient might alter his or her perceptions. Personal change is difficult because change implies an alteration in the way the person sees the world, a frightening and anxiety-provoking prospect. This may be particularly so when 'core' constructs are involved — those constructs that deal specifically with perceptions of the self. The idea in this kind of therapy is to loosen the patient's theories so that new and more helpful ones can be formed. Conversation plays an important part, with the therapist challenging and adding to the patient's constructs, but Kelly advocated more active methods as well. The patient might be encouraged to 'role play' for example: he might be given a personality sketch of an individual and asked to act as if he were that person for a brief period:

> The client is to eat the kind of food they think this person would eat, read the books they would read, respond to other people in the way in which this person would respond, dream the dreams this person would dream, and try to interpret their experiences entirely in terms of this 'person'. It should be made clear to the client that this is a limited venture and that after a fixed period it will come to an end and they will revert 'to being themselves'. It must be made clear that the fixed role is in no sense being set up as an ideal, it is merely a hypothesis for them to experiment with, a possibility for them to experience. During the short period of fixed-role enactment the client sees the therapist frequently to discuss the interpretation of the fixed role, to consider the kind of experiences they are getting and to play the role with the therapist.
>
> At the end of the fixed role enactment it is hoped that the client will have experienced behaviours from people of a kind not likely to have been elicited by their usual 'self'. They will have been forced into a detailed psychological examination of this imaginary person and thereby have been less centred on themselves. Above all, they may have begun to suspect that a person is self-inventing and that they are not necessarily trapped forever inside their own autobiography and their own customary thought and behaviour. (Ref. 15, p. 14)

An appealing aspect of the repertory-grid technique is that it can be used to assess the progress and outcome of therapy. The distance between elements and their position relative to constructs might change, for example, so that the 'self' matches the 'ideal self' more closely. Furthermore, the actual constructs elicited by the grid may alter, providing further evidence of change.

Aaron Beck

Kelly's repertory-grid technique provides a way of making explicit an individual's personal theories about the world. The notion of personal theories is also central to Beck's work, but, unlike Kelly, Beck argues that some theories are better than others, and that 'erroneous' perceptions can be identified. Just as a psychodynamic therapist would argue that no one has a perfect upbringing and that a certain amount of internal conflict is inevitable, Beck contends that everyone operates on some premises that are mistaken and that distort reality. As a therapist, he works from the patient's comments and the feelings underlying these comments in order to discover the rules that led to difficulty and the decision to seek help. The problem for both the therapist and the patient is to find these premises, examine them and to make changes if need be. An analogy can be drawn here between the use of rules of grammar and the use of these premises. When talking, people do not consciously form their sentences. They do not have to take care to place the subject before the verb because this rule is so well learned. Similarly, when interpreting a situation, people do not consciously reflect on the rules they use in making sense of that event. But when learning a new language, it is necessary to consider what is being said very carefully, taking time to place the parts of speech in their correct order, for instance. In Beck's therapy, the patient is encouraged to consider the rules he uses: first to consider how premises can be self-defeating, and second to experiment with new premises that had not been previously considered. In order to illustrate how the learning of this new language operates, it is helpful to provide an illustration of the approach. The medical student in this example is having difficulty in asserting himself in various situations:

Patient:	I have to give a talk before my class tomorrow and I'm scared stiff.
Therapist:	What are you afraid of?
Patient:	I think I'll make a fool of myself.
Therapist:	Suppose you do . . . make a fool of yourself . . . Why is that so bad?
Patient:	I'll never live it down.
Therapist:	'Never' is a long time . . . Now look here, suppose they ridicule you. Can you die from it?
Patient:	Of course not.
Therapist:	Suppose they decide you're the worst public speaker that ever lived . . . will this ruin your future career?
Patient:	No . . . But it would be nice if I could be a good speaker.
Therapist:	Sure it would be nice. But if you flubbed it, would your parents or your wife disown you?
Patient:	No . . . They're very sympathetic.
Therapist:	Well, what would be so awful about it?
Patient:	I would feel pretty bad.
Therapist:	For how long?
Patient:	For about a day or two.
Therapist:	And then what?
Patient:	Then I'd be OK.
Therapist:	So you're scaring yourself just as though your fate hangs in the balance.
Patient:	That's right. It does feel as though my whole future is at stake.
Therapist:	Now somewhere along the line, your thinking got fouled up . . . and you tend to regard any failure as though it's the end of the world . . . What you have to do is get your failures labelled correctly — as failure to reach a goal, not as disaster. You have to start to challenge your wrong premises. (Ref. 16, pp. 250 – 51)

For Beck it is not necessary to look for underlying unconscious motives for the student's anxieties. The cause of the difficulty lies within the assumptions that the student makes about himself and his environment. Another facet of Beck's cognitive therapy that is illustrated by this excerpt is that it is based on logical inference: the therapist plays the role of a teacher who points out the patient's faulty reasoning. He argues that many of the rules that predispose people to various disabilities can be outlined and discussed in therapy, and that there are several that recur frequently. The reader may find some of his or her own unstated assumptions in the following list:

1. In order to be happy, I have to be successful in whatever I undertake.
2. To be happy, I must be accepted (liked, admired) by all people at all times.
3. If I'm not on top, I'm a flop.
4. It's wonderful to be popular, famous, wealthy: it's terrible to be unpopular, mediocre.
5. If I make a mistake, it means that I'm inept.
6. My value as a person depends on what others think of me.
7. I can't live without love. If my spouse (sweetheart, parent, child) doesn't love me, I'm worthless.
8. If somebody disagrees with me, it means he doesn't like me.
9. If I don't take advantage of every opportunity to advance myself, I will regret it later. (Ref. 16, pp. 255 – 56)

These rules are often accompanied by a series of 'shoulds':

1. I should be the utmost of generosity, considerateness, dignity, courage, unselfishness.
2. I should be the perfect lover, friend, parent, teacher, student, spouse.
3. I should be able to endure any hardship with equanimity.
4. I should be able to find a quick solution to every problem.
5. I should never feel hurt; I should always be happy and serene.
6. I should know, understand, and foresee everything.
7. I should always be spontaneous; I should always control my feelings.
8. I should assert myself; I should never hurt anybody else.
9. I should never be tired or get sick.
10. I should always be at peak efficiency. (Ref. 16, pp. 255 – 256)

In particular, Beck has been interested in depression. This difficulty can be seen in many ways (for example some psychodynamic theorists consider depression to be the result of anger, which is turned in toward the self rather than being expressed towards others), but Beck prefers to see it in terms of faulty premises. He suggests that there is a triad of cognitive patterns that force the person to view events in a particular way. The first component is the pattern of interpreting experiences in a negative way. Life is seen as a series of burdens and obstacles, all of which detract from the quality of life. This cognition is often associated with loss of friends, time or money. The second component involves negative self-perceptions — of being inadequate or unworthy in some way — and is often associated with self-reproach and self-castigation. The third component consists of negative views about the future, which seems unremittingly difficult and full of continuing deprivation. Beck contends that if depressed people can be given evidence to illustrate that they can, indeed, attain goals, or if they can be helped to re-evaluate their present performance, their depression will be lessened[17, 18]. Some preliminary results suggest that therapy based on this view might be more effective than chemotherapy[19].

54

2.4   Personality Tests

Projective Techniques

Two of the best known projective tests are the Thematic Apperception Test (TAT) and the Rorschach Inkblot Test. In both instruments the person is presented with vague and ambiguous pictures and asked to describe them. There are no right or wrong descriptions, the assumption being that the way the person makes sense of the pictures is a reflection of personality. The important attributes of personality are said to be shown through the use of repeated themes. If, for example, an individual often describes the pictures in terms of parent – child relationships, then his relationship with his parents might be particularly important for that person. The TAT consists of 20 cards, showing vague and ambiguous scenes. In fact, one of the cards is blank. The examiner asks the person to concoct a story that suggests what led up to the event shown, what is presently occuring, and what the outcome may be. The kinds of stories a person tells are said to indicate his aspirations and needs. The Rorschach includes 10 inkblots in reds, greens and blacks. People are asked to suggest what the inkblots might represent and the responses are coded in terms of their number and the parts of the inkblot that are included in the description. The actual content is not considered to be so important, unless the description is very unusual.

Projective techniques have not been well accepted by psychologists for several reasons. One requirement of a measuring instrument is that observations taken at one time are similar to observations taken at another. In addition, it is important to have agreement between different observers when applying the measure in the same circumstances. The *reliability* of projective techniques is not good, since the same description of the TAT or Rorschach materials produces differing interpretations from different examiners. Another important requirement of personality instruments is that they measure what they purport to measure (i.e. underlying personality factors) rather than something else (e.g. what the examiner wants to hear). This is termed *construct validity*. There is evidence that responses on projective techniques are subject to temporary mood changes in the individual: if, for example, people are asked not to eat breakfast before describing the pictures on the TAT, they are more likely to give responses concerning food. In general, projective techniques seem to be sensitive to transient states as well as to longer-term ones. A further difficulty with projective techniques is that they are not particularly suitable for research purposes. Examiners require long training in order to interpret the responses and even then the materials do not lend themselves easily to numerical assessment. For testing large numbers of people, instruments that can be scored easily and provide data that can be readily analysed using statistical techniques are preferred.

Such difficulties with projective materials have led many psychologists to question their usefulness in assessing personality. However, it has been argued that they can be helpful in providing a global view of individuals when precise descriptions are not needed. They may, for instance, be useful in opening conversation between a therapist and a patient when the patient is feeling unsure or hesitant[20, 21].

Personality Questionnaires

Although psychotherapists argue that their concepts are applicable to everyone, their ideas have developed through working with people who have sought psychiatric assistance. Although these theories might apply to this specialized population, they may not be appropriate for everyone. Because psychotherapists do not use 'common sense' terms, this can easily lead to misinterpretation of their theories. For these reasons, and the problems of reliability and validity mentioned in the discussion on projective techniques, descriptive approaches to the study of personality have gained popularity amongst experimental psychologists. These are more easily open to measurement and are based on common-sense terms. When describing a person, the reader may well use a series of adjectives — honest, shy and hardworking, for example. Someone else might be described as less honest and shy but more outgoing and independent. Such descriptions illustrate that people have everyday ways of understanding personality that not only include adjectives but also scales as well — one individual might be more or less shy than another. Psychologists have systematized this approach in studying personality by attempting to provide instruments that measure the extent to which a person possesses certain characteristics, or *traits*, and to compare the results with others.

The method of personality assessment that has generated most research is the self-report questionnaire, in which subjects are asked questions about their behaviour or their thoughts, and are given a choice of answers, often a simple 'Yes' or 'No'. The decision about which questions (or *items* as they are usually called) are included depends on the purpose of the questionnaire. There are three main ways of selecting items. First, the items may be suggested through observation. For example, several clinicians have noted that patients with coronary heart disease often have distinctive personalities, characterized by striving for achievement, competitiveness and impatience. This constellation of traits has become known as the Type A personality, as compared to those who do not have these characteristics (known as Type B personalities). Jenkins *et al.*[22] constructed several items from interviews and observations that seemed to tap this distinction, arriving at the Jenkins Activity Survey.

Second, items may be selected empirically. Perhaps a researcher aims to distinguish people who belong to two groups, such as those who have been diagnosed as neurotic and those who have not been so diagnosed. The investigator could ask many questions of the people in each group and then subsequently use only those items that a majority of one group answered one way and the other group the other way. These items could then be later used as a diagnostic tool, assuming, of course, that the diagnosis of the original criterion group was a valid and reliable one and that the selection of the original control group was representative of the general population. This empirical approach was used in

56

the development of the Minnesota Multiphasic Personality Inventory (the MMPI), which is widely used in the United States. The MMPI contains 13 scales, each of which is intended to differentiate between various criterion and control groups. The scales include hypochondriasis, depression and social introversion – extraversion. Like the Jenkins Activity Survey, the MMPI is purely descriptive and there is no explanation given why the people in the various groups answer in particular ways or why they came to enter that group in the first place. Although some of the items are obvious (e.g. 'I am happy most of the time' is an item on the depression scale) others are less so (e.g. 'It takes a lot of argument to convince most people of the truth' in the same scale). The inclusion of an item is not dependent on being obviously applicable, but only on whether or not it discriminates.

An example of how the MMPI could be used in practice is given by a study on reactions of cancer patients to their diagnosis. The questionnaire was given to 133 newly diagnosed patients who were followed-up monthly for the next 6 months. A social worker, who did not know the MMPI results, took several measures of their emotional distress, so that the patients could be divided into those who showed a high degree of emotional distress and those who showed a low degree of distress. The highly distressed group scored higher on several scales of the MMPI, including emphasis on physical complaints, depression, anxiety and withdrawal. About 75% of the patients could be classified as showing high or low distress by the MMPI results, suggesting that the question-naire might be used to predict patients' reactions to the diagnosis[23].

A third approach to the design of personality questionnaires is based on factor analysis. Essentially, this method involves correlating subjects' answers on one item with their answers on all other items. In some cases the subjects would give similar responses to a group of questions: if they scored high on one they would score high on others. In other cases, the scores on one item would not correlate with scores on others. Each group of items which correlate or cluster together constitute a factor, and this factor is given a label that reflects the kinds of items that were found to cluster together. For example, people might respond to items about their relationship with parents and with friends in similar ways that may be appropriately be subsumed under a factor labelled 'dependency'. Factors may be selected to be independent of each other, so that an individual's score on one factor should not be related to his score on others.

In practice, the development of personality questionnaires often involve all three approaches. The Jenkins Activity Survey was first developed on the basis on observations, but later, items found not to discriminate between coronary and non-coronary patients were dropped. In the development of the Maudsley Personality Inventory (and the later versions, the Eysenck Personality Inventory and the Eysenck Personality Questionnaire)[24, 25], Eysenck originally chose many items on the basis of observation, factor-analysed them, and finally made adjustments according to the criterion-group approach. He suggests that there are three important factors — psychoticism, neuroticism and introversion – extraversion. The Eysenck Personality Questionnaire (EPQ) consists of 90 items, each of which is answered by a 'Yes' or 'No'. The individual's responses are compared to a large sample of others' answers in order to discover how unusual the responses are, so that this questionnaire, like the others mentioned, does not give an absolute measure of personality but simply a relative one. Someone is said to be extraverted, for example, if he replies to more of the items in an extraverted way than most other people. The responses of this large sample are called 'norms' and it is important to take account of the characteristics of the normative population when making the comparison: the individual should be similar in age, sex and cultural background to the comparison group. Another feature of this questionnaire, again shared by others, is that psychoticism, neuroticism and extraversion – introversion are considered to be continuous rather than discrete entities. The assumption is that everyone possesses these traits to some extent.

One further aspect of personality questionnaires merits attention. It is important that the examiner has some idea of how honestly and carefully the person has answered the items. For several reasons, people may present a picture of themselves that is not an accurate one but, rather, a picture that is socially desirable. Some people may not want to admit, even to themselves, their foibles and embarrassing thoughts, so that questionnaires often include some indication of how honestly the person is reporting his personality. Most questionnaires include one or more 'Lie' scales, in which questions about common frailties are asked. For example, on the EPQ, questions such as 'Have you ever taken advantage of someone?' are included. If the person answers too many of these kinds of items in a socially desirable way, then the validity of his answers on the other scales is called into question.

An appealing aspect of Eysenck's questionnaire is that he, unlike most other trait psychologists, has not been content to provide a purely descriptive outline of personality. There is a common tendency to use traits to explain behaviour, but this is logically incorrect. Traits are inferred from behaviour and cannot, therefore, be used to explain it. For example, if someone behaves in an honest way, people are likely to attribute this behaviour to an underlying trait of honesty. If this person returns some money that he had found, his friends may explain this by saying 'Well, he returned the money because he is honest'. This is a tempting mistake to make, one that Eysenck has avoided. He considers the responses on the EPI and EPQ scales to be strongly influenced by genetic factors. Vulnerability to psychotic behaviour is considered to be inherited, the predisposition becoming apparent in disturbed environments. High scorers on the neuroticism scale (who are often upset and lack confidence) are thought to have over-reactive autonomic nervous systems, whereas high scorers on the extraversion scale (who are impulsive and sociable) are said to be cortically inhibited. Although there are some specific problems with this theory, particularly using biological explanations for social behaviour, the attraction of Eysenck's position is that he has attempted to provide an understanding of why people have certain traits rather than simply describing them.

It may seem that the best way to validate a personality questionnaire is simply to administer and score it and then go back to the individual and ask if the results reflect his or her personality accurately. If the person were to say yes, then the examiner might conclude that the instrument is a valid one. There is a major problem with this approach, however, as shown by a study[26] in which subjects were asked to fill out a questionnaire and then some days later were given a summary of their personalities. They were then asked to evaluate the summaries' accuracy, and most thought it was a good description of them. Although the subjects could not know it, all the summaries were the same, containing such vague statements as 'You have a tendency to be critical of yourself' and 'Your sexual adjustment has presented problems for you'. These statements could apply to anyone. Subjects' assessments of accuracy are unlikely, then, to provide a good indication of construct validity (a term mentioned earlier with respect to projective techniques).

Perhaps a better indication of the validity of a personality test would be if it could predict how someone behaves. There are two basic assumptions behind the use of personality questionnaires: (1) that they tap underlying dispositions that are relatively independent of circumstances, and (2) that people act consistently in different situations. If person A is more assertive, aggressive and honest than person B in one situation, then A should be more assertive, aggressive and honest in other situations as well. If a theory is unable to predict how someone will act, (i.e. it has little *predictive validity*) then it could be argued that it should be discarded.

Eysenck's theory has met with some success in these respects. In several objective tests (e.g. under experimentally imposed stress) high scorers on the extraversion and neuroticism scales give different results from low scorers. Reactions to drugs and sedation vary along lines similar to those that Eysenck's theory would predict (see Chapter 11). Other personality questionnaires that have been designed for specific purposes have also been useful. The Jenkins Activity Survey, for example, has been validated in a prospective study. Over 3000 people were monitored in a long-term study of the correlates of coronary heart disease. Some 8½ years after the initial tests were given, 257 males in the sample who were initially healthy had some kind of heart complaint. Even when serum lipids, blood pressure, obesity and smoking were taken into account, Type A men had over twice the risk of heart disease than Type B men. Of course, many of the Type As did not report heart disease and many Type Bs did, indicating that other factors besides personality were also significant[27, 28].

However, the relationship between scores on personality tests and observations of behaviour have often been found to be tenuous, correlations being quite low[29]. A similar lack of correspondence between what people say they would do and what they actually do in practice has been found in research on attitudes. Attitudes are said to be general predispositions to respond towards objects or people in positive or negative ways, but they have been found to be poor predictors of behaviour[30]. For example, LaPiere[31] in the 1930s sent out questionnaires to many proprietors of restaurants and hotels in the United States, asking them the question 'Would you accept members of the Chinese race as guests in your establishment?'. This question was taken as a measure of attitudes, and he related answers to this question to actual acceptance of a Chinese couple at these establishments. Although most replied that they would not admit such a couple (reflecting a prejudice of the time), in fact the couple were not turned away in any of the restaurants and hotels when this attitude was put to the test.

Similarly, there is evidence that how a person behaves in one set of circumstances often provides a poor predictor of behaviour in dissimilar situations. Ellsworth et al.[32] asked both the staff of a psychiatric hospital and the patients' family and friends for assessments of patients' behaviour: the way in which they acted in hospital showed little congruence with the ways they acted outside it. Patients who showed improvements in hospital were not necessarily those who were improved once they rejoined the community. Such studies have important implications for medical care. Simply because a patient appears hostile in a hospital or a consulting room may not provide clues as to his or her behaviour elsewhere. As mentioned above, there seems to be a strong tendency for people to cite personality variables as causes of behaviour, a tendency that may often be misplaced[33]. For example, physicians often attribute lack of compliance in their patients to an uncooperative personality, but there are few indications that this provides an accurate assessment of the reasons for their behaviour (see Chapter 13).

Such results have thrown personality and attitude theorists into some disarray. Many psychologists have argued that personality is simply an illusion, and advocated rejection of the concept. Although people do act consistently, perhaps this consistency is not due to personality factors but to recurring patterns in the environment. For example, people tend to appear the same over time because their physical appearance changes only slightly and they have many routines that they repeat daily. For some of these psychologists it is the consequences of behaviour that are significant and an analysis of these consequences will provide good predictors of how people will act (a possibility discussed in the next chapter). For others, the expectations that people have of behaviour form the important variables: the roles that people play are seen to be of prime importance (see Chapter 6).

Despite the lack of correspondence between traits and behaviour and between attitudes and behaviour, the common-sense impression that internal dispositions are related to behaviour persists. In reply to these criticisms, personality theorists have sought more subtle and complex explanations of this relationship. Perhaps part of the difficulty is that an assumption behind the use of personality questionnaires is that everyone can be measured on every trait, without regard for the importance of these traits for each individual. However, only certain traits may be central to a person's personality and only these should be used to predict how he or she will behave. In studies where this distinction is made (e.g. Bem and Allen[34]), prediction of consistency is much improved. Perhaps, too, consistency for some kinds of traits is greater than that for others:

although honesty may vary across situations, cognitive tests (such as those on intelligence, see Chapter 5) provide reasonably good predictors of actual performance.

Other psychologists have advocated an intermediate position between those who argue that traits are significant (if only the important ones were isolated) and those who argue that the environment is crucial. They suggest that a useful approach is to consider behaviour as influenced by the environment, but also that people choose the situations in which they act and select the significant aspects of the situation upon which to respond. These responses subsequently affect the character and course of these situations. Instead of considering behaviour to be the product of either personality traits or situational determinants, the argument is that they interact, mutually influencing behaviour[35]. This position implies that, as advocated by the cognitive theorists discussed earlier in the chapter, it is the meaning of each situation that is important, and if psychologists are to be able to predict behaviour, it is these idiosyncratic meanings that need to be explored.

Summary

Three major trends in the study of personality are considered, psychodynamic, cognitive and descriptive approaches.

Although psychodynamic theories have developed significantly since the work of Freud, with greater emphasis on interpersonal relationships rather than considering an individual in isolation, many of his original concepts remain influential. Most psychodynamic theorists believe that normal development can be considered as a series of stages. Each stage places new demands on the individual, many of which are concerned with relationships with others, particularly the parents. Psychological problems are said to arise when these demands are too difficult to cope with. These problems are 'worked through' in psychotherapy, a term encompassing various techniques by which a patient is able to gain insight about his or her feelings. Measuring the success of psychotherapy is problematic because of difficulties in defining what a cure might be. However, some ways of evaluating progress do exist. Although Freud originally classified psychological difficulties according to their aetiology, the system now in use depends on symptomatology and has three broad distinctions: neurosis, psychosis and personality disorders. The scheme implies that a state of normality can be identified, although in practice, normality can be defined in many ways.

Although psychodynamic theorists place emphasis on the unconscious, cognitive theorists are more concerned with the conscious workings of the mind. Some, like Kelly, liken people to scientists who try to make sense of, and predict, events in their everyday lives. Everyone has his or her own theory, which is said to be the individual's personality. Beck, another cognitive theorist, believes that psychological problems are associated with certain erroneous beliefs. Treatment consists of helping the patient to identify and correct such unhelpful beliefs.

Unlike the first two approaches, which were developed by therapists through their work with patients, descriptive approaches to personality have been primarily the domain of experimental psychologists and tend to be the most open to measurement and statistical analysis. Personality questionnaires are composed of statements or *items* that are selected either by observing differences between groups, identifying differences between groups by research or through factor-analytic methods. Although these questionnaires often simply describe people as possessing certain traits without explaining why they behave as they do, Eysenck has developed a theory to account for the differences, based on genetic factors. Difficulties in validating personality questionnaires have led some psychologists to consider the situation in which the behaviour takes place as well as the particular individual.

Suggested reading

Two books that provide introductions to psychotherapy are Storr[6] and D. Brown and J. Pedder, *Introduction to psychotherapy*, Tavistock Publications, London, 1979.

References

1. Sullivan, H.S., *The interpersonal theory of psychiatry*, Norton, New York, 1953.
2. Erickson, E.H., *Childhood and society*, Pelican, Harmondsworth, 1965.
3. Whitehorn, J.C. and Betz, B.J., A study of psychotherapeutic relationships between physicians and schizophrenic patients, *American Journal of Psychiatry*, 1954, **111**, 321 – 331.
4. Rogers, C.R., *On becoming a person*, Constable Publishers, London, 1967.
5. Rogers, C.R. and Truax, C.B., The therapeutic conditions antecedent to change *In* Rogers, C.R., Gendlin, G.T., Liesler, D.V. and Truax, C.B., *The therapeutic relationship and its impact*, University of Wisconsin Press, Madison, 1967.
6. Storr, A., *The art of psychotherapy*, Secker and Warburg, London, 1979. Reproduced by permission of Secker & Warburg and A.D. Peters & Co. Ltd.
7. Silverman, L.H., Psychoanalytic theory: 'The reports of my death are greatly exaggerated', *American Psychologist*, 1976, **31**, 621 – 637.
8. Raimy, V.C., Self-reference in counselling interviews, *Journal of Consulting Psychology*, 1948, **12**, 153 – 163.
9. Slater, E. and Cowie, V., *Genetics of mental disorders*, Oxford University Press, London, 1971.
10. Preiss, J.J., Self and role in medical education, *In* Gordon, C. and Gergen, K.J. (eds.), *The self in social interaction*, Wiley, London, 1968.
11. Brockman, J., D'Arcy, C. and Edmonds, L., Facts or artifacts? Changing public attitudes towards the mentally ill, *Social Science and Medicine*, 1979, **13A**, 673 – 682.
12. Whatley, C.D., Social attitudes towards discharged mental patients, *Social problems*, 1959, **6**, 313 – 320.
13. Farina, A., Mental illness and the impact of believing others know about it, *Journal of Abnormal Psychology*, 1971, **77**, 1 – 5.

14. Fazio, R.H., Effrein, E.A. and Falender, V.J., Self perceptions following social interaction, *Journal of Personality and Social Psychology*, 1981, **41**, 232 – 242.
15. Rowe, D., *The experience of depression*, Wiley, Chichester, 1978.
16. Beck, A.T., *Cognitive therapy and the emotional disorders*, International Universities Press, New York, 1976.
17. Loeb, A., Beck, A.T. and Diggory, J., Differential effects of success and failure on depressed and non-depressed patients, *Journal of Nervous and Mental Disease*, 1971, **152**, 106 – 114.
18. Beck, A.T., Rush, J., Shaw, B.F. and Emery, G., *Cognitive therapy of depression*, Wiley, London, 1979.
19. Goldberg D., Cognitive therapy for depression, *British Medical Journal*, 1982, **284**, 143 – 144.
20. Anastasi, A., *Psychological testing* (3rd edn.), Macmillan, London, 1968.
21. Cronbach, L.J., *Essentials of psychological testing* (3rd edn.), Harper and Row, London, 1970.
22. Jenkins, C.D., Rosenman, R.H. and Freidman, M., Development of an objective psychological test for the determination of the coronary-prone behaviour pattern in employed men, *Journal of Chronic Diseases*, 1967, **20**, 371 – 379.
23. Sobel, H.J. and Worden, J.W., The MMPI as a predictor of psychosocial adaptation to cancer, *Journal of Consulting and Clinical Psychology*, 1979, **47**, 716 – 724.
24. Eysenck, H.J., *The scientific study of personality*, Routledge & Kegan Paul, London, 1952.
25. Eysenck, H.J. and Eysenck, S.B.G., *Psychoticism as a dimension of personality*, Hodder and Stoughton, London, 1976.
26. Forer, B.R., The fallacy of personality validation: A classroom demonstration of gullibility, *Journal of Abnormal and Social Psychology*, 1949, **44**, 118 – 123.
27. Rosenman, R.H., Brand, R.J., Jenkins, C.D., Friedman, M., Straus, R. and Wurm, M., Coronary heart disease in the Western Collaborative Group Study, *Journal of the American Medical Association*, 1975, **233**, 872 – 877.
28. Matteson, M.T. and Ivancevich, J.M., The coronary-prone behaviour pattern: A review and appraisal, *Social Science and Medicine*, 1980, **14A**, 337 – 351.
29. Mischel, W., Toward a cognitive social learning reconceptualisation of personality *Psychological Review*, 1973, **80**, 252 – 283.
30. Wicker, A.W., Attitudes versus actions, *Journal of Social Issues*, 1969, **25**, 41 – 78.
31. LaPiere, R.T., Attitudes versus actions, *Social Forces*, 1934, **13**, 230 – 237.
32. Ellsworth, R.B., Foster, L., Childers, B., Arthur, G. and Kroeker, D., Hospital and community adjustment as perceived by psychiatric patients, their families and staff, *Journal of Consulting and Clinical Psychology, Monograph Supplement*, **32**, 1968.
33. Ross, L., The intuitive psychologist and his short comings: Distortions in the attribution process *In* Berkowitz, L. (ed.), *Advances in Experimental Social Psychology*, vol. 10, Academic Press, New York, 1977.
34. Bem, D.J. and Allen, A., On predicting some of the people some of the time, *Psychological Review*, 1974, **81**, 506 – 520.
35. Endler, N.S. and Magnusson, D., *Interactional psychology and personality*, Wiley, London, 1976.

3
The Behavioural Approach

3.1 Introduction

The previous chapter discussed three trends in personality research — psycho-dynamic, trait and cognitive theories. Common to all three approaches is the notion that 'personality *is* something and *does* something. . . . It is what lies *behind* specific acts and *within* the individual' (Allport[1], p. 48). Behaviour was considered to be an outward manifestation of inner drives, traits or cognitions. Unusual or maladaptive behaviour would therefore reflect an underlying problem, only 'signalling' the real difficulty. Although theorists in this tradition have become increasingly concerned with environmental influences on behaviour, the focus of interest has been on individual differences and inner predispositions to behave in certain ways.

Some psychologists were dissatisfied with the personality approach, particularly with the psychodynamic theories. These psychologists argued that the postulated inner states that were said to underlie behaviour could never be understood scientifically. They found that when the symptom alone was treated, only infrequently did the patient return with another manifestation of a problem: little evidence was found for symptom substitution. Although the psychodynamic approach implied that deviant behaviour was in some way fundamentally different from normal behaviour and the experiences involved in normal development differed from those of abnormal development, the approach advocated by the psychologists discussed in the present chapter implied the opposite: that behaviour which could be considered unusual or maladaptive was acquired in the same way as other, more desirable, behaviour. Instead of developing principles in clinical settings with small samples of patients and uncontrolled case studies, they argued, the science of psychology should be firmly based in the laboratory. Only experimental studies could be used to critically evaluate the validity of a theory or the efficacy of a therapy. This approach thus considered intuition and insight inadequate in themselves for the study of man's behaviour.

Many of the studies mentioned in this chapter are based on experiments with non-human animals, such as rats and pigeons, in artificial laboratory situations, such as learning to press a lever in order to gain a drink or a pellet of food. The reader may feel that this work provides a poor basis for forming conclusions about how humans learn, with their apparently greater ability to understand and interpret situations. Simply because rats seem to learn in a certain way does not necessarily mean people learn in the same way. And what similarities could there be between pressing a lever and studying for an exam?

There are several answers to such criticisms. First, the use of lower animals in experiments means that some of the ethical problems involved in experimenting with humans can be overcome. Just as society considers it more acceptable to first test drugs on rats before trying them out on humans, so too is it more accepting towards keeping them hungry or thirsty or giving them electric shocks. It seems likely that many of the methods that can be used to alleviate human distress described in this chapter would not have been discovered if only human subjects had been used. (Of course, many people in our society argue that animals should not be used for any kind of experimentation.) A second reply to this criticism is empirical: many of the principles and theories developed through work with rats do seem to apply to humans as well. However dissimilar humans and non-humans may be, there are also many similarities. For psychologists, the term 'learning' is used in a wide sense, applying to many kinds of adaptive changes. The argument is that, in principle, there is little difference between lever-pressing and studying, since they both result in consequences that aid the organism. In the first case it is food to relieve hunger, whereas in the second a pass mark provides a qualification that, in turn, might lead to a job.

The first part of this chapter considers the development of an approach that considers behaviour and behavioural difficulties to be due to environmental influences rather than intrapsychic variables. Refinements have been made to this approach as experimental studies indicated currently held theories were inadequate. In chronological order, the respondent (or classical) model, the instrumental (or operant) model and the observational model have been suggested as ways of explaining how the environment influences behaviour. Most recently, these theories have been expanded to include cognitions. Applications to *behavioural medicine*, which are derived from these models are described. Here, these techniques are termed behaviour therapy or behaviour modification to distinguish them from psychotherapies that involve techniques based on the personality theories of the previous chapter (but note that some writers use the term psychotherapy to include behavioural treatments). These behaviour therapies are relevant because they are used by many clinical psychologists who form part of the paramedical services increasingly associated with general practitioners and hospitals. Parents, too, are sometimes taught such behavioural techniques to reduce their children's problem behaviours, and physicians themselves have been encouraged to make use of them. Many further applications of behaviour therapies to medical problems are outlined in later chapters. Knowledge of the underlying theory is necessary for an understanding of all these therapies.

In addition, the change in emphasis of these theories compared to those of the previous chapter (from inner states to external determinants) has important implications. Foremost amongst these concerns the direction psychological treatment should take. Is there any point in attempting to understand the inner workings of a patient's mind or of helping him to come to terms with childhood experiences if these have little effect on his behaviour? Do behavioural theories provide more useful guidelines for therapy? The chapter concludes with an evaluation of some of the many studies that have attempted to compare therapies based on the two different types of theory: behavioural therapies versus psychotherapies.

3.2 Respondent Conditioning

Pavlov's Experiments

The origins of the respondent or classical conditioning approach are considered to lie with Pavlov (1849 – 1936), a Russian physiologist who studied the digestive system of dogs. He used the concept of a 'reflex' to describe the unlearned and predictable response of producing saliva and stomach digestive juices when food was tasted. All reflexes (others include withdrawal from a painful stimulus and eye-blinking in response to a puff of wind) were thought to have adjustment or protective purposes. He noticed that after several feedings his dogs would begin salivating not only to the taste of food but to the sight of food and even to the sight of the handler who regularly fed them. It seemed as though a connection or association had been made between the sight of food (and the handler) and salivation. He called salivation in this instance a conditioned response, because its occurrence was conditional upon a prior association between seeing the food and tasting it.

Pavlov hypothesized that many such associations could be learned, and performed several experiments to test this prediction. Typically, a stimulus that the animal was likely to notice but that had no prior association with salivation was presented — a light for example. This stimulus was then followed closely in time by food, which normally elicited salivation. Several pairings, or acquisition trials, were conducted in this way. In order to test for the presence of an association, the light was turned on but no food presented: if salivation occurred, a conditioned reflex had been formed. Pavlov showed that many previously neutral stimuli could come to elicit salivation, even though the response may be somewhat weaker (e.g. fewer drops of saliva) than to the original unconditioned stimulus (the food). The more pairings made, the more similar did the conditioned reflex become to the unconditioned one (i.e. the quantity of saliva increased). This finding suggested one means of measuring the strength of the conditioned reflex, in that as the number of drops of saliva increased, the conditioned reflex could be said to be stronger. After a period of time, the response to the conditioned stimulus alone became progressively weaker. Gradually, fewer and fewer drops of saliva were elicited by the light. These trials are known as extinction trials, and provided another measure of the strength of the reflex: the more trials it took before the response was extinguished, the stronger the conditioned reflex could be said to be.

Pavlov came to view the learning of associations between unconditioned and conditioned stimuli as the fundamental building block of all behaviour, contending that learning could be reduced to associations between unlearned reflexes and previously neutral stimuli. He worked out elaborate theories about cortical inhibition and excitation that are still accepted in part by some psychologists and psychiatrists, notably Eysenck whose personality theory was mentioned in the previous chapter.

Although Pavlov's results were important in their own right, perhaps his greatest influence has been in providing a method of studying *behaviour*, as distinct from inner thoughts, images and imagination. An important debate at the turn of the century was between those philosophers and psychologists who thought that man's inner life was the proper area of study and those who disputed this, arguing that these inner states could never be scientifically validated or measured. It was impossible, they claimed, to know if one person has the same image of an event as another person, or to prove that imaginary images exist at all. If this inner life could not be measured, how could psychology discover the laws that govern man's actions? The only way anything could be discovered about a person was from his behaviour — everything else is inferred. Taking classical physics as their model, these psychologists wanted to find mathematical equations that could predict how someone would behave in a given situation. It was behaviour that was important, not the subjective feelings of an individual. This school of thought came to be known as *behaviourism*.

Pavlov's experiments explored many questions consistent with behaviourism. For example, did the timing of presentation of the unconditioned and conditioned stimuli affect the strength of the conditioned reflex? Or, can an animal learn to discriminate between two very similar stimuli? However important the answers to these questions might be, the exciting prospect for psychologists was that they could be answered at all. Unanswerable questions about inaccessible thoughts need not be considered. Here was a method for understanding how an animal adapts to its environment during its lifetime — a contribution that seemed as important as Darwin's.

Perhaps the best known example of the application of his methods to the study of human learning is provided by Watson and Raynor[2] in their study of little Albert and the white rat. Originally, Albert was shown a white rat: he seemed interested in it and wanted to play with it, showing no obvious aversive behaviour towards the animal. Although it may be proper to question the ethics of this study, Watson and Raynor showed how a fear of situations could be learned. They did this by pairing a loud noise (a hammer striking a steel bar) with presentation of the rat, so that each time Albert saw the rat he would also hear the unpleasant noise. Very quickly (after 6 trials) Albert's behaviour changed: he began to show distress at the sight of the rat in the absence of the noise. Further, the distressful behaviour seemed to generalize to other objects similar in appearance to the rat, so that white rabbits, cotton wool and fur coats also elicited the distress. Thus, stimuli that had a similar physical appearance to the original conditioned stimulus also elicited the fear response, a phenomenon termed 'generalization'.

Owing to experiments such as this, the classical conditioning model and the behaviourist perspective gained many adherents. Although conditioned fear responses could not always be shown to be learned in this way, it was argued that many fears could be the result of conditioning. For example, fear of the dark could be learned if darkness was paired with a disturbing experience, such as a loud noise. Several studies conducted in the laboratory showed how this effect could work with several conditions. For example, Rachman[3] presented photographs of women's boots with slides of sexually stimulating women: after several pairings, the men in the study exhibited sexual arousal (as measured by penile volume increase) to the boots alone, and this arousal generalized to other kinds of footwear. Perhaps many fears and sexual difficulties were learned in a similar way outside the laboratory. If so, then there are certain implications for treatment.

Treatments Based on Respondent Conditioning

Instead of examining the patient's inner conflicts, the respondent conditioning paradigm suggests that it is first necessary to discover the patterns of conditioning that led people into difficulty and to modify the learned responses. Perhaps new patterns of more adaptive behaviour could be learned. The second implication concerns the way in which this relearning could be accomplished: in keeping with the emphasis on using techniques discovered and validated in the laboratory, principles such as extinction, the pairing of conditioned and unconditioned stimuli and generalization would be employed. Further, if a method

68

did not alter a patient's behaviour significantly, then it would be discarded and new possibilities explored. Several methods have been developed, including aversion therapy, flooding and systematic desensitization.

Aversion therapy. This kind of therapy is designed to reduce the frequency of behaviour that is considered undesirable. The idea is to pair the undesired behaviour with a noxious stimulus, thus making the behaviour unpleasant and likely to be avoided, just as little Albert avoided the white rat. Any aversive stimulus could be paired with any undesired behaviour in theory, but in practice there are cultural and methodological constraints. A particular behaviour, for instance, may become more or less acceptable depending on current social values and knowledge. In the 1960s and early 1970s homosexuality was considered undesirable. There are many papers in the literature from this time exploring the effect of aversion therapy on homosexuality, but as this sexual practice has become more acceptable, fewer reports have been published. Conversely, smoking has only been viewed as undesirable in recent years, reflected by an increase in the number of studies attempting to modify this behaviour.

There are various practical considerations. The order in which the stimuli are presented is important: it is better to present the stimulus that leads to the undesired behaviour before the aversive stimulus in order for conditioning to take place (called forward conditioning) rather than the other way around (backward conditioning). Perhaps more significant is the research on the long-term effects of aversion therapy. Not all researchers have reported long-term benefits. Often, the effects of aversion therapy diminish in the continued absence of the aversive stimulus. It could also be argued that, even if aversion therapy was consistently effective, the patient was not 'cured': for an alcoholic patient, for instance, a cure might involve an ability to have one or two drinks only, like a non-alcoholic.

Finally, the ethics of aversion therapy have played an important role in the reluctance of many psychologists to use this technique. It is not always clear why someone seeks therapy for a problem. Many of the people who seek assistance for sexual deviations, for example, only do so after they have been detained by law or have been isolated by family and society, so that it is important to question whether it is reasonable to subject patients to aversive stimuli for the sake of society rather than the individual. Given the cultural relativity of many behaviours, psychologists are often unwilling to pursue this kind of treatment.

An interesting form of aversion therapy that reduces this ethical problem somewhat is covert sensitization, in which the patient is asked to imagine the aversive stimulus, rather than experience it. There is evidence that this approach is effective. An example of the technique is the following, used in the treatment of an obese woman with a particular liking for apple pie:

> I want you to imagine you've just had your main meal and you are about to eat your dessert, which is apple pie. As you are about to reach for the fork, you get a funny feeling in the pit of your stomach. You start to feel queasy, nauseous, and sick all over. As you touch the fork, you can feel food particles inching up your throat. You're just

69

about to vomit. As you put the fork into the pie, the food comes up into your mouth. You try to keep your mouth closed because you are afraid that you'll spit the food out all over the place. You bring the piece of pie to your mouth. As you're about to open your mouth, you puke; you vomit all over your hands, the fork, over the pie. It goes all over the table, over the other peoples' food. Your eyes are watering. Snot and mucous are all over your mouth and nose. Your hands feel sticky. There is an awful smell. As you look at this mess you just can't help but vomit again and again until just watery stuff is coming out. Everybody is looking at you with shocked expressions. You turn away from the food and immediately start to feel better. You run out of the room and, as you run out, you feel better and better. You wash and clean yourself up, and it feels wonderful. (Ref. 4, p. 462)

However, covert sensitization does raise a theoretical challenge for behaviourists, since it involves pairing not two observable, external events but images of two behaviours. In order to account for the success of this technique, it is necessary to postulate the existence of mental images within the patient, otherwise the treatment would not be effective. Further, the patient has learned something — has adapted to the environment — not through the pairing of two stimuli alone but also through the verbal instructions of the therapist. Strict behaviourism seems to be inadequate in this case.

Flooding.   This is another technique that uses the classical conditioning model. The approach is based on the possibility that once fears and phobias are learned they are not extinguished because the patient never places himself in the fear-eliciting situation again. For example, a person who is afraid of the dark will avoid dark places and thus the strength of the response will not diminish. Therapists who use flooding encourage the patient to confront the situation repeatedly until they discover that dark places (or spiders or snakes) are not really all that frightening.

There are several case studies in the literature indicating that flooding is an approach that can provide good results in certain conditions, such as agoraphobia. Sreenivasan et al.[5] report the effects of flooding on a young girl who had been extremely fearful of dogs for about 5 years. The fear did not lessen in response to other kinds of therapy, and flooding seemed justified in this case. A passive and friendly dog was chosen and taken off the leash while the girl was in the room:

For the first session, Colleen was apprehensive for several hours before. On arrival in the treatment room she was anxiously scanning the area for the dog. When the dog was led in she froze, visibly paled and her pupils were dilated. Staff talked reassuringly to Colleen, but when the dog was freed she jumped on a chair. She cried and pleaded that the dog should be placed on its leash. Gradually she relaxed slightly but stayed on the chair, becoming anxious and entreating if the dog moved towards the chair. Two of the staff played table tennis and tried unsuccessfully to persuade Colleen to join them. In the second session she was equally anxious but would get down from the chair or table she stood on for a few seconds but was never at ease. Prior to the third session Colleen appeared excited, although she expressed fear and dislike of the sessions. She managed to take part in the table tennis game for brief periods, sitting on the table if the dog ambled towards the table. In the fourth session she could pat the dog if it was not facing her. In the sixth session she tolerated the dog in her lap, and then took the dog for a walk holding the leash to the amazement of her parents who happened to arrive. After this, she was able to take the family pet for a walk and then to go for a drive with the puppy in the car. (Ref. 5, pp. 257 – 258)

After only six sessions of about an hour her fears appeared to subside, as measured by the therapist and subjectively validated by the girl herself. Further, she was no longer troubled by thoughts about dogs attacking her and was now doing well in school. Although the authors note the effectiveness of flooding in this case, they felt that systematic desensitization (considered below) would be less stressful and should precede flooding.

Systematic desensitization. Whereas flooding involves long periods of intense experience with the feared object, systematic desensitization involves a gradual approach to the feared object, usually in imagination, while the patient is deeply relaxed. The technique was developed by Wolpe[6] and its existence is due to his sharp observations rather than to classical conditioning theory itself. Wolpe was conducting research on learning, which included giving cats electric shocks. When the voltage was turned on, the cat would show great distress — rapid respiration and howls. At first, this behaviour ended when the shock ended, but after a few trials the responses continued with increasing strength until the cat would not even eat in the experimental cage. Refusal to eat generalized to the rest of the laboratory and to similar laboratories. Nor did it extinguish.

Wolpe hypothesized that the cat's anxiety about the shock inhibited eating — that fear and eating were in some way incompatible. He reasoned that if food were made available in a situation that was very dissimilar to the cage, anxiety would be lower and feeding would be likely to take place. He studied this possibility by offering food in a dissimilar room and, indeed, the cat began to eat. The animal was then fed in increasingly similar rooms to the laboratory, until it was able to eat within the cage, behaviour that was not shown beforehand. It appeared that eating inhibited anxiety, just as anxiety inhibited eating, so that they were incompatible and reciprocal. This suggested that if behaviour that was incompatible with anxiety could be encouraged, then the anxiety provoked by a stimulus (the cage in the case of the cat, perhaps an exam in the case of humans) could be lowered.

When used with patients, muscle relaxation (rather than food) is used. Relaxation inhibits anxiety by producing physiological states (low heart and respiration rates) opposite to and incompatible with anxiety. The first step in this therapy is to train the person in deep muscle relaxation, generally by tensing and relaxing muscles. Then the patient is asked to rate his anxieties about the particular event under consideration, say taking an exam, so that a hierarchy of anxiety-provoking situations can be developed. The anxiety might be very low a month before the exam but rise as it approaches, reaching a peak while walking to the examination hall. The actual desensitization procedure involves the therapist in relaxing the patient and taking him through the rated anxieties step by step, asking the patient to imagine himself in the situations. Whenever the patient indicates anxiety, he is asked to stop imagining the scene and more relaxation (for 20 – 30 s perhaps) is given. By slowly going up the scale the relaxation counter-conditions the anxiety to the stressful event. Many therapists actually take their patients to the real fear object (i.e. *in vivo*) as well as relying on imagination.

There are many studies that illustrate the efficacy of these kinds of treatments for some kinds of conditions. For example, Munby and Johnston[7] treated agoraphobic patients (people fearful of open or crowded spaces or of taking journeys by bus or train). These patients were given various treatments based on the classical conditioning model, including desensitization and flooding (both in imagination and *in vivo*). For three different groups of patients, the assessors' ratings of agoraphobia indicated that the treatment reduced severity at 6 months after completion and that this improvement was maintained many years later. Further, there did not appear to be any evidence of symptom substitution: careful questioning by the research worker did not reveal any evidence of the appearance of new neurotic disorders.

Such results are consistent with the classical conditioning model, suggesting it can account for some of man's learning and provide effective treatment for behavioural difficulties. It does, however, have problems in accounting for all learning. One difficulty is that imagined scenes of anxiety are effective in therapy, indicating that cognitions are important for understanding such behaviour. A second problem with this approach is its essentially passive nature. Pavlov argued that learning comes about because events happen to occur at about the same time and these become associated within the organism. But this point of view neglects the fact that animals often actively explore their environment and appear to make attempts to influence events. They are active operators as well as passive recipients and rarely wait about until a stimulus occurs. It was the recognition of the importance of this aspect of behaviour that led psychologists in the 1930s to explore another area of learning — instrumental learning.

3.3 Instrumental Conditioning

This kind of learning is called instrumental or operant, because it recognizes that animals operate upon their environment. That is, they actively seek to modify their surroundings by their actions. According to this model of learning, it is the consequences of behaviour that determine what an animal will do. When a positive consequence occurs, the animal is more likely to repeat the behaviour; if the consequences are negative, less likely to repeat it. Usually, the behaviour is random in first instance. For example, a rat running through a T-maze (Fig. 3.1) is equally likely to turn right or left as it runs up from the starting box. But when it happens to turn right, it finds food, and if it is hungry this is a gratifying result. In time, it will tend to turn to the right more often than not if placed back in the starting box. The rat has learned that a right turn results in food. The speed of learning would be affected by the intensity of the rat's hunger (which could be manipulated by denying it access to food for a specified time) and by the amount of food it would find.

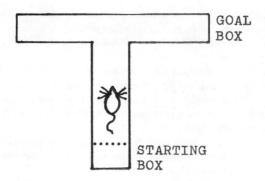

GOAL BOX

STARTING BOX

Fig. 3.1   A T-maze.

The food in this example is called a reinforcer, a concept that plays an important part in understanding operant behaviour. A reinforcer could be any experience (food, water, praise) that increases the probability of occurrence of a piece of behaviour. If the reader has attempted to train a dog by giving the animal biscuits when the desired behaviour is shown, positive reinforcement has been used. By giving a biscuit when a stick is retrieved, for example, the dog is more likely to fetch the stick again. Operant conditioning is not limited to animal behaviour. If the reader has been rewarded in any way for behaviour in the past (e.g. relieving a headache by taking an aspirin) operant conditioning could be said to have occurred. Any relief of the headache would make it more likely that aspirin would be taken again on another occasion. B.F. Skinner, a leading proponent of operant learning, has written extensively about the ways that the principle of reinforcement can be applied to humans, notably in his novel about the utopia *Walden Two*[8].

Reinforcers can be positive or negative. In the case of a positive reinforcer, *presentation* increases the probability of a response, whereas the *removal* of a negative reinforcer increases the chance that a response will occur. A hungry rat will learn to press a bar in order to obtain food through positive reinforcement if, when the bar is pressed, food arrives. The rat will also learn to press the bar, through negative reinforcement, if an aversive stimulus like an electric shock is terminated by bar pressing. An everyday example of this is a mother picking up a crying infant. If the baby stops crying when picked up, the probability of the mother repeating the same behaviour increases since the cessation of the baby's crying provides her with reinforcement. Punishment is not the same as negative reinforcement. Technically, punishment is an event that *reduces* the probability of behaviour. This can occur when a positive reinforcer is withdrawn (e.g. a parent might refuse to talk to a child when he has been ill-behaved) or when an aversive stimulus is presented (e.g. a parent might reprimand a child).

Reinforcers can also be primary or secondary. Primary reinforcers are those that satisfy basic biological needs, such as hunger or thirst. Secondary reinforcers are events that have become rewarding through their association with primaries. Money is an obvious example: cash will increase the probability of behaviour not because it is innately reinforcing, but because people have learned that they can satisfy their needs with it. It then takes on reinforcing characteristics of its own.

This short description of operant learning indicates that there are some basic similarities between this kind of conditioning and respondent conditioning. There is the same emphasis on behaviour rather than inner mental states. There has also been a similar concern with extinction, stimulus generalization and the timing of stimulus and response. Operant learning theorists are interested in the strength of the stimulus – response (S – R) bond, measured by how long the responses take to disappear (i.e. extinction) and by counting the number of responses the animal makes in a given time.

The differences between the two models are also noteworthy. Whereas classical theorists saw learning as a passive process, operant theorists consider animals to be actively seeking consequences in the environment. The experimenter's behaviour is different in each case as well. In the classical approach, the unconditioned stimulus is presented to the subject just after the conditioned stimulus (light after food) and the response follows. Under the operant model, the reinforcer is not given until the desired response is obtained. The desired behaviour is encouraged by the method of successive approximations, or 'shaping'. If, when training a dog to fetch a stick, the trainer waited for the correct behaviour, the procedure would take a long time to learn. It is unlikely that the dog would wait quietly until the stick was thrown, then wait for the command to fetch it, and then return to the trainer's side by chance. Instead, the trainer will reward the dog for each small step that approximates to the desired behaviour. At first, a biscuit might be given for running up to the stick. When this response is well learned, the trainer may withhold reward until, by chance, the dog returns the stick. Eventually, no reward would be given until the correct sequence of actions is performed. The trainer could also begin pairing praise with the dog biscuits during the procedure, until praise has attained secondary reinforcing characteristics and biscuits would no longer be needed.

Shaping has been used successfully in treating human behavioural difficulties, particularly those people with severe developmental disabilities. One case study involved a 3-year-old girl who was mute and severely physically handicapped. Although her physical handicaps responded to treatment, she remained mute. She did, however, occasionally make faint grunts, and these vocalizations were reinforced until gradually she was able to 'reply' to the therapist. The reinforcements given were songs, short nursery rhymes and jogging on the therapist's lap. Although her progress was not outstanding, she was given a good prognosis, quite different from the institutionalization that she would otherwise have faced.[9]

Treatments Based on Instrumental Conditioning

Operant learning procedures thus gave psychologists another powerful tool for predicting and changing behaviour. The theory suggested that, by discovering the reinforcement contingencies involved in maladaptive behaviour, it would be possible to change these contingencies and substitute more appropriate reinforcement patterns. This conceptualization has proved useful in work with children. Some children become disruptive, disturbing classes at school and being difficult to control at home. Although many children do this occasionally, constant disruption is a problem for teachers and parents and, in the long run, for the children themselves. Some children become very seclusive, refusing to take part in social play and preferring to stay on their own. Again, although such behaviour is sometimes desirable, prolonged isolation from others may be considered maladaptive.

Where a psychotherapist might see the children and their families in such cases for verbal psychotherapy, a behaviour therapist using the operant model might confront such difficulties directly, first observing the child's behaviour and the behaviour of others around him. The aim would be to discover the frequency of the problem behaviour and its function: the context in which it occurs and the reactions it evokes from others. For example, in one case, teachers attended to one child when he was seclusive but not when he was sociable[10]. Whenever he sat alone he was talked to and concern was shown, but whenever he joined the other children, his contact with the teachers lessened. Effectively, the teachers were punishing the child's social behaviour by withdrawing the social reinforcements he received when alone. When this was pointed out to the teachers, they stopped rewarding seclusion and began to reward co-operation with other children. As a result, the child's tendency to play alone lessened and he began to play with the other children. When the old set of reinforcements were re-introduced to test whether the teachers' attention was in fact the important variable, the child again retreated to seclusion.

This study illustrates the importance of giving reinforcement until the desired behaviour is rewarded by natural social consequences. Simply providing reinforcement until the desired behaviour is obtained is not adequate. Unless the child is rewarded for sociability by those around him beyond the treatment programme, little long-term success would be expected and extinction would occur.

This study also illustrates several important features of operant behaviour therapy. First, there is the functional analysis of the behaviour to be modified, depending upon careful observation and description. The undesired behaviour must be described in very specific terms so that even small steps towards the desired (or target) behaviours are initially rewarded and the behaviour is shaped efficiently. Second, the reinforcers must be chosen to suit each individual, since what might be reinforcing for one person might be aversive to another. For example, the opportunity to have a snack might be attractive for one person, but not to another who has anorexia nervosa. The reinforcers are often chosen on the basis of observation. If a patient is particularly fond of a food, that food may be a suitable reinforcer: if he chooses to sit on a particular chair when possible, an opportunity to do so is a reinforcer. Parents use this regularly. Since children often play when they have the opportunity, play can be used as a reward, as in

'If you finish your supper you can go out and play'.

Once the target behaviours and the reinforcers appropriate to the individual case are chosen, the treatment procedures can be started. Generally, positive aspects of behaviour are emphasized by the introduction of the reinforcers at the appropriate times. Decreasing the probability of undesirable behaviour is a secondary consideration. Coercive procedures (e.g. threats) are rarely used, and undesirable behaviour is left to extinguish. Besides, if positive behaviour is being produced, there is less time available for undesirable behaviour, and this kind of behaviour is effectively punished since it delays the availability of positive reinforcements.

Punishment *per se* has its effects on behaviour, however, and has been used in extreme circumstances. Lang and Melamed[11] describe a case in which a 9-month-old child was vomiting persistently, weighing only 12 pounds. When various physical and psychological treatments were unable to discover the cause or alleviate the problem, punishment was used. In an attempt to save the child's life, an electric shock was administered to the infant's leg when he was about to vomit. This treatment had quick and dramatic effects: the vomiting ceased almost immediately and the child began to gain weight.

These operant techniques have gained wide acceptance amongst educational and clinical psychologists. They can be adapted to fit individual cases and provide reasonably clear guidelines about how to perform therapy. There is increasing interest in their application to encourage patients to follow their doctor's advice. Compliance with medical instructions is surprisingly low and is considered in detail in Chapter 13. An operant analysis can be used to enhance compliance, as outlined by Zifferblat[12]. He argues that whether or not a patient follows advice is a function of environmental events that immediately precede and follow the prescribed behaviour. If the patient can feel or observe that 'this is the time to take my medication' easily and unambiguously, compliance would tend to be high. A headache or an upset stomach, for example, would provide these clues. If, however, there is no obvious signal, the probability of compliance would be low. This could occur if a drug is given as a preventative measure: by the time the patient realizes medication is necessary, it is already too late. The events that follow the prescribed behaviour are also seen as significant. If taking medication is followed by pleasant consequences, for example pain relief, it is likely to occur. If there are no immediate and pleasant consequences, then the probability of following advice would be low. An individual on a weight-reducing diet may find it difficult because any loss of weight will occur in the long term; in the short-term the consequences are unpleasant. Thus Zifferblatt argues that compliance can be increased if the signals are made explicit and unambiguous (perhaps by using a buzzer) and by providing rewards (perhaps money) when the medications themselves are not intrinsically pleasant. An example of the application of these principles is given by a study on haemodialysis patients. Each time their weight or potassium level was within acceptable standards, they were given coupons that could be redeemed for such rewards as a shorter dialysis session, foregoing a complete dialysis session or purchasing material goods. Over the 7-week study, the patients'

76

weights changed in the desired direction[13].

Biofeedback is another technique that can be considered in terms of operant conditioning principles, in that a person is rewarded each time certain behaviour is shown. The important distinction is that this required behaviour is internal rather than external: lower muscle tension, for example, rather than pressing a lever. The internal behaviour is monitored and rewards are given to people via lights or tones, which reflect changes in the internal behaviour. Biofeedback thus provides a way of controlling certain internal states. When biofeedback is used with animals (and this is where the research originated) the rewards are given directly via pleasurable brain stimulation.

The technique has aroused considerable interest. It has indicated that some functions that had previously been thought to be autonomic (e.g. heart rate, blood pressure) can be controlled through higher-level processes. This implies that a patient with, say, high blood pressure might be helped to lower it without the use of drugs. Since there is concern about placing people on hypertensive drugs indefinitely, biofeedback provides an attractive alternative. Kristt and Engel[14] studied a few patients whose high blood pressure had required doctors' care for the previous 10 years. The patients were asked to control their systolic blood pressure — sometimes they were asked to lower it, sometimes to raise it. Keeping a light illuminated provided the patients with the information that they were exerting control. All patients were able to alter their systolic blood pressure, some more effectively than others. Kristt and Engel also took measures several months later and found that the effects of biofeedback were not transient.

There are several methodological problems with many studies of biofeedback, including the study discussed above. In order to say that the effects are directly attributable to biofeedback, there would need to be a control group of subjects who were treated in exactly the same way as the 'treatment' group (hooked up to the biofeedback equipment, asked to concentrate on the light and so forth), but whose feedback was not contingent on changes in internal state. It is possible that the beneficial effects might have resulted from some other aspect of the therapy sessions, such as concentrating on the light or being hooked up to the apparatus. Biofeedback is often used in conjunction with relaxation techniques similar to those mentioned earlier under systematic desensitization, and there are some very encouraging results[15].

3.4 Observational Learning

A type of learning that neither the classical nor the operant approaches explain adequately is observational learning. The work of Albert Bandura has stimulated much research into the role and importance of this kind of learning. He was interested in the fact that people were able to repeat a performance, often without error, when there was no obvious reinforcement for this learning provided to the subject. Even when children in one study were not informed in advance that correct imitations would be rewarded, as much learning was displayed as when incentives were promised[16]. There are several reports of dolphins and chimpanzees also learning in this way. For example, chimps raised in experimenters' homes have been seen to sit at typewriters striking the keys and to apply lipstick in front of a mirror without prior tutoring[17]. Particularly charming are the descriptions of dolphins kept in zoos, who often imitate their handlers' behaviour. For example, just as divers use scrapers to remove algae growth from their tanks, dolphins have been known to grasp loose tiles in their mouths and to scrape the viewports of the tanks. They have also been seen to release air bubbles, just like the divers. There are many examples of such learning in humans. For instance, much of the learning involved in becoming a member of a profession involves observation. Watching a consultant during rounds provides much information for a medical student about behaviour with patients.

Several explanations have been given for these findings. It may be the case that imitation is in itself pleasurable and so external rewards or punishments are not necessary for learning. Another explanation is that the observer expects to be treated in a similar way to the person watched, so there is 'vicarious' reinforcement. Several studies have shown that this is at least part of the explanation. For example, children in one study viewed aggressive behaviour that was sometimes rewarded and sometimes punished. When given an opportunity to imitate, the children acted as if vicarious reinforcement was taking place: those who saw aggression rewarded tended to be aggressive, whereas those who saw it punished showed no imitative behaviour[18]. Other studies have indicated that when a prohibited behaviour is not punished, it is as if it was rewarded, since imitation increases in this circumstance.

Treatments Based on Observational Learning

The emphasis in this kind of social learning is on the importance of models, their behaviour and the consequences of their behaviour. Extensive research has been conducted in various situations on the characteristics of models that are effective in encouraging imitation (high prestige and similarity to the observer are important), on how the modelling should be accomplished (e.g. phobic patients benefit more from fearful models gradually overcoming their fear than initially unfrightened models) and on how this type of learning could be used clinically. The latter has resulted in two important techniques: the use of models in helping patients cope with anxieties (such as phobias and hospitalization) and social skills training.

Coping with anxieties. The idea behind the use of observational learning in treating anxieties and phobias is that behaviour that the observer has previously regarded as hazardous in some way is repeatedly shown, under various circumstances, to be safe. Through vicarious reinforcement, the observer is encouraged to perform the actions that he had previously shunned. Someone with a phobia about snakes, for example, is more likely to approach snakes after seeing a model handle one without negative consequences. A variation of this method is participant modelling, which involves the therapist first modelling the desired behaviour and then the patient repeating the performance, at his own pace, until imitation is achieved. This combination of modelling and participation seems particularly effective.

More relevant here perhaps is one study that has used the technique to help patients cope with their fears of medical treatment. Some methods for assisting the patient in hospital were discussed in Chapter 1, and the idea of peer modelling was mentioned there: children who watched a realistic film of another child receive an injection were able to cope with the procedure better than children who watched an unrealistic film or who saw no film. Similar research has been conducted on admission to hospital and surgery[19]. Films were shown to children between 4 and 12 years of age, who were about to enter hospital for surgery (e.g. tonsillectomies). None of the children had been in hospital previously, and two groups of children were matched for sex, age, race and type of operation. One group saw a film of a child who hesitated before entering hospital, who showed some anxiety during the admission procedure and who talked with the surgeon and anaesthetist about what to expect. After waking in the recovery room, he regained his composure as he prepared to go home. He talked about his feelings about his stay, as did other children in the hospital playroom. The uncomfortable aspects of the operation were balanced by a rewarding atmosphere, with medical staff and the mother on hand to give comfort and support. He was given a present after the operation and was shown leaving the same way as he arrived, which included carrying his toy dog, Ruffy. The control children were also shown a film but it was not related to hospitals. This film, about a fishing trip, controlled for length of time watching a film, interest value and a peer model coping with a new experience. Several measures were taken at different times. The results of the palmar sweat index (taken as a measure of emotional factors) are shown in Fig. 3.2a and those from observers' ratings of anxiety (as shown by crying and trembling hands) in Fig. 3.2b. On both measures, the children who were able to observe a model go through the hospital procedure and arrive safely home again showed better adjustment both just before the operation and after it (some 3 – 4 weeks later). Results such as these indicate that modelling is a powerful procedure in helping patients to overcome their anxieties about medical care.

Social skills training (SST). SST has been used with considerable success with people who do not have any well defined difficulties but whose relationships with others are in some way inadequate. Although it has proved useful for patients with impaired relationships, SST has also been used in business and manager – employee relations. As in the behaviour therapies previously mentioned, this type of learning is not primarily concerned with bringing about changes in inner personality states, but in learning useful behavioural skills. This could apply equally to a manager who alienates his employees as to a patient who complains of an inability to get along with other people. Unlike most behaviour therapies, however, SST is often instructional in its approach (the therapist explains the effect of the behaviour) and uses videotaped

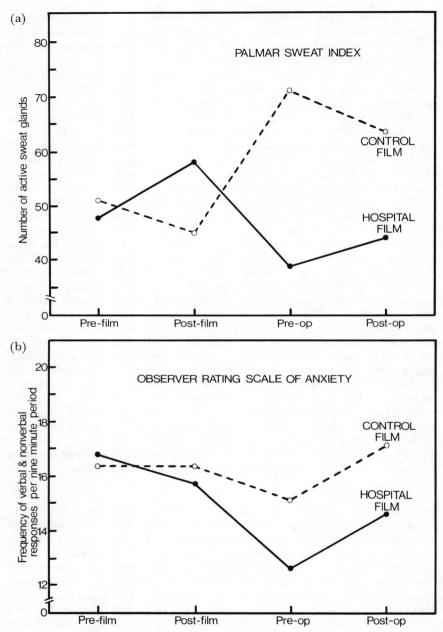

Fig. 3.2 **Preparation for hospitalization and surgery. Indications of anxiety shown by the children in the experimental and control groups across the four measurement periods. (a) shows the number of active sweat glands, and (b) the verbal and non-verbal indications of anxiety. (Reproduced from B.G. Melamed and L.J. Siegel,** *Journal of Consulting and Clinical Psychology,* **1975, 43, 511–521. Copyright 1975 by the American Psychological Association. Reprinted by permission of the publisher and author.)**

feedback to show the person how he functions.

Several methods are used. *Role playing* involves the person acting in situations that approximate to the real ones. An excessively shy person, for example, might role play someone who engages another in conversation. By practising the skill in a relatively non-threatening situation, some of the anxieties can be allayed. *Role reversal* is similar, in that an artificial role-play is used, but in this case the person takes the role of the other individual with whom he has difficulty. In many medical schools, students are asked to role-play patients, to help them appreciate patients' reactions to medical care. Another technique is *modelling*, in which actors or therapists demonstrate effective ways of behaving. Watching a peer handle a difficult situation seems particularly effective. The *instructional* component of SST entails giving information about non-verbal communication. For instance, eye gaze is very important in conversation, indicating interest and attention. Someone who does not look at his conversational partner may seem disinterested and unfriendly, making it difficult to achieve satisfactory social relationships. The instructor might suggest to his patient 'When you're listening to someone, show that you're interested by looking at him more often'. Finally, there is the *feedback* component. Social skills can be likened to other kinds of skills, such as riding a bicycle. In order to learn to learn to ride a bike, it is necessary to acquire knowledge of results, the effect of a shift of weight on balance for example. Similarly, videotapes provide an opportunity for the patient to see and hear himself less subjectively, and when he cannot see where he has gone 'wrong' the instructor can point out the difficulty. The uses of this training are various, including marriage guidance and the rehabilitation of adolescent offenders and psychiatric patients[20]. A method that uses SST in helping students and medical staff learn to interview patients is discussed in Chapter 12.

3.5 Cognitive Learning

Although advocates of the kinds of learning previously discussed may disagree about the relative importance of different environmental characteristics, they hold in common the view that it is not necessary to consider intra-psychic variables in order to predict behaviour. Although most take the individual's unique circumstances and learning history into account (some events may be reinforcing for some people but not others), little or no emphasis is placed on the inner workings of the mind. In many respects, this is quite satisfactory, since the models are able to account for man's behaviour much of the time (at least in restricted environments). This is a valid criterion for any theory. In other respects, the theories are not so appealing. First, cognitive factors appear to play a role in some learning (for example in the case of covert sensitization) and, second, learning sometimes occurs without any apparent association between behaviour and consequence.

In exploring the effect of cognition on learning, one research method has been to lead different groups of subjects to have different expectations or beliefs about the situation, but then to give all the same learning contingencies. If cognition were not important, then there should be little difference between the responses of various groups. Perhaps cognitive factors would have least effect in the case of classical conditioning, where Pavlov considered learning to be on an autonomic level. In one study, all subjects were given the same contingencies — when certain words embedded in a list were said, an electric shock followed. However, one group of subjects was informed about these signal words, while the other group was lead to believe that there was no association between words and shocks. The researchers found that whereas the heart rates of the first group of subjects increased when they heard the signal words, little association was found for the second group[21]. Apparently, the subjects' understanding of the situation was important. In another experiment, when subjects were told that an aversive event no longer followed a stimulus, their affective reactions were promptly eliminated, whereas subjects not so informed showed a gradual decrease[22]. It seems that the classical conditioning model, with its emphasis on behaviour alone, cannot account for these results.

Similarly, operant conditioning, with its emphasis on reinforcement, does not provide an explanation for all learning, since prior knowledge of reinforcement contingencies affects the behaviour of human subjects. In one of many studies on this topic, different groups of subjects were given different information about the timing of reinforcement. One group was told that they would be rewarded for their operant behaviour on average once per minute, a second group was told that rewards would be forthcoming exactly once per minute, and a third group every 150 responses. In fact, all groups were rewarded on average once per minute. The dependent measure was the response rate shown by the subjects: if the objective reinforcement contingencies were most important, the subjects would be expected to show a similar response rate whatever their instructions, but if their behaviour was mediated by understanding, differences would result. Differences between the groups were found. The first group gave an average of 65 responses per reinforcement, the second group 6 responses and the third group 260 responses. Thus, the subjects' *beliefs* about the consequences of their behaviour had an important effect on it, in that they regulated their performance in accord with their expectations[23]. In order to account for these results, it is necessary to postulate the existence of an internal monitoring system that gives meaning to behaviour and to reinforcements[24].

Latent learning provides another example of the importance of inner states. This kind of learning is shown when a subject is able to perform a task well, not because he has been reinforced for it previously but simply because he has had an opportunity to explore the task requirements beforehand. In this case, reinforcement seems to be responsible not for learning, but only for the performance of a task. In the classic experiments, some rats were allowed several days to wander around a complicated maze, while another group of rats were regularly rewarded with food if they found their way to the goal box. As soon as the first group of rats were similarly rewarded, they were able to find their way through the maze as quickly as the always-rewarded rats, indicating that learning had taken place without reinforcement[25]. This finding suggests that inner maps or cognitive structures are learned through experience, but that this learning becomes apparent only if some incentive is given for performance.

One explanation for these findings has been given by Bandura[26]. He suggests that the critical factor in learning is not simply that events occur together in time, but that people become able to predict them and summon up appropriate actions. Thus, the CS in Pavlov's experiments provides a predictive signal for the presentation of food. Extinction occurs when the animal discovers that the signal is no longer predictive. Similarly, it may be that operant methods are useful in changing behaviour because the subject learns that the consequences of his behaviour depend on his actions in a predictable way: if he performs X in all probability Y will occur.

Treatments Based on Cognitive Learning

Such an argument has important consequences for those who hold that only behaviour should be studied in psychology. Since studies have shown that man's inner mental state plays a significant role in his behaviour, there has been a major and important shift in learning theory, a shift away from changing behaviour alone towards changing beliefs and cognitive structures as well. If it is people's assumptions about how the world operates that are critical, then these assumptions should be considered and changed where appropriate. The similarity between this position and that advocated by some of the therapists discussed in Chapter 2 — Kelly and Beck — is striking. Although there are many differences in their approaches and theories, both they and the cognitive learning theorists contend that it is the individual's perceptions of the environment and of himself that are significant in changing behaviour. This recent shift in learning theory thus approaches the position that considers personality variables important in therapy. Cognitive learning theory represents a kind of synthesis between the behaviouristic and psychotherapeutic positions.

Just as respondent, instrumental and observational learning approaches have suggested means of treating patients with medical and psychological difficulties, cognitive learning theory has indicated ways of helping patients. Self-instruction and self-control are two such methods.

Self-instruction.　The reader may have noticed that when he or she learns a new skill, this learning is often enhanced by instruction and observation. For example, when first learning to drive a car, it is usual to ask a competent driver what he is doing when he starts the car, changes gear, brakes and so on. This provides some information about driving. The first time in the driver's seat is usually accompanied by a series of instructions by an experienced driver. After some practice, the teacher's instructions become unnecessary and the learner is able to run through the instructions silently. Eventually, the instructions to himself cease, and the driving is performed automatically without conscious thought.

This sequence of events — from overt instruction to automatic execution — is typical of much learning. Although it is usually associated with learning physical skills, it is also found in cognitive development. Children often talk to themselves when playing with puzzles, for example. Recent research has indicated that self-instruction can be used to modify many problem behaviours, such as social isolation and hyperactivity. Meichenbaum and Goodman describe a study in which the behaviour of hyperactive children was modified.

These children were said to have impulse-control problems, in that they did not stop to consider their behaviour before performance. The treatment involved five steps:

1. An adult model performed the task (e.g. copying of patterns) while giving detailed self-instructions like 'Okay, what is it I have to do? . . . draw the line down . . . then to the right . . . I'm doing fine so far. Remember, go slowly . . . even if I make an error I can go on slowly and carefully . . . Finished. I did it'. (Ref. 27, p. 117)
2. The hyperactive child then performed the task under the adult's direction.
3. The child performed the task while instructing himself out loud.
4. The child whispered the instructions to himself.
5. The child guided his performance with private speech.

When compared with control groups, children who had undergone this training procedure did significantly better on several tasks involving self-control, a result that was maintained 1 month later. This may have been because the children had learned a new way of coping with their environment by monitoring what they were doing rather than acting impulsively[27]. This result is particularly important since drug treatment with hyperactive children usually ceases to be effective when medication ceases[28]; children apparently attribute their ability to cope with their impulsiveness to the medication[29]. A method of modifying behaviour which has lasting effects has obvious advantages.

An application of self-instructional training that may be of more personal relevance to the reader concerns test anxiety. The deleterious effects of high anxiety in the performance of complex tasks is well documented, and is a problem often encountered by students taking important exams. Part of the difficulty seems to be that highly anxious students tend to be self-deprecating about their performance and ruminate on the performance of others in the examination hall. There seems to be a failure to attend to the relevant aspects of the task, with irrelevant thoughts intruding frequently. In an attempt to help students with this problem, they were encouraged to become aware of their thoughts and self-verbalizations during exams. They were then asked to imagine themselves taking an exam, but instead of ruminating on irrelevant thoughts, to instruct themselves positively, for instance, to say to themselves, 'This is a difficult exam, I'd better start working at it' rather than 'I'm really nervous. I can't handle this'. Compared to students who were waiting to take the cognitive-modification programme, this procedure had a significant effect on grades and self-reports of improvement[30].

Self-control. Self-control techniques do not involve 'Use your willpower' or 'Pull yourself together' admonitions. Self-control methods, which are used to alter specific behaviours rather than traits, are much more detailed and structured than these kinds of advice. It is the patient himself who is the agent of his own change, hence there are fewer moral problems with this technique than some other methods. There are two main components. First there is careful observation of the conditions that evoke the undesired behaviour. Someone who wanted to stop smoking, for instance, would be encouraged to monitor the occasions when a cigarette is taken. This could be done by keeping a diary of the circumstances in which smoking occurs, the number smoked and so on. Since people are not particularly accurate at observing their own behaviour, the therapist would provide instructions on how this charting could be accomplished. Observation is important, but it is not sufficient, since it may have little effect on behaviour by itself.

The second component of self-control involves the idea of self-reward, in which the patient gives himself rewards contingent on his behaviour. This can be encouraged by either direct instruction or by modelling. In the case of direct instruction, the therapist tells his patient to choose something pleasant whenever he reaches a certain standard of behaviour. When he has no cigarette with his morning coffee, he could have a piece of cake, for instance. In modelling, the individual observes someone rewarding himself for performing a certain action, and is encouraged to do the same. Once people have learned to reward themselves in this way, the behaviour is typically maintained for longer periods of time than when reinforcement is always given by the experimenter or therapist. Self-punishment, by contrast, has relatively little effect on self-control[31].

The difference between self-control and self-instruction is nicely illustrated by some research that explored the self-control shown by students attempting to study. Students were initially asked to examine their own study methods, noting when and where they usually revised. To increase motivation, the students were also requested to make lists of all the reasons why they should study. Two methods were used to increase self-control. The first involved stimulus control: the students were encouraged to use only one or two places for study, places not associated with behaviour incompatible with studying. This method was based on the notion that the environment has an important effect on behaviour. The second method involved asking the students to reward themselves whenever they studied for a specified length of time. At first, this time was short, about 20 min, but this increased as the programme progressed. They chose their own reinforcers, which could have been food, cigarettes, seeing a film. The students were also taught to graph the number of hours they spent studying, so that they could see the results of their efforts. The programme was supplemented by information about the *SQ3R*, a method outlined in Chapter 4, that teaches students to skim over their reading before they begin in earnest and to rephrase, in their own words, the material they are learning. The results were very encouraging. A significant improvement in grades in the university exams was found for these students, compared with those not involved in the programme and those who dropped out after the introduction. Although these researchers could not attribute the results to self-reinforcement alone owing to the design of the experiment, others have shown more clearly that self-reinforcement is effective in changing study patterns.

Self-reinforcement has proved effective in modifying many problem behaviours, such as eating and speech disorders. Compliance with medical advice has recently become an increasingly important topic of study. One diabetic patient, who had been admitted to hospital on three previous occasions for hypoglycemia, was encouraged to maintain self-care procedures through the use of self-reinforcement. Finding cigarettes pleasurable, he was instructed to reward

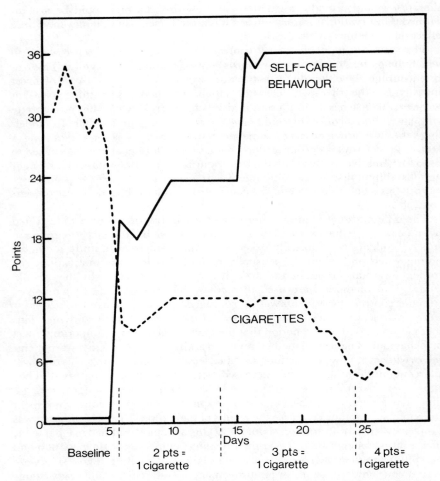

Fig. 3.3 The effect of self-reinforcement on self-care for one diabetic patient. (Reproduced from Karasu and Steinmuller, *Psychotherapeutics in Medicine*, 1978, by permission of Grune & Stratton.)

himself whenever he performed his self-care tasks (testing his urine, adjusting his insulin supply and keeping to an appropriate diet). Gradually, more and more tasks were required before he could reward himself. The results of this reinforcement scheme are shown in Fig. 3.3, which indicates a clear increase in self-care[32]. Interestingly, a corresponding decrease in the number of cigarettes was also found.

3.6 Comparing Therapies

The search for evidence that indicates that one kind of therapy is superior to others is a relatively recent one, but there are perhaps thousands of studies addressed to the issue of treatment efficacy. The topic is an important one, having many practical implications. If one treatment can be shown to be more effective than another, then therapists could have a responsibility to use the superior treatment for the good of their patients. The type of approach a therapist advocates may not only affect the treatment used but also which signs and symptoms will be observed and altered. In one study, for example, psycho-dynamic therapists and behaviour therapists viewed the same film of a person said to be a patient — they interpreted his actions in very different ways[33]. Broadly speaking, studies in this area have been concerned with distinguishing between different behaviour therapies or with distinguishing between behaviour therapy and verbal psychotherapy.

Different Behaviour Therapies

The usual approach is to assign patients with similar severity and types of diffi-culties randomly to one of three groups. Two of the groups would be treated by two different methods (for example systematic desensitization and modelling), whereas the patients in the third group would serve as waiting-list controls. Baseline measures would be taken before treatment, and a follow-up conducted some months after treatment is completed. As well as experiments that have considered differences between treatments, researchers have been interested in ascertaining the most important aspects of any one procedure. Self-instruction, for example, involves several steps: are all of these necessary or can one or more of them be left out without detriment?

Although answers to many of these questions are beyond the scope of this text (Kazdin and Wilson[34] provide a consideration of some of them), several general principles have appeared:

1. Generally, behaviour therapies have proved effective as compared with waiting-list control groups in the treatment of phobias, some sexual dys-functions and compulsions. However, many of these comparative studies have relied on university undergraduate recruits — volunteers who might not ordinarily have sought help for their difficulties.
2. There are many individual case studies in the literature testifying to the efficacy of behaviour therapy. Although these cases provide evidence, a

therapist is unlikely to seek to publish instances where his or her therapy has not been successful.

3. Treatments that involve the patient in actually engaging in the feared behaviour are more effective than those that rely on imagination. *In vivo* treatments, such as participant modelling, produce more change than, say, modelling alone.

4. Studies using cognitive-behaviour modification have generally proved superior to the more traditional kinds of behaviour therapies, providing better generalization with less cost in therapists' time. Another attraction of the cognitive approach is that it overcomes many of the moral problems associated with classical and operant methods. Often they are used in conjunction with each other. For example, if a therapist finds that his patient is unwilling to give self-instructions without prompting, reinforcements might be provided for such statements.

5. Programmes that use multiple treatments have tended to be more effective than those that use a single method. This may be because many psychological difficulties have several components, and each approach is best suited to a different component. Fear of spiders, for example, can involve physiological reactions, subjective perceptions and behavioural actions. Each component might best be altered by a different kind of therapy: a classical approach for the physiological component, a cognitive approach for the subjective one and an operant approach for the behaviour. Perhaps a fear is caused via the classical conditioning model, but is maintained through the operant: for example a person may run out of a room whenever a spider is sighted, thus gaining some relief from the feared stimulus. By combining several methods, each component is treated.

Psychotherapy versus Behaviour Therapy

The important distinction made in this book between these two broad types of therapy is that the former conceives of the patient's presenting complaint as only a symptom of the underlying 'real' difficulty, whereas the latter considers the presenting complaint *as* the real problem, with little attention paid to inner states. There have been few areas in psychology that have been so extensively researched or passionately debated as these alternative viewpoints. The controversy reached its height in the 1960s and early 1970s, when several researchers who saw behaviour therapy as the most efficacious challenged the psychotherapists to justify their treatments. Those who believed in the importance of insight and interpersonal relationships cited evidence indicating that it was the interest and concern shown by the behaviour therapists that were the ingredients of change, and argued that the practitioners of behaviour therapy were unaware of the role that their warmth and caring had on patients' improvement. For example, when behavioural techniques are used, 'warm' therapists obtain better results then 'cold' ones, indicating that the personality of the therapist and his relationship with his patient has an effect on recovery. Behaviourists countered this by arguing that psychotherapy involved positive reinforcement of certain behaviours by the therapists, punishment of others, and attempted to redefine psychotherapy in learning theory terms. Who is right?

At first sight, the question seems to be an easy one to answer. Simply assign patients to either psychotherapeutic or behavioural treatments and compare their recovery rates. A particularly good example of research of this kind has been conducted by Sloane and his colleagues[35]. Unlike most studies, there was a fairly large sample ($N = 94$) and a follow-up was conducted 1 year after the completion of treatment. They used clinically experienced therapists in both behavioural and psychotherapeutic groups, and there was little subject attrition. (This is important, since those who leave therapy may differ from those who remain: if there was a high drop-out rate in one condition but not the other, the comparison may be biased in some way.) The patients were moderately disturbed (neurotic) and were given 4 months of treatment. Assessments were taken from the therapists, their patients, an independent assessor and the patients' relations, both before and after treatment.

In general, there was little difference between the two groups, both of whom did better than the waiting-list controls. About 80% of the patients in the two therapeutic groups showed improvement according to the independent assessor. This study has been widely cited by psychotherapists in defense of insight therapies, but there have been criticisms from the other side. Behaviour therapists have noted that the independent assessor was a psychiatrist who was likely to favour psychotherapy. Even though he assessed the patients blind, that is without knowing their treatment condition, it was possible that he gained some knowledge about the treatment during the assessment interview, perhaps introducing some bias. Another criticism was that the patients in this study were mostly young, verbally competent, intelligent and successful — the kinds of patients who traditionally do well in psychotherapy. A more representative sample of the population may have given different results.

The history of other similar studies has been that one side or the other has found something to criticize in the experimental design. An alternative to designing the 'perfect' experiment has been suggested by Smith and Glass[36]. They conducted a statistical review of about 350 studies that examined this issue, of which about 50 had adequate control groups. Most reviewers take a 'voting' system approach: if 15 studies support a viewpoint and 5 are against, the reviewer might conclude that the evidence is weak but supportive. Such an approach does not take the *size* of any effect into account, however. If, for instance, the 5 against showed highly significant results, whereas the effects in the other 15 were much less strong, the voting system could be quite misleading. Smith and Glass took the effect size into account in their analysis, so that a study that strongly supported one side or the other was weighted more heavily than a study that found only slight differences. Overall, their analysis showed the difference between treatments to be very small indeed, suggesting that psychotherapies and behaviour therapies were equally effective. This approach also has its critics. There are two main difficulties with such an analysis. First, it relies on the comparability of different assessment measures, assuming that self-report questionnaires, interviews and observations are equally valid and reliable, an assumption questioned in the previous chapter. Second, the quality of the studies are not taken into account. Many of Smith and Glass' sample of studies were not as well designed as the Sloane study mentioned above.

Several suggestions have been put forward to account for the apparent lack of difference between the effectiveness of psychotherapies and behaviour therapies. One contention is that each has *specific effects*[37]: that is, a particular therapy is appropriate for particular conditions and particular patients. According to this view, the same type of therapy would be inappropriate in treating all complaints, or even the same complaint in two different patients.

An alternative view is that, rather than psychotherapies and behaviour therapies having different strengths and weaknesses, they are equally effective because they have many similar features[38]. The *common behaviours* used by the two types of therapist may be responsible for changes in their patients. If it is these common behaviours that are significant, then a therapist may not require specific training and long experience in order to be effective. Several features found in both types of therapy have been outlined:

1. Motivation of client. Whatever the therapeutic method, patients who are motivated to succeed do better. If a patient enters therapy because of a referral (from school, the courts) he is less likely to benefit than if he sought assistance on his or her own initiative.

2. Socially sanctioned healer. All forms of therapy involve a 'healer' who is recognized by society. Whether the therapist uses behavioural or verbal techniques, the patient comes to someone who society has sanctioned to help others.

3. Some verbal relationship. A behavioural psychologist involves his patient in verbal exchanges even if his techniques are non-verbal in nature. In order to elicit the patient's difficulties the therapist must show concern, caring and willingness to help. Understanding, acceptance and respect are central to all therapies.

4. Some kind of rationale for therapy. Each therapeutic procedure is underpinned by a theory. When a patient seeks help, he is often confused and unable to make sense of why he feels as he does. It may be the case that any explanation of his suffering will do, as long as it provides some rationale for why he became depressed or phobic or whatever. This belief system removes some of the mystery surrounding his complaint.

5. Hope. One characteristic distinguishing patients who seek assistance for their difficulties from those who do not is their sense of helplessness and demoralization. All therapies hold out hope for the patient that his suffering will be diminished. Many patients improve spontaneously after an initial interview. Perhaps the expectation that assistance will be given is responsible for this effect.

6. Opportunity to confide in a trusted individual. The opportunity to confide in another person seems to have particularly important consequences in therapy. Behavioural therapists often find their patients talking about many aspects of their lives not specifically being considered in treatment.

90

Summary

The theories we have about how behaviour is acquired affect how we attempt to help people who experience psychological difficulties. Some theorists believe that behaviour is guided mainly by an individual's personality (inner drives, conflicts, etc.), leading to the psychotherapies; others believe such a subjective view is unscientific and rely mainly on external, observable events to account for learning. This chapter considers the theories held by the latter group of psychologists and their resulting treatments.

In classical conditioning, associations between unconditioned and conditioned stimuli are viewed as the fundamental building blocks of all behaviour. Various treatments are based on this model: aversion therapy, where an undesired behaviour is paired with a noxious stimulus; flooding, where patients confront the feared stimulus, and systematic desensitization, where an incompatible response, such as relaxation, is paired with the anxiety-provoking situation. Classical or respondent conditioning theories view behaviour as being acquired passively, but it is clear that individuals learn actively, by relating actions to consequences. This is recognized in instrumental learning theories, where actions which are reinforced or rewarded are repeated, whereas those that are not, die out. Conversely, undesired behaviour can be reduced by ceasing to pay attention to (i.e. ceasing to reward) it. Some learning seems to come about through observing the actions of others, and this is not accounted for by either classical or operant learning. Imitating others' behaviour has helped individuals cope with previously stressful situations or in developing social skills. In the latter case, observation of their own videotaped interactions provides important feedback.

Although these theories are able to predict behaviour much of the time, particularly in restricted environments, they do not consider the individual's beliefs and values. In addition, learning occurs when there are no apparent rewards. These considerations have led to methods of helping patients that take cognitive factors into account, such as structured self-instruction and self-control techniques.

Although these different forms of behaviour therapy have been shown to be effective, with those incorporating real-life situations and those involving a cognitive element being superior, their value compared to psychotherapies has proved difficult to assess. This may be because each is effective but only in defined situations, or because the common aspects involved in both, such as the opportunity to talk to somebody, are actually what is relevant.

Suggested Reading

S. Rachman and G. Wilson, *The effects of psychological therapy*, Pergamon, Oxford, 1980, and R. Williams and W. Gentry (eds.), *Behavioural approaches to medical treatment*, Ballinger, Cambridge, Mass., 1977, provide reviews of various applications of behaviour therapy, the latter being more medically oriented.

P.C. Kendall and S.D. Hollon (eds.), *Cognitive-behavioural interventions*, Academic Press, London, 1979, show how the cognitive approach can be applied to psychological difficulties.

Many of the issues raised in the last part of this chapter are considered in S. Garfield and A. Bergin (eds.), *Handbook of psychotherapy and behaviour change*, Wiley, Chichester, 1978.

References

1. Allport, G.W., *Personality: A psychological interpretation*, Holt, New York, 1937.
2. Watson, J.B. and Raynor, R., Conditioned emotional reactions, *Journal of Experimental Psychology*, 1920, **3**, 1 – 14.
3. Rachman, S., Sexual fetishism: An experimental analogue, *Psychological Records*, 1966, **16**, 293 – 296.
4. Reprinted with permission of author and publisher from Cautela, J.R., Covert sensitization, *Psychological Reports*, 1967, **20**, 459 – 468.
5. Sreenivasan, U., Manocha, S.N. and Jain, V.K., Treatment of severe dog phobia in childhood by flooding: A case report, *Journal of Child Psychology and Psychiatry*, 1979, **20**, 255 – 260.
6. Wolpe, J., *The practice of behaviour therapy*, Pergamon Press, New York, 1969.
7. Munby, M. and Johnston, D.W., Agoraphobia: The long-term follow-up of behavioural treatment, *British Journal of Psychiatry*, 1980, **137**, 418 – 427.
8. Skinner, B.F., *Walden Two*, Collier Macmillan, London, 1976.
9. Kerr, N., Meyerson, L. and Michael, J., A procedure for shaping vocalisations in a mute child, *In* Ullman, L.P. and Krasner, L., *Research in behaviour modification*, Holt, Rinehart and Winston, London, 1965.
10. Harris, F.R., Wolfe, M.M. and Baer, D.M., Effects of adult social reinforcement on child behaviour, *Young Children*, 1964, **20**, 8 – 17.
11. Lang, P.J. and Melamed, B.G., Case report: Avoidance conditioning therapy of an infant with chronic ruminative vomiting, *Journal of Abnormal Psychology*, 1968, **74**, 1 – 8.
12. Zifferblatt, S.M., Increasing patient compliance through the applied analysis of behaviour, *Preventative Medicine*, 1975, **4**, 173 – 182.
13. Hart, R.R., Utilization of token economy within a chronic dialysis unit, *Journal of Consulting and Clinical Psychology*, 1979, **47**, 646 – 648.
14. Kristt, D.A. and Engel, B.T., Learned control of blood pressure, *Circulation*, 1975, **51**, 370 – 378.
15. Patel, C., Marmot, M.G. and Terry, D.J., Controlled trial of biofeedback-aided behavioural methods in reducing mild hypertension, *British Medical Journal*, 1981, **282**, 2005 – 2008.
16. Bandura, A., Grusec, J.E. and Menlove, F.L., Observational learning as a function of symbolisation and incentive set, *Child Development*, 1966, **37**, 499 – 506.
17. Hayes, K.J. and Hayes, C., Imitation in a home-raised chimpanzee, *Journal of Comparative Physiological Psychology*, 1952, **45**, 450 – 459.
18. Rosekrans, M.A. and Hartup, W.W., Imitative influences of consistent and inconsistent response consequences to a model on aggressive behaviour in children, *Journal of Personality and Social Psychology*, 1967, **7**, 429 – 434.
19. Melamed, B.G. and Siegel, L.J., Reduction of anxiety in children facing surgery by modeling, *Journal of Consulting and Clinical Psychology*, 1975, **43**, 511 – 521.

20. Urey, J.R., Laughlin, C. and Kelly, J.A., Teaching heterosexual conversational skills to male psychiatric inpatients, *Journal of Behaviour Therapy and Experimental Psychiatry*, 1979, **10**, 323 – 328.

21. Chatterjee, B.B., and Eriksen, C.W., Cognitive factors in heart rate conditioning *Journal of Experimental Psychology*, 1962, **64**, 272 – 279.

22. Grings, W.W., The role of consciousness and cognition in autonomic behaviour change, *In* McGuigan, F.J. and Schoonover, R. (eds.), *The psychophysiology of thinking*, Academic Press, New York, 1973.

23. Kaufman, A., Baron, A. and Kopp, R.E., Some effects of instructions on human operant behaviour, *Psychonomic Monograph Supplements*, 1966, **1**, 243 – 250.

24. Postman, L. and Sassenrath, J., The autonomic action of verbal rewards and punishments, *Journal of General Psychology*, 1961, **65**, 109 – 136.

25. Tolman, E.C., Cognitive maps in rats and men, *Psychological Review*, 1948, **55**, 189 – 208.

26. Bandura, A., *Social learning theory*, Prentice-Hall, Englewood Cliffs, 1977.

27. Meichenbaum, D., *Cognitive behaviour modification*, Plenum, New York, 1977.

28. Douglas, V., Are drugs enough? To treat or train the hyperactive child, *International Journal of Mental Health*, 1975, **4**, 199 – 212.

29. Whalen, C. and Henker, B., Psychostimulants and children. A review and analysis, *Psychology Bulletin*, 1976, **83**, 1113 – 1130.

30. Meichenbaum, D., Cognitive modification of test anxious college students *Journal of Consulting and Clinical Psychology*, 1972, **39**, 370 – 380.

31. Thorensen, C.E. and Mahoney, M.J., *Behavioural self-control*, Holt, Rinehart and Winston, New York, 1974.

32. Fordyce, W.E., Behavioural methods in medical practice, *In* Karasu, T.B. and Steinmuller, R.I., *Psychotherapeutics in medicine*, Grune and Stratton, London, 1978.

33. Langer, E.J. and Abelson, R.P., A patient by any other name, *Journal of Consulting and Clinical Psychology*, 1974, **42**, 4 – 9.

34. Kazdin, A.E. and Wilson, G.T., *Evaluation of behaviour therapy*, Ballinger, Cambridge, Mass., 1978.

35. Sloane, R.B., Staples, F.R., Cristol, A.H., Yorkston, N.J. and Whipple, K., *Psychotherapy versus behaviour therapy*, Harvard University Press, Cambridge, 1975.

36. Smith, M.L. and Glass, G.V., Meta-analysis of psychotherapy outcome studies, *American Psychologist*, 1977, **32**, 752 – 760.

37. Kiesler, D.J., Experimental designs in psychotherapy research, *In* Bergin, A.E. and Garfield, S.L., *Handbook of psychotherapy and behaviour change*, Wiley, London, 1971.

38. Murray, E., and Jacobson, L., The nature of learning in traditional psychotherapy, In Bergin, A.E. and Garfield, S.L., *Handbook of psychotherapy and behaviour change*, Wiley, London, 1971.

4
Memory

4.1 Introduction

I gave S. a series of words, then numbers, then letters, reading them to him slowly or presenting them in written form. He read or listened attentively and then repeated the material exactly as it had been presented. I increased the number of elements in each series, giving him as many as thirty, fifty, or even seventy words or numbers, but this, too, presented no problem for him.

    . . . if I gave him a series of words or numbers, which I read slowly and distinctly, he would listen attentively, sometimes ask me to stop and enunciate a word more clearly, or, if in doubt whether he had heard a word correctly, would ask me to repeat it. Usually during an experiment he would close his eyes or stare into space, fixing his gaze on one point; when the experiment was over, he would ask that we pause while he went over the material in his mind to see if he had retained it. Thereupon, without another moment's pause, he would reproduce the series that had been read to him.

    The experiment indicated that he could reproduce a series in reverse order — from the end to the beginning — just as simply as from start to finish; that he could readily tell me which word followed another in a series or reproduce the word which happened to precede one I'd name. He would pause for a minute, as though searching for the word, but immediately after would be able to answer my questions and generally made no mistakes.

    It was of no consequence to him whether the series I gave him contained meaningful words or nonsense syllables, numbers or sounds; whether they were presented orally or in writing. All he required was that there be a three-to-four-second pause between each element in the series, and he had no difficulty reproducing whatever I gave him. (Ref. 1, pp. 9 – 11)

Unfortunately, very few people are able to learn and remember material as quickly as this. It would certainly make the learning of complex medical information less difficult. Nevertheless, that such material can be remembered at all is a substantial feat. Upon reflection, it becomes clear how vital memory is in everyday life. Not only would it be impossible to study a subject (and how could the area of study develop in the first place?) but also to have conversations, to recognize faces and to find one's way home. These are highly sophisticated operations that require a considerable degree of competence. Indeed, when memory is disrupted through organic damage, these abilities are sometimes lost and cause great personal distress.

In Chapter 1 an information-processing model describing perception was outlined. According to this model, there are three stages involved in perception — sensation, interpretation and memory. These stages are interdependent, so that the sensation of events is related to processes connected with interpretation (e.g. selective attention). Similarly, these first two stages are both affected and influenced by memory. The individual's past experiences determine to some extent how events are interpreted: the case of the physician who diagnosed all his patient's complaints in terms of a previous illness is an illustration of this. It is tempting to consider the memory stage as a rather straightforward process: information is learned and it is either remembered or forgotten. However, such a view is not consistent with either personal experience or experimental evidence. Sometimes a piece of information cannot be recalled when every effort is made, only to find it popping up later. The reader may have had the experience of entering a room and the smell or the appearance causing recall of incidents that had not been considered for months or years. Some information is very difficult to learn, whereas other information can be recalled without any apparent intention to remember it. Research into these processes has provided clues about how memory might be made more accurate, and has several practical applications.

4.2 Studying Memory

Early Experiments

One way to study memory might be to give a person a list of words or a passage of prose to learn and ask him or her to repeat the material back again. The experimenter could manipulate the number of words or the time allowed to learn them and test for the accuracy of recall. This basic strategy was used in the 19th century by Ebbinghaus who was one of the first psychologists to study memory in a systematic way. He made several important contributions to memory research. He argued that psychologists would have to be careful in choosing the material they used. If, for example, the word 'horse' were to be used as part of a list, a subject might be able to remember it accurately simply because he owned one and the word 'horse' had personally meaningful connotations. It would be difficult to gain an accurate picture of how people learn and remember, he reasoned, if material that could be affected by past experience were used. In fact, many words could have this kind of meaning, so he argued that 'nonsense syllables' — such as KYH or ZIW — should be used instead. Today, the use of nonsense material in memory experiments is said to affect *encoding*. It is easier to encode meaningful material than nonsense syllables. In addition, Ebbinghaus showed how memory was open to experimental study by meticulous use of his own memory capacity. Typically, he would learn a list until he could repeat it accurately. By varying the number of nonsense syllables to be learned and by varying the time between learning and recall, he was able to formulate some general principles. His work indicated that most forgetting occurred within the first few hours, that forgetting was retarded if the material was 'overlearned' (i.e. instead of stopping his reviews of the lists when the material was accurately recited for the first time, he would recite it once or twice more) and that as the amount of material increased the time taken to learn it increased in greater proportion. In a long list, syllables at the beginning (primacy effect) and syllables at the end (recency effect) were more likely to be recalled than those in the middle. These principles have stood the test of many later studies. Additionally, Ebbinghaus developed measures to test his learning and memory capacity. One criterion was the number of times a list had to be repeated until it could be recalled perfectly. Another was the time taken to relearn a list that was committed to memory some time previously and only imperfectly recalled later — called 'savings'. For example, he may have been able to recall only a few nonsense syllables from a list learned a week before. It seemed that they had been forgotten. However, it required less time to learn to recite this list again than it did to learn a whole new list of syllables, indicating that they had not been completely forgotten.

Ebbinghaus also distinguished between recall and recognition. The reader may have experienced the 'tip of the tongue' phenomenon, the certainty that a piece of information is known but cannot be recalled: someone's name, perhaps, or an important fact on an exam. Once the name or fact is given, it can be recognized. Apparently, the information was in *storage*, but could not be easily *retrieved*. Recognition of faces, at least in laboratory experiments, is particularly good. In several studies, subjects have been shown hundreds of pictures of different faces, yet are able to recognize a single repeated picture with great accuracy.

Thus, memory seems to involve three stages: learning information (encoding), keeping it (storage) and retrieving it (through recall or recognition). These three processes are not independent, since the way in which material is encoded or the length of time it is in store affects how accurately and completely it can be retrieved.

Types of Storage

One notable feature of memory is that, over time, recall of information tends to become more and more difficult. It is as if memory of the material decays in some way. However, it has proved difficult to demonstrate decay experimentally and, in any case, not all memories decay in a straightforward way. Why is it possible to remember some events so well while others seem to be lost? For example, most people who were adults at the time can remember the circumstances of President Kennedy's death — what they were doing at the time, who told them the news — with considerable clarity. It would be necessary to explain why some memories decay whereas others do not.

Many psychologists consider memory retention in terms of type of storage, distinguishing between three types of store — sensory, short-term and long-term. Although there is disagreement about the length of time information remains in each store or, indeed, whether these types can be distinguished at all, the 3-store hypothesis has proved helpful in memory research and it is this model that will be discussed here. The first type — sensory store — may last less than a second and seems to be based on an auditory or visual after-image. If this information is not given attention it fades and seems to be permanently lost. If, however, this information is attended to, it enters short-term storage. As this sentence is read, the previous one will be in short-term store and will be available for only about 20 – 30 s if it is not rehearsed or reviewed. The classic study on this second, or short-term, store (STS) was performed by Peterson and Peterson[2]. They asked their subjects to remember 3 letters (a nonsense syllable). If the experimenters did not make any further demands on the subjects, they could be expected to remember the syllable for a considerable length of time because they could recite it to themselves. However, in order to prevent any rehearsal, the subjects were asked to count backwards by 3s from, say, 309 as fast as possible. Without rehearsal, the probability of recall diminished quickly, as shown in Fig. 4.1: after 18 s, less than 10% of the information could be recalled. Peterson and Peterson argued that this experiment showed that there was a fundamental limitation in memory capacity. If information is not rehearsed soon after it is seen or heard it will not be possible to retrieve it.

There is another limitation to STS — the number of items that it can hold. If subjects are asked to repeat back a series of letters immediately, they can do this accurately until the number of letters approaches 8 or 9. The reader will have little difficulty in repeating:

A S D F G

but is much less likely to be able to recall:

Q W E R T Y U I O P

after a single reading. The limitation of STS is considered to be about 7 items plus or minus two. It is important to note that it is not the number of symbols or letters that is crucial. Rather, it is the number of meaningful relationships that is limited. For example, it is more difficult to recall 8 syllables like:

SUN ON LY RAINS RARE IT NY DAYS

than the following 8-syllable sentence:

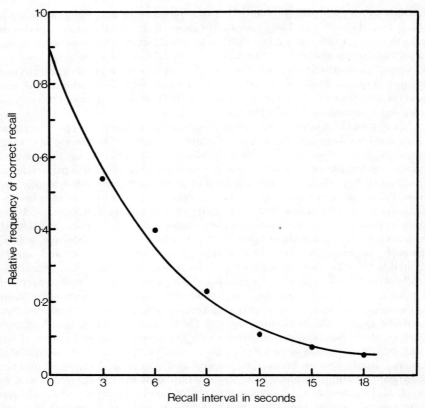

Fig. 4.1 Correct recalls of nonsense syllables as a function of recall interval. The intervals were filled by asking subjects to count backwards by 3s. (Reproduced from L.R. Peterson and M. Peterson, *Journal of Experimental Psychology*, 1959, 58, 193–198. Copyright 1959 by the American Psychological Association. Reprinted by permission of the author.)

IT RARELY RAINS ON SUNNY DAYS

The difference is that the sentence is meaningful whereas the syllables are not. It is not the number of symbols or digits that is limited in STS, but the number of meaningful units or 'chunks'. The sentence 'It rarely rains on sunny days' has only a few chunks of information — the number of syllables is not so important. Further, such chunking draws on information in long-term store relating both to grammatical aspects of sentence construction and the sense of the words.

This chunking illustrates the relationship between short-term and long-term storage. Long-term storage (LTS) is considered to hold past experiences that have been integrated from STS. Forgetting from LTS seems to be very slow and its capacity is considered to be very large indeed. The transfer from STS may be biochemical or anatomical[3] in nature, although it has proved difficult to specify the processes involved. An important feature of LTS is its active nature. Far from being simply a warehouse full of past experiences, holding memories that can be accurately recalled, LTS changes or reconstructs memories. There are many similarities here with interpretation. As shown in Chapter 1, people tend to attend selectively to stimuli, concentrating on those aspects of the environment that are relevant to their purposes and interpreting them in ways which are consistent with previously held beliefs. LTS is also affected by meaning and experience. After a period of time, material recalled from LTS may not necessarily correspond to that which was originally learnt but may be distorted to fit into themes or ideas. It is as if the gaps in memory are filled with pieces of general information about the world. Inferences are made and integrated into memory. An illustration of how memory is a constructive process is provided by Loftus and Palmer[4]. They showed subjects a film of a traffic accident and then asked them questions about the speed of the vehicles in one of two ways. Some subjects were asked 'About how fast were the cars going when they smashed into each other?', whereas another group heard the question 'About how fast were the cars going when they hit each other?'. The first question elicited a much higher estimate of speed. This difference could have been due to response bias (i.e. the subjects in the 'smashed' condition might have thought the researcher wanted a high estimate and so provided it). Alternatively, the wording of the question may have actually affected the memory of the event. In order to test between these possibilities, the experimenters asked the subjects to return a week later. Without viewing the film again, they were asked some more questions about the accident. The hypothesis that the original questioning had actually affected the memory was tested by asking about details that had not occurred in the film. There was no broken glass shown, but over twice as many of the subjects in the 'smashed' condition remembered broken glass than those in the 'hit' condition. Loftus and Palmer suggested that our memories of events are determined not only by the perception of the event itself but also by information gained after it. Other studies have indicated that prior experiences, too, can modify memories. It seems that the longer the interval between witnessing an event or reading a passage, the greater the change in memory. This phenomenon, the tendency for information in LTS to become consistent with other information, is called 'effort after meaning'.

Thus, although forgetting (or, more correctly, inability to retrieve information) is important in itself, the distortions in retrieved memories due to 'efforts after meaning' are important in much psychological research and medical practice. Whenever a subject in a psychological experiment or a patient under the care of his general practitioner is asked for retrospective data, there is the possibility that the memories will be matched not simply to events but also to previous and subsequent experiences. People may be more likely to remember and embellish an event if it is followed by a change in health, for example (see Chapter 10 on stress), or to forget a doctor's advice if it does not easily fit into a pre-existing pattern of memories and expectations (see Chapter 12).

There is also growing evidence that eye-witness accounts of accidents or crimes are not reliable indicators of the actual events. Although in laboratory studies subjects are able to recognize a photo of a face embedded in hundreds of others but shown only once previously, this accuracy does not seem to hold in real-life situations. By using simulated assaults, several studies have indicated that innocent bystanders are sometimes identified as the assailant, and that subjects remember the perpetrators to be taller and heavier than was actually the case.

4.3   Memory Aids

The previous section of the chapter discussed some of the methods psychologists have used to study recall of information and the three types of store. This section describes some of the research that applies to aiding retrieval. Here, the emphasis will be on aids that affect the three interdependent processes of encoding, storage and retrieval, but there are many situations in which external aids, such as a diary to remember appointments, are probably more appropriate. It is often easier to put information in a place where it is easily accessible than to try and put it into long-term storage. Some of the techniques designed to aid recall discussed below may be familiar to the reader because they are in common use.

Repetition and Rehearsal

The most commonly used technique for transferring information into long-term storage is repetition or rehearsal of the information. Several studies have shown that material that is repeated after it is first encountered is more likely to be recalled or recognized[5]. A more complex question concerns the timing of repetition. Several studies have shown that immediate rehearsal is of particular value. Other research has indicated that the time between rehearsals is also important. For example, one investigator had two groups of subjects read a passage 5 times. For half of the subjects, the readings were all done at one sitting, whereas for the other subjects they were spaced over 5 days. Retention was tested three times: immediately after the fifth reading there was little difference between the groups. After 2 weeks, however, the second group performed some 20% better than the first, and after 4 weeks some 25%. By spacing the repetitions over time, more information was retrieved. Thus, although an immediate rehearsal is helpful, subsequent repetitions should be spaced over time for maximum transfer to LTS rather than being massed into a short time interval.

Context

The situation or state of mind of the learner affects how completely information can be retrieved. Two studies on physical context illustrate how subjects can remember more accurately in the situation in which they learned the material than in different situations. In one of the studies, subjects were asked to learn associations between pairs of words, e.g. COW and BALL, whereas during the testing phase the experimenter gave one word and the subject was asked to recall the other. On the first day, they learned a list of these pairs in a windowless room, the experimenter was neatly groomed in tie and slacks and the paired-associates were shown on slides. On the second day they learned a new list, but this time in a tiny room with windows, the experimenter dressed sloppily in jeans and the paired-associates presented via a tape recorder. On the third day, the subjects were divided into two groups, half going to the first room, half to the second and were asked to recall as much of the material they had learned on the previous two days as they could. If the context in which information is learned aided retrieval, then the subjects would be expected to recall more of the associates learned in the room where they were tested. Indeed, on average, 59% of the lists were recalled in the same setting, only 46% in a different one[6]. In the other study, members of a subaqua club were asked to learn lists of words both on shore and under water: those words learned on shore were recalled better there, whereas those learned under water were recalled better under water. It seems that contextual elements become associated with memories and can be used to aid recall.

Physiological state has also been shown to affect retrieval. Eich *et al.*[7] had their subjects learn a list of words, half after smoking a marijuana cigarette and half after smoking a regular cigarette. They were tested for recall 4 hours later after half the subjects in each group were given a marijuana cigarette to smoke. As expected, those who were intoxicated while learning performed more accurately if they were again given marijuana before recall, whereas those who were not intoxicated during learning performed better if non-intoxicated during recall. Incidentally, the results do not suggest that intoxication aids recall, since the non-intoxicated learners did better than the intoxicated regardless of whether they were given a marijuana cigarette.

Elaboration

The illustrations given earlier about the active nature of long-term storage indicate how memories are matched into themes and previously held meanings. This process can result in distortion, but it can also aid accuracy. Although Ebbinghaus argued for the use of nonsense syllables in memory research, some recent theorists have contended that such a strategy is artificial: people do not, in their everyday lives, try to remember nonsense. Instead, they try to remember meaningful material that is comprehended and integrated into already existing memories. This principle has been called elaboration, and is based on the idea that information that is integrated with meaningful material — called a deep level of processing — is more easily retrieved than information that is superficially processed. Two studies illustrate how the level of processing can make it easier to encode and retrieve information. Bobrow and Bower[8] asked their subjects to learn several short noun – verb – noun sentences. As a measure of recall, the experimenters gave them the first noun and the subjects were to give the second. In one condition the subjects were given a full sentence:

for instance, the sentence 'The cow chased the ball' was given for the nouns COW and BALL. In the second condition, only the two nouns were given, and the subjects were asked to make up their own sentence, using their own choice of verb. Those in the second condition were thus required to think more deeply about the meaning of the nouns and the possible relationships between them. When tested, the subjects in the first condition gave only 29% of the correct answers, whereas those in the second gave 58%.

The second study is even more interesting. In all of the research so far mentioned in this chapter, the subjects were explicitly asked to learn and remember the material presented to them. Although intention to learn does have an effect on recall, one of the more surprising results of recent memory research is that intention is not necessary for remembering. Hyde and Jenkins[9] showed their subjects lists of words, each word for about 3 s. In one condition they were asked to check whether each word contained the letters *e* or *g*, and in another condition they were asked to rate the pleasantness of each word. The experimenters also gave half the subjects in each group different instructions. Some were told that the true purpose of the experiment was to learn the words: this was called the intention group. The other half of the subjects were not told that the true purpose concerned memory, but were simply told to rate the words for pleasantness or check for letters: the incidental group. Thus, there were four different groups, each with different combinations of tasks and instructions. After performing the tasks, all subjects were asked to remember as many words as possible. Some of the results are shown in Table 4.1. Subjects' intentions had only a minimal effect on accuracy of recall, since the intentional and incidental groups remembered about the same percentages of words in each task. However, those who rated the pleasantness of the words recalled a significantly higher percentage than those who checked for letters. The subjects' intention was not important, only the degree of elaboration. As in the Bobrow and Bower study, the subjects presumably had to search their memories to rate pleasantness, thus involving a deep level of processing and resulting in unintentional remembering of the words.

A particularly effective way of elaborating information is to formulate questions about the material, preferably before it is read. This can be accomplished

Table 4.1 Percentages of Words Recalled as Determined by Task and by Instructions to Remember

(Reproduced from T.S. Hyde and J.J. Jenkins, *Journal of Verbal Learning and Verbal Behaviour*, 1973, **12**, 471 – 480, by permission of Academic Press Inc.)

	Rate pleasantness	Check letters
Incidental	68	39
Intentional	69	43

in several ways. The headings of the sections of this chapter, for example, could be translated into questions and the sections read in order to answer them. This section titled 'Elaboration' might prompt questions such as 'What is elaboration?' or 'How could elaboration be useful in studying for exams?'. Several studies have indicated that question-asking is helpful in retaining information. Holmes[10] gave one group of subjects a list of 20 questions before reading a passage, whereas another group simply read the passage. When tested, not only was the first group more successful in recalling the answers to the 20 questions previously asked, but also on another 20 as well. This result was replicated by Frase[11]. He asked his subjects to read a passage, making up questions for themselves on one-third of the material, reading to answer another's questions for one-third, and simply reading the remaining third. When asked about the passages, the subjects were able to recall 70%, 67% and 50%, respectively. Questions asked before or during reading seem to have maximum effectiveness, and conceptual questions (those which are aimed at the general theme of a passage) appear to be more powerful aids to memory than specific-fact questions.

Organization

Much more information can be remembered if it is organized rather than random. Bower *et al.*[12] asked subjects to learn lists of words, presented in two different ways. For some subjects, the words were given in an organized manner (for example, the words 'limestone' and 'granite' under the heading 'masonry'; 'gold' and 'silver' under the heading 'rare metals'), whereas for other subjects the words were presented in random fashion. Recall was two to three times better when material was organized in this way. Words can also be organized in a narrative. In another study, which seems to use both organization and elaboration, Bower and Clark[13] asked subjects to learn 12 lists of 10 unrelated nouns. This was accomplished by either simply studying and rehearsing the words or by a narrative chaining method, in which the subjects were asked to construct a meaningful story around the words to be remembered. It is important in studies on memory that the subjects in various conditions are allowed to have the same amount of time to study the material, or differences in recall might simply be due to differences in study time. In many of the experiments mentioned above, this was accomplished by restricting the amount of time the material was available, say 3 s per word. In this particular study, the experimenters wanted to give the subjects in the narrative condition as much time as they wanted to construct a story, so they used a *yoked* design: a subject in the narrative condition was conducted through the experiment and then a subject in the rehearsal condition was given the same amount of time to study the words. This was repeated for each pair of subjects, thus ensuring an equal study time in the two conditions. A typical story of a subject in the narrative condition was as follows:

A VEGETABLE can be a useful INSTRUMENT for a COLLEGE student. A carrot can be a NAIL for your FENCE or BASIN. But a MERCHANT of the QUEEN would SCALE that fence and feed the carrot to the GOAT.

When they were later asked to recall all 12 lists, retrieval was 6 – 7 times better in the narrative condition than the rehearsal condition.

For the reader of this book, some of the organizational work has already been carried out. Since this chapter is called 'Memory', the reader could expect to learn about factors affecting remembering. The reader can assist organization by previewing or surveying the chapters before they are read. Each chapter in the book has a list of contents at the beginning. By skimming over the contents, expectations about the information to be discussed can be raised and the material more easily organized. There is evidence that this approach is effective. In one study a group of subjects were shown how to skim over headings and summaries before they settled down to read. When given a new passage to read, this group read 24% faster than, and as accurately as, subjects not given these preparatory instructions.

Use of mnemonics provides another method of organizing material. The quotation at the beginning of this chapter described the abilities of an individual with an apparently limitless memory capacity. He seemed able to transfer information from STS to LTS accurately and retain it over long periods of time. Long and complex lists of words could be remembered some 15 years after they were first learned, even if they were nonsense words or in an unknown language. Indeed, his problem was in trying to forget information. S. used mnemonics in order to perform this feat. Essentially, the process involves both elaboration and organization. The first step is to form an association between the material and an item that already exists in memory. The second step is to organize these items. Many people use mnemonics, such as the rhyme '30 days has September, April, June and November. . .'. S. used images of well known streets near his home to organize his memory. In learning a list of words, for example, he would visualize the objects they represented and place them in prominent positions so that he would notice them as he walked by them in imagination.

In the absence of much experimental evidence, however, it is difficult to evaluate the effectiveness of mnemonics. There are several popular books and some applications of mnemonics to medicine. For example, the causes of dementia might be remembered by using the mnemonic device DEMENTIAS, in which each letter stands for a cause[14]:

Deficiency disorders
Ethanol (alcohol) and other drugs
Myxoedema
Encephalitis
Neoplasm
Trauma
Inflammation
Atherosclerosis
Sugar low: hypoglycemia. Senility. Schizophrenia

It is important, of course, that the mnemonic vehicle be readily accessible and unlikely to be forgotten.

4.4 Effective Study

Several suggestions for more effective study have already been made. The spacing of rehearsal, the use of context, elaboration and organization can all be expected to assist the transfer of information from STS to LTS and the retrieval of this information. Preparation for exams might be aided by studying the nature of past examinations in the subject area. The type of exam can influence how material should be studied. In one experiment, students were given a passage to read and then examined on it. One group of the subjects was told that they would receive short-answer open questions, whereas the other expected multiple-choice questions. However, half of each group was given the kind of test they did not expect, so that their preparation may have been inappropriate. As predicted, those who received the expected type of test did better than those who received the unexpected one[15]. Additionally, legibility of writing is an important factor in essay-type tests. By giving different groups of teachers the same essays written either clearly or illegibly, several studies have shown that legibly written work receives higher marks.

Many suggestions for efficient and accurate study have been outlined in the SQ3R method: Survey, Question, Read, Recite, Review. Although not all of these stages have been experimentally validated, the package as a whole has been shown to be effective in aiding recall (see Chapter 3 under the heading 'Self-control'):

Survey 1. Glance over the headings in the chapter to see the few big points which will be developed. This survey should not take more than a minute and will show the three to six core ideas around which the rest of the discussion will cluster. If the chapter has a final summary paragraph this will also list the ideas developed in the chapter. This orientation will help you organize the ideas as you read them later.

Question 2. Now begin to work. Turn the first heading into a question. This will arouse your curiosity and so increase comprehension. It will bring to mind information already known, thus helping you to understand that section more quickly. And the question will make important points stand out while explanatory detail is recognized as such. This turning a heading into a question can be done on the instant of reading the heading, but it demands a conscious effort on the part of the reader to make this query for which he must read to find the answer.

Read 3. Read to answer that question, i.e., to the end of the first headed section. This is not a passive plowing along each line, but an active search for the answer.

Recite 4. Having read the first section, look away from the book and try briefly to recite the answer to your question. Use your own words and name an example. If you can do this you know what is in the book; if you can't, glance over the section again. An excellent way to do this reciting from memory is to jot down cue phrases in outline form on a sheet of paper. Make these notes very brief!

Now repeat steps 2, 3 and 4 on each succeeding headed section. That is, turn the next heading into a question, read to answer that question, and recite the answer by jotting down cue phrases in your outline. Read in this way until the entire lesson is completed.

Review 5.   When the lesson has thus been read through, look over your notes to get a bird's-eye view of the points and of their relationship and check your memory as to the content by reciting the major subpoints under each heading. This checking of memory can be done by covering up the notes and trying to recall the main points. Then expose each major point and try to recall the subpoints listed under it. (Ref. 16, p. 28)

4.5   Clinical Implications

There are two main ways in which memory research may be relevant to clinical practice: first, in understanding how doctors might impart information to aid patients' recall, and second, in the diagnosis and monitoring of people with certain types of brain damage.

As discussed above, one important aspect of memory is that simply because someone has been told something, it cannot be assumed that this will necessarily be remembered. In the section on remembering in Chapter 13, ways in which doctors can present advice to patients to make it more likely to be retained are described. These include being aware of the primacy effect (material given early in the consultation is more likely to be remembered), stressing the crucial aspects and not giving patients too much to remember. Elaboration and organization of the information may assist recall. For doctors who have to transmit bad news to their patients, it seems to be the case that people in a shocked state retain little of what is said to them. This could apply equally to informing someone of a terminal prognosis as to telling parents that their child is handicapped. As one mother recalls, when asked what she was told during the consultation when she first heard her child had Down's Syndrome: '. . . I can't really remember; I think we were too shocked at the time that anything else he said just went into one ear and out the other' (Hannam[17], p. 26). This implies that it would be important for doctors to make themselves available on subsequent occasions and to be prepared to repeat information which has already been given.

Apart from understanding these 'normal' memory processes, techniques developed from memory research have proved useful with patients suffering from memory impairments. Like personality and intelligence tests, tests of memory can provide significant clinical data. They can assist in diagnosis[18], they can be used to monitor changes in a patient's condition and they can give the patient some insight into his difficulties and suggest ways in which these might be overcome. Situations in which these possibilities might be used are provided by studies of ageing and brain damage.

Increasing age has been shown to affect memory in several studies. For example, Fig. 4.2 illustrates the learning curves for two groups of trainee taxicab drivers. In order to qualify for a licence to work in London, taxi drivers had to learn the layout of streets and the positions of hotels and hospitals. Fig. 4.2 shows that the older trainees took longer to reach the criterion than the

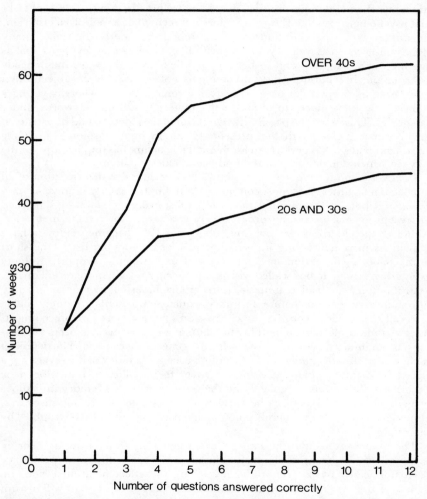

Fig. 4.2   Lengths of time taken by trainee taxi drivers to reach required levels of learning. The older subjects needed more time to answer 12 questions correctly. (Reproduced from A. Shooter, A. Schonfield, H. King and A. Welford, *Occupational Psychology*, 1956, 30, 204–215, by permission of the copyright holder, NFER-Nelson Publishing Company.)

younger ones[19]. Whether results such as these are due to physiological deterioration is debatable. Most studies of age-related decline in memory are cross-sectional (i.e. using different groups at different ages) rather than longitudinal (following the same group over time), so there are confounding variables present. Older subjects are generally less motivated than younger ones, they tend to be more anxious (which has deleterious effects on learning complex tasks) and younger subjects tend to have had higher and more recent formal education than older ones, so they may be more practised in the kinds of tasks that psychologists set them. Age itself does not seem to be a fool-proof criterion, since there is a wide variation of scores among the elderly: typically, many elderly subjects do as well as younger ones. There is, however, evidence that as age increases, subjects tend to become less flexible in the ways they encode information. In laboratory tasks involving lists of words, elderly subjects often rely on simple repetition as a strategy for remembering, whereas younger subjects are more likely to organize the material, subsuming words under categories. This raises the possibility that recall in the elderly could be assisted if the information given to them is presented in an organized fashion — i.e. if the organizational work is performed for them. This, again, has implications for the ways in which doctors present their advice to elderly patients.

Dementia is the term given to profound and progressive deterioration of all intellectual faculties. It is most commonly found in the elderly, known as *senile dementia*. Ribot, in 1904, argued that memory loss in dementia was most marked for recent events, becoming progressively less severe for remote memories. Although the elderly in general (only about 5 – 10% become senile) do have difficulties in remembering information such as a shopping list in the short term, Ribot's contention has not received experimental support. Remote events do not seem to be recalled with greater accuracy than more recent ones[20].

Brain injury can lead to amnesia. Retrograde amnesia refers to the difficulty in remembering events before an injury: concussed patients are often unable to recall the incident causing the concussion or the events just preceding it. Anterograde amnesia is an inability to retain new experiences, as occurs following a brain injury or during recovery from a general anaesthetic. The degree of such post-traumatic amnesia is in fact often used as an index of the severity of a closed head injury. Patients usually recover their ability to remember new experiences but rarely completely fill the retrograde gap. Memory difficulties in general are considered to be early warning signals of organic disorders, although anyone who is severely emotionally disturbed may also be troubled by forgetfulness.

The hippocampus and the Papez Circuit generally (hippocampus – fornix – mamillary bodies – thalamus – ungulate cortex – hippocampus) have been implicated by several studies exploring the effect of brain lesions on memory. It seems that bilateral damage to any part of this circuit will disrupt memory. Some of the more striking case studies are those reported by Milner[21]. In an attempt to relieve patients of severe epilepsy, and when more conservative treatments had little effect, the mesial parts of both temporal lobes were removed, thus destroying two-thirds of the hippocampus bilaterally.

Disconcertingly, the operation led to severe memory impairment in several patients. For example:

> . . . ten months after the operation the family moved to a new house which was situated only a few blocks away from their old one, on the same street. When examined by Scoville and Milner, nearly a year later, H.M. had not yet learned the new address, nor could he be trusted to find his way home alone, because he would go to the old house. Six years ago the family moved again, and H.M. is still unsure of his present address, although he does seem to know that he has moved. Moreover, his mother states now, as she did in 1955, that he is unable to learn where objects constantly in use are kept; for example, although he mows the lawn regularly, and quite expertly, she still has to tell him where to find the lawnmower, even when he has been using it only the day before. His mother also observes that he will do the same jigsaw puzzles day after day without showing any practice effect, and read the same magazines over and over again without ever finding their contents familiar. The same forgetfulness applies to people he has met since the operation, even to those neighbours who have been visiting the house regularly for the past six years. He has not learned their names and he does not recognize any of them if he meets them in the street. Conversely, he cannot now be left alone in the house, because he has been known to invite total strangers in to await his mother's return, thinking that they must be friends of the family whom he has failed to recognize. This last example shows that H.M. is aware of his memory difficulty . . . (Ref. 21, pp. 113 – 114)

Brain-injured patients require assistance in several ways. There have been some recent attempts to help them recover their memory capacity. Training in mnemonics, elaboration and organisation seem to be leading to promising results[22, 23]. Equally important are the personal and social aspects of memory loss. There is a growing realization of the usefulness of psychotherapeutic assistance for brain-injured patients and their families. Therapists have noted the great personal distress associated with brain injury, notably depression and anxiety. Coming to terms with such a loss seems similar to mourning the loss of a close friend or relative (see Chapter 10). Whether the injury is due to a stroke or to surgery, as in the case of H.M. described above, the offer of psychotherapeutic help is an important aspect of patient management.

Summary

In research on memory, three stages are often distinguished: encoding, storage and retrieval. Encoding involves the initial registration of information. Traditionally, psychologists have used artifical materials (lists of letters or unrelated words) in their experiments, in order to reduce contamination from past experience. More recently, there has been growing interest in the use of meaningful material, such as prose extracts, because this is thought to provide a more accurate picture of how people remember in their everyday lives outside the laboratory. The second stage of memory involves storage. Many psychologists use a three-store model — sensory, short-term and long-term. Sensory and short-term stores operate for short periods of time and have limited capacity, whereas long-term store can contain information for decades and has no easily measured limits. A notable feature of long-term store is its dynamic nature: memories seem to change in order to become consistent with past experiences and expectations. The third stage, retrieval, involves the recall of information from store or the recognition of information when it is encountered again. These three stages appear to be interdependent, in that the way information is encoded seems to affect how accurately it can be retrieved.

Several methods can be used to aid memory. These include not only rehearsal and repetition, but also ways in which new material can be elaborated or organized to integrate it with previously stored material. If new information can be associated with already held memories, retrieval is less difficult. Although illustrating ways of presenting information to make it more readily remembered, the methods can be used as aids for effective studying, to help patients remember their physicians' advice and to assist individuals who suffer memory impairments.

Suggested Reading

G.R. Loftus and E.F. Loftus, *Human memory: the processing of information*, Wiley, London, 1976, consider many of the points discussed in this chapter in more detail.

References

1. From *The Mind of a Mnemonist: a little book about a vast memory* by A.R. Luria, © 1968 by Basic Books, Inc. By permission of Basic Books, Inc., Publishers, New York and Jonathan Cape, Ltd., London.
2. Peterson, L.R. and Peterson, M., Short-term retention of individual items, *Journal of Experimental Psychology*, 1959, **58**, 193 – 198.
3. Dunn, A.J., Neurochemistry of learning and memory: an evaluation of recent data, *Annual Review of Psychology*, 1980, **31**, 343 – 390.
4. Loftus, G.R. and Palmer, J.C., Reconstruction of automobile destruction: an example of the interaction between language and memory, *Journal of Verbal Learning and Verbal Behaviour*, 1974, **13**, 585 – 589.
5. Spitzer, H.F., Studies in retention, *Journal of Educational Psychology*, 1939, **30**, 641 – 656.
6. Smith, S.M., Glenberg, A. and Bjork, R.A., Environmental context and human memory *Memory and Cognition*, 1978, **6**, 342 – 353.
7. Eich, J., Weingartner, H., Stillman, R.C. and Gillin, J.C., State-dependent accessibility of retrieval cues in the retention of a categorised list, *Journal of Verbal Learning and Verbal Behaviour*, 1975, **14**, 408 – 417.
8. Bobrow, S. and Bower, G.H., Comprehension and recall of sentences, *Journal of Experimental Psychology*, 1969, **80**, 455 – 461.
9. Hyde, T.S. and Jenkins J.J., Recall for words as a function of semantic, graphic and syntactic orienting tasks, *Journal of Verbal Learning and Verbal Behaviour*, 1973, **12**, 471 – 480.

10. Holmes, E., Reading guided by questions versus careful reading and rereading without questions, *School Review*, 1931, **39**, 361 – 371.
11. Frase, L.T., Prose processing, *In* Bower, G.H. (ed.), *The psychology of learning and motivation*, vol. 9, Academic Press, New York, 1975.
12. Bower, G.H., Clark, M.C., Lesgold, A.M. and Winzenz, D., Hierarchal retrieval schemes in recall of categorised word lists, *Journal of Verbal Learning and Verbal Behaviour*, 1969, **8**, 323 – 343
13. Bower, G.H. and Clark, M.C., Narrative stories as mediators for serial learning, *Psychonomic Science*, 1969, **14**, 181 – 182.
14. Shipman, J.J., *Mnemonics and tactics in surgery and medicine*, Lloyd-Luke Ltd, London, 1978.
15. d'Ydewalle, G. and Rosselle, H., Test expectations in text learning, *In* Gruneberg, M.M., Morris, P.E. and Sykes, R.N. (eds.), *Practical aspects of memory*, Academic Press, London, 1978.
16. 'Steps in the SQ3R Method' on pages 32–33 in *Effective Study*, *4th edition*, by Francis P. Robinson. Copyright 1941, 1946 by Harper & Row, Publishers, Inc. Copyright © 1961, 1970 by Francis P. Robinson. Reprinted by permission of Harper & Row, Publishers, Inc.
17. Hannam, C., *Parents and mentally handicapped children*, Penguin, Harmondsworth, 1975.
18. Walsh, K.W., *Neuropsychology*, Churchill Livingstone, London, 1978.
19. Shooter, A., Schonfield, A., King, H. and Welford, A., Some field data on the training of older people, *Occupational Psychology*, 1956, **30**, 204 – 215.
20. Warrington, E.K. and Sanders, H.I., The fate of old memories, *Quarterly Journal of Experimental Psychology*, 1971, **23**, 432 – 442.
21. Milner, B., Amnesia following operation on the temporal lobes, *In* Whitty, C.W.M. and Zangwill, O.L., *Amnesia*, Butterworths, London, 1966.
22. Grafman, J. and Matthews, C.G., Assessment and remediation of memory deficits in brain-injured patients, *In* Gruneberg, M.M., Morris, P.E. and Sykes, R.N. (eds.), *Practical aspects of memory*, Academic Press, London, 1978.
23. McDowall, J., Effects of encoding instructions and retrieval cuing in recall in Korsakoff patients, *Memory and Cognition*, 1979, **7** 232 – 239.

5
Intelligence

5.1   Introduction

Most people, at some time in their lives, undergo tests of ability. They may be overt, such as an examination in school designed to give an indication of how well a student has learned a subject, or they may be less obvious, such as a manager unobtrusively assessing the ability of a worker. These kinds of tests are very specific: the interest is only in one aspect of a person's life, often at a particular time. Psychologists have attempted to gain a more general measure of ability through the development of IQ (Intelligence Quotient) tests. These are used by many educational and clinical psychologists in their assessments of, say, a child who is not doing well in school or an adult whose capacities may have been damaged by a stroke or an accident. In such cases, IQ tests may aid diagnosis. The child whose school grades are low might have some basic inability to learn or, alternatively, have emotional or interpersonal problems. If a high score were achieved on an IQ test, this could effectively rule out the former possibility, so that an educational psychologist might suggest that psychological problems were responsible for the school difficulties. Since IQ tests measure various abilities, the particular difficulties experienced by a patient who has suffered a stroke can sometimes be pinpointed and rehabilitation programmes devised[1].

112

Although there are a wide variety of suggested definitions of 'intelligence', as measured by IQ tests it basically refers to an ability to solve problems and to think in the abstract. Measurements of this ability run into numerous problems: for instance, can it meaningfully be regarded as one global ability or does it refer to several independent abilities such as perceptual acuity, memory and word fluency? Can it be measured without taking into account a person's motivation to succeed at the task? Is it possible to devise tests that measure aptitude rather than prior learning? Once a measurement has been made, does it show that a person has inherited greater intellectual endowment, or does it reflect the individual's experiences? What, if anything, does current performance indicate about a person's future capabilities?

Although it is important to remember that, in some societies, there is not even an equivalent concept, in Western societies intelligence is highly prized. Until the Eleven-plus examination was abolished in Britain, this IQ test determined the type of secondary education for many people: a graded system that assumed that intellectual performance on a couple of occasions at age 11 was a reliable predictor of future educational prospects. Those who scored highly were given opportunities to develop more abstract, academic skills, whereas those who scored lower were regarded as suited to more practical tasks. In this context, the suggestion that certain classes or races have, on average, lower measured IQs than others has led to heated debate. The field of IQ testing has been characterized by confrontations between those extremists who claim too much for an IQ score — that it can accurately predict a person's future capabilities — and those who consider IQ tests useless because of the bias in the tests towards white, middle-class culture and because they sample only a limited range of behaviour.

In this chapter we look at how people have studied intelligence, with particular attention to the development and use of IQ tests. The various factors affecting people's scores on these tests, such as age, experience and genetics are examined, and the usefulness of the concept is explored. In addition to their use in educational settings, IQ tests can identify people with degenerative diseases as well as those with mental handicaps, and can be used as a way of monitoring the progress of such people.

5.2   Measurement of IQ

Several ways of measuring intelligence have been explored. As far back as 1884, Galton tried, unsuccessfully, to relate head size and reaction times to intellectual performance. More recently, attempts to relate the speed of brain functioning through EEG recordings to intellectual performance have had slight success, but producing low correlations. The most successful approach to intellectual measurement has been the IQ test.

The forerunner of current individual IQ tests was a scale developed by Binet at the beginning of the century at the request of the Paris authorities. They wished to identify those children who would not benefit from the educational system. Binet's original test, was, thus, designed to predict school success, a need probably bound up with the increasing technology of the developing industrial society. By giving a large sample of children various problems to solve, he identified items that could be done by, on average, half the children of each age. For example, he found that half the 6-year-olds could repeat a sentence of 16 syllables, half the 8-year-olds could count backwards from 20 to zero, half the 9-year-olds could name the days of the week, and half the 10-year-olds could name the months of the year. His test consisted of a set of these age-graded items. When the test was administered to a particular child, he or she would initially be presented with the items for an age lower than his or her chronological age and then given successively harder items until several in a row were failed in order to establish the child's mental age.

The formula

$$\frac{\text{Mental age (MA)}}{\text{Chronological age (CA)}} \times 100$$

was later developed, to provide the intelligent quotient or IQ. To simplify somewhat, in the case of an 8-year-old child who passed only the items expected of an average 6 year old, the IQ would be $6/8 \times 100 = 75$, whereas the IQ of a child whose answers indicated the ability of a 10 year old would be $10/8 \times 100 = 125$. An 'average' child, with a mental age equivalent to the chronological age, would have an IQ of 100.

The original Binet test was updated and revised by Terman at Stanford University in 1916 to provide the Stanford – Binet intelligence test. This has itself undergone several revisions, but remains in common use, along with a test developed along similar lines by Wechsler (the Wechsler Intelligence Scale for children or WISC). In the 1960 revision of the Stanford – Binet, an 8-year-old child would be asked to define certain words (e.g. a straw, an orange, an envelope, a puddle), to point out absurdities in statements ('An old man complained that he could no longer walk around the park as he used to; he said that now he could only go half-way round and then back again'), to say how two things were alike and how they differed (e.g. sea and river) and to indicate comprehension of situations by answering questions appropriately ('What's the thing for you to do when you are on your way to school and think you are going to be late?')[2]. There are also various tests for children below the age of 2 years, such as those devised by Griffiths and Cattell[3]. In the latter, a 6-month-old infant would be expected to pick a cube off a table; to lift a cup from a table; to finger his reflection in a mirror; to reach out for objects with one hand and to stretch persistently towards an object that was just out of reach.

All of these are individual tests — the examiner tests one person at a time and various items are included. Some IQ tests have been devised for groups, such as Raven's Progressive Matrices, a non-verbal test in which a pattern has to be selected to complete a sequence[4]. One of the less difficult items from this test is shown in Fig. 5.1. Raven's Progressive Matrices is often used in conjunction with the Mill Hill Vocabulary Scale, another paper-and-pencil test that can

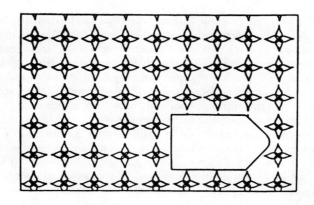

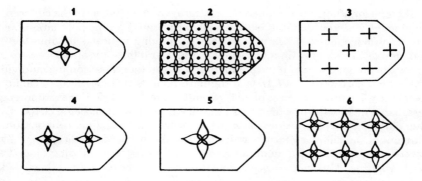

Fig. 5.1   An example of an item from Raven's Progressive Matrices. The sequence in the top part of the figure has to be completed by one of the six alternatives at the bottom. (Reproduced from J.C. Raven, *Standard Progressive Matrices*, 1958, by permission of J.C. Raven Ltd.)

easily be given to large groups of people at one time. Respondents are asked to write the meanings of several words, such as 'continue' and 'putative'. A second section of the test requires the correct meaning of a target word to be underlined out of a list of possibilities; for instance, for the word WHIM, a synonym from the list:

complain	noise
tonic	fancy
wind	wish

has to be selected.

Beyond the age of about 16 years, the formula $100 \times MA/CA$ ceases to apply. It is not easy, for example, to find items that can be done by 23-year-olds but not by 22-year-olds; for adults, mental age ceases to maintain its relation to chronological age. An IQ can still be calculated for an adult, however, by comparing his performance with that of a large group of people of similar age. This is the same principle that many personality theorists have used in developing their tests for assessing personality. It is not the absolute score that is important, but how this compares with others' scores, so it is important to use a comparison group that is similar to the person being tested. It would make little sense, for example, to compare the IQ scores of an American astronaut with those of a rural farm worker in England, or to compare either of these with the scores of an Australian aborigine. Although the astronaut would be likely to score higher on IQ tests than the aboriginal, the former could not be said to be more intelligent. Only if people come from similar social backgrounds can the comparison be made. When an IQ test has been given to a large group of people it is said to be 'standardized' for that population and their results are called 'norms'.

IQ tests for adults are designed so that the average is 100, as in the children's versions. IQ is considered to be 'normally distributed' in the population, and this knowledge allows a curve to be constructed that indicates the number of individuals likely to obtain a particular score. To do this, it is also necessary to know the range of scores in the population, i.e. whether there could be individuals with IQs of 200 or − 10. In fact, standard IQ tests are devised so that almost everybody lies within a range of 90 IQ points, from 55 to 145. For those scoring less than 85, there have been several classifications, new terms being adopted as the old ones were considered to have developed negative connotations. Currently, the following terms are used: O − 20, profound handicap; 20 − 35, severe handicap; 35 − 50, moderate handicap; 50 − 70, mild handicap and 70 − 85, borderline. This range was previously covered by the terms idiot, low-grade imbecile, high-grade imbecile and moron or feeble-minded person. There are marked biological as well as psychological differences between the severely handicapped (IQ less than 50) and the mildly handicapped (IQ greater than 50)[5].

Reliability and Validity

The results of IQ tests can only be taken seriously if they can be shown to be reliable (i.e. the same result would be obtained by different testers or on different occasions) and valid (i.e. the tests are measuring problem-solving abilities and abstract thinking rather than, say, prior experience and training).

Reliability can be measured in various ways: by seeing if people achieve a similar score on subsequent administrations of the test; by preparing alternative or parallel forms of the test and seeing whether people score similarly on both, which eliminates the practice element involved in doing the same test again (the Stanford − Binet has parallel forms: L and M); or by comparing scores on one half of the test with scores on the other half (split-half reliability).

One way in which reliability is maintained is by standardizing the way the

116

tests are given, so that each testing is seen as a well controlled experiment. Manuals describe precisely how the tests must be administered and the psychologists must follow this agreed procedure, down to the exact words. Instructions are given about establishing rapport with the testee and there is evidence[6] that feeling comfortable with the examiner does improve test-score results. The sex and race of the examiner also influence the results obtained[7, 8].

As far as validity is concerned, IQ tests do correlate with academic achievement, the original purpose behind Binet's scale. The Stanford – Binet and WAIS correlate between 0.40 to 0.60 with school grades. IQ test results also correlate with occupational achievement, and the average IQ of people in different jobs (such as lawyer or butcher) has been found to correlate with independent rankings of how intelligent such workers would be considered to be. Within more restricted ranges, however, IQ correlates less well with achievement. Doctors in the top and bottom thirds of their graduating class displayed only very slight differences in the quality of practice thereafter and even these decreased after the first few years[9]. However, the IQ test was not designed to discriminate between people of similar high (or low) ability, but rather to distinguish between the high and low scorers. Since almost everyone who goes to university will have a high IQ, this lack of correspondence would be expected. Nor are IQ tests designed to measure divergent or creative thinking, an ability that may be important in this context. There are, however, tests that have been devised to measure creativity[10].

The validity of IQ tests in certain contexts has been brought into question because of their cultural bias. Obviously, someone with a poor grasp of English would be at a disadvantage on items that depend on understanding instructions or rely on knowledge of vocabulary. Less obviously, people from different social classes within a culture use language differently. Not only are there differences in grammar, there are also likely to be differences in vocabulary. One study[11] of the errors in IQ tests looked at an item in which subjects were asked to pick out the word that did not belong with the others in the list:

cello, harp, drum, violin, guitar

85% of the children from homes of high socioeconomic status chose 'drum', the intended correct answer, but only 45% of the children from homes of low socioeconomic status. These latter children most commonly answered 'cello', an unfamiliar word that they thought did not belong. The high socioeconomic status children were more likely to at least have heard the word.

Attempts have been made to develop 'culture-fair' tests that do not rely on linguistic ability. However, it is clear that cultural influences extend beyond language: the motivation to succeed at the task may be quite different, for instance, and it now seems apparent that, although some tests may be less culture-biased than others, no test is culture fair. This means it is impossible on the basis of IQ tests to say people from one culture are more intelligent than people from another. This has been well demonstrated by a study[12] investigating groups of children in various parts of the world. Each group showed definite variations in the pattern of abilities. Children in underdeveloped countries

117

sometimes surpassed Western standards in some tasks, but scored very low on others. Such studies illustrate that the global concept of intelligence provides only a crude measure. Certainly, any interpretation of IQ test scores must take into consideration the individual's background.

5.3 Factors Affecting IQ

Genetics

An individual's score on an IQ test is generally considered to be a function of both heredity and environment. It would be surprising if genetics had no effect, since it plays a role in many other attributes. Certainly, a defect in an individual's genetic make-up can lead to impaired intelligence: a genetic defect that affects one in every 2000 babies born to women in their 20s but one in 50 babies born to women in their 40s is Down's Syndrome. This condition is often called Mongolism because of the babies' slightly Eastern appearance. 47 chromosomes are present instead of the usual 46. It is not clear what causes this, but it may be related to maternal exposure to radiation (X-rays). It is not believed to be hereditary. The condition is always associated with severe mental handicaps. No physical way of ameliorating this condition is known, although, along with other genetic abnormalities, it can be detected *in utero* by testing a small sample of amniotic fluid. In some areas, all pregnant women over the age of 35 are routinely offered this amniocentesis test. Down's Syndrome accounts for a quarter of all cases of severe mental handicap.

The role of the environment is also of consequence since genes provide only a potential for growth and do not determine its course independent of the environment. The importance of genetics in height, for example, is clear, but the general population in Western countries has been becoming appreciably taller over the last generations. This seems to be due to better diet and living conditions. Specific gene mutations that affect IQ highlight the complexity of the inter-relationship between nature and nurture. Children born with phenylketonuria (PKU) used to suffer brain damage owing to the build-up of phenylalanine in toxic quantities in the bloodstream. Now, however, every infant is routinely tested a few days after birth (the Guthrie test), and in the rare cases that the condition is detected, amelioration is possible by the provision of a special diet, largely fruit and vegetables and as low as possible in phenylalanine. Galactosemia is similar; a single gene defect leaves the patient unable to metabolize galactose. If not detected, this can lead to mental retardation. Once identified, the treatment is again mainly dietary. In both cases, by providing the right environment, the potentially damaging effects of the individual's genetic make-up are averted.

There is considerable disagreement about the relative importance of genetic and environmental influences. Some hold that heredity is primarily responsible for scores in IQ tests, others argue that environment is the critical factor. This debate, which is found among geneticists as well as psychologists, has been

118

fiercely argued by both sides, with accusations (some justified) of fraudulent reporting of data. It is not possible adequately to summarize the debate here, except to make some general points.

The problem in disentangling the effects of genes and environment is that people who are related to one another genetically are usually related to one another socially as well. If they live in the same household, they will have many shared experiences, so that any correlation between their IQs could just as easily be attributed to similarities in environment as to similarities in genetic endowment. Attempts to separate these effects include studies on monozygotic twins who have been separated from birth and studies of children who have been adopted.

Some investigators have given IQ tests to monozygotic (MZ) twins who have been separated at or near birth and compared them with twins who have been reared together. If genetic influences are most important, then there should be little difference between both kinds of twins, but if environment is critical, there should be a high correlation between the IQs of twins reared together, but not between the separated twins. In fact, the correlations are about the same and high: about 0.70 for twins reared apart, 0.85 for twins reared together. Results such as these have not been accepted by the environmentalists (notably Kamin), who have argued that the environments for the separated twins were really very similar. For example, in one study, many of the twins were raised in related branches of the parents' family, such as by the biological mother's sister. Only 13 of the 40 pairs in this sample were reared in unrelated households: for these, IQs correlated 0.51, whereas for the 27 pairs reared in related families, the correlation was 0.83. The environmentalists argue further than even the correlation of 0.51 can be misleading, since many of these were reared by friends of the biological mother[13].

Adoption studies provide another means of separating environmental and genetic effects. Some research compared the IQs of biological parents and their offspring with the IQs of adoptive parents and their adopted child. In the first case, both environmental and genetic factors operated, whereas in the second, only environmental. Under the genetic model, the relationship between biological parents' IQs and their child's IQ should be much stronger than the adoptive parent – child relationship. Some early studies indicated that this was the case, suggesting that environment plays a relatively small part and heredity a large one. However, some later studies, using a somewhat different design, have questioned this conclusion. Here, the comparison has been between parents and their adopted child and the same parents with their biological child. They found little difference. The recent studies, using more reliable and valid measures of IQ, should, perhaps, be given more weight than the earlier work.

Another point to make about this research is that measuring IQ is not like measuring height or weight. In these latter instances, the relationship between the examiner and the subject to be measured is not a social one. The emphasis placed on the standardization of the way IQ tests are given is precisely because scores are open to social influences, as discussed in the previous section. An examiner who encourages the client to try harder or who is warm and reassuring

119

may obtain different results from an examiner who does not show these qualities. If IQ tests were only measuring an innate ability, we would not expect to find such systematic differences. At least in part, measuring IQ is a social process, and this means that when doing research using IQ tests the examiner should be 'blind' to the purpose of the study. This point is illustrated by a study in which children were tested using the Stanford – Binet by graduate students in psychology. The students were asked to test two children each, being led to believe that one was capable of high academic achievement whereas the other had shown only poor academic ability. In fact, there was no such systematic sorting of children, yet the examiners' results corresponded to their expectations. Those children said to be more able attained significantly higher scores than those said to be less able[14]. The environmentalists point out that blind testing has not always been used in the studies mentioned above. In one study concerning separated twins, a correlation of 0.77 was reported between the IQs of twins reared apart, very similar to that of twins reared together (0.76). Besides the possibility that this result might be due to related environments, the same investigator tested 35 of the 40 separated twins. For the remaining five pairs, two different examiners gave the tests. There is the possibility that the examiner expected to find similar IQs and unconsciously biased the administration of the tests. For the five pairs tested by different examiners, the correlation was 0.11 and there was a mean difference of 22.4 points between the twins, whereas for the other 35, the correlation was 0.84 with a mean difference of 8.5 points. It may well be that other factors are operating here (the twins tested by the two different examiners may have been systematically different from the others in some way), but it does point out the importance of 'blind' testing.

There are several other criticisms made by the environmentalists of the studies. Some of these are statistical, others having to do with design. There is always a problem for any reader who is not able to consult all the primary sources in a subject. A reviewer (or writers of a book on psychology) will inevitably have theoretical predilections that will result in biases of some kind, selecting certain studies for mention or reporting only certain results. Even going to the original paper does not solve the problem altogether, since a researcher may report only those results which support his or her hypothesis. Such biases are not necessarily conscious, as shown in Chapter 1, and part of the reason for careful research design is to minimise these biases as far as possible.

Finally, some discussion of the heritability index is required. This is a statistic that indicates the extent to which a trait can be inherited. The implication sometimes drawn from studies on IQ is that if the heritability index is found to be high, then intellectual ability is mainly genetically determined and environmental changes would have little effect. Such a view would have important social consequences. For example, there is a mean difference of about 15 IQ points between American whites and American blacks. If IQ scores are mainly due to genetics, the argument might run, educational or social-enrichment programmes established to reduce this difference might be expected to have limited effect. It might also suggest to some that all blacks would score lower than all whites.

Such conclusions are unwarranted, for several reasons. First, the heritability index is calculated for a particular society at a particular time. As a population statistic, it does not apply to specific individuals (there is considerable overlap between black and white populations, so that many blacks score more highly than many whites), nor is it unchanging over time. As Eysenck (a leading proponent of the genetic position) puts it:

> 'Because in a given population heredity accounts for 80% of the variance in IQ and environment for 20%, it does not follow that these proportions would be the same for a given individual in that population, or in other cultures or in the same culture at a different period in history . . . . While the figures quoted give an approximate idea of the position as it is now, it is by no means certain that had these studies been carried out 200 or 300 years ago, results would have been the same. It seems quite likely that in those days environment played a much more important part than it does now, so that heritability would probably have been somewhat lower.' (Ref. 15, p. 59).

In other words, heritability is a function of the similarity of the environment as well as genes.

A second point concerns the relative importance of genetics and environment. Using Eysenck's figures, the proportions are 80 to 20. This does not mean that inheritance is four times as important as environment. In order to calculate their relative significance, the square root of 80 over 20 is taken, which is 2.00[15]. Genes would be twice as important as environment, leaving a large amount of leeway for educational and social progress. When other, lower, estimates of heritability are used, its relative importance decreases correspondingly.

The debate between the two camps is likely to continue for some time yet. As in some other areas of psychology, it is those studies that have important social implications that are most critically examined, each side looking for flaws in the other's research. In practice, it may be impossible to distinguish between the effects of nature and nurture, since the effects of genes depend on the environment they act in. Children who are given 'good' genes by their parents are also likely to live in an enriched environment, with plentiful books, lots of conversation and encouragement to do well at school. Any genetic potential is more likely to be fulfilled in such conditions.

Environment

The effect of a wide range of environmental circumstances on intellectual ability (again, as measured by IQ tests) have been studied, including the prenatal environment, family, social class and education. Environment is taken to mean physical as well as social influences. The effects of specific environmental factors are difficult to disentangle in practice, and there is no unified theory available at present. Generally, the data indicate that the earlier and more sustained an intervention, the greater is its influence.

121

Prenatal influences.   Influences on the foetus in the womb can affect the IQ of the child, and these influences depend on their timing, an organ system being most sensitive when it is developing most rapidly. Although in most cases of mental handicap no physical cause can be discovered, if the mother catches rubella (German Measles) in the first three months of pregnancy, for instance, the infant's hearing system may be impaired and heart defects or other physical abnormalities caused. Syphilis in the mother is passed to her infant in 25% of cases, and the child may be subnormal. The number of brain cells in the child is reduced if the mother's diet is inadequate (too little protein or too few calories) particularly in the final three months of pregnancy, and maternal alcoholism has been shown to lead to mental handicap in the child. Certain drugs taken by the mother during pregnancy can also affect the child. The effects of maternal smoking in pregnancy are not clear, but one study[16] found children of mothers who smoked during pregnancy were, on average, 3 months behind their peers on general intelligence at age 11 years. Although this is a small effect, it is also a preventable one. Children from multiple births often have lower IQs, though this could be due to diminished parent – child interaction through having to share the attention of parents, rather than to prenatal factors. During the birth process itself, the infant's brain is extremely susceptible to damage. Lack of oxygen during birth (anoxia) is estimated to prevent one baby in 1000 from reaching a 12-year-old level of functioning.

Family/social class.   Numerous studies have shown clear relationships between parental social class and both the IQ and scholastic achievement of their children (e.g. Douglas[17]). Part of this social-class influence may be related to differences in the quality and quantity of language used in the home. In residential nurseries, it has been shown that the quality of children's verbal environment and the richness of their activities were significant determinants of early cognitive development. Many studies have found marked social-class differences in the language used by parents to their children[18, 19], which put working-class children at a disadvantage on traditional IQ tests compared to middle-class children. A review by Rutter and Madge[20] of children reared in isolated or poor communities concluded that the longer the privation, the more intellectual development was impeded. The quality of the parent – child interaction and the range of experiences available to the child were among those aspects of the environment that were most important in this connection. Further, they point out that it is not the amount of stimulation, but rather the quality, meaningfulness and range of experiences available to the child that are important.

Parental attitudes to learning and education and the literacy of the home may also be part of the social-class related influences, as, indirectly, are poor material circumstances such as poverty, overcrowding and lack of basic household facilities. More important, there is a high correlation between large family size and low attainment, larger families also tending to be those with less financial and material resources. The different forms of social disadvantage all tend to affect the same group of families. Verbal skills are particularly affected. Certainly, McCall *et al.*[21], comparing children whose IQ scores increased over

122

time with those whose IQ scores decreased, found the former had parents who stressed intellectual tasks and achievements more. Additionally, there is some evidence that first-born children (particularly boys) tend to have higher IQs and to achieve more than later-born children.

Education.   Education has been shown to affect IQ, but to account for much less of the variance than features of family and home, perhaps because there is less variation between schools than between homes, and because the measures taken have tended to be rather crude. There have been various attempts to help children from disadvantaged homes by means of compensatory education, generally at pre-school level. Perhaps the best known of these is the Head Start programme in the United States. This was initiated in 1965 as an 8 weeks traditional nursery-school programme for children from low-income families. The programme was set up after only 3 months' planning, with rather imprecise goals and unclear criteria on which to base evaluation. It was based on the assumption that disadvantaged children could make use of the same kinds of experience as children from privileged homes. Evaluation concentrated on IQ gains, and little effect was found. It is possible that other measures, for instance of social skills or language ability, might have been more appropriate. Other, more focused projects have shown IQ gains of 10–15 points, especially where there has been emphasis on the development of language. As well as highlighting the necessity for focused projects, the Head Start programme illustrated that once intervention ceased, gains seemed to be lost. Attempts to continue intervention programmes into the primary grades have shown that beneficial effects can be maintained. Involving parents with such intervention programmes also seems to have measurable, beneficial effects.

A recent study[22] combines many of these factors. Forty children were selected at birth whose mothers had an IQ of 80 or below. Twenty of the children served as a comparison group, being given no special attention. The other children were given extensive educational advantages — attending a centre for 7 hours a day, 5 days a week. The programme included assistance in language, thinking and sensorimotor skills. Their mothers, too, were included, being given vocational and child-care training. Both groups of children were periodically tested, and after the age of 14 months differences between the groups became apparent. At about 5 years of age the experimental group children averaged 120 IQ points, whereas the control group childen had an average IQ of about 95. Attempts at compensatory education that involve the family and that continue into the school years seem the most likely to succeed.

Age

Studies on the effects of ageing do not fall easily into either the genetic or environmental categories. Since growing involves both maturational and experiential influences, both factors apply. Although IQ tests assess current intellectual functioning, the underlying assumption is that they imply something about future performance. Many studies have looked at the stability of IQ

123

over time. Before 1 year of age, test results bear little relation to results a year later, not because the tests are particularly unreliable (an infant will be likely to respond to a moving light or the sound of a bell in the same way on successive testings in the short term), but because these early tests sample a different, and greatly reduced, range of behaviours compared to tests for older children. Indeed, before 1 year of age, parental IQs provide a better predictor of the child's future IQ than infant tests. Differing test content is a source of change over time in all child IQ tests, but the older the child becomes, the more likely it is that similar items will be sampled. Even by 2 years, IQ results do correlate with those obtained, say, a year later, though they still bear little relationship to adult functioning.

Even when correlations between successive testings are quite high, this can mask quite substantial changes in IQ over time. Hindley and Owen[23] point out that with a correlation as high as 0.76 from age 5 to 8 years, the median change is still expected to be 9 IQ points. Between 3 and 17 years, half of their sample changed by more than 10 points, a quarter by 20 points or more. They concluded:

> In the primary school period alone, a quarter will change by at least 15 points. Moreover, the tester cannot know towards which end of the spectrum any child will fall. Thus, selecting children for different types of school at 11 years, though perhaps administratively convenient, is very hazardous from the standpoint of the educational welfare of the individual child. (Ref. 23, p. 346)

Although Hindley and Owen accept that test unreliability and changing test content may account for some of this change, some reflects true changes in ability over time.

Mental abilities that require speed and extensive use of short-term memory peak at about 30 – 40 years and then decline. Those that tap general knowledge, however, show little decline with age. The first type, which generally involve tackling novel problems, has been suggested to reflect a kind of 'fluid' or non-specialized type of intelligence, which indicates an individual's capacity to adapt to new situations, in contrast with the second type, suggested to reflect 'crystallized' intelligence or ability resulting from accumulated wisdom. Two tests described previously are sometimes used to measure these two types of intelligence: Raven's Progressive Matrices, requiring the solution of new problems, is believed to reflect changes in capacity; whereas the Mill Hill Vocabulary scale, drawing on past experience, is a more resistant test, reflecting 'crystallized' intelligence.

The exact nature of the decrement in mental processes with age depends on the methods used to collect the data. Cross-sectional studies, where a sample of the population of various ages (say 20, 40, 60, 80) are tested on one occasion, produce different results from longitudinal studies where the same group of people are tested on successive occasions as they reach different ages. Cross-sectional studies may run up against non-age-related differences between generations — younger people are more attuned to the whole ethos of intelligence testing, for example. Longitudinal studies are biased by non-random factors in drop out[24]. In addition, it appears that a relatively sudden drop in IQ may occur up to 5 years before death (the terminal drop) which affects results[25]. The rate of decline in IQ relates to occupation; people in intellectually demanding occupations do not decline in mental abilities as early as others in less demanding jobs.

The distinction between fluid and crystallized intelligence is an important one when considering the needs of the elderly. Having difficulty in adapting to new problems or strange situations may make hospitalization more stressful than for a younger person. There is some evidence that whenever possible the elderly should be treated at home in order to minimize these effects (Chapter 10). Further, simply because an elderly person may have difficulty in adapting to new surroundings does not necessarily mean that he or she cannot cope in familiar ones. Thus, assessments of ability and behaviour made outside the home may not provide a true reflection of abilities within it.

5.4 Development of Intelligence

The intelligence tests so far described are empirical, simply identifying tasks that an average child of a particular age can do. The researchers who devised the early tests were not primarily concerned with explaining how such skills develop. Some theorists have argued that there is a sequence of stages through which every child progresses. The idea is that the order of these stages is common to all, although some children may pass through them more quickly than others. Certain theorists have placed great weight on maturation (growth processes that are governed by automatic, genetically determined signals), whereas others have placed more emphasis on learning. Both processes are involved to some extent: for example, maturation is clearly important in the infant's ability to reach or to walk, but there is evidence that both skills can be hastened by experience[26, 27]. A major proponent of the maturation approach is Arnold Gesell who, with several co-workers, made many detailed observations of infants' and pre-school children's abilities. By examining large groups of children, Gesell charted the normal (or average) course of development. An individual child's abilities could then be compared with this data. The tests devised from this work are easy to administer, score and interpret, being concerned with the average age at which such skills as smiling, sitting without support or standing holding on to furniture emerge[28]. Such normative studies of development form the basis of routine paediatric assessments. By checking all children in this way as a matter of course, developmental lags can be carefully monitored, allowing the early detection of sensory or mental handicaps and early intervention to deal with these. Gesell believed behaviour unfolded in a sequence of stages, determined by inherent maturational mechanisms and in accordance with the law of developmental direction — that behaviour becomes organized from head to foot. That is, the lips lead, eye muscles follow, then neck, shoulders, arms, trunk, legs and lastly, feet. Although this work shows the average ages at which skills emerge, it is important to realize that there is a large normal range of ages at which skills develop. The average age of walking is 14 months, for example, but many children do not accomplish this until some months later.

A more active view of the developmental process is taken by Piaget. Rather than simply accumulating experiences or maturing physically, he argued, the child comes to understand the world through actively working with, modifying and organizing these experiences. Like Gesell, Piaget believed that, to achieve these understandings, a child goes through a series of distinct stages. Each stage builds on the previous ones and, once new concepts are mastered, allows the child to explore new aspects of the environment. The precise ages at which such developments take place seems to depend on how they are measured (e.g. what tasks the child is given to perform, the wording of the requests[29]), but Piaget's important contribution has been to encourage psychologists to consider children's conceptual development as well as their ability to perform on certain tasks, which the IQ tests concentrate upon. Although IQ tests are based on the premiss that younger children simply do less of the things that older children or adults do, Piaget highlights qualitative differences in their modes of thinking.

There are several different stages in his theory. The relationship between movement and perception dominates the earliest stages (up to 2 years). Many of the basic ideas that we all take for granted, such as the fact that hands are a part of one's body, that objects have permanence even when they cannot be seen and that it is possible to have an effect on the environment (e.g. by shaking a rattle) are learned in the first year. During later stages, language becomes important. The development of symbolic thought enables the child to engage in pretend play: a box may become a house, a car or a spaceship. Still later, by manipulating and experimenting through play, such concepts as conservation are discovered: for example, that a lump of clay contains the same mass regardless of its shape, or that a volume of water is unchanging no matter what the shape of the container. The child needs to see the materials manipulated in order to achieve these understandings, and it is not until the age of about 11 years that reasoning can take place independently of concrete objects. The developing ability to use abstract thought enables the adolescent to examine and question general principles of human behaviour or to consider metaphysical ideas. For Piaget, such new concepts cannot be taught — the child must discover them for himself. The provision of a suitable environment can increase a child's opportunities to make such discoveries.

For those dealing with children who are ill, Piaget's theory makes it clear that the child's understanding of concepts such as health and illness may be very different from an adult's view. The concept of cause and effect is a very complex one in medicine, and it may not be until the age of 9 or 10 that a child can understand these ideas. Children often consider illness to be a punishment for bad or prohibited behaviour. Similarly, children's views about death are often different from adults'. Below the age of about 5, death may be confused with 'going away' for a short time or with sleep. It, too, might be seen as a form of punishment. Later, death becomes more final and inevitable, but it is not until adolescence that most children can view it is a philosophical way[30].

There are also implications for asking children to participate in certain situations. Schwartz[31] examined the effects of hospitalization of a purely research nature on children from 4 to 18 years of age. The researchers gave each child and the parents careful preparation before the research work began, explaining its purposes, duration and possible benefits. Later, however, despite having been told the purpose of the hospitalization was research, there was no indication that any of the children under the age of 11 understood why they were in hospital. This abstract idea was apparently beyond their capacity to understand, and, therefore, their consent to participate could not have been 'informed'.

Piaget's theory holds that children are motivated to explore their world. Experiments with primates, too, indicate that satisfying curiosity is inherently reinforcing: monkeys will learn to press levers in order to look outside their cages. Curiosity may be as important a motivator of behaviour as the biological pressures of hunger and thirst. Besides the problems associated with separation from the parents (see Chapter 7) hospitalization may have disturbing effects on the child if these cognitive requirements are not met. The opportunity to explore and experiment with their world may be restricted in hospitals due to staff shortages or lack of toys and space. Particularly when chronic illnesses requiring lengthy stays in hospital are involved, a chance to play may be crucial for well-being[32].

5.5   Use of Intellectual Assessments

Although, as discussed above, IQ scores obtained from infants have low correlations with later scores, scales based on the work of Gesell are widely used, especially by paediatricians and Health Visitors. Using this approach, sensory and mental handicaps can be diagnosed in infants during the first year of life, as shown by Illingworth[33]. Although the earlier the diagnosis is made the better, since the environment can then be structured to optimize development, it is important to ensure that re-assessments occur: 21% of Illingworth's sample were not, at future testings, intellectually handicapped on any criterion, despite their earlier scores.

In educational settings, standard IQ tests, such as the WISC, have proved useful in assessing individual children who have problems at school. They provide a way of seeing whether a child's difficulties are due to below average intelligence for which a remedial programme might be suggested, or whether there are sensory difficulties, such as impaired vision or hearing; or whether there are specific perceptual difficulties, such as dyslexia, that would affect a child's ability to read but not affect his score on an individually administered IQ test. The different subscales of the WISC allow a comparison between verbal and performance measures (the latter comprising manipulation or arrangement of blocks, beads, etc.) that can pinpoint more specific problems.

In psychiatric settings, individual IQ tests of adults can provide helpful information. Stress at work, for instance, could arise from lack of capacity to cope with a too-demanding job or could result from a person's over-capacity in an undemanding job. Some clinical conditions cause deterioration of intellectual performance, leading to dementia. In the early stages, such conditions can resemble other psychiatric disorders. In conjunction with psychiatric evidence, IQ tests may enable elderly people with intellectual difficulties associated with functional, treatable disorders to be distinguished from those related to more severe degenerative senile processes[34]. The course of any deterioration can be charted by testing at different time intervals. It is very important to take account of the state of the patient during the testing, and the nature of the referral may provide clues; for instance, someone showing signs of depression may be particularly handicapped on timed items.

The use of intellectual assessments in paediatric and educational settings can identify people with mental handicaps. Care of mentally handicapped people has changed in recent years. It is now recognized that long-stay hospitals, into which they were often admitted as a matter of course, provide an unsuitable environment (see Chapter 6). Most mentally handicapped people require not medical but educational help, not institutional care but housing in ordinary small homes within the community. Although IQ tests can be helpful in identifying mental handicaps (traditionally defined as IQs less than 70), they do not provide information on appropriate care. Despite low capacity, many mentally handicapped people can, with time, learn to cope effectively with familiar situations. Their adaptive behaviour, or ability to cope independently, is what is important, and there are tests available that attempt to measure this[35, 36]. Stage approaches to intellectual development may also be helpful in assessing and treating mentally handicapped people. Early stimulation of handicapped children by parents has been found to produce significant gains compared with controls[37]. Self-help guides for parents of mentally handicapped children have been produced, based on Gesell's work. As well as enabling parents to chart their child's progress, they indicate the next likely step in development, allowing parents to provide opportunities for the child to practise the necessary skills. Piaget's stages have been taken as the basis of educational work with severely handicapped adults as well as children[38].

Finally, an important use of intellectual assessments is as dependent measures in research studies with children. Changes in IQ have been perhaps the most frequently used way of showing the differential effects of programmes of education or assessing the effects of certain forms of care, such as long-term residential care (Chapter 7). The ready availability of these tests may have led to their over-use: for instance, in studies assessing the relative benefits of different forms of pre-school education, is increased IQ the most important criterion, or would assessments of social skills or attitude to school be more appropriate? In order to understand the implications of such studies, it is important to be aware of the strengths and weaknesses of the IQ tests on which they rely.

Summary

Intelligence, like personality, is an abstraction. It is not possible to touch or feel intelligence, only to observe its effects. It is usually measured by IQ tests that seem to provide reliable and valid indicators of current intellectual performance. However, IQ tests are strongly geared towards white, middle-class culture despite attempts to develop 'culture fair' tests. Although predictive of the future average performance of groups of people, there are often large changes in particular individuals, indicating that caution is necessary in the interpretation of test results.

Although intelligence undoubtedly has some genetic basis, the importance of heredity has been fiercely disputed. There are major environmental influences, such as the prenatal environment, a person's family, social class and education. Tests assessing intellectual performance can identify particular problems, such as mental handicap or intellectual deterioration. A crucial distinction can be made between the capacity to solve novel problems and abilities amassed due to experience. Although the former deteriorates with age, the latter does not. This distinction is important for both old people and mentally handicapped people. Mentally handicapped people have limited capacity, but during their development ability to handle familiar situations may continue to increase as a result of experience. Both old people and mentally handicapped people may thus be able to cope effectively in familiar situations despite low measured IQ on some tests.

IQ testing is not based on a theory of intelligence, but rather on the premiss that children acquire more skills as they grow older. Piaget's theory of intellectual development, however, illustrates qualitative differences between the thinking of children at different ages. This theory suggests that intelligence develops through an invariant sequence of stages, and has implications for education and the care of sick children.

Suggested Reading

Reference 15 provides a flavour of the debate between the genetic and environmental positions on IQ, whereas N. Madge and J. Tizard, Intelligence (Chapter 21), *In* M. Rutter (ed.), *Scientific foundations of developmental psychiatry*, Heinemann Medical Books, London, 1980, give a more general review.

References

1. Walsh, K.W., *Neuropsychology*, Churchill Livingstone, London, 1978.
2. Terman, L.M. and Merrill, M.A., *Stanford – Binet Intelligence Scale: Manual for the third revision*, Harrap, London, 1961.
3. Anastasi, A., *Individual differences*, Wiley, London, 1965.
4. Raven, J.C., Court, J.H. and Raven, J., *Manual for Raven's Progressive Matrices and Vocabulary Scale*, HK Lewis and Company, London, 1977.
5. Clarke, A.M. and Clarke, A.D.B. (eds.), *Mental deficiency: the changing outlook* (3rd edn.), Methuen, London, 1974.
6. Sacks, E., Intelligence scores as a function of experimentally established social relationships between child and examiner, *Journal of Abnormal and Social Psychology*, 1952, **46**, 354 – 358.

7. Pederson, D.M., Shinedling, M.M. and Johnson, D.L., Effects of sex of examiner and subject on children's quantitative test performance, *Journal of Personality and Social Psychology*, 1968, **10**, 251 – 254.
8. Watson, P., Can racial discrimination affect IQ? *In* Richardson, K. and Spears, D. (eds.), *Race, culture and intelligence*, Penguin, Harmondsworth, 1972.
9. Becker, H.S., Geer, B. and Miller. S.J., Medical education, *In* Freeman, H.E., Levine, S. and Reeder, L.G. (eds.), *Handbook of medical sociology* (2nd edn.), Prentice-Hall, Englewood Cliffs, 1972.
10. Hudson, L., *Contrary imaginations*, Penguin, Harmondsworth, 1966.
11. Eells, K., Davis A., Havighurst, R.J., Herrick, V.E. and Tyler, R.W., *Intelligence and cultural differences*, Chicago University Press, Chicago, 1951.
12. Vernon, P.E., *Intelligence and cultural environment*, Methuen, London, 1969.
13. Kamin, L.J., *The science and politics of IQ*, Lawrence Erlbaum Associates, Maryland, 1974.
14. Hersh, J.B., Effects of referral information on testers, *Journal of Consulting and Clinical Psychology*, 1971, **37**, 116 – 122.
15. Eysenck, H.J. and Kamin, L., *Intelligence: the battle for the mind*, Multimedia Publications, Amsterdam, 1981.
16. Butler, N.R. and Goldstein, H., Smoking in pregnancy and subsequent child development, *British Medical Journal*, 1973, **4**, 573 – 575.
17. Douglas, J.W.B., *The home and the school* Panther, St. Albans, 1967.
18. Hess, R.D. and Shipman, V.C., Early experience and the socialisation of cognitive modes in children, *Child Development*, 1965, **36**, 869 – 886.
19. Bernstein, B., A sociolinguistic approach to social learning, *In* Gould, J. (ed.), *Penguin survey of the social sciences*, Penguin, Harmondsworth, 1965.
20. Rutter, M. and Madge, N., *Cycles of disadvantage*, Heinemann, London, 1976.
21. McCall, R.B., Appelbaum, M.I. and Hogarty, P.S., Developmental changes in mental performance, *Monographs of the Society for Research in Child Development*, 1973, **38**, Whole number 150.
22. Garber, H. and Heber, F.R., The Milwaukee project, *In* Mittler, P. (ed.), *Research to practice in mental retardation*, University Park Press, Baltimore, 1977.
23. Hindley, C.B. and Owen, C.F., The extent of individual changes in IQ for ages between 6 months and 17 years in a British longitudinal sample, *Journal of Child Psychology and Psychiatry*, 1978, **19**, 329 – 350.
24. Siegler, I.C. and Botwinick, J., A long-term longitudinal study of intellectual ability of older adults, *Journal of Gerontology*, 1979, **34**, 242 – 245.
25. Riegel, K.R. and Riegel, R.M., Development, drop and death, *Developmental Psychology*, 1972, **6**, 306 – 319.
26. White, B.L., Castle, P. and Held, R., Observations on the development of visually-guided reaching, *Child Development*, 1964, **35**, 349 – 364.
27. Zelazo, P.R., Zelazo, N.A. and Kolb, S., 'Walking' in the newborn, *Science*, 1972, **176**, 314 – 315.
28. Frankenburg, W.K. and Dodds, J.B., The Denver developmental screening test, *Journal of Pediatrics*, 1967, **71**, 181 – 191.
29. Bryant, P., *Perception and understanding in young children*, Methuen, London, 1974.
30. Blos, P., Children think about illness: their concepts and beliefs, *In* Gellert, E. (ed.), *Psychosocial aspects of pediatric care*, Grune and Stratton, London, 1978.
31. Schwartz, A.H., Children's concepts of research hospitalisation, *New England Journal of Medicine*, 1972, **287**, 589 – 592.
32. Crocker, E., Play programmes in pediatric settings, *In* Gellert, E. (ed.), *Psychosocial aspects of pediatric care*, Grune and Stratton, London, 1978.

33. Illingworth, R.S., The predictive value of developmental assessment in infancy, *Developmental Medicine and Child Neurology*, 1971, **13**, 721 – 725.
34. Savage, R.D., Britton, P.G., Bolton, N. and Hall, E.H., *Intellectual functioning in the aged*, Methuen, London, 1973.
35. Gunzberg, H.C., *The P-A-C Manual*, National Association on Mental Deficiency, London, 1969.
36. Nihira, K., Foster, R., Shellhaas, M. and Leland, H., *AAMD Adaptive Behaviour Scale for children and adults*, American Association on Mental Deficiency, 1974.
37. Gath, A., Parents as therapists of mentally handicapped children, *Journal of Child Psychology and Psychiatry*, 1979, **20**, 161 – 165.
38. Woodward, M., The application of Piaget's theory to the training of the subnormal, *Journal of Mental Subnormality*, 1962, **8**, 17 – 25.

6
The Social Context

6.1   Introduction

Traditionally, many of the psychological processes discussed in previous chapters have been considered to be relatively independent of the situation in which they occur. However, it has become clear that fuller understanding of such attributes as personality, memory and intelligence can be achieved by taking into account the circumstances in which they are shown. For example, it seems necessary to study *what* people remember and *where* the material was learned in order to understand the processes involved in recall. Similarly, when an individual's IQ is considered, it is important to take not only his early environment into account, but also his relationship with the examiner. The setting in which people act — which includes both the physical and the social setting — has important influences on their behaviour.

This chapter turns to some of the research that has investigated these influences. Sometimes the distinction between psychology and the other social sciences becomes blurred. Some of the work described is usually considered to be within the province of sociology, which is concerned with the behaviour of groups of people rather than individuals. Perhaps the most important observation to a sociologist is that societies manage to exist at all. Since there does not seem to be anyone who directs us to have a government, to build schools, hospitals and prisons or to develop immunization programmes, the very existence of these phenomena can be seen as a remarkable achievement.

Whether a society is technologically advanced or 'primitive', it has several institutions and customs that ensure it continues to work. Central to the sociologist's explanation of such phenomena is the concept of *expectation*. The idea is that all of us have expectations of how others should behave and they have expectations of us. As children grow up in society, they learn what is expected of them from family, friends and in school. If these requirements are not met, then steps will be taken to sanction the individual concerned — the legal system provides one institutionalized means of sanctioning people who do not meet certain kinds of expectations. Within society, there will be several different groups of people with their own particular set of expectations about other groups. In the medical school system, teachers have expectations of students (e.g. that they will turn up to lectures and take exams) and students of teachers (e.g. that they should set fair exams and mark them justly). When a doctor is on the ward, he or she has expectations of patients, and they of the doctor. A sociologist is primarily concerned with how different groups of people have different ideas about what behaviour is appropriate and how these groups relate to each other.

In order to discover and explain these behaviours, sociologists have traditionally performed their research in real-life situations, bringing interview, questionnaire or participant observation methods to bear on the topic. (In the latter case, the investigator finds a position in the organization he wishes to study and explores it from the 'inside'.) For example, a sociologist might interview patients from general practices in order to find out about their expectations of how doctors should behave. In one such study, three different kinds of expectations were identified. *Background expectations* concerned people's ideas of what a consultation is generally like, depending on the particular illness. A thorough examination would be expected for some symptoms, but not for others. *Interaction expectations* concern how the doctor will react to and assess symptoms. In a group practice, for example, a patient may come to realize that the physicians differ in their approaches and will select the doctor whose approach is most favoured for a particular problem. The third type of expectation concerns the *actions* the physician will take. Before patients arrive, they have expectations of what the doctor should do for them, which might involve writing a prescription, for example. In this study it became clear that patients were dissatisfied when their expectations were not met for any apparent reason. If the doctor did not listen to their worries or if the patient did not agree with the doctor's advice, this was a cause for complaint to the researcher. For example, one woman explained:

> I had a bout when I was not sleeping at all and I used to lay awake hours and hours in the night and it was worry about my mother it was . . . she was ill at the time . . . and I was really — worked myself to such a pitch, you know, and I was trying to tell him (the doctor) but I couldn't get the words out, you know, I was so choked inside. And he just sort of — 'Oh well, it's your mother, is it, is that what you are worried about?' And I said 'Yes' and he said, 'We're doing all we can for her', and that was all. 'Take some tablets', he said, and he gave me some tablets. He wasn't interested, I just got over it myself. (Ref. 1, pp. 74 – 75)

133

Sometimes, a sociologist might test the importance of an expectation by deliberately breaking the rule involved. For example, in one study in California, the investigator knocked on a bank door during business hours, waiting for someone to come and open it rather than walking straight in. This would be appropriate behaviour at a private house, but not, it seems, in a public place: the police were called. By contrast, social psychologists have usually attempted to understand social influence in the controlled conditions of the laboratory. Although these studies often seem artificial and far removed from real-life, they do have advantages. It is often easier to pinpoint those factors that are responsible for behaviour. By randomly assigning subjects to various conditions, many extraneous factors, such as personality, can be cancelled out.

Many of the topics covered in this book draw on research that falls within the domain of social psychology, such as studies on attraction (Chapter 9). This chapter concentrates on studies of how people behave in specific circumstances, such as in times of emergency. In many respects, however, the actions and expectations of other people are always involved in behaviour and in medical care. When the polio vaccine was first placed on the market, for example, it was not simply the medical view that influenced decisions to have it, but the opinions of friends and relatives as well[2].

Even the actions of those from another culture can have an effect. This point is nicely illustrated by an outbreak of the plague in Manchuria at the turn of the century. The Manchurians had a cultural taboo against hunting sick marmots. Since these animals often harboured the plague *bacillus*, this cultural expectation effectively prevented transmission of the disease to the hunters. Around 1910, a change in women's fashions in Europe suddenly resulted in a huge increase in demand for the fur of the marmot. Many inexperienced Chinese hunters who did not have the same cultural taboos began trapping every animal they could find, especially the sickest who were the easiest to catch. The plague carried by these marmots was transmitted to the hunters and when the hunters gathered together the disease was passed between them. A change in fashion in Europe thus indirectly caused a widespread epidemic of pneumonic plague in Asia[3].

6.2   Social Influences

It is clear that much of our behaviour is influenced by the actions of others. For example, a student might be reluctant to ask a question in a lecture if other members of his class never spoke up. In certain situations, the actions of other people can elicit behaviour that may seem unlikely or surprising. Three specific aspects are considered here. The first, termed 'Bystander Intervention', concerns people's reluctance to intervene in emergencies. If other bystanders are unresponsive, a particular individual is less likely to take the initiative. People's willingness to perform unkind and undesirable actions when asked to do so in an authoritative way, forms the second topic. Third, the tendency for some people to conform to others' erroneous views rather than to voice their own opinions in public is examined.

Research in this area was motivated by a particularly nasty murder in New York City in 1964. A woman was killed in the street while a large number of people in a nearby apartment block could hear but made no attempt to help her, not even by telephoning the police. This was especially disturbing because the assault took place over more than an hour and her distress was obvious. Reactions to this incident included condemnation of the residents and warnings of the imminent breakdown of society, but it also demonstrated to social psychologists that they lacked knowledge about how people react in such situations. Research on the variables that affect how people help each other has been conducted in both naturalistic and laboratory settings, and it is this latter type of research that is discussed here.

Usually this topic has been explored by staging incidents. The approach has been to recruit subjects on the basis of taking part in a psychology experiment, but they are misled as to its purpose. They might be told that the study involves memory or filling out questionnaires. At some point the experimenter finds an excuse to leave the subjects alone in the room. After some minutes, an emergency is staged — sounds of someone falling in the next room, or smoke coming from under a door. The measure taken is whether the subjects do something about it, either trying to find the experimenter or entering the room where the incident has occurred.

The question is: What factors affect whether the subjects will give help? One possibility was suggested through interviews with the witnesses of the New York murder. Many mentioned that they had thought 'someone else' would contact the police. It was as if the responsibility for helping was diffused, so that in the end nothing was done. In order to test the importance of this factor, Darley and Latane[4] led subjects to believe that they were to take part in a group discussion about personal problems. In order to avoid embarrassment, they were told, each person in the study would sit alone in a booth and talk with others through a microphone, each in turn. The experimenter said that he would not be listening. One group of subjects was told that they would discuss their problems with one other person, a second group was told that two others would be taking part, and a third group that there would be five others. Thus, different subjects thought that they were in groups of varying sizes. In fact, there was only ever one person in the experiment, the others' voices being on tape. On the first round of discussion, one of the voices indicated that he was prone to having epileptic seizures. When it was his turn on the second round, he made a few calm comments but then it seemed that he was having a seizure.

The experimenters reasoned that if diffusion of responsibility were an important factor in bystander intervention, then subjects who believed themselves to be in a large group would be less likely to leave their booth and give aid than those who believed they were part of a small group. This hypothesis was supported: 85% of those who thought themselves to be the only ones listening to the seizure sought help, 62% of those who thought there was one other person who could give aid, and only 31% of those who thought there were four others.

135

Thus, it seems that the decision to give aid is related to the number of others who are also available to give assistance.

Of course, it could be argued that some people did not give help because they were sceptical about the genuineness of the incident. It was, after all, a psychology experiment. However, at the end of the study all subjects were interviewed and none thought that the emergency was faked. Besides, there was no apparent reason why subjects in the large-group condition would believe this more often than those in the small-group condition. Nor was there any evidence that the subjects who did not help were callous, uncaring individuals — at the end of the experiment when they were asked why they had not helped, they reported feeling very upset by the experience.

Interviews with the subjects pointed towards another possible reason why aid was not given. Several volunteered the information that they were unsure that the situation was, in fact, an emergency. There was some ambiguity in their minds about whether help was actually required. It seemed that since emergencies are very rare in most people's lives, it takes some time to make sense of what is going on before action is taken. In order to test the importance of interpretation, Darley and Latané introduced a confederate into an experiment. They reasoned that in times of ambiguity people look to the reactions of others to help them make sense of what is going on, and if this confederate was instructed not to react to an incident, the subject would be less likely to give help. In this next experiment, they constructed three conditions. In one, the subjects were left alone in a room; in a second condition two subjects who were strangers to each other were left together; and in the third the subject was placed with a confederate. All were told that they were part of a market-survey study and the experimenter was said to be a representative of the company. After she asked the subjects to fill out several questionnaires, she indicated that she would do some work next door and would return in 10 – 15 min. The subjects saw her go into the next room, screened from them by a curtain:

> While they worked on their questionnaires, subjects heard the representative moving around in the next office, shuffling papers, and opening and closing drawers. After about four minutes, if they were listening carefully, they heard her climb up on a chair to get a book from the top shelf. Even if they were not listening carefully, they heard a loud crash and a woman's scream as the chair fell over. 'Oh my God, my foot . . .', cried the representative. 'I . . . I . . . can't move . . . it. Oh, my ankle. I . . . can't . . . can't . . . get . . . this thing off . . . me.' She moaned and cried for about a minute longer, getting gradually more subdued and controlled. Finally, she muttered something about getting outside, knocked the chair around as she pulled herself up, and limped out, closing the door behind her. (Ref. 5, p. 58)

In order to ensure that all subjects heard the same accident, it was recorded on tape, but they had no way of knowing this. Intervention could have been made in several ways in this study — by going into the room, by looking for help or, simply, by calling through the curtain to ask the representative if she were hurt. While the accident occurred, the confederate in the third condition was instructed to look up, to stare quizzically at the curtain, shrug the shoulders and then return to the questionnaires.

The results supported the hypothesis that interpretation was significant. In the first (alone) condition, some 70% of the subjects intervened. When two strangers were working together, the number fell to 40%. This is both a replication and an extension of the previous study. In the personal-problems experiment, the subjects could not hear or see anyone else: apparently this was not a critical factor, because the responsibility was still diffused, despite subjects being able to see the reactions of someone else. In the third (confederate) condition, only 8% of the subjects made an attempt to help: by seeing someone not react to the incident, the subjects were less inclined to treat it as an emergency that merited assistance.

Other studies, and studies in naturalistic settings as well, have supported the influence of these two factors. In some situations there may be little ambiguity about the meaning of an incident (as in the case of the murder) and in such cases diffusion of responsibility may be significant. In others, it may be difficult for the people involved to interpret the incident. Here the reactions of others may be important. One additional point that can be made about these studies, relevant to other work in social psychology, is that once such findings become widely known, the effect itself may no longer be present. The reactions of people who had seen a film describing this research were compared with those of people who had not seen the film to a staged incident on the street: more of the informed subjects gave assistance. Psychology can reflect back and influence society as well as provide clues about its operation.

Obedience to Authority

As in the case of research on bystander intervention, that on obedience was motivated by real-life experiences, particularly the murder of Jews during World War Two. Milgram[6] sought to gain some understanding of why so many German officials had obeyed their orders. There are likely to be many valid answers to this question, but he was interested in the relationship between obedience and authority. In his experiments, subjects were recruited from a wide range of age and social groups, so that his results cannot be said to apply only to university students. They were told that the experiment involved memory, testing the theory that people learn more quickly when they are punished for making a mistake. The subject's job was to help someone to learn some paired-associate words. For example, when the word 'blue' was given, the word 'box' was to be supplied. If this association was not recalled, the learner was to be given a shock by the subject and this shock was to be more intense the next time an error was made. Each subject saw the learner strapped into a chair and was then seated in front of a shock generator. This had a total of 30 switches, labelled from 15 volts to 450 volts. The intensity of these shocks was also indicated, from 'slight shock' to 'danger, severe shock'. The shocks were said to be painful, but not to cause any permanent tissue damage.

Actually, the learner was a confederate and the shock generator was fake. The confederate was instructed to protest as the level was increased, then to shout and scream and finally to fall silent. The experimenter was to prod the subject if

137

he baulked at giving the shocks, saying that he would accept all responsibility for the consequences. But there was no physical coercion and no promise of greater payment. The experimental question was to see how far up the shock levels the subjects would go before they refused to obey the experimenter.

Before this study, Milgram canvassed colleagues', friends' and psychiatrists' predictions of the results. They felt that only a minority of subjects would continue to obey the experimenter for long and that only a tiny number would go up to the 450-volt level. The reader might wonder if he or she would agree to take part in the study at all. Nevertheless, 25 of the 40 subjects tested went all the way to 450 volts despite the apparent pain involved. Was this due to malevolent or sadistic personalities of the people involved? It seemed not, since most showed clear signs of distress and conflict, despite their obedience. In other experiments, the nature of the situation was shown to have an effect. When the subject and learner sat side by side, only 16 of 40 went to 450 volts, and when the subject was actually responsible for placing the learner's hand on an electric grid, only 12 out of 40. Other factors had less effect. Many of the studies were performed within the auspicious confines of Yale University and it was thought that perhaps this may have had an influence. However, when the laboratory was transferred to an old building in the centre of the city, little difference was found.

These are not isolated results, being replicated many times. Their relevance to medical care has been illustrated by a study of nursing staff and their relationship to doctors. Here, the researchers were interested in whether or not nursing students would comply with an order from a doctor that should not have been obeyed according to the hospital's rules. While on the ward, the nurse received a telephone call from the ward doctor requesting her to give some tablets. There were two problems with this call. First, it was against hospital policy for medication to be given on the basis of a telephone call: the doctor should have signed the order before the drug was given. Second, the doctor requested that twice the maximum daily dosage should be given, as it was stated on the package. When a nurse received the call, she was unobtrusively observed to see if she did, in fact, give the medication (which was actually glucose): 21 nurses fulfilled the request out of 22 nurses studied. This result could not have been due simply to their being unaware of the inappropriate dosage, since 11 later said that they realized the discrepancy[7]. Milgram concluded from his work that the subjects in his study were willing to apply the electric shocks because the experimenter said that he would accept responsibility for the consequences. A similar process may have been operating here. It seems that obedience to authority happens in naturally occurring situations as well as in the psychology laboratory.

These studies also indicate that people are not particularly good at predicting how they would behave in unusual circumstances. Just as the reader might predict that he or she would, of course, give help to someone who had an accident or would refuse to give apparently painful shocks in a psychology experiment, so too did another sample of student nurses indicate that they would refuse to obey the doctor's orders when they were inappropriate. Of 21 nurses who were not involved in the study, all said that they would not give the medication. Assuming that these nurses were no different than the ones who participated, and there was no reason to suspect they were, it seems likely that they, too, would comply under the circumstances.

Conformity

Another example of social influence on behaviour is provided by a series of studies performed by Asch[8]. A kind of conformity was mentioned in Chapter 1, where some studies on the autokinetic phenomenon were discussed. The reader may remember that Sherif and Sherif placed subjects in a dark room and shone a faint light some distance away. This light appeared to move after a short time. The extent of the movement was vague and ambiguous and the Sherifs were able to show how subjects' judgements could be influenced by confederates' reports. Asch argued that this was really a poor test of conformity in a true sense, because of the ambiguity. The subjects may have thought that one judgement was as good as any other and simply went along with the confederate. A better test of conformity would be to give clear, unambiguous stimuli: Asch reasoned that under these circumstances conformity would not occur. Accordingly, he presented subjects with materials similar to those shown in Fig. 6.1. On the left is a card with one line on it. The subjects' task was to choose which of those shown on the card on the right was of the same length. Like the Sherifs, Asch used confederates in his study. Typically, one subject would give his report after four others (confederates) had given theirs. On the first two trials, all went well with no problems for the subject, but on the third trial (and occasional others) he heard the other four give a wrong answer. Faced with this

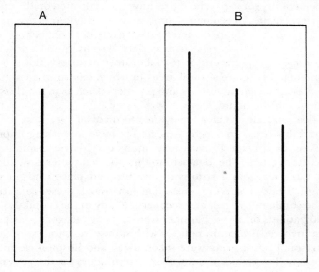

Fig. 6.1   Materials similar to those used in Asch's experiments[8].

139

clear discrepancy, the question was what would the subject do? To some extent, it seemed to depend on the subject himself. Some never conformed, others almost always. Over a large number of trials and many experiments, conformity was found on about 35% of test trials. The probability of conformity could be influenced by several factors, but most especially by the presence of one other person who did not conform, where the incidence was reduced to only about 6%.

It is possible to make both too much and too little of Asch's studies. Conformity with his materials was less than the Sherifs', indicating that more ambiguous stimuli are associated with greater conformity. Observations of the subjects indicated that they were under considerable strain, suggesting that they were aware of the oddity of the situation. However, many situations in everyday life are very ambiguous, much more so than Asch's material. Others' responses may be important in resolving such situations, whether they be accidents as in the Latané and Darley studies, the interpretation of X-rays, the usefulness of medication for a particular patient or diagnosis. The confederates in Asch's studies can be considered to have provided information about what kind of answer was appropriate in the situation. When, for example, diagnosis is problematic, as it often is, conformity with the opinions provided by other physicians may be significant in influencing treatment.

6.3 Environmental Influences

Although the work discussed so far has emphasized the influence of other people on behaviour, some psychologists have concentrated on the effects of the physical environment. An ecological approach to behaviour is taken, involving studies designed to investigate the inter-relationship between behaviour and the surroundings in which it occurs. A wide variety of techniques have been used — from well controlled experiments in the laboratory to observations in naturalistic environments. There are several areas in which environmental psychology has provided assistance to architects and planners, such as in the classroom, the playground and in the home.

One application that has clear relevance to medical care is in the design of hospitals, and this research can be expected to have increasing importance in the near future. During the 19th century, many psychiatric hospitals were built on the outskirts of cities. The idea behind this was that patients should be taken away from the stresses and strains of city life and placed in quiet, isolated surroundings. Besides serving custodial functions, these conditions were thought to be conducive to rest and recovery. Many of the hospitals were large, having 1000 patients or more. Families were not encouraged to visit (if only by the distance involved). Certain policies within these hospitals were advocated. Patients' personal possessions were taken away and hospital clothing issued. This was designed to reduce the number of reminders for the patients of their past experiences. These measures appear harsh, but for some people at least they were based on high ideals and therapeutic intentions. However, there was an unfortunate by-product of this treatment, in that many patients became dependent on the institution and indifferent or even antagonistic to leaving. They were said to be institutionalized and it became difficult to integrate such people back into the community. It was as if they came to consider the hospital their permanent home. There are people in psychiatric institutions today who were placed there in the 1920s because they were considered ill by the standards of the time.

One result of this problem of institutionalism is a change in policy towards treatment procedures within existing buildings. During the 1950s and 1960s there were many attempts to minimize the difference between hospital and community. Personal possessions were allowed and more patient privacy provided. Wing and Brown[9] described how they examined three psychiatric hospitals, called A, B and C. Hospital A was considered the most progressive, allowing most of the patients personal possessions (their own clothes instead of institutional ones, their own toothbrushes, a locker to keep books, etc.) and opportunities to engage in meaningful constructive work. Hospital B shared some of these characteristics, but there were also instances of an institutional atmosphere. Not many patients, for example, possessed scissors or a mirror, and fewer baths were screened from onlookers. Hospital C was considered the least progressive, with only few activities provided, little or no privacy and few personal possessions being allowed. The staff of this hospital were also more restrictive, the patients requiring permission to leave the ward or to use the kitchen to make a drink. Wing and Brown then took several measures of the patients' behaviour. They found that Hospital C had more severely ill patients, a result that could not be attributed to condition at admission. These patients were more likely to be socially withdrawn, isolated and passive, as well as to spend much of their time 'doing nothing'. They were also more likely to want to stay in the hospital. There seemed to be a gradation between the hospitals, so that these observations were more common in Hospital C than B then A.

Although this study was correlational, their suggestion that differences in patient behaviour were due to the effects of the hospital environment was given further support when they examined the hospitals over a period of time. As physical conditions improved, so too did the clinical condition of the schizophrenic patients. In two hospitals, conditions improved and then deteriorated again: the patients' conditions showed a similar pattern. The lack of privacy and the paucity of organized activities were thought to be responsible for these effects. Other studies have implicated drab colours on the walls and large multi-occupant bedrooms as further deleterious factors. Wing and Brown[10] argued that many of the features associated with the condition of schizophrenia were due to the under-stimulation presented by these large institutions.

Influenced by such research, there have been several attempts at changing the atmosphere in psychiatric hospitals over the last decades. For example, Holahan and Saegert[11] report a study on remodelling a psychiatric ward. In this particular hospital they were able to find two nearly identical wards; in both the walls were dirty and the furniture was worn and uncomfortable. One ward was chosen for improvement. The walls were painted with bright colours and new furniture purchased. In order to create privacy, the large dormitory was divided into more personal two-bed sections, and small areas of the large day ward were informally sectioned off to provide the opportunity for intimate talk. The second ward acted as control so that the effects of the remodelling could be evaluated.

Patients were randomly placed on one of the two wards and 6 months later the investigators returned. Instead of observing all the patients all of the time (which would be very expensive and time-consuming) they took *samples* of behaviour. Twenty-five patients on each ward were randomly selected for study and their activities at 5-min intervals were noted over several days: whatever they were doing at this point was recorded. Sampling in this way has several advantages. Practically speaking, fewer researchers are needed, but also a better indication of the activity on the ward can be gathered. The same amount of observation time could be used observing the ward for one entire day only, but then the results might be strongly affected by unique circumstances. There might be a plan to take several residents out on a trip from one ward but not the other; some patients may be ill, which could bias the results towards inactivity; the ward might be short-staffed that day owing to a snowstorm. By taking several small samples of behaviour over several days, short-term influences such as these even out. Those in the remodelled ward were found to be significantly more sociable with other patients, with staff and with visitors and less likely to be passive and isolated, suggesting that the difference in environment had effects on the patients' behaviour. The researchers also took some measures of attitudes toward the ward and correlated these with the patients' activity levels. Those patients who most liked the remodelled ward tended to be those who were most active, whereas those who most liked the control ward were those who were least active (especially those who slept much of the time). Since many hospital staff place a high value on social contact, these results indicate that providing bright colours and opportunities for privacy is conducive to good treatment.

Although these findings are suggestive, they are not conclusive. The behaviour of the patients in the remodelled ward may have differed from those of the control ward not because of the character of the new conditions but because they were made to feel special simply because changes had taken place. Direct evidence for this possibility comes from a study attempting to relate working conditions to factory output. A small group of workers who constructed telephone relays were chosen to see how their output could be increased. The system of payment was manipulated, pay originally depending on the output of the whole factory, but during the experiment other criteria were used at different times, such as depending on the output of this small group. Rest periods were introduced, then lengthened, then increased in number. Later, a light lunch was provided by the company, then work stopped one half-hour early. From the experimenters' viewpoint, this seemed a good way of testing the effect of various working conditions. By trying each possibility in turn, those conditions that assisted output could be introduced to all of the workforce, whereas those which had no effect could be rejected. The results, however, were unexpected: whether there were more or fewer rest periods, whether there were longer or shorter days, each condition produced a higher rate of output than the one before. It seemed that the workers considered themselves to be special because they were treated differently and that, knowing the output was to be measured, worked harder and more efficiently. This phenomenon is known as the 'Hawthorn effect', after the factory where the research was done. A similar effect may have been operating in the study of psychiatric wards. The staff, who were seemingly aware of the purpose of the experiment, might also have felt that they were special; they might have made more effort to socialize with, and help, patients and their attitude might have been communicated to the patients themselves.

This problem can be found in other studies. In one experiment, a carpet was laid in one ward for disturbed women, and another ward with an old tiled floor served as a control. Both patients and staff were found to modulate their voices more in the carpeted ward, the patients were less irritable and excitable and some previously incontinent patients requested toilet facilities[12]. In another investigation, the seating arrangements on the wards of a psychiatric hospital were changed. Originally, all the chairs were lined up beside one another along the walls. In order to talk, the patients had to pivot 90 degrees, and it was difficult to hold a conversation with more than one person at a time. The arrangement of chairs was then altered, so that they were grouped around small tables holding magazines. As a measure of the effect of this change, the number and length of conversations between patients were recorded. As shown in Table 6.1, the new arrangement was associated with more interactions, both brief and sustained, than the old one[13]. Because of the Hawthorn effect, it would have been better if an adequate control ward could have been studied in both investigations (perhaps in the study on the effects of the carpet another ward could also have been given a new floor, such as linoleum), but such research has had an important effect on the environment in many hospitals.

Occasionally there are naturally occurring situations that have many of the features of well controlled laboratory experiments. Such a situation is described

Table 6.1 Number of Brief and Sustained Interactions per Day when Seating Arrangements in a Psychiatric Ward were Changed

(Reproduced from *Personal Space* by Robert Sommer, © 1969, by permission of Prentice-Hall, Inc., Englewood Cliffs, New Jersey.)

	Number of interactions	
	Brief	Sustained
Old arrangement	47	36
New arrangement	73	61

in a study on the effects of ward design in a large medical hospital. Three different ward designs were incorporated into the hospital as it was built. One ward was designed in a wheel shape, with the nurses' station in the centre and the bedrooms radiating from it. Another ward was built in an L-shape, with the nurses' station at the junction of two corridors. A third was rectangular, containing two parallel aisles with the bedrooms on either side and the station sited between them. On many measures, the radial design was found to be better than the L-shaped or rectangular wards: there were fewer absences and fewer accidents among the nursing staff and they were observed to spend more time with their patients. When the doctors and patients were asked to rate their impressions, the radial ward was again favoured[14].

These studies on hospital design and decoration have had several effects. There is increasing resistance amongst those who care for the psychiatrically ill and mentally handicapped against the building of large hospitals set apart from the community. Not only does this old policy seem to be counter-productive in terms of caregiving, it also stigmatizes the patients who live in the institutions. Being set apart physically makes contact with community facilities more difficult, providing less opportunity for the development of skills required to live independently. Equally, 'ordinary' people rarely encounter the psychiatrically ill or mentally handicapped people who inhabit such institutions and thus have little opportunity to begin to understand their problems. Accordingly, current policies stress the need to accommodate these people in smaller units sited within the community. Although there can be opposition to the provision of sheltered housing in residential communities, this may be due more to the incongruous buildings that are often constructed than to the residents themselves[15]. Another result of this research is a greater awareness on the part of caregivers of the effect of the physical environment which they present to their patients. If the setting is not conducive to treatment, the positive effects of medical care could be reduced. This point is taken up further in later chapters when the influence of the hospital environment (Chapter 10) and the arrangement of furniture in the consulting room (Chapter 12) are considered. Many medical and nursing staff have also become more aware of the effect that medical equipment can have on their patients. Workshops that have attempted to help staff see this equipment from the patients' viewpoint have been undertaken, as in this example:

> Distances seemed three times as long on crutches as they had previously. It took a very long time to go down the hallway in a wheelchair; when one person wheeled another, the speed of passage was very important. Wheeling a person at ordinary walking speed seemed much too fast; the person in the chair felt as if he were a bowling ball going down the alley. . . . Riding on the gurney, a long flat table with wheels, made a number of people nauseous; the ceiling became the visual environment and the overhead lights went flashing by bang bang bang in a very annoying manner. (Ref. 16, p. 44)

Some researchers have taken a broader view of the effects of the environment, being concerned with how changes in living conditions can have significant effects on the health of the general population. Indeed, it has been argued that such changes are more important than medical interventions. McKeown[17], for example, provides evidence from various sources that indicates that many of the most notable improvements in health care over the last century or so are due to changes in sewage treatment, diet and housing rather than the scientific and technological advances of medicine. The incidence of death due to tuberculosis provides an example of this. The death rate from this disease has declined continuously since about 1840, as shown in Fig. 6.2. This is unlikely to be due to medical advances alone since the incidence was falling rapidly before the causal organism was identified and before medical treatments became generally available. Although chemotherapy and vaccination undoubtedly contributed to the decline in mortality, their effect appears to be relatively small compared to that of environmental change.

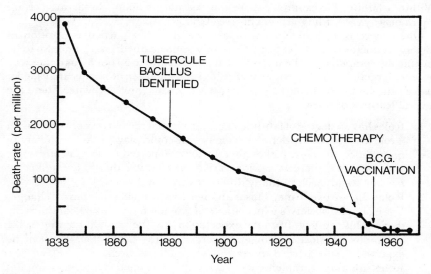

Fig. 6.2 **Annual death rates from tuberculosis in England and Wales from 1838. (Reproduced from T. McKeown,** *The Role of Medicine,* **1979, by permission of Basil Blackwell Publisher.)**

6.4 Roles

The previous sections of this chapter have shown how knowledge of certain social and physical aspects of a situation can help predict how someone will behave. This section considers how people decide to request medical assistance. In order to understand the research bearing on this topic, however, it is first necessary to discuss three important concepts used by both sociologists and social psychologists, the ideas of norms, roles and socialization.

People's beliefs about what behaviour is customary and proper in a society are termed *norms*. In different societies, different norms operate. There seems, for example, to be a norm for children to take their father's surname in our culture, but this is not the case in other cultures. Within a society, there are also differences, such that different groups of people have different expectations about what behaviour is admissible. In many factories, for example, there are norms about how quickly a worker should do his or her job. If the work is done too quickly or too slowly, sanctions might be applied against the individual. Norms change over time as well. There was a time when all medical students were expected to attend lectures in very respectable clothes, but now this is often required only when on the wards. This idea of norms provides one way of understanding how society operates: the relationships between people in any group can be described in terms of the expectations of how they should act. Within a family, for example, there may be norms about discussing certain topics or ways of settling arguments (see Chapter 9).

Often there is a cluster of norms associated with a particular position in society. A doctor could be expected not only to be neatly dressed, but also to be technically competent, to be interested in patients and to go out of his or her way in an emergency. The activities that fulfil such a cluster of norms are called a *role*. Examples of other roles are father, teacher, daughter and wife. There are several features of roles:

1. Roles have a degree of latitude. This means that the norms connected with a role are not strictly defined. Two people could play a role adequately in quite different ways. Although a doctor is expected to dress neatly when with patients, there is a wide variety of clothing that is acceptable; a teacher could teach in many different ways, and so on.
2. Roles change over time. This is another way of saying that norms change. For example, society's expectations of women have altered considerably during this century, from the expectation that they should not undertake strenuous physical and mental exercise to the belief that they can be expected to take part in sports and academic research.
3. Roles are often complements. To say that someone is a teacher implies that there are students to teach. A doctor cannot be a doctor unless there are patients, nor can someone be a parent unless there are children. In order for an individual to perform a role, there must be someone playing the complementary role. This complementarity may affect the way roles are adopted: a physician who adopts an authoritarian approach to doctoring may restrict the patient into a submissive position during the consultation.
4. Different roles are sometimes in conflict. An individual is likely to play many different roles in society; sometimes a student, sometimes a friend, sometimes a son or daughter. Each role has associated norms which can be in conflict. As a student the person may feel independent but as a son or daughter certain concessions to parental authority might be expected. Similarly, a person may be both a doctor and a husband or wife, having

expectations from patients and a spouse that may be incompatible. Within a role there may also be conflicting expectations. Where all members of a family have the same doctor, the treatment of one member may affect others, as when a young daughter seeks contraceptive advice. It is not simply a question of what might be right or wrong in such situations, but a problem of conflicting expectations and how these are handled.

The process of learning, understanding and fulfilling norms and roles is a vital part of social development. During this process, people become increasingly aware of others' expectations and more skilful at fulfilling them. Known as *socialization*, this learning continues throughout life. There are expectations involved in being a patient, for example, so that when someone is admitted to hospital he or she will experience a period of uncertainty until the norms are discovered and the role can be enacted. When they enter the wards for the first time, medical students often report a similar sense of uncertainty until they find out what is expected of them. Thus, socialization can be seen in terms of predictability[18]. Once a person is familiar with norms and is adept at acting-out roles, his behaviour will be predictable to others, and if everyone has the same familiarity with requirements, then the way people act will be mutually predictable. The patient will have a good idea of how the doctor will behave and the doctor will be correct in his expectations of how the patient will act.

The Sick Role

Like other forms of behaviour, the ways someone acts when ill are regulated by norms. There are certain expectations of sick people. To some extent, these depend on the particular circumstances (one ward sister might have very different ideas of how a 'good' patient should act from another, for example), but there seems to be some norms that apply to most patients. As outlined by Talcott Parsons[19], these include both rights and obligations. One right involves exemption from many social responsibilities — someone who is ill is not required to go to work or, perhaps, to take exams. This means that if an individual can manage to convince others that he or she is indeed ill, these social responsibilities can be avoided. A second right is that the person cannot be expected to take care of himself or to remove the illness by willpower. That is, the person is not required to 'pull himself together' and get on with social duties. When a person is admonished in this way, there is the implicit message that the presence of illness is not accepted. These rights are balanced by some obligations: the person should want to get well, should seek medical advice and should co-operate with these experts. If these obligations are not fulfilled, the individual could be said to be breaking the norms concerning illness.

Like many other roles, certain qualifications are required before the sick role can be taken up. First, the person must have a condition that has been defined by the culture to be a medical problem. Our society's views on what constitutes an illness have changed in some respects over time. Alcoholism is one example: it is increasingly being seen as a symptom of a disease rather than as a sign of moral failure. Until recently, the alcoholic could not take on the sick role

147

because the condition was not considered to be a medical problem. This is a particularly good example because there is continuing disagreement about this condition, many arguing that it is not a medical problem at all[20]. Different societies also have different criteria for defining illness. To use an example mentioned in Chapter 2, Australian aborigines often hear voices and see visions, a condition considered normal in their culture but as a sign of schizophrenia in ours. It is not the condition itself that is significant but the meaning and consequences of symptoms, and these are partly culturally defined.

A second qualification that a person will have to fulfill involves acquiring some validation of the difficulty. A physical sign is most readily accepted (e.g. a broken leg or a high temperature), but a functional complaint (e.g. a headache) will usually be acceptable as long as it does not occur too frequently. Perhaps the best method is to convince an expert of the problem. When a child, the reader may have used a parent for such validation (perhaps in order to get a day off school), but for an adult the doctor is the prime source of validation. Difficulties sometimes arise when a patient complains of a problem but the doctor can find no physical indication of it. In such circumstances, the doctor may suggest further tests, may consider psychological problems, or may decide the patient is malingering.

Third, before the sick role can be taken up, it has to be accepted by the person involved. It is tempting to assume that whenever a person has a symptom — is in ill-health — then he or she will consult a physician about it. According to this assumption, the physician would see all the people in the practice who are ill. This is mistaken. Sometimes, for instance if the condition is incapacitating, the person has little choice in the matter, but in most cases there is a decision involved. There is a problem here in defining health. If it is defined as the absence of symptoms, then it appears that most people are unhealthy much of the time. Evidence for this statement comes mainly from two different kinds of studies. Some researchers have tried to gain an idea of the health of the general population not by consulting medical records but by screening large numbers of people in the community. In one sample of over 3000 people, only 15% were considered to be free from disability, ranging from psychiatric disorders to respiratory problems[21]. Another kind of study has involved asking people to keep a diary of how they felt each day for several days or weeks. Here, again, there is strong evidence that people have symptoms much of the time. In one survey of this kind lasting for 1 month, symptoms (such as headaches, backaches and abdominal pains) were recorded about one day in three, lasting an average of 1.6 days[22]. There is also evidence that there is much psychiatric illness in the community that does not come to the attention of the general practitioner or psychiatrist[23].

These studies have several implications. First, they indicate that a general practitioner will see only a proportion of the people in the practice who have a medical difficulty. In the screening study mentioned above, some 39% of the difficulties found were not known to the general practitioner, some of these meriting immediate care. Second, the results mean that medical records do not provide an accurate indication of illness in the community. This has implications for much research such as that on the relationship between stress and illness discussed in Chapter 10. Third, it makes the problem of who contacts the doctor and why the choice was made at a particular time, an interesting and important one.

The Decision to Consult

Several factors have been identified as being important in the decision to seek medical help for both physical and psychiatric complaints. Broadly speaking, these can be grouped into those concerning the interpretation of symptoms and those concerning social and personality variables.

First, there is the problem of interpretation. As discussed in Chapter 1, signs and symptoms have meaning only in so far as they fit into a larger context in which past experience plays an important part. Robinson[24] asked mothers to keep diaries of the signs of illness in their families along with a description of how they reacted to and interpreted them. Clearly, there was a considerable degree of uncertainty about the meaning of these upsets. The mothers would often adopt a 'wait and see' strategy, so that a child might feel quite ill for several days or wet the bed on several occasions before a decision to see the doctor would be taken. 'After all', they wrote, 'the problem might only be temporary'. Once they decided that the signs were, indeed, indications of an important illness, steps were taken. Another researcher interviewed myocardial infarction patients about their perceptions at the time of the attack. Often, they first tested alternative explanations for the pains they were feeling, and only after the pains worsened was action taken. For example:

> I just felt rotten. I had a pain in my chest and I thought it was indigestion. I'd been rushing in the lunch hour and lifted a heavy box and all this sort of thing and it was, oh, three-quarters-of-an-hour after the actual rush that I felt the pain. (Ref. 25, p. 89)

Similarly, psychiatric illness can be difficult to interpret. In one study, the process involved in interpreting psychiatric illness in the family was explored by asking the spouses of patients about their perceptions once the decision to admit to hospital was made. Initially, unusual behaviour was put down to a physical condition or to a normal response to a crisis. There were attempts to 'normalize' the behaviour by finding explanations for it or by looking for similar behaviour in others who were not ill. Only when these strategies did not work satisfactorily on several occasions was the decision taken to seek assistance[26].

Related to the importance of interpretation are studies concerned with perceived health. Simply because a physician considers a symptom to be serious does not mean that lay members of the public do as well. The discrepancy can be large. In one study, two out of three elderly people who were rated as being in unfavourable health by their physicians gave themselves favourable reports, whereas one in five who saw themselves as being in poor health had physicians who considered them to be in good condition[27]. Part of this discrepancy might be due to differences in how doctors and their patients view the seriousness of symptoms. When asked about the suitability of self-care for a number of signs,

149

doctors placed more emphasis on self-care for some (e.g. 'difficulty in sleeping for about a week'), less for others (e.g. 'more than one headache a week for a month') than did patients[28].

Other research has been conducted on the social factors influencing the decision to consult a doctor. The problem may be seen as one of delay: because many patients waited until the disease had been present for several weeks or months, one question was: 'Why did they delay so long?' Here, such demographic characteristics as age, sex and social class of the patients were analysed, but these variables seemed only mildly related to delay. An examination of individuals' particular circumstances, however, was more informative. Through interviewing patients, it became clear that a visit to the doctor involved costs as well as gains. Although there might be some gain in physiological health, there might also be several psychological and social costs. Economics seemed to play a part, not only because of any fees (many studies being conducted in the United States) but also because of time taken off work. It might be difficult to find someone to look after children, and so on[29, 30]. Some of these factors are illustrated by the following quotation:

> I wish I knew what you mean by being sick. Sometimes I felt so bad I could curl up and die, but I had to go on because of the kids who have to be taken care of, and besides, we didn't have the money to spend for the doctor. How could I be sick? Some people can be sick any time with anything, but most of us can't be sick, even when we need to be. (Ref. 31, p. 30)

This kind of approach to delay has been criticized by some researchers, suggesting as it does that people would 'naturally' go and see their doctor if these obstacles were not in the way. This view, it is argued, does not portray the decision process at all well. In the survey study mentioned above[21] for example, only about one in every 37 symptoms resulted in consultation with the physician. It seems unlikely that so many obstacles could be present for people so much of the time. Zola[32] described how he came to view the issue somewhat differently. While interviewing people in an out-patient department of a hospital, he noted that many were attending with difficulties that had bothered them for some time. His question became 'Why are you coming now?' rather than 'Why didn't you come before?' He noted that they were attending not simply because there were reasons not to previously, but because their symptoms were beginning to interfere with their normal activities. He suggested that people often learn to accommodate themselves to their disabilities and only when this accommodation is upset in some way (which might be the worsening of a condition or equally a new social demand) is action taken. Patients of Anglo-Saxon origin were more likely to attend when the difficulty came to interfere with physical or work activities, whereas those of Italian origin were more likely to come when inter-personal relationships were affected. It also seemed that a condition was sometimes used for inter-personal reasons — to relieve the person of unwanted social duties, perhaps, as in the following example:

Carol Conte was a 45-year-old, single book-keeper. For a number of years she had

150

been both the sole support and nurse for her mother. Within the past year, her mother died and shortly thereafter her relatives began insisting that she move in with them, quit her job, work in their variety store, and nurse their mother. With Carol's vacation approaching, they have stepped up their efforts to persuade her to at least try this arrangement. Although she has long had a number of minor aches and pains, her chief complaint was a small cyst on her eyelid (diagnosis: fibroma). She related her fear that it *might* be growing or could lead to something more serious and thus she felt she had better look into it now (the second day of her vacation) 'before it was too late'. 'Too late' for what was revealed only in a somewhat mumbled response to the question of what she expected or would like the doctor to do. From a list of possible outcomes to her examination, she responded, 'Maybe a "hospital"(ization) . . . "Rest" would be all right . . .' (and then in a barely audible tone, in fact turning her head away as if she were speaking to no-one at all) 'just so they (the family) would stop bothering me.' Responding to her physical concern, the examining physician acceded to her request for the removal of the fibroma, referred her for surgery, and thus removed her from the situation for the duration of her vacation. (Ref. 32, p. 685)

According to this view, social factors act as 'triggers' that set the decision to seek aid in motion.

Others have looked at factors associated with family background that affect the decision to consult. From their work, it appears that not only is the interpretation of the nature of the condition affected by the family setting, but the decision as to whether it merits professional assistance is also negotiated here. For most people, the decision to consult the doctor is an inter-personal process and, thus, affected by the needs and expectations of the family group. The influence of the mother seems particularly significant. Mechanic[33] showed that mothers tended to treat their children's illness like their own: those mothers who were more likely to take medication or to visit the doctor for themselves, were also more likely to give medication to their children and to take them to see the doctor.

It seems possible, then, that some people are more ready to take up the sick role than others, given the same degree of disability. This was explored in one study by giving students a questionnaire designed to measure this inclination. Briefly, they were asked to indicate how likely it was that they would report to the University Health Service if they had been feeling unwell or had a specified temperature. They could answer certainly, probably, not very likely or very unlikely to these items. When the medical records were later consulted, those who had indicated a high tendency to adopt the sick role did, indeed, attend the health service more frequently[34].

The same study also provided some support for Zola's triggering hypothesis. Students who reported that they were nervous or lonely made more use of the medical facilities, supporting the view that psychological difficulties make the decision to consult more likely. Another possible interpretation of this last result (discussed in more detail in Chapter 10) is that these psychological difficulties actually contributed to the onset of disease.

In summary, the evidence indicates that the relationship between symptom and action is mediated by several social and psychological factors. It seems necessary to consider the presentation of symptoms against the total background of the patient's daily life and relationships with others. In this context many writers have made a distinction between disease and 'illness behaviour'. Disease might be considered a good term for the objective pathology, whereas the term 'illness behaviour' might be used to describe the processes of evaluation and action connected with the perception of symptoms. It may be more useful to consider the decision to consult a physician as a result of difficulties in continuing a life-style rather than as a result of the disease itself[35]. Seen in this way, illness becomes an indication of impaired capacity rather than an indication of disease[36]. If this is the basis upon which a person consults a doctor, it seems likely that some consultations will not be about diseases at all, but rather about interpersonal relationships and emotional difficulties. It would also seem that curing a disease is not the same as curing an illness, so that medical care would involve more than physiological measures.

It is relevant to mention here the possibility that the sick role is expected of some groups of people for whom it is inappropriate. This may be especially so for those whose disability is chronic rather than acute, and for those more in need of emotional and educational assistance than medical. The disagreement about whether alcoholism is a disease was mentioned previously: similar disagreements can be found concerning the mentally handicapped. An interesting analysis of how blind people come to take on the sick role and the associated behaviours expected of them is given by Scott[37]. He suggests that blindness is a social role that people who have serious difficulty in seeing or who cannot see at all learn how to play. Blind people are often seen as a homogenous group — docile, dependent and reacting with gratitude to assistance. Scott argues that much of this behaviour is socially determined, in that many of the patterns that are assumed to be the result of the condition are actually the result of the socialization processes. This may be equally true of many groups of people who are placed in institutions: unusual or disturbed behaviour might be due to their circumstances rather than their original condition.

Relinquishing the Sick Role

It seems, then, that the presence of a disease is not an adequate reason to consult a doctor for many people. Although it is the case that the more severe the symptom the more likely it is that the individual will consult, there is no one-to-one relationship between the two. Similarly, recovery from a condition may not automatically return the individual to the previous state of activity. Research on this possibility has been mainly concerned with patients recovering from myocardial infarction (MI) and this is reflected in the studies mentioned below. It is possible that the problems faced by these patients may differ from those encountered by people with other conditions.

Many of the investigators have used return to work as their measure of recovery. Several have found that about 50% of MI patients never take up employment again, although this proportion has been steadily falling over recent years. Part of this effect is due to early voluntary retirement, but many individuals may become invalids through psychological and social rather than cardiac problems. It seems that there is long-lasting distress for a sizeable minority of patients, and if measures of distress include personality and social difficulties in adjustment as well as vocational ones, the proportion rises significantly[38, 39].

The way the patient comes to see his health appears to be the important variable, rather than the medical view. For example, Garrity[40] related the severity of the heart attack in 71 patients to various social and psychological indicators 6 months later. No relationship was found between severity and return to work, but the way in which the individual perceived his current health was a reasonably good predictor. When they were asked about their general morale, similar results were found: morale correlated with health perception but not with severity of attack. This study implies that the patient's perceived state of health is more important than his objective state of health, although the study could be criticized on the grounds that the measure of objective health was taken several months earlier and was therefore not a good indication of the patient's present condition. However, another investigation has shown that there is a close relationship between signs of cardiac damage at an initial observation and signs some months later, so that this criticism is unsupported. In this latter study[41] similar results to Garrity's were found: non-cardiac social and psychological factors were almost equally common as causes of invalidism as were cardiac indicators.

There is also evidence that recovery may be related to a person's general ability to cope with problems and difficulties in his life. Querido[42] followed up patients who had undergone hospital treatment. When admitted, two assessments were made. One was based on the medical, technical and somatic side of the problem, a decision being made by a general physician as to whether the prognosis was 'favourable' or 'unfavourable'. The second assessment was made by a team consisting of a social worker and psychiatrist as well as a general physician. They looked at the patient's psycho-social case history and obtained additional information as necessary in order to judge whether the patient could be considered 'distressed', meaning the patient was not able to handle his problems and was hampered or burdened by them. This did not indicate the presence of problems *per se*: a patient could be under stress, but if the team considered he was able to handle these problems, 'distress' was not considered to be present. Six months after discharge the patients were visited in their homes and their medical condition relating to the original hospital treatment was evaluated as satisfactory or unsatisfactory. Of the 1630 patients in the study, 1128 had been given favourable clinical prognoses. Their condition at follow-up is shown in Table 6.2. Patients without distress were more than twice as likely to do well as those considered to be distressed. Perhaps, with the right kind of help, more of those suffering distress might have been able to achieve a satisfactory outcome.

If recovery is affected by perceptions of health and ability to cope, the question arises as to what factors influence these perceptions. Many social psychologists have argued that our sense of self — our identity — results from others' reactions to us. The only way we can gain some idea of our abilities is to

153

Table 6.2

Follow-up condition related to prior team assessments for patients who had been given favourable clinical prognoses. 75 % of the patients judged to be without distress at the initial assessment had a satisfactory outcome, but only 35 % of the patients considered to be in distress. (Reproduced from A. Querido, *British Journal of Preventative and Social Medicine*, 1959, **13**, 33 – 49, by permission.)

Follow-up condition	Team assessment		
	No distress	Distress	
Satisfactory	497	163	
Unsatisfactory	168	300	
Total	665	463	1128

test them and see what effect they have on others. If other people find them praiseworthy, we are likely to have a good self-image, but if others find them lacking, we may come to consider ourselves inadequate in some respect. For example, it is likely that the reader's self-image was enhanced when an application was accepted by a medical school, but perhaps would become less positive if exams were failed. Similarly, people who have suffered a disease may undergo changes in their self-image, depending on the reactions they receive from others. If the individual is expected to be incapable in some way, the sick role may become part of the self-image. Since the sick person is not responsible for performing many social duties, return to work may not be contemplated if this role has become integrated within the self-concept. If this way of seeing the problems of rehabilitation has value, then the length of time a patient waits for treatment — i.e. the length of time he occupies the sick role — should be related to outcome. A recent examination of patients who had undergone surgery for a coronary bypass supports this idea. A group of 30 men were interviewed before the surgical procedure and again 1 – 2 years later. At follow-up, a large proportion continued to experience difficulty. 83 % were unemployed and 57 % sexually impaired, for example. The waiting time before surgery was associated with these rates: significantly more patients showed long-term impairment if they waited more than 8 months than if the operation was performed within this time. The researchers noted that those patients whose symptoms were prolonged showed 'damaged' self-concepts[43].

Another way of examining the difficulties a person might experience as a result of a condition is in terms of the support given by the family. Some of the evidence that suggests that a supportive family has a protective effect against illness is discussed in Chapter 10, but there are also indications that it can either aid or hinder rehabilitation as well. For example, Litman[44] found that three-quarters of those who had a supportive family had a good response to rehabilitation from various conditions, whereas three-quarters of those whose family was not considered to be a source of strength and assurance during recovery were considered to have a poor rehabilitation record. Support may be important for other family members, too, and may be obtained from outside the immediate family network. In one study[45], the resources available to the spouse of MI patients were found to be of significance. Those women who reported that they, too, were given educational and emotional support by professionals, friends and relatives, were more likely to have husbands who were at work and who had recovered from the condition than those who reported few such supports. It may be that one way to help a patient is to help his or her relatives.

Rehabilitation seems particularly difficult for patients whose conditions are chronic and painful. Some psychologists have argued that behaviours associated with such conditions, such as inactivity and complaints of pain, are maintained by reinforcements. In taking this behavioural approach (see Chapter 3), there is no implication that the patient is consciously attempting to gain sympathy or attention, only that these reinforcements are commonly given to patients with such difficulties. Fordyce and his colleagues[46] applied this approach to patients whose conditions seemed intractable, in that they failed to respond to other forms of treatment. They first identified the reinforcement contingencies that maintained the undesired behaviour and then tried to alter these patterns. Instead of rewarding complaints of pain, they rewarded activity and accomplishment. Although this treatment approach did not solve all the patients' problems, there was a marked increase in activity levels for most.

Summary

The ways in which people act are not determined solely by intrapsychic variables but are affected by the environment, both social and physical. There are some social situations in which people tend to react in undesirable ways, such as not helping in emergencies and following orders or conforming to others' views even when these are clearly mistaken. Certain factors affect these tendencies, such as the number of people present and their reactions. Aspects of the physical environment have been implicated in institutionalization, and social activities in psychiatric hospitals have been shown to increase with improved ward conditions. In acute hospitals, too, the physical environment can affect patient care and the efficiency of staff.

One specific social situation is considered in detail: people's decision to request medical assistance and their recovery from illness. Many symptoms go untreated, and the decision to consult a doctor depends on several social and psychological factors as well as the severity of the symptoms. These include the person's perception of his state of health and the extent to which ill-health interferes with everyday activities. Similarly, recovery from illness is related only indirectly to objective state of health. Here, too, measures of general ability to cope and self-image can be used to describe the process of achieving full

155

recovery. Rehabilitation may be helped through the use of behavioural techniques.

Suggested Reading

D. Canter and S. Canter, *Designing for therapeutic environments*, Wiley, Chichester, 1979, provide reviews of research in several aspects of environmental psychology.

There are several books concerned with the sick role and medical sociology generally. Two that extend the outline given in this chapter are D. Tuckett, *An introduction to medical sociology*, Tavistock Publications, London, 1976, and J.A. Denton, *Medical sociology*, Houghton Mifflin, London, 1976.

References

1. Stimson, G. and Webb, B., *Going to see the doctor*, Routledge & Kegan Paul, London, 1975.
2. Merrill, M.H., Hollister, A.C., Gibbens, S. and Haynes, A.W., Attitudes of Californians towards poliomyelitis vaccination, *American Journal of Public Health*, 1958, **48**, 146 – 152.
3. Dubos, R., *Man, medicine and environment*, Mentor, New York, 1968.
4. Darley, J.M. and Latané, B., Bystander intervention in emergencies: diffusion of responsibility, *Journal of Personality and Social Psychology*, 1968, **8**, 377 – 383, adapted from Latané, B. and Rodin, J., A lady in distress: Inhibiting effects of friends and strangers on bystander intervention, *Journal of Experimental Social Psychology*.
5. Latané, B. and Darley, J.M., *The unresponsive bystander*, Appleton-Century-Crofts, New York, 1970.
6. Milgram, S., *Obedience to authority: an experimental view*, Harper and Row, New York, 1974.
7. Hofling, C.K., Brotzman, E., Dalrymple, S., Graves, N. and Pierce, C.M., An experimental study in nurse-physician relationships, *Journal of Nervous and Mental Disease*, 1966, **143**, 171 – 180.
8. Asch, S.E., Effects of group pressure upon the modification and distortion of judgements, *In* Guetzkow, H. (ed.), *Groups, leadership and men*, Carnegie Press, Pittsburg, 1951.
9. Wing, J.K. and Brown, G.W., Social treatment of chronic schizophrenia: a comparative survey of three mental hospitals, *Journal of Mental Science*, 1961, **107**, 847 – 861.
10. Wing, J.K. and Brown, G.W., *Institutionalism and schizophrenia*, Cambridge University Press, Cambridge, 1970.
11. Holahan, C. and Saegert, S., Behavioural and attitudinal effects of large-scale variation in the physical environment of psychiatric wards, *Journal of Abnormal Psychology*, 1973, **82**, 454 – 462.
12. Lee, R., The advantage of carpets in mental hospitals, *Mental Hospitals*, 1965, **16**, 324 – 325.

13. Sommer, R., *Personal space*, Prentice Hall, Englewood Cliffs, 1969.
14. Trites, D.K., Galbraith, F.D., Sturdavant, M. and Leckwart, J.F., Influence of nursing-unit design on the activities and subjective feelings of nursing personnel, *Environment and Behaviour*, 1970, **2**, 303 – 334.
15. Dalgleish, M. and Matthews, R., Living as others do, *Community Care*, June 26th, 1980.
16. Sommer, R., *Design awareness*, Holt, Rinehart and Winston, New York, 1972.
17. McKeown, T., *The role of medicine*, Basil Blackwell, Oxford, 1979.
18. Kelvin, P., *The bases of social behaviour*, Holt, Rinehart and Winston, London, 1971.
19. Parsons, T., *The social system*, Free Press, New York, 1951.
20. Robinson, D., The alcohologist's addiction, *Quarterly Journal of Studies on Alcohol*, 1972, **33**, 1028 – 1042.
21. Epsom, J.D., The mobile health clinic: a report on the first year's work, *In* Tuckett, D. and Kaufert, J., *Basic readings in medical sociology*, Tavistock Publications, London, 1978.
22. Banks, M.H., Beresford, S.A.A., Morrell, D.C., Walker, J.J. and Watkins, C.J. Factors influencing the demand for primary medical care in women aged 20 – 24 years, *International Journal of Epidemiology*, 1975, **4**, 189 – 195.
23. Goldberg, D. and Huxley, P., *Mental illness in the community*, Tavistock Publications, London, 1980.
24. Robinson, D., *The process of becoming ill*, Routledge & Kegan Paul, London, 1971.
25. Cowie, B., The cardiac patient's perception of his heart attack, *Social Science and Medicine*, 1976, **10**, 87 – 96.
26. Radye-Yarrow, M., Schwartz, C.G., Murphy, H.S. and Deasy, L.C., The psychological meaning of mental illness in the family, *Journal of Social Issues*, 1955, **2**, 12 – 24.
27. Suchman, E. and Phillips, B., An analysis of the validity of health questionnaires, *Social Forces*, 1958, **36**, 223 – 232.
28. Cartwright, A., Minor illness in the surgery: a response to a trivial, ill-defined or inappropriate service? *In Management of minor illnesses*, King Edward's Hospital Fund, London, 1979.
29. Blackwell, B., Drug therapy: patient compliance, *New England Medical Journal* 1973, **289**, 249 – 252.
30. Adam, S.A., Horner, J.K. and Vessey, M.P., Delay in treatment for breast cancer, *Community Medicine*, 1980, **2**, 195 – 201.
31. Koos, E.L., *The health of Regionville*, Columbia University Press, New York, 1954.
32. Zola, I.K., Pathways to the doctor — from person to patient, *Social Science and Medicine*, 1973, **7**, 677 – 689.
33. Mechanic, D., Influence of mothers on their children's health attitudes and behaviour, *Pediatrics*, 1964, **33**, 445 – 453.
34. Mechanic, D. and Volkart, E.H., Stress, illness behaviour and the sick role, *American Sociological Review*, 1961, **26**, 51 – 58.
35. Alonzo, A.A., Everyday illness behaviour: a situational approach to health status deviations, *Social Science and Medicine*, 1979, **13A**, 397 – 404.
36. Gallagher, E.B., Lines of reconstruction and extension in the Parsonian sociology of illness, *Social Science and Medicine*, 1976, **10**, 207 – 218.
37. Scott, R., *The making of blind men*, Russell Sage, New York, 1969.
38. Doehrman, S.R., Psycho-social aspects of recovery from coronary heart disease: a review, *Social Science and Medicine*, 1977, **11**, 199 – 218.
39. Mayou, R., Foster, A. and Williamson, B., Psycho-social adjustment in patients

one year after myocardial infarction, *Journal of Psychosomatic Research*, 1978, **22**, 447 – 483.

40. Garrity, T.F., Social involvement and activeness as predictors of morale six months after first myocardial infarction, *Social Science and Medicine*, 1973, **7**, 199 – 207.
41. Nagle, R., Gangola, R. and Picton-Robinson, I., Factors influencing return to work after myocardial infarction, *Lancet*, 1971, **2**, 454 – 456.
42. Querido, A., An investigation into the clinical, social and mental factors determining the results of hospital treatment, *British Journal of Preventative and Social Medicine*, 1959, **13**, 33 – 49.
43. Grundle, M.J., Reeves, B.R., Tate, S., Raft, F. and McLaurin, L.P., Psychosocial outcome after coronary artery surgery, *American Journal of Psychiatry*, 1980, **137**, 1591 – 1594.
44. Litman, T.J., The family and physical rehabilitation, *Journal of Chronic Diseases*, 1966, **19**, 211 – 217.
45. Finlayson, A., Social networks as coping resources, *Social Science and Medicine*, 1976, **10**, 97 – 108.
46. Fordyce, W.E., Fowler, R.S., Lehmann, J.F. and DeLateur, B., Some implications of learning in problems of chronic pain, *Journal of Chronic Diseases*, 1968, **21**, 179 – 190.

PART 2
Human Development

7
Early Social Relationships

7.1 Introduction

The study of child development has many branches, such as the stages of physical development, the development of intelligent thought (Chapter 5) and personality development (Chapter 2). In this second part of the book, the emphasis is on social relationships, and this chapter is concerned with how such relationships develop. Research in this field provides information that can be practically applied in detecting inter-personal problems and suggesting ways in which they might be overcome. In the delivery room, for instance, medical staff witness the first social encounter between a baby and its parents, which can be related to future family difficulties. Some researchers believe that separation from the primary caregiver can markedly affect the development of the child, a belief that has important implications for medical practice where such separations are imposed if children are admitted to hospital or if the mother goes to hospital for the birth of a sibling. Children in long-term care are typically involved in a greater number of social relationships than children brought up at home, and these tend to be less constant. The professional's understanding of the effects of such relationships on the development of children owes much to the systematic study of these situations.

Some variables, such as the influence of specific aspects of an adult's behaviour on an infant, lend themselves to experimental study: adults can be asked to alter their behaviour systematically while the effects on the infant are recorded. Another way to study these aspects is to observe naturally occurring situations and to monitor their outcome. This type of approach underlies much of the work with infants and children in areas such as separation and long-term care, where it would clearly be unethical to produce the required conditions experimentally. To assess long-term effects, the same children would, ideally, be studied for several years, but such 'longitudinal' studies are expensive and time-consuming, so that many researchers resort to a 'cross-sectional' design, comparing samples of children at different ages.

That the new-born child can develop into a socially aware and competent individual in just a few years is intriguing. The process appears to be remarkably complex and unlikely, given the amount of information that a child must learn and the range of skills a child must master. A child of 5 or 6 years of age would be expected to speak in a way that adults could understand without difficulty and to be learning about such abstractions as time, space and number. But some other abilities are not so obvious. For example, you could observe what happens next time you make a purchase. Typically, the customer brings his hand up with the money as the vendor moves his hand forward as well: the money is exchanged midway between them. After the exchange both customer and vendor withdraw their hands while change is counted. This dance of the hands is then repeated: the vendor offers the change and the customer's hand comes up to meet his half-way. If this series of moves is not respected, certain conclusions may be drawn. Initially, if the vendor's hand is waiting in position before the customer's arrives, the vendor may be seen as somewhat grasping; if the customer's arms do not fall to his side while he waits for change, he may be seen as impatient or rude. The rules and roles involved in even such a simple social encounter are remarkably complex.

Without an awareness of these rules an individual would find it difficult to communicate with others. *Socialization* is the term given to the process whereby the individual becomes reasonably predictable to others and other people become predictable to him. To the extent that the customer and the vendor in the hand dance are mutually predictable, they can be said to be socialized. Similarly, most people living in Western cultures could be expected to be married to only one person at a time, not simply because there are laws against bigamy but rather because polygamy would not be consistent with their values and beliefs. A different pattern of socialization could be expected in some other cultures, in which having more than one spouse is thought to be not only morally acceptable but socially desirable, as an indication of wealth and status.

The aim of this chapter is to explore the beginnings of socialization, particularly the importance of the relationship between parent and infant. The topics that are covered here can be grouped under two headings. The first concerns social behaviour, concentrating particularly on the patterning of early relationships. Although it may be said that society influences the child more than the child influences its society, it has become increasingly clear that this is only a matter of degree and that a fuller understanding of socialization involves taking both types of influence into account. In the second part of the chapter, the

162

possibility that the quality of early relationships has long-term effects on the child is explored.

There are many other aspects of social relationships that, although not covered here, are currently arousing much interest. Most of the research mentioned in this chapter concerns the mother – child relationship: recently there has been an increased interest in the father – child relationship as well[1]. Another aspect of early social relationships is the effect of the arrival of a sibling on the parents and their first-born child. Presumably because of the increased demands on the mother due to the new infant, there is a marked decrease in positive interactions between the mother and the first child, with an increase in controlling or prohibitive statements[2]. The significance of play in social and cognitive development has also been studied. Amongst the primates, the time between birth and adolescence lengthens as we go up the phylogenic scale. This has led to the suggestion that an opportunity to play has evolutionary advantage: the individual has a chance to learn about social relationships and about the use and construction of tools in a relatively pressure-free environment[3].

7.2 Social Behaviour

Prenatal Influences

The process of socialization is often considered to begin only after birth, but the kinds of experience that the child will encounter and influence begin at conception. The foetus itself is a socializing agent for its parents. They begin to adapt to the child by attending prenatal clinics, preparing a cot and clothes and telling friends and relatives. Conversely, the mother's state of health and social position has considerable effect on the unborn infant. Sontag[4] examined the relationship between the mother's emotional state and the activity of the foetus. Not only did activity in the womb increase during stressful periods in the mothers' lives, but the nature of this stress affected foetal movements. When the stress was intense but brief, Sontag found only a transitory increase in activity. However, when the stressful events continued over a long period of time, activity increased up to ten times the normal level and did not decline so quickly. In an earlier study, it was found that mothers who had experienced long periods of severe anxiety during late pregnancy were more likely to have children who were highly active and intolerant of delays of feeding. Crandon[5] gave mothers-to-be a questionnaire designed to measure anxiety and then reviewed their records for the incidence of obstetric complications. On several measures, as shown in Fig. 7.1, those who scored highly on the questionnaire (N = 34) had more complications than those who had low scores (N = 112). However, it may have been that those women who were highly anxious were those who had been informed that they were at risk: it is not possible to form conclusions about a causal link here.

Nevertheless, such results have led to an increasing interest in the usefulness of preparing parents for childbirth. Although the weight of evidence indicates

163

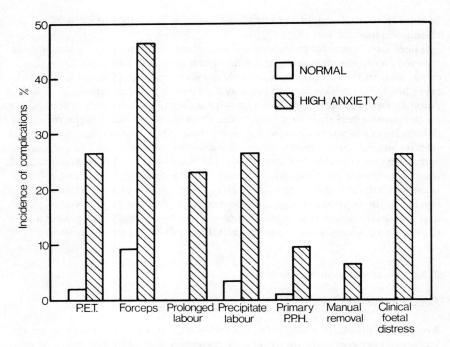

Fig. 7.1   The incidence of complications during childbirth for women who were highly anxious and those who were not. (Reproduced from A.J. Crandon, *Journal of Psychosomatic Research*, 1979, 23, 109–111, by permission.)

that preparation is useful, methodological problems are common in studies in this area[6]. Participation in prenatal classes is highly related to socio-economic status (those of the higher social classes being much more likely to attend), making it difficult to specify the reasons for any differences between those who have attended and those who have not[7].

The degree of stress that a pregnant woman experiences may affect the date of birth. Newton *et al.*[8] studied mothers who gave birth to full term (at least 37 weeks), moderately premature (33 – 36 weeks) and very premature (less than 33 weeks) infants. Although there were no significant differences between these groups in age, gravidity and parity, levels of psychological and social stress were higher in mothers of pre-term infants than full-term infants. In the week preceeding the onset of labour, mothers of pre-terms were more likely to have undergone a major life event, such as marital separation, unemployment of the husband or the death of an immediate family member. Eighty-four percent of the very premature group indicated that a major event had occurred.

Many other social and psychological factors have been found to be related to the state of the unborn infant. It has been repeatedly shown that infant mortality occurs more frequently in the lower socio-economic classes than in the higher ones. The marital status of the mother is also significant. Weeks[9] found that pre-maritally conceived but legitimately born infants (i.e. the mother had married between the time of conception and birth) were less likely to survive than post-maritally conceived infants. Although this effect seems valid regardless of the age of the mother, Weeks reports that there is also substantially higher risk of infant death for mothers 15 – 17 years of age than those older.

One difficulty with survey studies such as this is interpretation of the data. The higher mortality of infants conceived when the mother was unmarried may be due to several factors. There may be nutritional differences, for example, or poorer living conditions. Another possibility is the stress involved in 'shotgun' marriages. Perhaps it is society's attitude to pre-marital conceptions that affects the mother and thence the foetus. Similarly, it may be that the effect of mothers' age on infant mortality is a simple function of physiological immaturity on the part of the mother or, alternatively, the social significance of young parenthood. To the extent that young mothers-to-be are fearful of the reactions of others to the condition, they might be expected to hide their pregnancies and delay seeking medical advice. Chase and Nelson[10] found that the incidence of infant mortality was related to the timing of the first visit to an ante-natal clinic. The incidence was 6.6 per 1000 live births if the mother paid her first visit within the first 11 weeks of pregnancy, rising to 9.7 per 1000 if she waited until 12 – 27 weeks, and to 16.1 per 1000 if she attended a clinic after 27 weeks or not at all. Another study relating to the effect of physiological immaturity was conducted in Sweden. When a concerted effort was made to encourage young women to attend prenatal clinics, the mortality rate for young mothers was not signifi-cantly different than that for older women. These studies suggest that the lack of prenatal care may be responsible for the high incidence of infant mortality in young women.

Abilities of the Neonate

Even without any evidence to guide a theorist, it would make good sense to hypothesize that infants are in some way biologically primed for social inter-action because their chances of survival would be increased. An early researcher observed the behaviour of young infants, particularly before feeding: after a few days of life, the infants became increasingly restless just before they were due to be fed, and this increase occurred whether they were on a 3-hour or a 4-hour schedule. They had apparently already learned their caregivers' patterns of behaviour. After 8 days of observation, the infants on the 3-hour schedule were changed to a 4-hourly feeding: the level of restlessness increased substantially after 3 hours for this group initially but soon they, too, showed the 4-hour cycle of quiet and restless activity.

It has been suggested that an infant's cry acts as a kind of key that unlocks an innate mechanism for caregiving in humans. Bowlby[11] has argued that infants are genetically programmed to cry when distressed or when out of contact from their caregivers. Three patterns of crying have been distinguished — a basic rhythmical cry, a pain cry and an angry cry — and mothers have been found to attend to these different patterns appropriately. At first sight, it appears that crying provides an example of an innate ability in the newborn that triggers off innate responses in adults, but there are indications that this view is too simplistic since other factors affect caregivers' responses to a cry. For example, Western mothers respond to crying much more slowly than those living in the foraging Zhun/twa tribe. Infants in this Botswanan society rarely cry (other signals are used by mothers to anticipate hunger), but the cry when it occurs is treated as an emergency signal. It then brings an immediate response. In the United States, by contrast, about 17% of cries of first-borns were ignored and that response was delayed for from 10 to 30 min for one-third of the cries[12]. Further, experienced women are better than inexperienced women at discriminating between different kinds of cries. Thus, although it appears that crying is an important signalling mechanism for the infant, it is open to cultural and personal variation[13].

Incidentally, there is no evidence that attending to infants when they cry leads to greater demands for attention. In fact, observations suggest the opposite. Ainsworth and her colleagues[14] observed mothers and their children at home, noting particularly the frequency and speed with which mothers attended to their infants' cries over the first year of life. The results indicated that those mothers who intervened (by picking up, touching, playing with the children) were less likely to have infants who cried frequently or for long periods than mothers who ignored or responded slowly to the cries. At least until 1 year of age, maternal responsiveness did not reinforce the crying — rather, it reduced its probability.

Smiling and hearing are two other abilities of infants that have important social consequences. Neonates are able to locate sounds and attend to them visually. Further, they will not only attend preferentially to human voices over impersonal clicks, but also to a female voice rather than to a male one[15]. An infant who can respond, even in such a rudimentary way, is likely to prove rewarding for the caregiver. Similarly, since adults find smiles attractive, smiling may be an evolutionary advantage. It is an endogenous activity for the first weeks after birth, occurring at the rate of about 11 smiles per 100 min. It is present in blind infants and in all cultures, suggesting that it is innate.

The infant's appearance, particularly the eyes, may also be important to survival and social interaction. Sight and eye contact appear to have a significance greater than the purely cognitive. Infants as young as 3 weeks look at human faces and objects resembling faces more than other stimuli. Roskies[16] describes mothers who were considering institutionalizing their children soon after birth when they found they had been affected by thalidomide. These mothers remembered the decision to keep their children within the context of an engagement of eyes. Perhaps the most dramatic evidence of the importance of eye contact for the mother – infant relationship comes from a study conducted by Klaus and Kennell[17]. They filmed 12 mothers and their new-borns shortly after birth. The mothers were given their naked babies in privacy, except for the presence of a camera and sound-recording equipment. Besides touching the baby in a fairly predictable way (first tentatively with the fingertips and later with the palm of the hand), most mothers encouraged the infant to waken and open its eyes with comments like 'Let me see your eyes' and 'Open your eyes and then I'll know that you love me'. Several of the mothers reported that they felt closer to their children once they had achieved eye contact (see also Macfarlane[18]). In a later chapter, the possibility that lack of parental interest in the infant's eyes may be an indication of high risk for child abuse will be raised.

The research discussed above suggests that infants possess several attributes that increase the probability that adults will take an interest in and care for them. Neonates are able to learn quickly, are able to signal their needs and are visually attractive. With the growth of sociability much of the new-born's behaviour comes to be predictable to the adults who care for him or her. The study concerning infants' level of activity before feeding is a case in point. Individual infants also exhibit reasonably stable patterns of crying, perhaps making it easier for adults to interact with them. When predictability is difficult to achieve, as is the case with brain-damaged children, frustration and lack of parental care may result. Prechtl[19], in a description of interviews with mothers of brain-damaged children, indicated that these mothers tended to reject their infants more than mothers of normal children. Robson and Moss[20] conducted retrospective interviews with mothers in their third post-natal month, and concluded that a mother's feelings of attachment with her child decreased if crying, fussing and other demands did not lessen. They describe one woman in particular who was enthusiastic about her pregnancy but later wanted little to do with the child. The child did not respond to holding, smiled infrequently and showed little eye-to-eye contact. This child was later found to have brain damage. When mutual predictability between caregiver and child is difficult to establish, their relationship may be unsatisfactory.

Parent – Infant Interaction

The age at which infants engage in interaction has been variously estimated — the more recent the estimation, the younger it is thought to occur. Much evidence on this problem has been provided by T.B. Brazelton, a paediatrician. Although he and his colleagues rarely present any statistical analysis of their data and although it is not always clear how systematically their observations have been made, their insights have stimulated research in this area considerably. These researchers report they could predict, from filmed records of a baby's behaviour at 4 weeks of age, whether he was looking at his mother or an object[21]. Further, the behaviour of infants at 4 weeks of age towards strangers was similar to that towards inanimate objects[22]. This result may mean that infants of this age can discriminate between individuals or, alternatively, that strangers are not as skilled as family members at eliciting the familiar patterns of interaction.

Brazelton and his colleagues have also explored the effects of a non-responsive mother on the infant. In this study, the mothers were asked to present a still, mask-like face to their infants instead of their usual animation.

167

Infants initially oriented and smiled, but then sobered, became quiet and looked away. Several cycles of looking, smiling and then looking away were reported. Eventually, when repeated attempts failed to achieve a response, the infant withdrew into 'an attitude of helplessness, face averted, body curled up and motionless' (Brazelton et al.[23], p. 143). When the mothers returned to their more usual form of behaviour the infant, after an initial period of 'puzzlement', began to smile and return to their usual cycle of interaction.

Related to this experimental study is a case description of a naturally occurring distortion of a similar kind. It seems that in order to develop a full range of adult facial expressions, visual information from others is necessary. Without this information, a mask-like appearance is often present, as is sometimes found in adults who have been blind from birth. Some effects of congenital blindness in a mother on her infant's behaviour have been examined by Brazelton. At 4 weeks of age the (sighted) child was very alert, but would glance only briefly at her mother's eyes and would avert her face when the mother leaned over to talk. With the researchers, on the other hand, she 'greedily watched our eyes and followed every move'[23]. By 8 weeks, the infant reacted normally with the researchers but not with her mother. The infant still searched her face and eyes and then averted her own face. Not until some weeks later did the pair adapt successfully. Apparently, they had learned to use other modes of communication, such as the auditory, in place of the visual one.

Another approach to parent – infant interaction has concentrated on individual differences between infants, examining their 'behavioural style'. In an extended interview, Thomas et al.[24] asked mothers to describe their children not in terms of personality but in terms of their behaviour in several situations. They assumed that the parents could be used as an effective source of information about their children if they were asked about current situations and if the questions were quite specific. Their answers were validated by observing the children in different situations, and the issue of consistency was explored by observing them over a period of time. The researchers considered nine variables to describe infants' behavioural style adequately, variables that can be discerned as early as 3 months:

1. *Activity level*: the motor component present in an infant's functioning, including motility during bathing, eating, playing, dressing, etc. A low score means that the infant moves very little, while a higher score means, e.g. that the infant moves its arms and legs a lot, wiggles a lot, etc.
2. *Rhythmicity*: the predictability versus the unpredictability in time of functions like sleeping, eating and elimination. A low score means that the infant is mostly unpredictable, while a high score means that the infant is mostly predictable.
3. *Approach – Withdrawal*: the initial response to a new stimulus, such as food, toys, or a new person. A low score means Withdrawal, which is a negative response with fussing, crying, pulling away, etc. A high score means Approach, which is a positive response with smiling, cooing, moving closer, etc.
4. *Adaptability*: the adaptation (after the initial response) to a new stimulus, such as a new food. A low score means that the infant does not adapt or adapts very slowly to new stimuli, while a high score means that the infant quickly adapts to new stimuli.

168

5. *Intensity*: the energy level of response, irrespective of its positive – negative direction. A low score means mild responses like whimpering or smiling, while a high score means intense responses like hard crying, loud laughing, etc.

6. *Threshold*: the intensity level of stimulation that is necessary to evoke a response from the infant. A low score means a high threshold, i.e. the infant does not easily react to sounds, the temperature of food or bath water; while a high score means a low threshold, i.e. the infant reacts to noises of even low or moderate intensity, to small changes in the temperature of food, to a slightly wet diaper, etc.

7. *Mood*: the amount of happy, joyful behaviour, in contrast to unhappy and crying behaviour. A low score means that the infant often cries, whimpers, etc., while a high score means that the infant often smiles, coos, etc.

8. *Attention – Persistence*: the length of time that a given activity is pursued by the infant (Attention Span) and the continuation of an activity in spite of obstacles (Persistence). A low score means that attention span is short and that the infant, for example, tries only once or twice to reach for a toy. A high score means, e.g. that the infant plays for a long time with the same toy and that he makes repeated attempts to reach for a toy if not successful on the first attempt.

9. *Distractability*: the effectiveness of extraneous environmental stimuli in interfering with or in altering the direction of ongoing behaviour. A low score means that such stimuli seldom interfere with the infant's ongoing activity, while a high score means that such stimuli often and easily interfere with ongoing activity. (Ref. 25, p. 4)

This system categorizes the infant in terms of how he or she *acts*. Subsequently, interviews have been replaced by questionnaires, which require less time in administration, scoring and interpretation. Parents are given alternatives to check off, and their replies are scored on one or more of the scales, as in the following examples from one version:

'The following is an example of a question which has three answer categories and which represents one temperament variable (Rhythmicity):

'When does the baby wake up in the morning?
(a) The time usually varies by more than an hour.
(b) Quite often at the same time, but sometimes more than half an hour earlier or later (than usual).
(c) At the same time (within half an hour of the usual time).'

Alternative (a) is scored as 0 points (low Rhythmicity), alternative (b) as 1 point, and alternative (c) as 2 points (high Rhythmicity).

The following is an example of a question with five answer categories, the question representing two temperament variables [mood and intensity]:

'What does the baby usually do when he is being dressed to go outside?
(a) He cries and kicks.
(b) He whimpers and wiggles.
(c) He stares solemnly, wiggles a little.
(d) He smiles and gurgles, wiggles.
(e) He laughs loudly, gurgles, kicks.' (Ref. 25, pp. 5 – 6)

Thomas and his colleagues have identified three main patterns among the children they studied. The 'Easy Child', pattern (which applied to about 40%

of the children) consisted of high Rhythymicity, positive Mood, Approach, high Adaptability and low Intensity. Children showing the opposite behavioural style were termed 'Difficult Children' (about 10%), and those characterized by low Activity, Withdrawal, low Adaptability, negative Mood and low Intensity were said to be 'Slow-to-warm-up Children' (15%). A large proportion (35%) could not be characterized by any of these three patterns.

The presence of these individual differences in infants suggests that there is no one 'correct' way of relating to them, since each has different requirements. A difficult child would require a different pattern of interaction than an easy one, as would a blind or otherwise handicapped child. Rhythmicity — or predictability — may be particularly important in this respect. Regularity of sleeping and eating patterns is important for parents because in being able to anticipate the infant's needs their feelings of competence are enhanced and they adapt their routines to fit the child's more easily. By contrast, an unpredictable infant requires a fresh decision to be made about the meaning of each cry or whimper, a most difficult task for parents who might be unsure about their abilities. This can put a strain on the relationship between caregiver and infant that might, in combination with further difficulties, lead to later problems.

Usually, as an infant matures, he or she becomes more predictable and more responsive. Similarly, a caregiver gains experience with a particular child and usually develops increased sensitivity to his needs and increased skill in meeting them. Unfortunately, this is not always the case. Parents of children who are severely mentally handicapped or who have sensory impairments may be faced with a continuing lack of predictability and responsiveness. Sometimes a parent might have unrealistic expectations about the degree of stimulation an infant requires, providing too much or too little. One comparison of the communication patterns between mothers with normal infants and mothers with Down's Syndrome infants found several differences. Although the Down's children were involved in as many interactive sequences as normal children, they took the initiative less often and their mothers tended to be more directive. This researcher recommended that mothers of Down's Syndrome children curb their activity so that the infants have an opportunity to learn to take the initiative[26].

Similarly, infants born prematurely differ from full-terms in their need for stimulation and are less interactionally responsive, even when their families are similar. Pre-term infants are more likely to break off the interaction than full-terms[27] and to look less at their mothers and their environment. Several studies have indicated that prematurity has an effect on the way mothers interact with their infants. They have been found to issue more directive commands and to poke, pinch and rock more frequently when their children are pre-term. They are also more likely to initiate communication than mothers of full-terms, who share this responsibility more equally with their infants. The lack of cues from children with cerebral palsy and the excess of cues from hyperactive children have been shown to affect the mother – child relationship. Brazelton has instituted a programme in which mothers are able to view themselves and their children on videotape in an attempt to call their attention to inappropriate behaviour. He notes that many unsatisfactory relationships are due to inordinately high levels of maternal stimulation: many mothers, when able to view themselves on tape, recognize this tendency. In other cases, the mother is not stimulating enough, and Brazelton is able to show how the infant responds to imitation. Although access to videotape may not be available to many in the caring professions, it is possible to draw attention to some of these considerations through simple observation.

There are some specific ways in which adults adapt their behaviour when communicating with children. Some researchers have been more impressed by mothers' imitation of their children than vice versa. Mothers would often unwittingly protrude their tongues and open their eyes wide in imitation of their children's behaviour. Stern[28] notes that adults appear to match infants' tolerance for stimulus change and complexity. In his study of 18 mothers, adults used a slow tempo of speech, highly repetitive vocalizations, exaggerated facial expressions and gestures, and they also held their vowel sounds for longer than compared to their conversations with adults. In other words, they became more baby-like in their behaviour. These studies of parent – infant interaction illustrate the complexity and reciprocity of this relationship.

7.3 Long-Term Effects of Early Experience

The effect of early experience on later development has become one of the most intensively studied aspects of psychology, stimulated considerably by the work of John Bowlby. He reviewed the research on the intellectual and social development of children who had been separated from their mothers at an early age[29]. Many of these children had been brought up in residential institutions and were considered to be intellectually retarded (especially in language), to display excessive attention-seeking and unable to make close and trusting relationships with others. He attributed these effects to lack of a continuous, warm and intimate relationship with a single mother or mother-figure. Although he later pointed out that it could be beneficial if the child could be taken care of by other adults occasionally, he repeated his point that a single bond is crucial. He also believed there was a 'critical' period, such that if a child had not formed a bond by the age of 2½ – 3 years, the social and intellectual damage would be irreversible.

Central to his theory of *attachment* is the idea of a secure base. A mother may fulfill the needs of food and clothing, but it is equally important that she also provide a secure base from which the child can explore and develop self-reliance. For Bowlby, protection is seen as being fully as important as the more obvious biological needs. In many respects, his theory is consistent with a psychodynamic approach to personality development (Chapter 2): the infant's first relationship with a parent is seen to be critical for later development. If the parents — particularly the mother — do not provide a secure base, later development is said to be adversely affected. Trust and openness in later relationships will be much more difficult to achieve.

Bowlby has used several *ethological* studies of mother – infant behaviour to support his case. Ethological methods emphasize observation of behaviour in natural surroundings, and the observations are given an evolutionary explanation. This method of research was first used in zoology, Lorenz's descriptions of infant ducks becoming imprinted on their mothers being an example: they follow their mother soon after birth. He suggested that this response has an evolutionary advantage, keeping the chicks near their mother and thus less likely to wander away. Once an observation has been made, the researcher often attempts to manipulate the situation, systematically altering features until the important stimuli are discovered. In the case of imprinting, it seems that it is the first moving object that the chicks can discriminate that is important. Lorenz was able to arrange conditions so that the chicks became imprinted on him. Later studies have indicated that they could become attached to almost any moving object (gloves, cubes) and that they will attempt to mate with these objects when mature. The time when the moving object is shown to the chicks is important. There seems to be a critical period involved: if the moving object is shown after several days, the response is much less likely to occur. Thus, imprinting is the result of both innate and environmental factors. The application of ethological methods to children is more complicated, since infants reared in technologically advanced societies develop in very different conditions from the 'natural' environment, making it difficult to apply evolutionary explanations to their behaviour. Nevertheless, the emphasis on *observation* of how children behave has made this approach attractive to many psychologists.

Although Bowlby's theory is important in its own right, it is the way it has stimulated research into early social relationships that is of interest here. That so much research has resulted is partly due to the practical implications of his theory. One result is the easier access given to parents while their children are in hospital. Some of the conclusions derived from his theory have been less well accepted, such as his belief that it was beneficial for the child under 3 years of age if the mother was not employed outside the home. Similarly, if his critical period hypothesis is correct, this raises important questions about the possibility of successfully adopting older children who have never had the opportunity of forming a single continuous bond. Bowlby argued that the intellectual retardation found in residential nurseries was due to the absence of a bond with a single mother-figure, but more recent researchers have suggested that it was due to the unstimulating environment that characterized some institutions of this kind. The children were left in their cots for most of the day and given only routine care. Perhaps they failed to develop normally because they had little opportunity to play or to hear and speak to adults. Similarly, any lasting inability to form close relationships with others may have been due to the small amount of contact with an ever-changing staff. Perhaps it is not necessary to have a single bond for good social development, but it is necessary to experience some stability. Many studies have attempted to disentangle these various factors.

Four aspects of this research are discussed in the remaining sections of this chapter. The effects of separating the parent and the child are considered: first, the disruption of the parent – infant bond that may occur due to separation soon after birth; second, the effects of parent – infant separation due to factors such as hospitalization or marital disruption. In the third section, the effects of 'multiple' caregiving as may occur in residential nurseries or if the mother works are examined. The chapter concludes with a discussion of whether any adverse effects of such experiences on the child's development can be remedied later in life.

Bonding

That the period immediately after birth is particularly important or 'sensitive' for parent – infant bonding is based on evidence from various experimental and observational studies. The research conducted by Kennell and his colleagues has been particularly helpful in understanding the usefulness of the concept of a sensitive period. In an important experiment one group of women was given routine contact with their newborns: a glance of the baby shortly after birth, a short visit at 6 – 12 hours, and then every 4 hours of 20 – 30 min each for feeding over the first 3 days. This was the normal procedure at the hospital, so that this group of women and their children formed the control group. A second group of women were given this routine contact plus additional contact with their infants. They were given their naked babies to hold for 1 hour within the first 3 hours after birth and 5 extra hours per day over the next 3 days. Although the mothers in each group were comparable with respect to age, socio-economic status, colour, days spent in hospital and amount of pre-birth medication, Klaus and Kennell[17] found some striking differences in how the mothers in the two groups communicated with their children. After 1 month, the extended-contact mothers were observed to establish more eye contact with their children during feeding and to initiate more active play with their infants than the routine-contact mothers. Both groups were asked to keep diaries of their daily behaviour. Once again, the differences between the two groups suggested that the strength of the bond between the mother and the infant was related to the amount of contact shortly after birth. The extended-contact mothers reported thinking about the baby more frequently and staying at home more often than the control group. They also picked up the child more frequently when it cried, soothed their children more and were more likely to feed their children 'en face' (turning the head so that it was on the same plane as the infant's).

Early contact may have some long term effects as well. Kennell *et al.*[30] report that the differences between the groups still existed 1 year after the birth. Although about 50% of the mothers in both groups had returned to work by this time, most of the control-group mothers did not mention their baby when asked how they felt about this, whereas most of the extended-group mothers volunteered the information that they missed their children. At 2 years, there appeared to be differences in the way the mothers spoke to their children, with the extended-contact mothers asking more questions and issuing fewer commands[31] and differences in IQ have been reported at 42 months[32].

Another group of researchers has been interested in the effects of extended contact on child abuse and neglect. In their study, mothers were randomly assigned to either a control group, in which the mothers had 20 min of contact for feeding every 4 hours in the first 2 days post-partum, or they were assigned to a 'rooming-in' group, in which the child and his mother had an additional 6 hours together for each of these first 2 days. Although the children in these two groups did not differ in the frequency with which they visited the hospital for out-patient care or were ill, at least some were treated differently by their parents. Of the 277 children in the study, no rooming-in children were considered to have experienced abuse, neglect or non-organic failure to thrive, whereas nine control group children were considered to have suffered these conditions. Five of this group eventually died. These researchers concluded that mothers who were given close and extended physical contact with their newborn infants were less likely to abuse or neglect their children than women given more limited exposure[33].

Although these results have not been consistently replicated, and no other team of researchers have found such long-term effects[34], they have encouraged many obstetricians and paediatricians to make provision for early contact between the mother and her infant. Kempe and Kempe[35] have found that there is some predictive value in observing this first contact, their work indicating that the way a mother reacts to her child in the delivery room is related to the probability of later abuse and neglect (see Chapter 9). Other researchers have suggested that it may be possible to specify the optimal conditions for the establishment of the mother – infant bond. Kennell's work indicates that it is important that the mother hold her infant as soon as possible after birth. Fathers, too, seem to benefit from early contact with the newborn.

These findings also relate to the effects of pain-relieving drugs during labour. Several studies have indicated that these medications have some short-term effects, making the newborn drowsy and unresponsive[36]. By using short and simple tests on the child (such as Apgar scales, which measure heart rate, respiratory effort, reflex irritability, muscle tone etc.), some idea of the general health and responsiveness of the infant can be gained directly after birth. Pain-relieving drugs are associated with low scores on such scales. Since these activities may be important for the bonding process and the research cited here suggests the effects may be long-term, the use of these medications needs to be carefully considered.

Separation

A second aspect of Bowlby's theory of attachment concerns separation. Because of the need for protection, separation from the mother causes the baby distress — shown by the baby crying and attempting to locate her. Most babies show separation anxiety to some extent, usually between the ages of 8 to 24 months. It is usually most acute in novel situations. Many children also show anxiety in the presence of unfamiliar adults (stranger anxiety) between around 8 – 12 months. Bowlby suggests that these are examples of attachment responses in humans that have an innate basis and serve to protect the infant, keeping him close by the mother. The importance of the experience of separation has been studied in several ways, but most notably in those circumstances where the child enters hospital or where contact with a parent is lost due to divorce.

When children are placed in hospital, they may pass through three stages during their attempts to cope with the new environment. At first, they may show distress and protest, then misery and apathy followed, in the long term, by detachment and loss of interest in their parents. Older children are reported to show this pattern less frequently and less severely than younger children. Several researchers have used survey methods to explore the effects of hospitalization on children. Douglas[37] found that repeated hospital admissions in childhood were associated with a slight increase in enuresis, being most marked in children who underwent surgery. However, the interpretation of this finding must be cautious. Was the increase in bed-wetting due to the admissions or to the family background of these children? Children who are hospitalized frequently during the pre-school years are not altogether typical. For example, they are more likely to come from large families with parents who take little interest in their education. In addition, there appears to be considerable individual variation in how children react to hospitalization. Although 22% of children in one study showed some deterioration in their behaviour after having been in hospital (as indicated by their mothers), 10% showed some improvement[37]. Nevertheless, even when social class and the reason for hospitalization is taken into account, *repeated* admissions do seem to be associated with later disturbance[38].

This raises the possibility that some children may be more vulnerable to the experience than others. Can the minority of children who do show distress be predicted? Preliminary results reported by Brown[39] indicate that this might be possible. He conducted extended interviews with mothers, took observations of the patterns of mother – child interaction and observed the children (aged 3 – 6 years) on the hospital wards. Those children who, at home, were prone to spend much time with the family and stayed in close proximity to them were those who showed high distress in the hospital — they were upset, laughed little and were clinging when parents visited. Those children who were given more control over their own activities at home were likely to become involved with others on the ward and less likely to remain in bed. Thus, the high proximity and low-initiating children were most 'at-risk'. As in the case of other studies, the mothers' attitudes towards hospitalization were also relevant. Those who were anxious themselves about hospitals tended to have children who were withdrawn on the wards. Stacey *et al.*[40] report that those children who have poor relationships with adults and other children, who are socially inhibited or who are aggressive and uncommunicative before entering hospital are more likely to be disturbed by the experience. They also suggest that certain kinds of pleasant separations, such as having a baby-sitter or staying overnight with relatives, may prepare them for the stressful effects of hospitalization. A child coming from a secure background is less likely to be disturbed by the experience. The presence of a brother or a sister in the same hospital may result in less distress, as might the presence of the mother at admission. Nagera[41] provides a review of the literature on children's reactions to hospitalization and illness.

Although more than one interpretation of the results from these studies is possible, there is growing concern over the effects of hospitalization on young children, particularly when repeated admissions are necessary. It may be useful to consider these separations not as unique experiences that lead directly to disturbance but rather as part of the cumulative difficulties encountered by some children. The studies on psychological preparation for hospitalization and surgery discussed in Chapter 1 indicated that the stress involved could be reduced for children if adequate preparatory information was provided. The use of modelling via short films was shown to be effective in Chapter 3. Studies quoted above suggest that distress can be relieved further by providing emotional support for the child — e.g. by encouraging the mother to attend with her child at admission. There is also evidence that emotional support can be provided by nursing and medical staff. Fassler[42] assigned children who were to have minor surgery to one of three conditions. One group was given no information or emotional support during their stay. A second group was given emotional support alone, the experimenter reading a story to the children, giving them a set of toys to play with and talking with them about their interests, school and family. Little mention of hospitalization was made, but

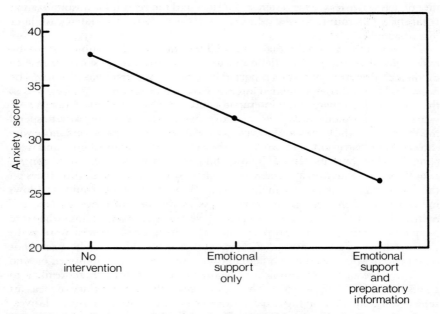

Fig. 7.2 Anxiety scores for hospitalized children who had received no intervention, received emotional support, or received both emotional support and preparatory information. (Reproduced from D. Fassler, *Patient Counselling and Health Education*, 1980, 2, 130–134, by permission.)

the procedure of this condition ensured that the children were given some emotional support. The third group was given this support, but also information concerning hospitalization; the children were given a set of toys to play with which included an operating table (providing an opportunity of talking about the treatment), they were shown a film about a child entering hospital (similar to that discussed in Chapter 3) and their concerns and fears about their stay were discussed. Thus, this condition provided emotional support plus information. Afterwards, each child was tested for his or her degree of anxiety. As shown in Fig. 7.2 those who were given no interventions were most anxious, followed by those who were given emotional support. However, the most effective intervention for reducing the children's anxieties before the operation was the combination of both emotional support and preparatory information.

A child can also be separated from his parents because of divorce, marital separation or death. If separation *per se* is the important variable, then all these could be expected to have similar consequences. This is usually not the case. Gibson[43], for example, found that only divorce and marital separation showed any association with delinquency (frequently used as an index of social adjustment) whereas death of a parent was not so related. Another study compared the rate of delinquency in families that had been disrupted because of divorce and separation with the rate in families where the parental relationship was quarrelsome and neglectful, but divorce had not taken place. They found significantly

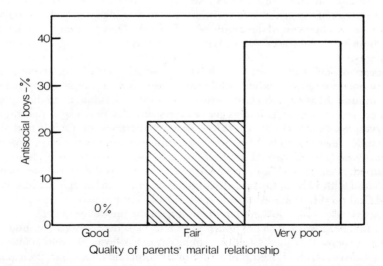

Fig. 7.3 Incidence of anti-social behaviour in boys as related to the quality of their parents' marital relationship (all boys living with both natural parents). (Reproduced from M. Rutter, *Journal of Child Psychology and Psychiatry*, 1971, 12, 233–603, by permission.)

less delinquency in the former type of family. Similarly, Rutter[44] examined the relationship between the quality of parental marriage and incidence of anti-social behaviour in the children. A linear relationship was found between these two variables, such that children showing anti-social behaviour were more likely to have parents with a very poor marriage. These results are illustrated in Fig. 7.3. Rutter also compared the incidence of delinquency in children who had been separated from their parents because of physical illness with those who had been separated because of family discord or psychiatric illness. The incidence of anti-social behaviour was some four times higher in the second group[45].

Some studies have examined the effects of youthful separation on mothers's later abilities to cope with and rear their own children. Frommer and O'Shea[46] divided mothers into two groups: those who complained of difficulties with their babies or their marriages in the first year of the babies' lives, and those who did not voice complaints. These researchers took the presence of complaints as a measure of difficulty. The mothers in the complaining group were more likely to have experienced separation from one or both parents before the age of 16 years and were more likely to report parental quarrelling when they were young. Similarly, Wolkind et al.[47] in a study of 500 primiparous women, related the women's early separation experiences to their psychological and social status at the time of pregnancy. They found that women who had been separated from their parents were more likely to be experiencing problems and to be troubled by minor physical complaints. The 20% of their sample who reported separation were also less likely to be married and more likely to be under the age of twenty. But these authors note that the separation per se should not be seen as the cause of the mothers' difficulties. They suggest that separation may be a sensitive index to the type of up-bringing that might lead to later problems.

Observational studies support this latter conclusion. Hall et al.[48] conducted 25 min of observation of mother – child interaction with a sample of mothers and their infants. Mothers who had come from families that had been disrupted by divorce, separation and, in this particular study, by death of a parent, were observed to talk with their infants less, to touch them less frequently and to look at them for fewer periods. Even when the time spent out of the room was taken into account (the 'disrupted' mothers were out of the room more) these effects remained. Also, only 35% of the disrupted mothers saw their babies as 'people', compared with 75% of the non-disrupted women, even though the researchers could find no differences between the children in these two groups.

These workers also collected information on the incidence of care away from home for these women. They found that although care away from home was closely associated with disruption, some women whose parental relationship was not disrupted had been taken care of by someone other than their parents for at least a month before the age of 16. The patterns of interaction with their children were similar to those of mothers who had not been taken care of away from home and whose parental relationship was good.

It appears from these studies that separation and disruption of the parent –

child relationship can be associated with long-term consequences. However, it may not be accurate to attribute these consequences to any single circumstance, such as separation due to hospitalization. Surveys that find that separation experiences distinguish between delinquents and non-delinquents or between women who had difficulty in coping with their children and women who do not, may, in fact, be measuring longer-term discord between the child and parents or between the parents themselves. Again, it may be more useful to consider separation as one of a series of difficulties, which have a cumulative effect.

Multiple Caregiving

Some questions do not lend themselves, either ethically or practically, to experimental testing. The problem of long-term parent – child separation is one such instance, hence the reliance on survey methods. The effects of caregiving by several adults is another example. Accordingly, attempts to answer this question have been made by examining naturally occuring situations in which infants have been given care by several adults. Of direct relevance to Bowlby's work are more recent efforts to extend and replicate his observations. In several reports, Barbara Tizard has explored the effects of residential nurseries on the cognitive and social development of children. She began by examining 65 children with an average age of 24 months. All of these children were born full-term and none was considered to have any physical or mental handicap. Her nurseries were, however, much more stimulating than those studied by Bowlby. Toys, mobiles and picture books were freely available, and staff were encouraged to communicate with the children.

On most measures, these children were very similar to a comparison group of working-class London children, except that they were less likely to approach strangers and their language development was slightly retarded. In further studies, Tizard has found little evidence of cognitive retardation. Tizard and Rees[49] reported their findings on the same children at 4 years of age. Some of them had remained in the institution and others had been restored to their natural mothers. Both restored and institution groups had IQ's similar to the working-class comparison group.

The children's cognitive development seemed to be related to the quality and frequency of staff contact. Tizard *et al.*[50] studied 85 children of 2 – 5 years of age who were being cared for in 13 residential nurseries. They found that the verbal abilities of the children were positively correlated with the frequency of informative staff talk, staff social activity and the frequency with which staff answered children's remarks. No evidence of developmental retardation was found in this sample.

These results suggest that although the quality of adult – child contact is important for cognitive and language development, it may not be necessary to have a single continuous relationship. The staff of these nurseries changed frequently, and close emotional contact was discouraged. The conclusions that can be drawn for social development are less clear, however. The development of trust in social relationships may require more than simply frequent contact with adults. Some continuity of care may well be important. In a follow-up to the earlier studies, Tizard[51] reports that at 8 years of age the institution-reared children seemed overly affectionate and 'clinging'. It is possible that this clinging was an attempt to obtain some sort of continuity of caregiving: a response to the frequent changing of caregivers. Related to this finding is research on the effects of adoption on later development. Tizard, in keeping with many studies, reports few social and emotional difficulties in the adopted children from her sample.

Other naturally occurring situations can be used to study the importance of multiple caregiving. Most of these studies suggest that being cared for by more than one adult does not necessarily have negative consequences. In Israeli Kibbutzim, children are 'shared' among all the adults present. Although there is some indication that parents may give more care and attention to their own offspring in practice, no evidence of cognitive or social deficits has been found in these children. Another situation is maternal employment, where mothers arrange for their children to be taken care of by another adult during their working day. Ethugh[52] concluded that employment itself was only weakly related to children's development and behaviour. If the home environment were disrupted because of marital difficulties or if adequate provision for supervision were not made, then problems may occur.

Evidence from other cultures also supports the idea that care could be given by more than one person without adverse effects. In many societies, several members of a family share the responsibility for caretaking (indeed, this often happens in ours) and breast-feeding is not necessarily given by the mother alone. From an evolutionary point of view it would be advantageous for an infant to be somewhat selective in forming attachment bonds, but having an inability to form more than one bond could have severe negative consequences. A sociobiological viewpoint would also support the importance of the whole family, since grandparents, older siblings and aunts and uncles would all have a greater opportunity to pass on their genes if they invested energy in the child and the child was receptive to this[53].

Conversely, there may well be a limit to the number of caregivers who could be helpful to the child. Insofar as good caregiving implies a sensitivity to a child's needs, this would require time and considerable contact. Some personal commitment on the part of the caregiver would be necessary for this. For the child — who also has a need for predictability — the different styles of interaction shown by a large number of adults may be disturbing. If only because time is required to form a relationship, it is likely that there is an upper limit on the number of people who could give satisfactory care[53]. For cognitive development, adequate stimulation and interest is needed, and it seems likely that for good social and emotional development at least one stable relationship, with commitment on the part of the caregiver, is required.

Resilience

Another conclusion that John Bowlby drew from his review of studies concerned the irreversibility of the effects of early deprivation. He argued that children would suffer a lasting inability to form close relationships if they had not been given the opportunity to do so before 2½ years of age. Many researchers have questioned the validity of Bowlby's conclusions in this respect. They suggest a child is not necessarily doomed to an unsatisfactory life because of an unsatisfactory childhood. Several naturally occurring situations can be used to examine the issue of the resilience of children in the face of early deprivation. It will be remembered that studies on mother – infant interaction indicated that premature infants sometimes provide less interesting and fulfilling responses for the mother than do full-term infants. If this early experience is so significant, then differences could be expected later in life, yet few differences have been found. In one study, patterns of interaction between mothers and their premature infants proved to be poor predictors of cognitive or social ability at age three[54]. Similar results have been found concerning the effects of perinatal anoxia. Although loss of oxygen at birth appears to affect the early mother – infant relationship, there is little evidence of an enduring connection between early morbidity and later psychological dysfunction[55].

Perhaps the strongest evidence that early deficits can be overcome comes from several case studies. Koluchova[56] describes the recovery of twin boys who were totally isolated from others from 18 months to 7 years of age. They were locked in a cupboard for most of this time. When they were eventually released, they could barely walk, suffered from rickets and their IQ's were in the forties. Although they were 18 months old at the time of their incarceration, this long period of isolation would be expected to have severe long-term effects on their intellectual and emotional development if early experience was crucial. However after 7 years of fostering in a supportive and emotionally caring home, they were found to have average IQ's and average social development.

Kagan[57] describes a girl of 14½ years of age who spent most of the first 30 months of her life in a small bedroom with no toys and a sister 1 year older than herself. When she was removed at 2½ years, she was severely malnourished and retarded in height and weight. At the time Kagan conducted his interview, she had spent 12 years in a foster home. He reported that her IQ was 88 (within the normal range) and that she gave an average performance on several cognitive tests. He noted that her interpersonal behaviour compared favourably with other adolescents.

It may be that the presence of a sibling in these two case reports helped those children considerably. There is increasing interest in the significance of friends in the social development of young children. There is evidence that without an opportunity to meet peers of a similar age, children are less likely to acquire social and communication skills. It has been argued that poor peer relationships are amongst the most powerful predictors of later social and emotional adjustment. One method of assisting troubled children with their difficulties has been to encourage play with peers, a method that has met with some success. Hartup and his colleagues describe a study in which children who were considered socially withdrawn or isolated were divided into three groups. One group acted as a control. The other two groups were encouraged to participate in special play sessions for 4 – 6 weeks: for half of these children the playmates were some 15 months younger, for the other half about the same age. The results indicated that exposure to children younger than the withdrawn children was particularly effective in reducing isolation — perhaps the younger playmates were less threatening than the same-age playmates. This study is particularly impressive because the ratings of isolation were made by people who did not know the purpose of the study (teachers) in a situation providing a good sample of the children's behaviour (the classroom)[58].

Another way of studying this issue of resilience is by examining cross-cultural patterns of child rearing. Not all cultures place the same emphasis on the early stimulation of the child as does the West. Guatamalan children, for example, are reared in virtual isolation for the first 3 years of life in order to protect them from evil spirits. They are given little contact with adults and not allowed to leave their homes. Yet, at adolescence, their cognitive development was reported as being adequate[57].

It is possible, of course, that the general failure to find enduring effects of early experience may be due to the insensitivity of methods currently used. Early deprivation and neglect are likely to have some long-term consequences — just as years of isolation in adulthood could be expected to affect an individual — but it appears that these consequences may have been over-estimated. Children seem more resilient and responsive to change than was thought a decade ago.

A more fruitful approach may be to consider early experience within the context of later circumstances. It could be concluded from the studies of early separation on later development that children who have difficulties in their first years are more likely to continue to experience difficulties as they grow, and that it is the cumulative effect that has significant consequences. This conclusion is not incompatible with the emphasis placed on mother – infant interaction earlier in the chapter. A mother and child may be able to cope with, say, a pre-term birth without undue difficulty, but further adverse experiences, such as a physical abnormality, immaturity in the mother or unavoidable and unwanted separations, may increase the risk of adversely affecting the development of the child.

Summary

Even before birth, the child is influenced by and influences his parents. The newborn infant has the ability to adapt to others' needs and schedules and has various characteristics that elicit caring responses. As early as 4 weeks after birth, parents engage in complex interactions with their children. This relationship can be distorted by either parent or child: for instance if the mother is insensitive to her child's needs for stimulation or if the child is developmentally delayed. In such cases, the needs of the two participants may conflict. Improvements in unsatisfactory parent – child relationships could be brought about by providing parents with an opportunity to view their relationship with the child more objectively, for instance by looking at videotapes of their interactions.

The period shortly after birth seems particularly sensitive for the formation of bonds between mother and child. This has implications for the management of childbirth. In older children, detrimental consequences of separation due to hospitalization appear to depend on the family background of the child. Distress is less if the parental relationship is good and if the child feels secure in his or her home environment. Similarly, multiple caregiving may not in itself affect a child's social development deleteriously. Although cognitive development seems to be related to the quality and frequency of adult contact, adequate social development may require continuity of care as well. It appears to be important that relationships are predictable and consistent. Children appear resilient to the effects of poor relationships early in their life; early deficits can be remedied. The bulk of the evidence suggests that isolated negative experiences have few long-term effects. Continuing adverse circumstances, on the other hand, may seriously affect later development. It seems that the continuing experience of adversity can have a cumulative effect on the child.

Suggested Reading

Several of the edited books referenced below (e.g Ref. 26) are helpful, particularly Rutter[45]. J. Osofsky (ed.), *Handbook of human development*, Wiley, Chichester, 1979, also considers many of the topics covered in this chapter. Another possibility is M. Rutter (ed.), *Scientific foundations of developmental psychiatry*, Heinemann Medical Books, London, 1980, which gives extensive coverage of many aspects of child development.

References

1. Lamb, M.E., Father – infant and mother – infant interaction in the first year of life, *Child Development*, 1977, **48**, 167 – 181.
2. Dunn, J. and Kendrick, C., The arrival of a sibling, *Journal of Child Psychology and Psychiatry*, 1980, **21**, 119 – 132.
3. Tizard, B. and Harvey, D., *The biology of play*, Heinemann, London, 1977.
4. Sontag, L.W., Implications of foetal behaviour and environment for adult personalities, *Annals of the New York Academy of Science*, 1966, **134**, 782.
5. Crandon, A.J., Maternal anxiety and obstetric complications, *Journal of Psychosomatic Research*, 1979, **23**, 109 – 111.
6. Beck, N.C. and Hull, D., Natural childbirth, *Obstetrics and Gynaecology*, 1978, **52**, 371 – 379.
7. Beck, N.C. *et al.*, The prediction of pregnancy outcome *Journal of Psychosomatic Research*, 1980, **24**, 343 – 351.
8. Newton, R.W., Webster, P.A.C., Binu, P.S., Maskrey, N. and Phillips, A.B., Psychosocial stress in pregnancy and its relation to the onset of premature labour, *British Medical Journal*, 1979, **2**, 411 – 413.
9. Weeks, J.R., Infant mortality and premarital pregnancies, *Social Science and Medicine*, 1976, **10**, 165 – 169.

10. Chase, H.C. and Nelson, F., A study of risks, medical care and infant mortality, *American Journal of Public Health*, 1973, **63**, Sept. Supplement.
11. Bowlby, J., *Attachment and loss*, Vol. 1 Attachment, Penguin, Harmondsworth, 1971.
12. Bernal, J., Crying during the first ten days of life and maternal responses, *Developmental Medicine and Child Neurology*, 1972, **14**, 362 – 372.
13. Murray, A.D., Infant crying as an elicitor of parental behaviour, *Psychological Bulletin*, 1979, **86**, 191 – 215.
14. Ainsworth, M., Bell, S. and Stayton, D., Individual differences in the development of some attachment behaviours, *Merrill-Palmer Quarterly*, 1972, **18**, 123 – 143.
15. Goldberg, S., Social competence in infancy, *Merrill-Palmer Quarterly*, 1977, **23**, 163 – 177.
16. Roskies, E., *Abnormality and normality: the mothering of thalidomide children*, Cornell University Press, Ithaca, 1972.
17. Klaus, H.M. and Kennell, J.H., Human maternal behaviour at first contact with her young, *Pediatrics*, 1970, **46**, 187 – 192.
18. Macfarlane, A., *The psychology of childbirth*, Penguin, Harmondsworth, 1978.
19. Prechtl, H.F.R., The mother – child interaction in babies with minimal brain damage, *In* Foss, B.M. (ed.), *Determinants of infant behaviour*, Vol. 2, Methuen, London, 1963.
20. Robson, K.S. and Moss, H.A., Patterns and determinants of maternal attachment, *Journal of Pediatrics*, 1970, **77**, 976 – 985.
21. Brazelton, T.B., Koslowski, B. and Main, M., The origins of reciprocity, *In* Lewis, M. and Rosenblum, L.A., *The effect of the infant on its caregiver*, Wiley, London, 1974.
22. Brazelton, T.B., Early parent – infant reciprocity, *In* Vaughan, V.C. and Brazelton, T.B. (eds.), *The family — can it be saved?*, Year Book Medical Publisher, New York, 1976.
23. Brazelton, T.B., Tronick, E., Adamson, L., Als, H. and Wise S., Early mother – infant reciprocity, *In* CIBA Foundation Symposium Vol. 33, *Parent – Infant Interaction*, 1975.
24. Thomas, A., Birch, H.G., Chess. S., Hertzig, M.E. and Korn, S., *Behavioural individuality in early childhood*, University of London Press, London, 1963.
25. Personn-Blennow, I, and McNeil, T.F., A questionnaire for measurement of temperament in six-month-old infants, *Journal of Child Psychology and Psychiatry*, 1979, **20**, 1 – 13.
26. Jones, O.H.M., A comparative study of mother – child communication with Down's Syndrome and normal infants, *In* Schaffer, D. and Dunn, J. (eds.), *The first year of life*, Wiley, Chichester, 1979.
27. Brown, J.V. and Bakeman, R., Relationships of mothers with their infants during the first year of life: effects of prematurity, *In* Bell, R.W. and Smotherman, W.P. (eds.), *Maternal influence and early behaviour* Spectrum, Holliswood, 1979.
28. Stern, D., A micro-analysis of mother – infant interaction, *American Academy of Child Psychiatry Journal*, 1971, **10**, 510 – 517.
29. Bowlby, J., *Maternal care and health care*, World Health Organization, Geneva, 1951.
30. Kennell, J.H., Jerauld, R., Wolfe, H., *et al.*, Maternal behaviour one year after early and extended post-partum contact, *Developmental Medicine and Child Neurology*, 1974, **16**, 172 – 179.
31. Ringler, N.M., Kennell, J.H., Jarvella, R., Navojosky, B. and Klaus, M.H.,

Mother-to-child speech at two years — effects of early post-natal contact *Behavioural Pediatrics*, 1975, **86**, 141 – 144.

32. Trause, M.A., Kennell, J. and Klaus, M., Parental attachment behaviours, *In* Money, J. and Musaph, H. (eds.), *Handbook of sexology*, Excerpta Medica, London, 1977.

33. O'Connor, S.M., Vietze, P.M., Hopkins, J.B. and Altemeir, W.A., Post-partum extended maternal infant contact, *Pediatric Research*, 1977, **11**, 380.

34. Svejda, M.J., Campos, J.J. and Emde, R.N., Mother – infant 'bonding', *Child Development*, 1980, **51**, 775 – 779.

35. Kempe, R.S., and Kempe, C.H., *Child abuse*, Fontana, London, 1978.

36. Aleksandrowicz, M. and Aleksandrowicz, D.R., Obstetrical pain-relieving drugs as predictors of neonate behaviour variability, *Child Development*, 1974, **45**, 935 – 945.

37. Douglas, J.W.B., Early hospital admissions and later disturbances of behaviour and learning, *Developmental Medicine and Child Neurology*, 1975, **17**, 456 – 480.

38. Quinton, D. and Rutter, M., Early hospital admissions and later disturbances of behaviour, *Developmental Medicine and Child Neurology*, 1976, **18**, 447 – 459.

39. Brown, B., Beyond separation: some new evidence on the impact of brief hospitalization on young children, *In* Hall, D. and Stacey, M. (eds.), *Beyond separation*, Routledge & Kegan Paul, London, 1979.

40. Stacey, M., Dearden, R., Pill, R. and Robinson, D., *Hospitals, children and their families*, Routledge & Kegan Paul, London, 1970.

41. Nagera, H., Children's reactions to hospitalization and illness, *Child Psychiatry and Human Development*, 1978, **9**, 3 – 19.

42. Fassler, D., Reducing preoperative anxiety in children, *Patient counselling and Health Education*, 1980, **2**, 130 – 134.

43. Gibson, H.B., Early delinquency in relation to broken homes, *Journal of Child Psychology and Psychiatry*, 1969, **10**, 195 – 204.

44. Rutter, M., Parent – child separation: psychological effects on the children, *Journal of Child Psychology and Psychiatry*, 1971, **12**, 233 – 260.

45. Rutter, M., Parent – child separation, *In* Clarke, A. and Clarke, A., *Early experience*, Open Books, London, 1979.

46. Frommer, E. and O'Shea, G., Antenatal identification of women liable to have problems managing their children, *British Journal of Psychiatry*, 1973, **123**, 149 – 156.

47. Wolkind, S., Kruk, S. and Chaves, L., Childhood separation experiences and psychosocial status in primiparous women, *British Journal of Psychiatry*, 1976, **128**, 391 – 396.

48. Hall, F., Pawlby, S.J. and Wolkind, S., Early life experiences and later mothering behaviour, *In* Schaffer, D. and Dunn, J. (eds.), *The first year of life*, Wiley, Chichester, 1979.

49. Tizard, B. and Rees, J., A comparison of the effects of adoption, restoration to the natural mother and continued institutionalisation on the cognitive development of 4 year old children, *Child Development*, 1974, **45**, 92 – 99.

50. Tizard, B., Cooperman, O., Joseph, A. and Tizard, J., Environmental effects on language development, *Child Development*, 1972, **43**, 337 – 358.

51. Tizard, B., Early experience and later social development, *In* Schaffer, D. and Dunn, J., *The first year of life*, Wiley, Chichester, 1979.

52. Ethugh, C., Effects of maternal employment on children, *Merrill-Palmer Quarterly*, 1974, **20**, 71 – 78.

53. Smith, P.K., Shared care of young children, *Merrill-Palmer Quarterly*, 1980, **26**, 371 – 389.
54. Bakeman, R. and Brown, R. Early interaction: consequences for social and mental development at three years, *Child Development*, 1980, **51**, 437 – 447.
55. Corah, N.L., Anthony, E.J., Painter, P., Stern, J.A. and Thurston, D.L., The effect of perinatal anoxia after seven years, *Psychological Monographs*, 1965, **79**, Whole number 596.
56. Koluchova, J., The further development of twins after severe and prolonged deprivation, *Journal of Child Psychology and Psychiatry*, 1976, **17**, 181 – 188.
57. Kagan, J., Resilience and continuity in psychological development, *In* Clarke, A. and Clarke, A., *Early experience*, Open Books, London, 1979.
58. Furman, W., Rahe, D.F. and Hartup, W.W., Rehabilitation of socially withdrawn preschool children through mixed-age and same-age socialisation, *Child Development*, 1979, **50**, 915 – 922.

8
Sexuality

8.1 Introduction

Sexuality is a topic that interests most people. Freud based his theory of personality development on sexual energy (although as shown in Chapter 2, his concept of sexuality was much wider than the everyday view of it). When a child is born, the first question asked is often about gender, indicating that this is a very important consideration. Expectations about people are affected by their gender, resulting in different ways of treating even very young children. During adolescence, interest in sexuality can become intense, often being a prime motivator of changes in appearance, interests and choice of friends.

Although there are obvious genetic and hormonal components affecting gender and sexual behaviour, the development of sexual behaviour is open to considerable variation depending on cultural and familial influences. Sexual functioning is emotional as well as physical, so that past experiences and the expectations of the individual play an important part in behaviour. The advent of safe and effective oral contraceptives has increased the opportunity for couples to enjoy their sexuality as fears of unwanted pregnancy recede. This chapter considers some of these social influences on sexuality.

There are several topics that are not covered in depth in this chapter although literature is generally available to the interested reader. Only brief mention is made of the physiological aspects of sexual response, although inadequate or inaccurate information about physiology and anatomy often contributes to

187

sexual difficulties. Nor is there much discussion of sexual myths, however widespread they may be. It is only 20 years since half the graduates and one-fifth of the faculty members of the five medical schools canvassed in one study believed that masturbation is a cause of psychiatric illness. In both these respects, the physician can have a crucial educational role. Additionally, the sexual problems faced by the physically or mentally handicapped are increasingly being recognized. Their sexual needs are often disregarded and it is sometimes the medical and nursing staff who may have to adjust their thinking on this. Finally, there is much research on the sexual 'deviations' such as incest and paedophilia. Both psychotherapeutic and behavioural methods have been used in treating these difficulties, and reviews can be found elsewhere (e.g. Leiblum and Pervin[1]).

8.2 Gender Identity

An important distinction is made between gender identity and sexual identity. The latter is a biological concept, relying on such characteristics as genitalia, hormonal levels and chromosomes. Gender identity, however, refers to a person's feelings and perceptions about whether he or she is male or female. This self concept seems particularly important. If the reader were asked to provide a self-description, it is likely that the first piece of information would be about maleness or femaleness. It is difficult to imagine a more basic attribute. Although obvious, an interesting feature of gender is its dichotomous nature; there are no shades of grey and there is no third category. It is vitally important to be one or the other. It seems to be common to all cultures that men and women be distinct types. During the mid 1960s, when long hair on men became fashionable, one of the more disturbing features of the fashion seemed to be that it was sometimes difficult to distinguish between the sexes. When confusion occurred, this was often a topic of conversation or curiosity.

It is tempting to conclude, then, that gender identity is biologically determined, unaffected by socialization processes. However, such an assumption has been called into question by several studies — many by John Money — on hermaphrodites, people who at birth show the physical characteristics of both sexes. Although it has been argued that this small sample of individuals is atypical, his results do raise the possibility that the sense of gender identity is strongly influenced by the environment. In most people gonadal sex, chromosomal sex, hormonal sex and external genitalia are consistent with each other giving unambiguous cues about gender. In hermaphrodites they are not, in that both male and female characteristics are present. In the case of testicular feminization, for example, the foetus is insensitive to androgens. Although the chromosomal sex is male, the external genitalia are female. In the androgenital syndrome (an excess of androgens) the internal structure of the chromosomally female foetus is unaffected, but the external genitalia sometimes resemble the male. The ambiguity of sex at birth means that, unlike most instances, a decision has to be made about gender. The choice is called the 'sex of assignment' and is important because parents and society react differently to boys and girls (see below under Sex Roles). Several studies with different kinds of hermaphrodites have indicated that this decision is a more reliable predictor of later gender identity and behaviour than chromosomal, hormonal or gonadal indices of sex. In Money's series of studies only about 5% of the cases showed indications of ambiguous gender identity or behaviour in later years[2].

Money does not claim that gender identity is purely environmental in origin. Rather, he suggests that innate mechanisms interact with environmental influences. Usually, these factors are consonant, but when innate and external influences are inconsistent, the environment can have a strong effect on whether individuals see themselves as male or female.

Occasionally, children are assigned one gender but later investigation indicates that a change would be appropriate. There is some disagreement about whether the timing of gender assignment is important. Early studies suggested that if gender is reassigned after 2 – 3 years of age, problems arise for the children, but some later research indicates that this may not always be the case. In some circumstances, gender reassignment can occur even as late as puberty without undue difficulty being experienced[3].

As mentioned above, one problem with these studies on hermaphrodites is that they are based on an atypical population. For most people, gender attributes are consistent with sexual ones, and Money's findings may not be applicable to this larger group of people. Before too much weight can be placed on the hermaphrodite studies, evidence is needed that genetically, hormonally and gonadally typical males or females can be reassigned. There is one such case in the literature, again reported by Money[4]. One of a pair of monozygotic twin boys lost his penis in a surgical accident at 7 months of age. At 17 months, his sex was reassigned on the opinion that a child without a penis could function more adequately as a female than as a male. Surgery and hormonal treatment were instituted (testes removed, a vaginal canal constructed and estrogen administered). The parents also began to treat the children differently with respect to attitudes to sex, domestic activities, career expectations and toys. They began to dress the child in dresses, blouses and ribbons. At nine years of age, the child had a normal female gender identity and engaged in typical female behaviours. Although it is important not to place too much emphasis on a single case, this report seems to illustrate the malleability of gender identity in a child whose sexual identity was unambiguous before the accident.

8.3 Sex Roles

As defined in Chapter 6, roles are those activities that fulfill others' expectations. When playing the role of a student, a person is expected to turn up at lectures, to take some notes and to write exams. Most behaviour is overlaid with what is perhaps the most important role of all: sex roles. Even though behaving like students, men tend to cross their legs in one way, women in another. If the topic of study is medicine, men are more likely to be doctors, women nurses.

Men are expected to be assertive and logical, women expressive and warm. A notion of what behaviour is appropriate for one's own sex is learned very early. By 3 years of age, children can discriminate between different classes of toys — boys tend to choose tools and vehicles, whereas girls choose prams and dishes to play with. By the age of 5 years, children have acquired knowledge about what are called 'role stereotypes' — that men dominate some professions, whereas women dominate others. Generally the roles that boys wish to take are those involving logical thought and objectivity, whereas the positions that girls expect to take are those requiring warmth and support.

Innate or Learned?

Those who hold that many of the differences in behaviour between men and women are innate rely on several kinds of evidence — genetic, hormonal and behavioural. The human embryo is initially neuter. If a Y chromosome is present, the primordial gonad differentiates into the testes, secreting hormones that promote male genital development. If these hormones are not present, the gonads develop into the ovaries. Those who hold that sex differences are innate point to these differences suggesting that these will have effects on behaviour and citing several examples. First, women, generally, find it more difficult to experience orgasm than men. Some sociobiologists argue that this is not due to society's restrictions on female sexuality but rather to biological function. For Wilson[5], orgasms serve two purposes: to tell the coital partners when to stop and to reward them for having begun intercourse. He argues that if women had orgasms as quickly as men, then coitus would be ended on 50% of occasions before male ejaculation, thus reducing the chances of conception. He suggests this behavioural difference is due to evolutionary pressure. A second argument comes from the work of cognitive psychologists. Traditionally, women are more adept at tasks involving the left cerebral hemisphere (verbal ability) and men at those involving the right cerebral hemisphere (spacial abilities). Third, differences in aggression have been found cross-culturally, with men tending to be more active and aggressive than women in most (but not all) societies. Fourth, there are several physiological differences at birth, male babies being heavier, taller, having higher metabolic rates and larger muscle-to-fat ratios. Finally, there are indications that prenatal exposure to the male hormone progestin (sometimes used to inhibit miscarriage) has an effect on later behaviour. Reinisch and Karlow[6] studied 16 boys and 10 girls whose mothers were given synthetic progestin during pregnancy. As compared with their siblings, they were more independent, more self-assured and more self-sufficient on a personality questionnaire measure. More evidence for the importance of hormones comes from a study on male pseudohermaphrodites born with a 5 α-reductase deficiency. Eighteen children who had female-appearing genetalia at birth were reared unambiguously as girls. At puberty, however, their male hormone levels increased naturally, and this resulted in the development of secondary sexual characteristics (a deeper voice, more hair, etc.). When studied as adults, 17 had transferred to a male gender identity and 16 to a male sex role. Their functioning seemed to depend on hormonal levels and not on previous environment[3]. These and other differences are taken to indicate that biology plays an important part in sex-typed behaviour.

Those who argue that sex roles are learned reject many of these arguments, believing instead that the observed differences between men and women are mainly due to parental and societal reactions to boys and girls. They, too, use evidence from several sources. Sociobiology, they say, provides an inadequate understanding of human sexual behaviour because, as suggested by Money's work on hermaphrodites, genetic and hormonal factors are open to environmental influence. The time women require to reach orgasm through masturbation is only slightly longer than men on average, suggesting more similarity in sexual response than some researchers have allowed. Similarly, some of the gender differences in cognitive functioning that have been well documented in the past are now beginning to fade in significance[7], a result that cannot be easily accounted for using a biological explanation. Cross-culturally, behaviour that is associated with men in some cultures has been found to be associated with women in others. For example, the Mundugmor women disliked childbearing and were as fierce and angry as the men; in the Tschambuli society, the men were given to adornment and gossip while the women showed comradely solidarity, were prone to hearty laughter and were responsible for food-gathering. Both the men and the women in the Arapesh society were expected to be gentle, sympathetic and non-aggressive[8].

Those who stress the importance of the environment have also pointed out an important aspect of statistical analysis: even when two populations are shown to differ significantly, there can be considerable overlap in scores between them. For example, one study found girls scored higher than boys on a test of creative thinking[9]. However, the scores are not dichotomous, as shown in Fig. 8.1: although the difference is significant statistically, the practical significance is debatable. It is not possible to predict the results on the basis of gender alone with great accuracy, since there is considerable overlap. Simply because two populations differ on average, does not preclude similarity between them.

Much of the work in this area concerns the differences in parental reactions to young boys and girls. Block[10] asked parents to agree or disagree with some statements. Parents of boys endorsed items such as 'I think a child should do better than others' whereas parents of girls tended to agree with items like 'I express affection by holding, hugging and kissing my child'. It seemed that boys were socialized along Protestant ethic lines, with an emphasis on achievement, competition and control of feelings, whereas girls were encouraged to develop close personal ties, to talk about problems and were given comfort and reassurance. Parents begin to describe the behaviour of their newborns along gender-stereotyped lines soon after birth. Girls are described as soft and fine-featured, whereas boys are seen as better co-ordinated, hardier and larger featured[11]. It may be, of course, that these differences do indeed exist in infants, so that this study alone is not adequate to show socialization differences. A better test of the hypothesis that adults react to and interpret infants' behaviour according to gender would be to lead adults to believe that the same infant was a boy or a girl

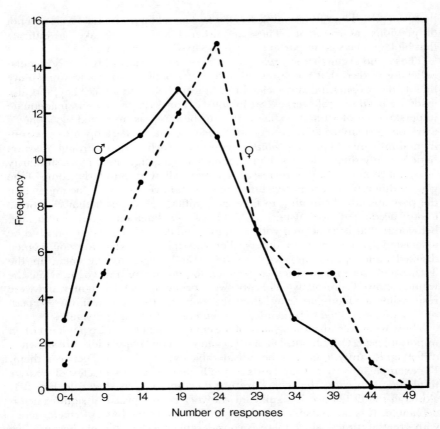

Fig. 8.1 Distributions of the scores for 60 boys and 60 girls on a test for creativity. Although the populations differ significantly, there is considerable overlap between their results. (Reproduced from R. Bhavnani and C. Hutt, *Journal of Psychology and Child Psychiatry*, 1972, 13, 121–127, by permission.)

and ask the adults to describe and play with the child. This research strategy has been followed in several studies. For example, in one experiment 200 students were shown a videotape of a 9-month-old infant. Half of the students were told that the infant was male, and half were told that the child was female. During the videotaped sequence, toys (a teddy bear and a jack-in-the-box) were presented to the infant and a loud buzzer sounded. The students' task was to describe the infant's responses to these occurrences. As predicted, the ascribed gender of the child affected the descriptions. Crying was usually perceived as anger in the 'male' child but as fear in the 'female', and the 'male' was seen as more potent and active. Apparently the students perceived what they expected to perceive. Other studies have shown that the toys adults choose to give to infants are similarly affected by ascribed sex. Interestingly, in some recent studies[12, 13], the findings have not been replicated, suggesting that socialization processes might be changing in this respect.

The different toys and reading materials actually received by children as presents have been examined. It seems that boys are given more vehicles, sports equipment and military machines than girls, who are likely to be provided with dolls, dolls' houses and domestic toys[14]. In a study of early school reading books, boy characters were portrayed as displaying more aggression, physical exertion and problem solving, whereas girl characters were more likely to engage in fantasy and to be obedient[15].

The problem here, as in the case of intelligence, is that it is difficult to disentangle the effects of nature and nurture. By the time differences in male and female behaviours can be distinguished in children, parental and societal influences are operating. Although girls as young as 12 weeks of age show greater attention to auditory stimuli than do boys, parents talk to girl infants of this age more than to boys. Is it the case that mothers talk more to their female infants because the girls are more interested and responsive? Or do girls become more responsive than boys because they are talked to more frequently?[16]. Although adults describe and play with 'male' infants differently than 'female' ones, is this due only to societal expectations, or have they found such differential behaviours to be effective in the past? The studies quoted above have been very short-term: would the subjects' descriptions and behaviours change with more contact?

Valuation of Sex Roles

Whatever the basis for the acquisition of sex-typed behaviour, many researchers have pointed out that male roles are more highly valued in Western society than female ones. Evidence for this proposition comes from many sources. One research strategy is to ask children which sex they would prefer to be: typically, more girls wish they could be boys than *vice versa*, one study finding a five-fold difference. In artistic and academic work, that done by men seems to be more highly valued than that done by women, independent of quality. Pheterson *et al.*[17] showed paintings to their subjects, crediting them to either male or female artists. When asked to evaluate the paintings, the subjects rated the 'men's' paintings higher than the 'women's' on such scales as technical competence and creativity. And it was only when the paintings were said to have won a prize were they evaluated equally. Similar results have been found with written materials. These results are all the more striking because the subjects in these experiments were female.

Success or failure at tasks also appears to have different meanings depending on the gender of the individual concerned. When attributing causes for success or failure, people often make a distinction between ability, task difficulty, luck and effort. Ability and effort are internal attributions, having to do with personality characteristics, whereas task difficulty and luck are seen to be outside the individual's control and are called external determinants. Thus, a student might blame failure in an exam to internal reasons (e.g. 'I didn't work hard enough') or to external ones ('The exam was too difficult'). The student might attempt to discover how classmates performed in order to make an attribution. When this analysis is applied to achievement and sex, some differences emerge in how people account for performance in men and women. In one study, subjects read a description of a highly successful doctor who volunteered for charity work while still in training, who increased the size of the practice and who was given an award as 'Doctor of the Year', the youngest person ever to have received it. Half the subjects were told that the physician was a man whereas the rest were told the physician was a woman, and all were asked to suggest why this doctor was so successful. Both male and female subjects considered that the woman physician worked harder than the man: to be equally successful, the woman physician would have to put more effort into her work. However, the reason why she would have to work harder was different for the male and female subjects. The males saw the woman as having less ability than the man, whereas the females perceived a greater task difficulty for her[18]. In a similar study, Feather and Simon[19] gave their subjects several statements that indicated that a man (or a woman) found himself at the top (or the bottom) of his class at medical school. They were then asked questions about the imagined reasons for this success or failure. In the condition where the woman succeeded, the subjects were more likely to attribute her success to an easy course than when the man succeeded. But when the man failed, this failure was seen as more likely to be due to the difficulty of the course than when the woman failed. Cheating was seen to be a less important cause when the man succeeded than when the woman succeeded. Moreover, when they were asked what they thought the future would hold for these students, the man was believed to be more likely to remain at the top of the class than the woman and less likely to continue at the bottom. It seems that the subjects in these experiments had different expectations of the performance of men and women, attributing different reasons for identical performances.

These studies rely on hypothetical situations rather than on actual observations of how men and women relate to one another. Perhaps a better test of the hypothesis that men and women have different status in Western society comes from analysis of conversations. A rather obvious, but important, feature of conversation is that only one person speaks at a time. A listener will usually wait until the speaker has finished before talking himself. There are some exceptions to this rule — interruptions — where the listener begins to talk before the speaker ends. Again, this is obvious, but it seems that interruptions are not randomly distributed between conversationalists, in that they are associated with status. Higher status individuals are more likely to interrupt than are those of lower status. So it may be that some measure of relative status can be gained by recording how two people talk to each other and counting the interruptions.

In studies of this kind, men interrupt women more often than *vice versa* (96% of the time in one investigation). This analysis has been applied to doctor –

patient communication as well. Since in the consulting room doctors are generally considered to have more power and status than their patients, an asymmetry in interruptions could be expected and, indeed, this has been found to be the case. An important qualification to this finding, however, is that the sex of the doctor is significant. One researcher who analysed consultations found that whereas male physicians contributed some 70% of the interruptions in their consultation with patients, female physicians initiated only 32%, even less when the patient was male[20]. If interruptions can be taken as a valid measure, then women doctors may either take on less status or be accorded less status by their patients than men.

Some writers have connected such differences in valuation with mental health. Women are more likely to request assistance for psychiatric difficulties in general than men, the ratio being 1.4:1, and where neuroses are concerned the ratio is even higher. They are more likely to be depressed, to suffer from suicidal thoughts and to attempt suicide, for example. Although this difference may be due simply to a greater likelihood of women expressing their difficulties (i.e. men may have as many problems but keep them to themselves), it has been argued that it is the way that women are valued that is responsible. In a society where tasks that require logical thinking and objectivity (the traditionally masculine qualities) are more highly valued than those requiring emotional support and warmth (traditionally feminine qualities), women may become depressed because their roles are undervalued. There is some evidence that levels of depression are determined by levels of self-esteem[21] and the cognitive psychologist Beck (Chapter 2) suggests that women have a culturally fostered tendency to see themselves as powerless and to undervalue their achievements[22]. This interpretation is supported by the research on the effects of employment on women: those who have a job are less likely to suffer depression, perhaps because employment heightens self-esteem (Nathanson[23] and Chapter 10).

It is possible also that physicians expect to find differences in symptomatology depending on the sex of the patient. Several studies have indicated that pharmaceutical advertisements have a strong effect on doctors' prescribing practices (see Chapter 12). Some have argued that the image of men and women put across by pharmaceutical companies has a similar effect, leading physicians to expect psychogenic symptoms to occur in women more frequently than in men. In an analysis of medical journals, advertisements for drugs aimed at psychogenic symptoms were predominantly illustrated with women, who were shown to be emotional, irrational and complaining. Advertisements for drugs for organic illness, on the other hand, predominantly depicted men, who tended to be non-emotional, stoic and rational (Ref. 24: see also Ref. 25). Although it is possible that such images may influence physicians' expectations of patients, there is little evidence to support this view. When clinicians were given short case histories said to be describing a man or a woman, no significant differences were found in the doctors' tendency to diagnose psychogenic versus organic problems. Regardless of ascribed sex, the problems (a headache or abdominal pains) were seen as being due to organic dysfunction[26].

195

There is an assumption in many people's minds that masculinity and femininity represent the ends of a single continuum. The ideal man might be considered assertive and instrumental, whereas women would be unassertive and passive. Women might be idealized as compassionate and expressive, whereas men would be low on these qualities. Women may be thought to be more dependent than men and less concerned with achievements. This model would place men and women on a single dimension: men would tend to fall at one end, women at the other. Although there are several stereotypes, few stand up to observational or experimental analysis[7].

Recently, psychologists have questioned the traditional assumption of a single dimension, exploring the possibility that masculinity and femininity are separate dimensions, each present in varying degrees in both men and women. In this model, the two dimensions are independent, so that an individual could score highly on both masculine and feminine characteristics, being both compassionate and assertive, for example. Such a person would be called 'psychologically androgynous' and would fall in quadrant A in Fig. 8.2. Someone who was high in masculine characteristics, but low in feminine ones would be termed masculine (quadrant B), and someone high in femininity and low in masculinity, termed feminine (quadrant C). Those who lie in the fourth quadrant (D) would be termed 'undifferentiated'.

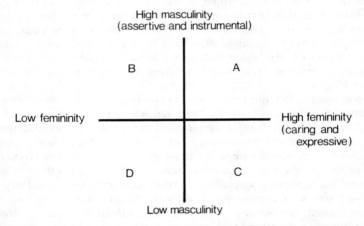

Fig. 8.2   In this model of masculinity and femininity, members of either gender can possess both masculine and feminine characteristics. The quadrants A, B, C and D are explained in the text.

There are now several self-report questionnaires designed to measure psychological androgyny. The Bem Sex Role Inventory (BSRI), for example, contains 20 items on each of the masculinity and femininity scales. The subject is asked to describe how well each item describes him or herself, placing an X where appropriate. An item on the masculine scale is:

Act as a leader

Never true – – – – – – – – Always true

and one on the femininity scale is

Affectionate

Never true – – – – – – – – Always true

An individual might answer near the 'Always true' end of both scales, and if many such items are endorsed, he or she would be considered androgynous. There is evidence that these individuals are more adaptable than those who are sex-typed, showing masculine or feminine behaviours depending on their appropriateness in different situations. An androgynous man is more likely to be nurturant (e.g. to smile, talk with and touch a baby or to show sympathy and understanding to a lonely person) than a masculine one, and an androgynous woman is more likely to resist social pressures to conform than a feminine one[27, 28]. Although there have been many criticisms of the concept of androgyny in general and the BSRI in particular[29, 30], the notion that individuals can be both masculine and feminine in behaviour and that this flexibility has advantages for adjustment has gained a firm foothold in psychology.

8.4   Sexual Behaviour

Clearly, there is a taboo in Western cultures about discussing sexuality and admitting to sexual problems. Although 60 – 70% of women and over 90% of men masturbate at some time (as reported in anonymous questionnaires and in-depth interviews), feelings of guilt abound. Similarly, although significant proportions of both men and women have homosexual experiences during their lives, being 'gay' continues to carry a social stigma. It has been argued that such behaviours are aberrant and a reflection of either immaturity or an abnormal upbringing, but this view has been questioned in recent years. One reason for this reconsideration is due to the work of cultural anthropologists — researchers who live with a tribe or society for several months or years and attempt to describe and explain their cultural patterns of behaviour. A cultural anthropologist might choose several aspects to focus upon. The beliefs of a people concerning the causes of a disease, the patterns of marriage and kinship (Chapter 9) or, relevant to the present chapter, sexuality might be described. Such studies illustrate the wide variety of sexual experiences that *homo sapiens* finds acceptable. Although homosexuality is abhorred in some cultures, it is accepted or encouraged in others[31, 32] for example. Meggit[33] describes the contrast between two cultures who have very different views about sexuality. In the Mae Enga tribe, men and women sleep apart, the men believe intercourse is debilitating and purify themselves afterwards, and bachelors swear sexual abstinence. The Mea Enga believe that contact with menstrual blood can cause

197

sickness and death. In contrast, the Kuma have a much less restrictive sexual code. Men and women share their sleeping quarters and girls select their sexual partners from both married and unmarried men. There are no taboos about intercourse during menstruation. Anthropologists often invoke economic reasons to explain their observations. For example, it has been suggested that the high population pressure experienced by the Mea Enga makes it necessary for there to be a mechanism that reduces the frequency of intercourse and thus limits fertility, whereas the Kuma have a relatively low population density[34]. The patterns of sexuality found in a culture may depend on the scarcity of resources to support the population.

Perhaps because of the taboos surrounding sexuality in the West, only recently have there been systematic attempts to describe and analyse sexual behaviour. Many of Freud's ideas reflected his cultural background, and his views on masturbation and the female orgasm have been severely criticized by many modern therapists. He considered many activities — such as homosexuality and the clitoral orgasm — to be due to a lack of progress through psychosexual stages and thus to be signs of immaturity. Alfred Kinsey is considered an important researcher because he sought to document the incidence of sexual behaviour in a large sample of people. By conducting in-depth interviews of some 18 000 individuals, he was able to show the mythological basis of many views of sexuality. For example, his results indicated that, to the apparent surprise of many, women can become sexually aroused quickly and enjoy and actively seek out sexual gratification. Two other important researchers are Masters and Johnson[35] who took detailed physiological measurements of male and female sexual arousal: they concluded that there are many similarities in the sexual responsiveness of men and women.

Despite these advances, there is a continuing difficulty in performing research on sexuality. The high refusal rates that investigators encounter attests to the embarrassment that people feel. Accordingly, many of the theories about sexuality are based on selected populations, often on those who present with sexual complaints, whereas relatively little is known about the rest of the population. It is not clear if ideas developed from therapy with patients are generally applicable. This is particularly problematic with sexual dysfunctions, but is also a problem with studies on abortion. Studies of contraceptive behaviour may also be biased in some ways, since the subjects in these studies are often university students.

Contraception

Most of the research on the use of contraceptives has concerned young unmarried women, with relatively few studies on adolescent men. This seems to be because the lives of these women are particularly likely to be disrupted if they become pregnant. Teenage girls have a higher incidence of obstetric complications during pregnancy than women in their twenties, which could be due to physiological immaturity or to extrinsic social factors, such as lack of prenatal care or heightened anxiety. There is also a greater risk of prematurity in infants

198

born to young mothers. In one study, 15 % of all infants born to women under 15 years of age weighed 2500 grams or less, 9 % to 19-year-olds, and 7 % to 20 – 25 years olds. There is also evidence that adolescent pregnancy is associated with long-term effects on both the mother and the father. In a large-scale survey, men and women who became parents while teenagers were compared with a group similar in socioeconomic status, IQ and age at marriage who did not have a child so early. At 5 and at 11 years after the birth, there were several clear differences in educational attainment. Only one-fifth of the women who gave birth before the age of 18 had completed secondary school, compared with three-quarters of the remaining women. Only 3 % of those who had a child before the age of 20 had completed university before the age of 29, compared to some 12 % of the control group. The younger mothers were also more likely to have less prestigious jobs, to have lower incomes and to be less satisfied with their jobs. Marital and fertility patterns were also different in the two groups, with the young parents having more children than planned and a higher incidence of divorce and separation. Of course, it is not possible to assign causality here, since early parenthood might be a symptom rather than a cause of difficulty.

There is little systematic evidence supporting the proposition that women who become pregnant at a young age are psychiatrically disturbed[36]. Any indication of psychopathology that might be discovered could just as easily be the result of the pregnancy and society's reactions to it. Other researchers have attempted to understand why effective contraceptives had not been employed. At first sight, the use of contraceptives appears to be a relatively simple operation, but in fact it requires a series of complex and difficult decisions. There must first be some prior awareness that sexual intercourse may soon occur. If it is not expected, it is unlikely that contraceptive precautions will be taken, perhaps accounting for the 50 % of women who report they did not take any precautions at their first intercourse. Second, there must be some public behaviour by one of the partners in order to acquire a contraceptive, which appears to be difficult for some. This difficulty has led to a debate about whether parents should be informed by physicians about their young daughter's requests for contraceptives, an issue involving questions of confidentiality. In this context it is important to note that there is little evidence that women become indiscriminate in their sexual behaviour after beginning to use the pill. There may, of course, be a reluctance to report more sexual partners, but Reichelt[37] found that the young women in one clinic claimed to have exactly the same number of partners 1 year after the initial prescription as before (the mean was 1.1 at both times). A third important decision about contraceptives is that they must be used consistently in order to be effective. For many methods, a fresh choice must be made on every occasion. Because there are so many steps involved, contraceptive use may break down at any one of several points. Using this analysis, it may be possible to determine the reason for contraceptive failure more accurately and make intervention more effective[38].

Another research approach has explored the personality characteristics of contraceptive users and non-users. A personality questionnaire that gained great popularity during the 1970s was the Locus of Control questionnaire. Earlier in the chapter the idea that people give different reasons for events was mentioned: the causes of an event could be external (luck and task difficulty) or internal (ability and effort) or a mix of the two. The Locus of Control questionnaire was designed to measure the extent to which an individual used internal or external attributions to explain events. A person with an internal locus of control has an expectation that he or she will be able to control the environment, either through ability or effort. Someone with an external locus of control expectation would tend to believe that outcomes are not contingent on personal qualities but rather on outside influences, such as luck. An example of an item on this questionnaire is the following:

'If you get on in the world it's because you're lucky'
Strongly Agree – – – – – – – – Strongly Disagree

The person is asked to place an 'X' somewhere between the two extremes to indicate strength of agreement with one or the other. Those who tend to disagree with this kind of item but agree with statements suggesting that ability and effort are important would be termed 'internals', and others who show the opposite tendency would be termed 'externals'.

This personality questionnaire has been shown to distinguish between contraceptive users and non-users. Lundy[39] asked 600 university students about their sexual behaviour and their use of contraceptives, and gave them the Locus of Control questionnaire. Concentrating on those who were sexually active, no significant age or social-class differences were found, but the contraceptive users were more internal than non-users. This result suggests that contraceptive use has something to do with a sense of control over the future, an indication supported by other studies (e.g. Steinlauf[40]). Another study compared couples who began to use contraceptives before their first pregnancy (early users) with couples who began to use them after the first pregnancy (late users). After controlling for socioeconomic status (which is an important variable — it seems that lower-income individuals have less confidence in any method), the early users reported greater emphasis on education and long-term goals. They had more faith in the future being predictable and were more willing to sacrifice short-term goals than the late users[41]. Incidentally, locus of control has been implicated in a wide range of health-related behaviours, with internals more likely to take a variety of preventative measures than externals[42].

The evidence concerning the importance of side-effects in the rejection of some contraceptive methods is not consistent. Although nausea, vomiting and depression are sometimes cited as reasons for abandoning the pill, it is not clear if these reports are due to pharmacological activity or to negative expectations about oral contraceptives. By including an inert substance condition in contraception studies (the women were asked to take additional precautions as well) some researchers have concluded that the complaints are psychogenic[43], whereas others have concluded otherwise[44]. In this context, it is interesting to point out the discrepancies between the effectiveness of contraceptive methods in clinical trials and in the general population. The condom has failed in 1 – 3 %

of clinical populations, but in 10 - 20% of the general population; the IUD 1 - 5% clinically, but 2 - 25% of users spontaneously expel it; the pill should fail in only 0.1 - 0.5% of cases theoretically, but fails in 4 - 7% of cases in practice. Simply because a method is effective in clinical trials does not mean it will be equally effective in widespread use.

Abortion

Studies on the psychological effects of abortion are plagued with methodological problems. In the main, this is due to lack of control groups on the one hand and poor measurement on the other. In order to assess the effects of abortion, it is important to take into account, first, whether or not the pregnancy was wanted — not all women who have an abortion have unwanted pregnancies (e.g. those whose pregnancies are terminated for genetic reasons) and not all women with unwanted pregnancies seek an abortion — and second, whether a request for abortion is refused — in answering questions about the effects of abortion, women (and their children) whose requests had been turned down as well as those whose requests had been granted need to be studied. Measurement is also poor in most abortion studies: estimates of disturbance are usually taken by one individual who knows the history of the women involved, so that judgements may be coloured by prior expectations. Only if the assessments are performed 'blind' (perhaps through the use of questionnaires) and in a way that is reliable, can the possible effects of observer bias be discounted.

Early reports on abortion often employed no control groups, relying mainly on psychiatrists' observations[45]. Prospective studies are rare, but they suggest that early termination of pregnancy has little adverse effect on most women[46]. There are nevertheless exceptions. Some women are distressed after abortion and this has led to attempts to identify them beforehand. In two recent studies, women were interviewed when they first requested an abortion and then followed up over the next few months. In one study[47] women who had a history of psychological and social instability, who had poor or no family ties and who had few friends, were found to be disturbed. In the other[48], lack of intimacy with the male partner and ambivalence about the decision to have an abortion were two variables that distinguished the women who became distressed from those who did not. Much more work needs to be done before firm conclusions can be drawn.

Women who have terminations because of diagnosis of genetic abnormality also seem to be 'at risk'. Donnai et al.[49] interviewed 12 women who had an abortion for this reason. Although all showed strain at the time of the interview, emotional recovery was considered to be good for seven of the women, fair for three of the women and poor for the remaining two women at 7 and 10 months after termination. The findings led the authors to change their clinical practice in similar cases, ensuring that a health visitor contacts the women while in hospital and offers future support.

In a long-term study (over 15 years), 90 children of women whose applications for abortion were refused were compared with 90 children of the same sex born in the ward at about the same time. The mothers were matched for age, parity and social class. The initially unwanted children were more likely to have an unmarried mother, to be born into a family where divorce occurred and to do less well at school than the wanted children. There was also evidence that they were more likely to have psychosomatic symptoms (headaches, stomach aches, etc.) and to be referred to a school psychiatrist[50]. Although these differences between groups were statistically significant, it should be noted that there were several other measures on which no differences were found: many of the unwanted children had satisfactory intellectual achievement and social adjustment, for example.

Several factors seem to affect the decision whether or not to grant an abortion. Religious and moral beliefs, rape, the possibility of a deformed child and danger to the mother's physical or mental health are all relevant. It is possible that an abortion is sometimes granted as a reward for conscientious contraceptive use or refused on the basis of irresponsibility. These possibilities were tested by giving subjects short case histories of women who had become pregnant and wanted an abortion. In order to give the experiment some real-life validity, the subjects were asked to imagine that they were members of a board that sat to consider abortion applications that included other members of the community. They were asked to read the case histories and to indicate whether they were in favour of or against granting the request. The histories were systematically varied in content: some women were said to have a casual relationship with the father, and others had a steady and involved one; some women were said to have become pregnant because of personal failure (e.g. not preparing for intercourse by forgetting to take contraceptives on a camping trip), whereas others had become pregnant because the method failed. The subjects in the study were more strongly in favour of granting an abortion when the conception was due to a failure of the method than when it was due to a failure of the person to use the method consistently, and when the relationship was steady than when it was casual. These results are interesting, because they show the subjects were more likely to confer motherhood on those women who were less able to plan their pregnancy and less likely to have the emotional support of the father. It was as if requests were withheld in order to punish inconsistent use of contraceptives and the less socially acceptable behaviour of having several sexual partners[51].

Sexual Dysfunction

The incidence of sexual dysfunction is difficult to estimate for several reasons. One concerns definition: a condition that presents a problem for one couple may not be a problem for another. Even if a definition could be agreed upon, a second difficulty is that people are reticent in disclosing their sexual patterns. Simply asking people about their sexual behaviour is unlikely to give an accurate picture: it would be surprising, for example, if a man in our society were as willing to volunteer the information that, say, he ejaculates prematurely as to volunteer that he has diabetes. Canvassing physicians for estimates on the basis on their experience seems to provide no better indication. When this was done in one study, there was a great range in the percentage of patients who presented with a sexual problem. As expected, physicians in some specialities (such as general practice and obstetrics) reported a higher incidence than others. But even within specialities there was a wide range of reported rates, from 1 to 60% in general practice, depending on the doctor canvassed. When the investigators attempted to understand this range, they found that characteristics of the doctors themselves were significant. Those physicians who routinely asked about sexual problems reported twice as many patients with sexual difficulties as those who did not, whereas doctors who were observed to be embarrassed while talking about sexual histories (as shown by blushing and fidgeting) had rates some five times lower than those who did not show such embarrassment. It seems that the willingness of patients to disclose and of physicians to inquire was associated with the doctors' own feelings about sexuality[52].

The sexual problems faced by the chronically ill and the handicapped are often significant in their lives. Those who have had a severe illness, such as myocardial infarction, are often unsure about the risks of sexual intercourse, even though the physiological 'cost' of coitus is comparatively modest. Attempts to counsel both the patient and the spouse have become common, reflecting the recognition of an important gap in caregiving. As might be expected from the research on the sick role (Chapter 6), the pattern of sexual activity in myocardial infarction patients bears little relationship to age or to severity of the attack: rather it depends almost entirely on the patient's and spouse's attitudes and fears[53]. Often, simply bringing these fears out into the open provides successful treatment.

One of the problems with research concerning the effects of illness on sexual functioning is that few investigators have inquired about the level of functioning *before* the onset of the disease. Even though there seems to be a high incidence of dysfunction after, say, myocardial infarction, causality cannot be attributed. It is possible that the kinds of people who suffer infarction are also the kind of people who have sexual difficulties. There is some evidence that this is so. Wabrek and Burchell[54] interviewed 131 patients about their previous sexual problems: two-thirds indicated difficulties before the infarction, two-thirds of these showing impotence. It may be that there is a cluster of symptoms associated with MI that includes sexual difficulties as well as competitive striving (see Chapter 2), but until the rates of impotence have been compared with those in the general population this remains hypothetical.

The psychological consequences of mastectomy have also received greater attention recently with the implications of less radical surgery being explored. Although there is a lack of controlled studies in this area — the usual approach is to interview women about their feelings and experiences — it would be surprising if this operation did not have an effect on sexual anxieties. In one study, almost a third of mastectomy patients who had had satisfactory sexual relations before the operation lost interest or ceased to enjoy them afterwards[55]. In another study, all of the 41 women approached showed an interest in psychological assistance. Once the immediate prospect of death had passed, practically without exception sexual concerns dominated their thinking. Sexual attractiveness was of central importance to their emotional functioning, and a major fear was that their partners would leave them. Counselling was found to be appropriate and useful[56].

People may have sexual problems arising from less obvious causes. Masters and Johnson outlined a learning theory approach to sexual difficulties. Their book, *Human sexual inadequacy*[57], published in 1970, has provided an important contribution to sexual therapy. They suggest that through cultural prohibitions or familial admonitions the naturally occurring growth of sexual skills is in some way inhibited. These past experiences are said to thwart sexual expression and increase fears of performance. Once the fear of failure has been aroused, the dysfunction operates in a vicious circle. For the man who is unable to attain an erection, his anxieties serve to interfere with the natural cycle of sexual arousal and are thus confirmed. The relationship with the sexual partner is also affected; as her concern is increased, she too is unable to enjoy her own sexuality.

Masters and Johnson's therapy is essentially an attempt to break this pattern. They seek to remove the goal-orientated basis of many of their patients' sexual encounters. Fear of performance is important, they reason, only if the partners are attempting to reach a goal of some kind, usually orgasm. If this goal is no longer required, they would then have the opportunity to respond spontaneously to the emotions and pleasures of physical sensation. Their technique for accomplishing this is termed 'sensate focus'. The therapists place a ban on intercourse for the first few days of therapy so that neither partner need fear failure. Each is instructed to give and receive sessions of gentle, non-sexually stimulating touch, for as long as both partners find it pleasurable. Sensate focus serves two purposes. First, as the name implies, it focuses the partners' attention on the physical sensations of their encounter, rather than on the fears that physical contact often engendered in the past. The second purpose of sensate focus exercises is to emphasize the importance of accurate communication between the partners. While indicating to each other which kinds of touch are pleasurable, the channels of sensory communication are being opened. Indeed, Masters and Johnson see their role primarily as catalysts to communication. For them, sexual dysfunction indicates that the most important channel of communication is disrupted, and sensate focus is designed to encourage the partners to share and understand each other's needs.

Accordingly, Masters and Johnson stress the importance of involving both partners. They do not consider it useful to treat one partner in isolation, since they see any form of sexual inadequacy as essentially a problem of mutual involvement. Because communication between partners is so significant, it would not be appropriate to treat only the person with the presenting difficulty. In fact:

> The marital relationship is considered as the patient . . . sexual dysfunction is indeed a marital-unit problem, certainly never only a wife's or a husband's personal concern. (Ref. 57 p. 3)

204

The focus on the relationship is aided by the use of co-therapists — one man and one woman. This has several advantages. The therapists can model a successful open relationship, where caring and reciprocity is shown. Each therapist can act as a kind of translator for the same-sex patient as they try to express their concerns and fears. The chances of a single therapist being too sympathetic to one partner at the expense of the other partner are reduced. Finally, the co-therapist who is not involved in an exchange has the opportunity to observe and then comment upon the situation, perhaps providing insights which an active therapist would not perceive. Masters and Johnson stress the necessity for therapists to have resolved their own feelings about sexuality before attempting work of this kind. This emphasis on self-examination applies to psychotherapeutic work in general, as discussed in Chapter 2.

The general format of education, discussion and sensate focus is followed for all patients with the next steps in the treatment programme depending on the particular type of dysfunction. However, the question of defining sexual dysfunction remains. Many objective measures (e.g. time taken to have an orgasm) do not seem adequate: if a couple is content with a given level of functioning it would not seem appropriate to diagnose dysfunction. For example, up to 25% of women may be non-orgasmic, but nevertheless report that they enjoy sex. Rather, it is defined in terms of the needs of the partners. A couple is said to be having difficulties if they are not satisfied with their sexual relationship.

Masters and Johnson's success rates are very high compared to many forms of psychological therapy with over 80% of difficulties being resolved. One criticism that has been levelled at their work was that they were highly selective about which couples were offered treatment. There was a sizable financial commitment, the couples had to be very highly motivated and it is possible these people were unrepresentative of the type of couple generally seeking assistance. In the last decade there have been several calls for increased flexibility in sex therapy. Some researchers have found good results using one therapist instead of two and by using other methods such as systematic desensitization (see Chapter 3). As greater experience is gained, methods can be expected to improve and to be more readily available to general practitioners. A notable contributor to these developments is Helen Kaplan[58] who has attempted to integrate the psychotherapeutic approach with the behavioural one. Whereas for Masters and Johnson the presenting sexual difficulty is seen to be the real problem, Kaplan considers the possibility that it could be an indication of another underlying problem, such as marital discord or depression. Seen in this way, sexual dysfunction would be treated within the larger context of the marital relationship.

Summary

One of our most basic attributes is our sense of gender identity. Although this may appear to be entirely biologically determined, studies have shown that environmental factors can have a strong effect on whether individuals see themselves as male or female. Sex roles refer to the activities which are expected of a person on the basis of their sex, men expected to be assertive and logical, women expressive and warm, for instance. Like gender identity, there is some controversy over the extent to which sex roles are innately determined or created by environmental influences: certainly, there is considerable variation in sex-linked behaviours cross-culturally and people treat even small babies differently on the basis of their sex. In Western society, male roles are generally more highly valued and attempts have been made to link this with women's greater susceptibility to psychological problems. Although masculinity and femininity have traditionally been seen as opposite ends of the same dimension, the view that they are independent factors, such that it is possible to have some characteristics of both (psychological androgyny) is gaining popularity.

Sexual practices vary widely both between and within cultures. Recent studies have attempted to dispel myths and misconceptions about sexual activities. Analysis of contraceptive use has shown several decision points at which effectiveness can break down and has isolated certain personality characteristics (internal locus of control) associated with contraceptive users. Attempts to study the effects of abortion indicate that, although early termination of pregnancy generally has little adverse psychological effect on most women, it can still be useful to isolate factors that identify those women who do experience difficulties.

The incidence of sexual dysfunction is difficult to establish through the reticence both of patients to tell and of their doctors to ask. Some illnesses and operations can lead to sexual difficulties, and psychological assistance may be valuable. Sexual dysfunctions can be successfully treated through therapy which views the problems as learned difficulties and suggests new, appropriate behaviours.

Suggested Reading

R. Unger, *Female and male*, Harper and Row, London, 1979, reviews much of the research on sex roles, taking mainly an environmental position. As an introduction to sexual medicine, E. Trimmer, *Basic sexual medicine*, Heinemann Medical Books, London, 1978, is useful. The January 1982 number of the *British Journal of Psychiatry* includes several reports from a symposium on sexual dysfunction covering different treatment approaches.

References

1. Leiblum, S.R. and Pervin, L.A. (eds.), *Principles and practice of sex therapy*, Tavistock Publications, London, 1980.
2. Money, J. and Ehrhardt, A.A., *Man and woman: boy and girl*, Johns Hopkins University Press, Baltimore, 1972.
3. Imperato-McGinley, J., Peterson, R.E., Gautier, T. and Sturla, E., Androgens and the evolution of male gender identity among male pseudohermaphrodites with 5 α-reductase deficiency, *New England Journal of Medicine*, 1979, **300**, 1233 – 1237.

4. Money, J., Ablatio penis: normal male infant sex-reassigned as a girl, *Archives of Sexual Behaviour*, 1975, **4**, 65 – 71.
5. Wilson, G., The sociobiology of sex differences *Bulletin of the British Psychological Society*, 1979, **32**, 350 – 353.
6. Reinisch, J.M. and Karlow, W.G., Prenatal exposure to synthetic progestins and estrogens, *Archives of Sexual Behaviour*, 1977, **6**, 257 – 288.
7. Maccoby, E.E. and Jacklin, C.N., *The psychology of sex differences*, Stanford University Press, Stanford, 1974.
8. Mead, M., *Sex and temperament in three societies*, Mentor, New York, 1950.
9. Bhavnani, R. and Hutt, C., Divergent thinking in boys and girls, *Journal of Child Psychology and Psychiatry*, 1972, **13**, 121 – 127.
10. Block, J.H. Conceptions of sex role, *American Psychologist*, 1973, **28**, 512 – 526.
11. Rubin, J.Z., Provenzano, F.J. and Luria, Z., The eye of the beholder, *American Journal of Orthopsychiatry*, 1974, **44**, 512 – 519.
12. Zucker, K.J. and Corter, C.M., Sex-stereotyping in adult-infant interaction, *American Journal of Orthopsychiatry*, 1980, **50**, 160 – 164.
13. Bell, N.J. and Carver, W., A reevaluation of gender label effects, *Child Development* 1980, **51**, 925 – 927.
14. Rheingold, H.L. and Cook, K.V., The contents of boys' and girls' rooms as an index of parents' behaviour, *Child Development*, 1975, **46**, 459 – 463.
15. Saario, T.N., Jacklin, C.N. and Tittle, C.K., Sex role stereotyping in the public schools, *Harvard Educational Review*, 1973, **43**, 386 – 416.
16. Lewis, M. and Weinraub, M., Origins of sex-role development, *Sex Roles*, 1979, **5**, 135 – 153.
17. Pheterson, G.I., Kiesler, S.B. and Goldberg, P.A., Evaluation of the performance of women as a function of their sex, achievement and personal history, *Journal of Personality and Social Psychology*, 1971, **19**, 114 – 118.
18. Feldman-Summers, S. and Kiesler, S.B., Those who are number two try harder, *Journal of Personality and Social Psychology*, 1974, **30**, 846 – 855.
19. Feather, N.T. and Simon, J.G., Reactions to male and female success and failure in sex-linked occupations, *Journal of Personality and Social Psychology*, 1975, **31**, 20 – 31.
20. West, C., When the doctor is a 'lady' *In* Stromberg, A. (ed.), *Women, health and medicine* Mayfield, Palo Alto, 1980.
21. Wilson, A.R. and Krane, R.V., Change in self-esteem and its effects on symptoms of depression, *Cognitive Therapy and Research*, 1980, **4**, 419 – 421.
22. Beck, A.T. and Greenberg, R.L., Cognitive therapy with depressed women, *In* Franks, V. and Burtle, V. (eds.), *Women in therapy*, Brunner/Mazel, New York, 1974.
23. Nathanson, C.A., Sex, illness and medical care, *Social Science and Medicine*, 1977, **11**, 13 – 25.
24. Prather, J. and Findell, L.S., Sex differences in the content and style of medical advertisements, *Social Science and Medicine*, 1975, **9**, 23 – 27.
25. Thompson, E.L., Sexual bias in drug advertisements, *Social Science and Medicine*, 1979, **13A**, 187 – 191.
26. McCranie, E.W., Horowitz, A.J. and Martin, R.M., Alleged sex-role stereotyping in the assessment of women's physical complaints, *Social Science and Medicine*, 1978, **12**, 111 – 116.
27. Bem, S.L., The measurement of psychological androgyny, *Journal of Consulting and Clinical Psychology*, 1974, **42**, 155 – 162.

28. Bem, S.L., Martyna, W. and Watson, C., Sex-typing and androgyny, *Journal of Personality and Social Psychology*, 1976, **34**, 1016 - 1023.

29. Kelly, J.A., Furman, W. and Young, V., Problems associated with the typological measurement of sex roles and androgyny, *Journal of Consulting and Clinical Psychology*, 1978, **46**, 1574 - 1576.

30. Pedhazur, E.J. and Tetenbaum, T.J., Bem Sex Role Inventory: a theoretical and methodological criticism, *Journal of Personality and Social Psychology*, 1979, **37**, 996 - 1016.

31. Evans-Pritchard, E.E., Sexual inversion among the Azande, *American Anthropologist*, 1970, **72**, 1428 - 1433.

32. Marshall, D.S. and Suggs, R.C. (eds.), *Human sexual behaviour*, Prentice-Hall, Englewood Cliffs, 1971.

33. Meggit, M., Male-female relationships in the highlands of Australian New Guinea, *American Anthropologist*, 1964, **66**, 204 - 224.

34. Sexton, L., Sexual interaction and population pressure in Highland New Guinea, Paper presented to the *22nd Annual meeting of the American Psychological Association*, New Orleans, 1973.

35. Masters, W.H. and Johnson, V.E., *Human sexual response*, Churchill Livingstone, London, 1966.

36. Shaffer, D., Pettigrew, A., Wolkind, S. and Zajicek, E., Psychiatric aspects of pregnancy in schoolgirls, *Psychological Medicine*, 1978, **8**, 119 - 130.

37. Reichelt, P.A., Changes in sexual behaviour among unmarried teenage women utilizing oral contraception, *Journal of Population*, 1978, **1**, 57 - 68.

38. Byrne, D., Jazwinski, C., DeNinno, J.A. and Fisher, W.A., Negative sexual attitudes and contraception, *In* Byrne, D. and Byrne, L.A. (eds.), *Explaining human sexuality* Harper and Row, New York, 1977.

39. Lundy, J.R., Some personality correlates of contraceptive use among unmarried female college students, *Journal of Psychology*, 1972, **80**, 9 - 14.

40. Steinlauf, B., Problem-solving skills, locus of control and the contraceptive effectiveness of young women, *Child Development*, 1979, **50**, 268 - 271.

41. Kar, S.B., Individual aspirations as related to early and late acceptance of contraception *Journal of Social Psychology*, 1971, **83**, 235 - 245.

42. Strickland, B.R., Internal-external expectancies and health-related behaviours *Journal of Consulting and Clinical Psychology*, 1978, **46**, 1192 - 1212.

43. Goldzieher, J.W., Moses, L.E., Averkin, E., Scheel, C. and Taber, B.Z., Nervousness and depression attributed to oral contraceptives, *American Journal of Obstetrics and Gynaecology*, 1971, **111**, 1013 - 1020.

44. Grounds, D., Davies, B. and Mowbray, R., The contraceptive pill, side effects and personality, *British Journal of Psychiatry*, 1970, **116**, 169 - 172.

45. Ekblad, M., Induced abortion on psychiatric grounds, *Acta Psychiatrica and Neurologica Scandinavia* (Supplement **99**), 1955, 1 - 238.

46. Gillis, A., A follow-up of 72 cases referred for abortion, *Mental Health in Society*, 1975, **2**, 212 - 218.

47. Belsey, E.M., Greer, H.S., Lal, S., Lewis, S.C., and Beard, R.W., Predictive factors in emotional responses to abortion, *Social Science and Medicine*, 1977, **11**, 71 - 82.

48. Shusterman, L.S., Predicting the psychological consequences of abortion, *Social Science and Medicine*, 1979, **13A**, 683 - 689.

49. Donnai, P., Charles, N. and Harris, R., Attitudes of patients after 'genetic' termination of pregnancy, *British Medical Journal*, 1981, **282**, 621 - 622.

50. Blomberg, S., Influence of maternal distress during pregnancy on postnatal development, *Acta Psychiatrica Scandinavia*, 1980, **62**, 405 – 417.
51. Allgeier, E.R., Allgeier, A.R. and Rywick, T., Abortion: reward for conscientious contraceptive use?, *Journal of Sex Research*, 1979, **15**, 64 – 75.
52. Burnap, D.W. and Golden, J.S., Sexual problems in medical practice, *Journal of Medical Education*, 1967, **42**, 673 – 680.
53. Rubin, I., Sexual adjustments in relation to pregnancy, illness, surgery, physical handicaps and other unusual circumstances, *In* Vincent, C.E. (ed.), *Human sexuality in medical education and practice*, Charles C. Thomas, Springfield, 1968.
54. Wabrek, A.J. and Burchell, R.C., Male sexual dysfunction associated with coronary heart disease, *Archives of Sexual behaviour*, 1980, **9**, 69 – 75.
55. Maguire, G.P., Lee, E.O., Bevington, D.J., Kucheman, C.S., Crabtree, R.J. and Cornell, C.E., Psychiatric problems in the first year after mastectomy, *British Medical Journal*, 1978, **1**, 963 – 965.
56. Witkin, M.H., Psychosexual counselling of the mastectomy patient, *Journal of Sexual and Marital Therapy*, 1978, **4**, 20 – 28.
57. Masters, W. and Johnson, V., *Human sexual inadequacy*, Little Brown, Boston, 1970.
58. Kaplan, H.S., *The new sex therapy*, Penguin, Harmondsworth, 1978.

9
Family Dynamics

9.1 Introduction

Although the family group is usually responsible for biological reproduction, it also plays a significant role in what can be termed 'social reproduction'. Many illustrations of this function have been given in previous chapters, particularly those on intelligence (Chapter 5) and the previous two on parent – child interaction and psycho-sexual development. It is through relationships with parents or caregivers that a child acquires much knowledge about him or herself and about the customs and expectations of society. The transmission of cultural information is not unique to *homo sapiens*: similar processes have been identified through observations of chimpanzees' behaviour.

Just as there are several ways in which the culture influences an individual, so, too, does each family have an effect. Within each family group, there will be several rules that are shared with the larger culture, but also many that are not. There may be taboos about discussing certain topics, for example, or certain accepted ways of dealing with conflicts. In one family, a conflict may escalate into violence, in another discussion may occur, and in a third the participants may avoid contact. Since children learn much through instruction by and observation of their parents, there is the possibility that intergenerational continuities arise in many spheres: children may grow up to use methods of coping with difficulties that are similar to those of their parents'. They may come to treat their children in the way that they themselves were treated when

210

young, or may create a relationship with their spouse similar to their parents' relationship. Reliable evidence of such a possibility is difficult to obtain because it often draws on people's memories of past events, memories that may change over time (Chapter 4). When cross-sectional studies are used, environmental changes may obscure any continuities. However, certain immediate factors have been shown to be related to such family problems as marital disharmony and child abuse. Awareness of the characteristics of such families may assist professional helpers to understand such problems and also to predict which families might be 'at risk'. Some of the variables associated with family discord are examined in the second half of this chapter, and ways of dealing with them, through family therapy, are also considered.

One specific sphere of family influence concerns illness. Most obviously, as a group of people living in close proximity with each other, it could be a source of disease. There is always the risk of contagion between members, for example, where infections are concerned. The implications of family life for psychiatric illness are more difficult to discern. There is evidence for both genetic and social influences in schizophrenia, and it is difficult to ascertain their relative importance. Another way in which the family can affect illness is in taking preventive measures. As well as transmitting societal norms and values, each individual family can be seen as a kind of subculture, with its own set of idiosyncratic ways of coping with illness. Some place more emphasis on prevention than others. The importance of good nutrition or views about the necessity of regular visits to the dentist are but two examples. The decision to consult the doctor is often taken within the family context. It seems that some families are more likely to consult than others, so in this sense the family can be involved in the recovery from illness (Chapter 6).

9.2 Family Systems

The contributions made by cultural anthropologists have been mentioned in earlier chapters. One notable aspect of their work is the observation of family systems in various cultures. There are several ways in which these systems can be described. Some anthropologists have placed emphasis on inheritance rights: is the parents' wealth equally distributed between all the children, amongst the sons only, or, as in some agricultural societies, is the farm passed on to the youngest son? When a son or daughter marries, does the couple live near the man's parents, the woman's, or are there no set rules about this? By describing societies in these ways, anthropologists have pointed out the wide range of customs open to and used by mankind.

There is a standard way of portraying family systems, as shown in Fig. 9.1. This illustrates a *nuclear* family comprising two parents and four children. The parents are represented by the circle (woman) and triangle (man) joined by a marriage bond, which is universally institutionalized in some form. The degree of ritual involved in forming this bond differs both between and within cultures. Sometimes it is accompanied by an important ceremony, at other times by

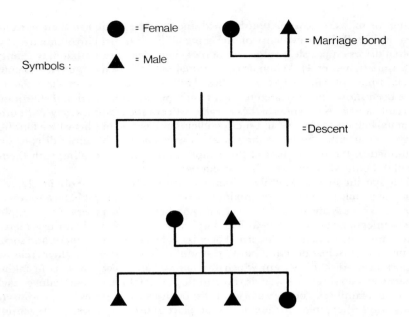

Symbols : ● = Female   ▲ = Male

● ▲ = Marriage bond

= Descent

Fig. 9.1   The nuclear family. A man and a woman are linked by a marriage bond and have four descendants.

simple agreement. So, too, does the strength of the bond vary. Divorce can involve complicated legal procedures or a simple statement on one partner's side that he or she wishes to end the obligation. When anthropologists use the term marriage they do not necessarily mean it in the way it is used in Western cultures. Rather, it is simply a socially recognized bond with obligations. It is likely that marriage, as a universal custom, has to do with the legitimization of parenthood (so the society knows to whom which children belong) rather than the legitimization of sexual relationships themselves. Fig. 9.1 also portrays the descent of three boys and one girl from these parents. Generally, the children live in the same household as the parents. There are some exceptions to this rule — such as Israeli kibbutzim[1] — but these are very rare. Even in kibbutzim there is an increasing trend for the children to live with their biological parents.

This virtually universal family system forms the basis of much anthropological research. Using this nuclear family as a basis, a wide variety of cultural customs can be described. One way in which they can be portrayed is in terms of the number of generations living together. In the independent nuclear family — common in the West — only two generations live together, the parents and their children. In this system, marriage ties are seen to be more important than blood ties — i.e. the couple's first obligation is to each other rather than to their parents. This type of family is short-lived (20 – 25 years), lasting only until the children leave home to begin their own nuclear families. It is found in both basic

212

and highly complex societies, where mobility is important. In the *extended* family system, more than one nuclear family live together in the same household. As pictured in Fig. 9.2, two nuclear families live together with the woman joining the male in his parents' household. This type of family can become very large, often including several generations, and be long lasting. Found predominantly in agricultural societies, it emphasizes blood-ties: the first obligations are to blood relatives and the marital obligations are relatively weak. Although the independent nuclear family system has been held responsible for many difficulties in Western cultures (e.g. parents can be isolated from familial assistance when rearing children), the extended family also has problems. The individual who marries into the extended family can feel isolated, and their interests are subordinate to those of individuals in the blood line. This analysis can be applied to our society; for example the kinship relations of East London residents were described in these terms by Young and Willmott[2]. Their evidence confirmed the view that there was a marked tendency toward matri-locality in the English working classes (i.e. when a couple married they tended to live near the woman's family of origin). Further, for family gatherings, the operative family was the wife's — the husband joined his wife's family as a kind of associate member. A variation of the extended family is the *joint* family, found in India. Here, the men and their wives stay in the family home until younger siblings are educated and married, at which time the wealth is divided up and the nuclear families become independent. In this system, the tie between brothers is particularly strong.

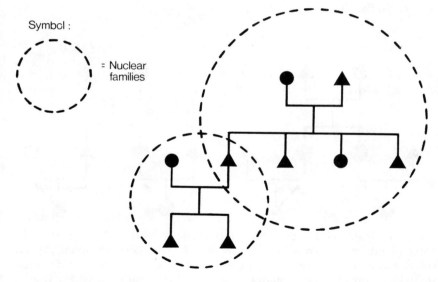

Fig. 9.2 The extended family. Three generations (two nuclear families) living in the same household.

Another way of describing family systems is in terms of the number of spouses that are socially acceptable. In the West the rule is monogamy, but only a minority of societies have a definite restriction on this. In most, *polygamy* is acceptable, in that there are no sanctions against having more than one spouse. There are two types of polygamy: *polygyny* (more than one wife for one man) is much more common than *polyandry* (more than one husband for one woman). The single husband or wife has definite financial and sexual obligations towards each spouse, and it is usually seen as a sign of economic status rather than of sexual attractiveness. In the more usual polygyny, the woman is often just as involved as the man in selecting a new wife and may exert pressure on him to do so. If both families live in the same household, her duties would be reduced by half (or more, since she would be the senior wife) and the status would reflect on her as well as her husband. Although polygyny is usually associated with wealth, polyandry is found in conditions of extreme poverty. In the very few societies where it is practised, it apparently serves to keep the birth rate down, thus reducing the strain on resources. By having more than one male in each family, the burden can be shared.

One other way in which anthropologists describe family systems is in terms of the rules of descent: descent through the father's line is called *patrilineal*, that through the mother's *matrilineal*. This is interesting because it sometimes affects the definition of incest. Although there is an almost universal taboo against sexual relations within families, who counts as 'family' depends on rules of descent. A purely genetic description is not adequate to predict this. Amongst the Trobrianders, for example, lineage is considered to operate through the mother. In Fig. 9.3, there are two examples of family trees. In Western society,

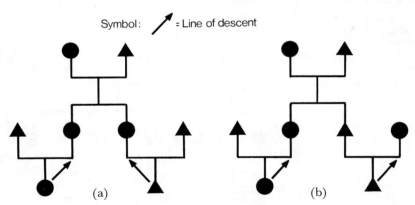

Symbol: ⟋ = Line of descent

(a)   (b)

Fig. 9.3 Rules of descent. The cultural definition of descent can affect rules about incest. In (a), the male and female grandchildren are considered to share the same mother because of the matrilineal line of descent: sexual relations between them are taboo. This is not the case for those in (b); they have different lines of descent and are considered potential marriage partners.

214

no difference would be seen in the relationships of the two pairs of grand-children, both being cousins, but the Trobrianders make an important distinction between them. Since the line of descent is matrilineal, the children in Fig. 9.3a are considered to have the same mother (the circle at the top), making them brother and sister. Sexual relations between them are taboo. Those in Fig. 9.3b, however, are considered to have different mothers, making sexual relations between them acceptable. In fact, this is a preferred marital bond in that culture.

Awareness of the great diversity of kinship patterns and cultural rules can help dispel *ethnocentrism*, the view that one's own culture provides the 'right' way of doing things and other systems are somewhat inferior. For instance, many readers will believe that the marriage tie is more important than the blood tie with parents, but this depends on cultural upbringing. Greater understanding of the behaviour of individuals may be achieved through knowledge of their cultural rules and norms.

This last point concerning ethnocentrism has particular relevance to medical care. Medical anthropology is the area of study concerned with describing how peoples of different cultures interpret and treat their illnesses. For example, Geertz[3] describes how the people of Java consult a *dukun* when ill, a person with great healing powers. The illness may be cured through the use of herbal medicines, spells or the intrinsic healing strength of the dukun. A person seeking assistance might be advised to re-bury their child's umbilical cord or to sleep the other way round in bed. The Javanese recognize that a particular recommendation may not work, but this does not destroy their faith in the medical system: 'Sometimes they cure you and sometimes they do not. The only difference is that you have to pay a Western doctor even if you die in his hands, while a good dukun expects payment only if he succeeds'.

Although we might find the practice of re-burying the umbilical cord both quaint and baffling, it should be pointed out that some standard medical procedures used in Western countries — such as the use of episiotomy during childbirth[4] — have little basis in experimental evidence. In the case of tonsil-lectomy it was faith in the benefits of technology and intervention that determined the wide-spread use of this procedure, not controlled studies. This is perhaps not so different from the faith the Javanese have in their dukun. It is likely that belief in the Javanese system is significant, but this also applies to Western medicine. Since many treatments involve a placebo effect (see Chapter 11), it seems important that both doctor and patient have confidence in the efficacy of a medication. Many herbal remedies do have properties that can be explained in Western terms, such as the presence of painkilling substances in coca leaves. Others are less obvious. The delay in exploring the effectiveness of acupuncture may be due to the (to us) nonsensical way it is explained in oriental cultures. In this case, ethnocentrism in medicine may have inhibited research into a potentially useful technique.

Many anthropologists consider a culture's medical system not only to be based on faith and belief but also as part of an overall pattern of adaptation to the environment. It cannot, therefore, be understood without reference to the economic and social conditions of the people. The same might be said of preventive measures. Some cultures have taboos on post-partum sexual relations, for example. These taboos tend to occur in societies where the diet is restricted: by ensuring that pregnancy does not occur, the mother's milk is kept high in nutrients thus increasing the infant's chances of survival. Although the explanation given might be different (offending the spirits is sometimes evoked as a reason for such customs) the practice has effective results. Similarly, there has been some discussion of the reasons why Western medicine does not find favour in many cultures or is not acceptable to recent immigrants to ours. Part of the reason seems to be that it does not fit easily into many value and belief systems. It can be difficult to persuade Asian women of the legitimacy of gynaecological examinations, for example.

Subcultural groupings are often evident within the larger culture. Although students at university may be quite dissimilar from each other in many respects, most will share the belief that higher education is of considerable value, a belief not shared by everyone in the larger culture. These similarities can be significant in many respects besides the medical. They also affect, for example, the choice of friends and marital partner, a topic that is considered in the next section.

9.3 Choice of Marital Partner

The choice of sexual/marital partner is influenced by several factors. Rules of *exogamy* sanction against marriage within a group: incest taboos are the most obvious example. However, there are also *endogamous* rules, which further limit the range of choice. These are rules against marriage outside a particular group. Here, racial and religious groupings are often important, in that sanctions are sometimes applied against marrying outside a particular race or religion.

Within these constraints, there is a considerable range of people who might be chosen. Obviously, this is not random, and the reader may well have his or her own ideas about the process. In fact, much of the research described below may seem little more than common sense. This is a criticism often aimed at research in the social sciences and this is an appropriate place to discuss the point. The main problem with common sense is that a homily can be found to fit almost any situation or any result that a psychologist might find. The bulk of evidence considered below, for example, indicates that attraction is related to similarity: people who like one another tend to be similar. This would be expected from the common sense description 'Birds of a feather flock together'. Thus, this research might be dismissed with an admonition that it is something that everyone knows anyway. However, if the research had found the opposite results, a similar criticism could also be made since, after all, 'Opposite attract'. There are several other homilies that might be used to explain research findings but, as shown in Table 9.1, such inconsistency makes the use of common sense untenable.

The process of choosing friends and a sexual partner can be regarded as

Table 9.1

Common sense seems to provide clear descriptions of how people behave. However, common sense is often contradictory — which homily is right? (Portions of Box 1.2 on page 8 in *Psychology: Making Sense* by David A. Statt. Copyright © 1977 by David A. Statt. Reprinted by permission of Harper & Row, Publishers, Inc.)

Look before you leap	but	He who hesitates is lost
Absence makes the heart grow fonder	but	Out of sight, out of mind
Great minds think alike	but	Fools seldom differ
Better the devil you know than the devil you don't	but	Familiarity breeds contempt
Birds of a feather flock together	but	Opposites attract

involving a series of filters[5]. The most basic filter has to do with physical distance, or propinquity. People are much more likely to have friends who work or live close by, and the likelihood of marriage decreases by something like the square of the distance between residences. One study found that 50% of couples lived within about one mile of each other before they were married. It can be difficult to distinguish propinquity from similarity of background. People who work or live close together are likely to have other features in common besides place of work or residence. Neighbourhoods in cities are usually stratified, with different social, economic and racial groups living in different areas. At a neighbourhood school or church we are likely to meet the same kinds of people as ourselves. Thus in survey studies similarity and proximity are confounded. Some researchers have attempted to demonstrate the importance of distance independently of similarity by studying students, who tend to come from similar backgrounds but whose place of residence on arriving at a university is determined by administrative authorities. Students are much more likely to become friends with others who share the same corridor, particularly the rooms next door, than those who are more distant. An example of this kind of research is provided by Segal[6] who examined the patterns of friendship among police trainees on a course. When they arrived they were assigned to seats and rooms on the basis of the alphabetical order of their surnames. At the end of the course they were asked to nominate their closest friend on the course, the results being shown in Fig. 9.4. This close association between physical distance and friendship illustrates the very important role of simple contact in the formation of friendships.

There are several reasons why distance is such a good predictor. The opportunity to meet, and easy accessibility afterwards, means that people will become increasingly familiar to each other. The more frequently a person is encountered, the more it is possible to predict how he or she will behave, which might in itself make social interaction less problematic between two individuals.

217

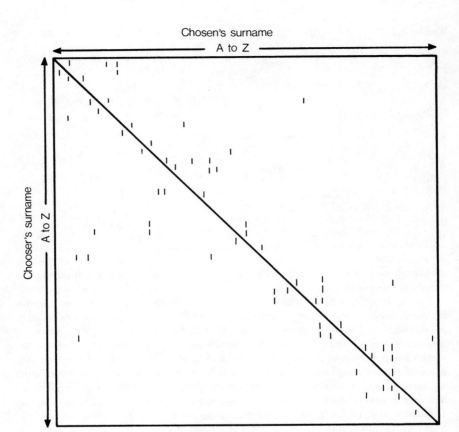

Fig. 9.4 Matrix of friendship choices. Those students whose surnames were adjacent alphabetically were given adjacent seats and later tended to choose each other as friends. (Reproduced from M.W. Segal, *Journal of Personality and Social Psychology*, 1974, 30, 654–657. Copyright 1974 by the American Psychological Association. Reprinted by permission of the author.)

Sheer familiarity itself may have positive consequences. Zajonc[7] showed his subjects a series of photographs. Some of them were repeated (up to 25 times), whereas others were shown only once or not at all. When asked to indicate how much they might like the person portrayed on each photograph, the subjects rated those whom they had seen a number of times more favourably than those they had seen infrequently. Thus, simply encountering a person on several occasions might make him or her more attractive.

Of course, friendships are not formed with everyone we meet. In the development of heterosexual relationships, physical attractiveness might be considered

the second filter. Given a degree of propinquity, this factor seems to be important in determining the frequency of future meetings, at least in the short term.
One of the classic studies in this area was performed on students who were just
entering university. They were given the opportunity to attend a dance as part
of their introduction to the university, being led to believe that a partner would
be arranged for them on the basis of computer matching. When they came to fill
out the required questionnaires, their physical attractiveness was rated very
roughly, by the experimenters. Partners were assigned randomly, and not on
the basis of computer sorting: the experimenters were interested in examining
the effect of physical attraction on their liking for one another. During the inter-
mission in the dance, the experimenters asked each partner, independently,
how much he or she liked the other: there was a significant tendency for the most
attractive people to be liked the most[8]. This result has been replicated several
times, indicating that physical attractiveness is a very important variable.
Several suggestions might be made about why this is so. It may be because of
social desirability: physical attractiveness in a partner is often seen as a desirable
social attainment. Another possibility has to do with the 'halo' effect mentioned
in Chapter 1, the tendency to generalize from one positive (or negative)
attribute to others.

In the longer term, matching of physical attractiveness seems to occur
between people. In a test of the similarity hypothesis, photographs were taken of
many men and women who had been together for some time. The physical
attractiveness of each person was rated by someone who did not know to which
couple he or she belonged. If couples did not match each other, a random assort-
ment of photographs into pairs should show a similar degree of correspondence
on ratings as that shown by the actual couples. The results indicated that there
was more correspondence between the actual couples than the random couples,
indicating that physical attractiveness was matched to some extent[9].

A third filter has to do with similarity of attitudes and personality.
Newcombe[11] was given the opportunity to assign newly arrived students at a
university to their rooms. He first gave them questionnaires to determine their
attitudes and then systematically placed the students. In some cases, those who
were similar to each other were assigned the same room, whereas in other cases
quite dissimilar students were placed together. Except for the study — which
involved questioning the students about their friendships later — there was little
intervention. Newcombe's results showed that similar room-mates generally
liked each other and became friends, whereas those who were dissimilar came to
dislike each other, choosing their friends elsewhere.

Research on personality variables have shown somewhat similar results. It
has been argued that partners choose each other on the basis of complementary
needs. A supportive person might marry someone who is dependent, for
example. Although there is some evidence in support of such complementarity,
for most personality characteristics similarity again seems to be important. For
example, Izard[12] gave personality questionnaires to an incoming class of
students, none of whom knew each other before entrance. Six months later,
they were asked to list the three most likeable and three least likeable members

of their class: the prior-to-acquaintance personality profiles were similar for the subjects and their 'most likeable' choices, but not for the 'least likeable' ones.

A further stage in the filtering process has to do with parents. They can affect choice in several ways. The most obvious is the use of pressure: in one study four-fifths of the parents interviewed admitted using pressure when their children showed interest in friends of whom they disapproved. More subtly, there may be effects of modelling. Although evidence is lacking in this area, some writers have contended that people often marry those who are similar in some way to the opposite-sex parent. This parent is considered to provide a model of how a spouse is expected to behave. Many readers of this book, if studying medicine, will be sons or daughters of physicians. Being born into this kind of family, they are more likely to live in a middle-class neighbourhood, attend better schools and to go to university than someone born into a lower-class family. They are also more likely to marry physicians themselves than the rest of the population.

The final stage in this filter theory has to do with desire to marry. In one study of couples introduced by computer matching (where similarity of background and interests are matched) the single best predictor of whether or not they eventually married was their agreement or disagreement with the item 'strong desire to marry soon'.

This is not to say that everyone will marry a person who lives nearby, who has similar attitudes and personality and whose parents approve of the choice, but these variables do describe marital patterns quite well. This tendency for like to marry like is called *homogamy* and it seems to have consequences for marital stability. Arranged marriages are often contracted on the basis of similarity of background and they usually result in close affectionate ties between partners. Several studies have explored variables connected with the ending of relationships. In comparisons between couples who have happy marriages and those who do not, the distressed couples are less likely to have similar backgrounds. The end of pre-marital heterosexual relationships is associated with discrepancies in age, educational aspirations, IQ and physical attractiveness[13]. The association between pre-marital pregnancy and marital instability could be because the usual courtship process is short-circuited[14]. Although it may be an over-simplification to suggest that there are causal effects at work here, there seems to be a correlational association at least.

9.4 Family Discord

The persistence of societal customs such as monogamy and polygamy suggests that children take on the values and beliefs held by their parents and their society as they grow up. This idea of continuity has prompted much research on such variables as economic and occupational status, crime and psychiatric disorder. In some cases, it is difficult to determine whether any continuities found are due to innate or cultural factors (e.g. in psychiatric difficulties), but it is likely that they both have an influence and that they interact. In some areas of study, such as social class, the existence of continuity is difficult to ascertain owing to the considerable mobility between classes in the last generations. Assignment to a particular class is usually based on type of occupation of the head of the family. There are social-class differences in child rearing — parents in the lower social classes tend to restrict their children more and talk to and play with them less[15] — but there is little evidence that these parents themselves were brought up in similar ways. Indeed, many report that they have reacted against their own upbringing, planning to bring up their children in quite different ways than they themselves were reared.

More support has been found for intergenerational continuity in other areas. Family size may remain similar through generations: one researcher found a significant association between the number of children a couple had and the size of their own families of origin[16]. Family discord and family violence may also reappear in later generations of the same family. Because of the social and medical implications, these areas will be discussed in some depth below.

Divorce

The ever-increasing rate and its social effects have made divorce an area of concern. It is not clear if this increase is due to more marriages breaking down, to more broken marriages ending in divorce (because of the relaxation in divorce laws and the lessening social stigma) or to a combination of these factors. Some researchers have attempted to specify the reasons for marital conflict by comparing couples whose relationship is distressed with those who are happily married. An important difference is in patterns of communication. The happily married not only tend to talk to each other more, but also to convey their feelings that they understand what is being said to them, to show more sensitivity to each other's feelings and to make more use of non-verbal signals such as eye contact and touching. Of course, these differences might just as easily be the result of discord as the cause. Other researchers have concentrated on social and demographic characteristics. Divorce is more likely for couples who marry after a short courtship, who marry because of pregnancy or who come from different social and economic backgrounds: in other words, when assortative mating does not occur. Yet other investigators have argued that personality characteristics are important. People who marry in order to escape from their parents' homes, who are over-dependent on their spouses or who are psychologically immature are also more likely to experience discord and divorce[17].

There is evidence that there is intergenerational continuity in divorce. In a large-scale survey, Langer and Michael[18] found that people whose parents had divorced or separated were twice as likely to have marriages that also ended in divorce or separation as those from intact homes. The reason for marital disruption seemed important: when the parental relationship was ended by the death of one parent, no effect was found. However, Langer and Michael's data also indicate that three-quarters of the divorced and separated adults came from intact homes, and in three-quarters of the intact couples at least one member had parents who had divorced or separated. There is no clear cause and effect operating here[19].

There has been particular concern about the effects of divorce or separation on children (reviewed by Bane[20]). As discussed in Chapter 7, it seems that it is not the divorce itself but the discord and disturbance that accompanies it that is most important. When comparisons are made between children whose parents are divorced and children whose parents remain unhappily married, few differences are found. In a comparison between single-parent and intact families, only in those instances where there was parental conflict was the children's self-esteem adversely affected[21]. In another study of 3000 women who were having their first child, those who had been illegitimate themselves or whose parents were divorced or separated were twice as likely to conceive or give birth before marriage, but if their parents' marriage was broken by death, no effects were found[22].

Perhaps a more useful way of considering marital conflict is not in terms of whether it results in divorce but rather how the conflicts are managed. It has been argued that all relationships involve a degree of conflict and that this should be accepted as an inevitable part of every marriage. According to this view, it is the way in which couples cope with their disagreement that is important, not whether these disagreements exist. This approach underlies much marital therapy, examined later in the chapter.

Violence in the Family

The incidence of violence in the family is difficult to ascertain. Part of the problem is definition. Does violent mean purely physical abuse, or does it also include nutritional and emotional neglect? Another difficulty concerns visibility. It is likely that only a small proportion of violent incidents are recorded by the police or by doctors. After a major newspaper ran a series of articles on child abuse, the incidence of reports increased 2 – 3 times in one city.

More important than incidence, perhaps, are the attempts to understand — rather than simply condemn — violence in the home. The origin of the laws against child abuse is an interesting one. Until comparatively recently, parents were considered to have every right to treat their children as they saw fit. One of the first legal challenges to this right was in New York City, in 1870. A church worker took the adoptive parents of a girl to court on the grounds that the child was suffering abuse. Since there were no laws against this, the action failed. However, there were laws against cruelty to animals and since the child was technically an animal, an action was brought under this law. Under these circumstances the action succeeded and new laws were drafted in both North America and Europe. Societies for the prevention of cruelty to children were formed in many countries shortly afterwards.

There seems to be continuing ambivalence about violence towards wives. In one study, subjects were given a description of a man and a woman fighting. The fight ended in unconsciousness for the woman. Half the subjects were told that the couple were husband and wife, the other half that they were not married. As a measure of how acceptable violence was between these couples, the subjects were then asked how severely the man should be punished. Significantly greater punishments were recommended for the unmarried man, indicating a greater acceptance of violence within the marital relationship than outside it[23].

Studies on the characteristics of people who use violence as a means of resolving family conflict have produced inconsistent results. Some researchers (but not all) have found child abuse to be most prevalent in the lowest social classes, but here again there is a problem of visibility: it is possible that violence towards children is actually more prevalent, or that it is more likely to be detected. Social and community workers more frequently visit families whose economic plight is apparent to welfare authorities, making evidence of abuse more visible and more likely to be reported to the police. For example, Gil[24] provides evidence that child abuse is associated with social conditions, such as low income, poor housing and unemployment. According to this viewpoint, the environment places stresses on the individual, violence being one possible result. The suggestion is that anyone could become an abusive parent given the circumstances. Others have argued that violence is due to personality disturbances — there is a higher rate of divorce, separation and minor criminal offences in abusive families, and depression in the mother is commonly found. She is also likely to have had her first child when very young. There seems to be some association between suicide attempts and abuse[25]. Another suggestion is that abuse is triggered by difficult children. Although only 7 – 8% of live births are premature, approximately 25% of abused children are born prematurely. Perhaps these infants are more difficult to rear because they fuss and cry more than full-term infants and give fewer rewards to their parents. Prematurity is also associated with young mothers who are under stress. Perhaps these women, because of their relative social immaturity, have greater difficulty in coping with their infant's demands. However, many of these results are difficult to interpret because comparison groups were not employed.

Another possible reason for this link between prematurity and abuse is failure of early bonding (see Chapter 7). Since the parents have only limited access to the child for the first weeks, the attachment between them may be weaker than usual. Relevant to this, Lynch[26] studied the relationship between ill health and child abuse. She used the siblings of abused children as the comparison group, reasoning that they were similar in many ways, and that the personalities of the parents would be relatively stable. She found several differences, including a higher incidence of abnormal pregnancies and deliveries and, important for the attachment hypothesis, a greater likelihood of separation between mother and child for the first 48 hours after birth and over the next 6 months. A later study indicated that abused children were twice as likely to have been in a special-care nursery after birth than a comparison group.

There is also the intergenerational hypothesis. Receiving or witnessing violence could be expected to have several consequences. From a psycho-dynamic point of view, the development of trust in parents is crucial, but this may be difficult to achieve when severe violence is experienced. Emotional as well as physical abuse may be interpreted as parental rejection with serious consequences for self-esteem and the growth of future relationships[27]. Although abuse rarely results in death, physiological and neurological impairment is not

223

uncommon, perhaps in up to 35% of cases[28]. The experience of violence as a child may have another important consequence: it may serve as a model for a method of resolving conflicts in later life. Gelles[29] interviewed 43 women who had suffered violence from their husbands. Forty of the 43 reported that they had been the victims of violence as children. Twenty-five reported that they had witnessed their parents being violent to one another. In a larger study of 150 women, over 80% reported that their husbands' parents had used violence, either towards their children or between themselves[30].

In the absence of control groups in these studies, it is not possible to say how high these figures are in comparison to the rest of the population. In fact, the incidence of the use of force in the population as a whole seems considerable. Many parents use some form of physical punishment towards their children, often at a very early age. One group of researchers interviewed mothers who were outpatients at medical clinics: one-quarter of the mothers had begun to use 'spanking' as a punishment before their children were 6 months of age[31]. In another study of university students, more than half reported actual or threatened use of violence from parents[32]. Gelles[33] conducted in-depth interviews with husbands and wives — about 60% had used physical aggression during a marital conflict. With such a high incidence of violence in the population, it is not possible to conclude that childhood experience with violence is closely associated with the use of violence in adulthood.

Nevertheless, it seems possible that as children grow they learn ways of coping with conflict. Several investigators have attempted to correlate ways of coping experienced as a child with favoured methods as adults. Owens and Straus[34] found such associations. Those who observed and received violence as children were more likely to have committed violence themselves as children and were more likely to approve of violent behaviour as adults (such as husband slapping his wife). In another study, students were asked to fill out questionnaires concerning the ways that they and their parents attempted to cope with conflicts. There were some similarities across generations: the way the parents coped with their differences between them (discussion, verbal aggression or physical aggression) were reflected in parent – child and sibling – sibling methods[35].

An important qualification is needed here, however. In many studies, an individual's own reports of past events are relied upon to give a picture of upbringing. There are two main reasons why this might be inadequate. First, there is the problem of *memory*. People may be more likely to remember their parents engaging in violence if violence has recently occurred in their own homes. Second, there is the question of *social desirability*. People might be more willing to admit parental violence to investigators if they have committed violence themselves. One research strategy in child-abuse investigation, for example, has been to compare the incidence of childhood experience with violence for abusive and non-abusive parents. If a difference was found, this might be due to the non-abusive parents being less likely to admit their negative childhood experiences. This point is nicely illustrated by recent research relating drug use by parents to drug use by their children. Some early studies

224

indicated that there was indeed a link present: children were more likely to use illegal drugs such as marijuana if their parents used tobacco and alcohol. In order to gauge drug use, the investigators asked the adolescents involved about both their own and their parents' habits. More recent research suggests that this result may be due to the way in which the studies were performed: when the parents themselves were asked about their use of tobacco and alcohol, no such association was found[36]. It is difficult to determine whether the parents' or their children's responses were the more accurate. For these reasons, much of the research in this area must be treated with caution and as exploratory rather than conclusive.

Prediction. The lesson from these studies is that there does not seem to be any one factor that is unique to violent families. Although as a group, abusive parents have been found to differ from the non-abusive, there is much overlap between the two populations, so that there is no one factor that can be pin-pointed as being solely responsible. Many parents who use violence come from deprived backgrounds, but not all with such childhood experiences become abusive. Similarly, many battered children are premature, but only a minority of premature children are battered. This has two implications. First, abuse might be more appropriately considered as lying along a continuum that includes nutritional and emotional neglect as well as physical abuse, so that it is a question of degree rather than of kind. When some 95% of parents report that they smack their children, 7% daily[15], it does not seem sensible to say that physical punishment itself is a sign of serious abuse. Second, it may be more fruitful to consider violence as a result of many factors, several of which in concert can make it more probable. The cumulative effects of prematurity in the child, youthfulness in the parents, social and economic stresses, personality and past experience with violence, may all contribute. This notion of accumulating experience and stress is similar to that mentioned in Chapter 7, where it was suggested that no single negative experience is likely to have long-lasting effects on personality development, but that continued deprivation might. Possibly, consideration of all of these factors will contribute to predictive power.

Accurate prediction is valuable because the resources open to doctors and the social services generally are limited. Services would be used inefficiently if too many *false positives* were identified — instances where violence is predicted to occur but where in fact it is unlikely. Conversely, *false negatives* — instances where unpredicted violence occurs — could have serious consequences. Thus, the problem in this kind of research is to minimize the number of these types of errors. In many research studies on prediction, the primary concern has been to minimize false negatives (often resulting in many false positives), based on the judgement that this is the less serious error to make.

The original studies on prediction involved in-depth interviews with parents who had abused their children, in the hope that some unique variables would show themselves. Such interviews highlighted several child-rearing patterns and expectations that seemed unusual and inappropriate. For example these parents seemed to treat their children as if they were much older and more

225

capable than they really were. The all-important comparison group was, however, missing in such studies — other research has indicated that a high proportion of parents have unrealistic expectations of their children. The interviews also suggested that abusive parents were more likely to agree with such statements as 'No one has ever really listened to me' and 'I have never felt really loved'. The problem here is that these interviews were conducted *after* the parents' violent behaviour had been recognized, so that the findings might have been affected by the reactions of the police and neighbours.

A method of predicting potential abuse that has had some success and is stimulating interest is based on observations in the delivery room and post-partum ward. In the delivery room, the concern is with the mother's reactions to her infant — is she ambivalent, disappointed, angry — and the support she is given by her spouse. In the post-partum period, continuing critical or disparaging remarks would be noted. The researchers indicate that some 75% of 'high risk' families can be identified through these observations, some of which are shown in Tables 9.2 and 9.3. Investigators in this field stress that their work is at an early stage: greater refinements can be expected in the near future[37].

Table 9.2 Signals in the Delivery Room Useful in Predicting Risk of Later Child Abuse

(Reprinted with permission from Helfer and Kempe, *Child Abuse and Neglect*, © 1976, Ballinger Publishing Company.)

A. Written form with baby's chart concerning parents' reactions at birth.
   1. How does the mother LOOK?
   2. What does the mother SAY?
   3. What does the mother DO?
B. The following phrases may help in the organization of information regarding observations for the above-mentioned form.
   1. Does the parent appear sad, happy, apathetic, disappointed, angry, exhausted, frightened, ambivalent?
   2. Does the parent talk to the baby, talk to spouse, use baby's name, establish eye contact, touch, cuddle, examine?
   3. Does the spouse, friend, relative offer support, criticism, rejection, ambivalence?
C. If this interaction seems dubious, further evaluation should be initiated.
D. Concerning reactions at delivery include:
   1. Lack of interest in the baby, ambivalence, passive reaction.
   2. Keeps the focus of attention on herself.
   3. Unwillingness or refusal to hold the baby, even when offered.
   4. Hostility directed toward father, who put her 'through all this'.
   5. Inappropriate verbalizations, glances directed at the baby, with definite hostility expressed.
   6. Disparaging remarks about the baby's sex or physical characteristics.
   7. Disappointment over sex or other physical characteristics of the child.

Table 9.3 Signals in the Post-partum Period (on the post-partum ward and in the well baby clinic) Useful for Predicting Risk of Later Child Abuse

(Reprinted with permission Helfer and Kempe, *Child Abuse and Neglect*, © 1976, Ballinger Publishing Company.)

A. Does the family remain disappointed over sex of baby?
B. What is the child's name?
   1. Who is he named for/after?
   2. Who picked the name?
   3. When was the name picked?
   4. Is the name used when talking to or about the baby?
C. What was/is the husband's and/or family's reaction to the new baby?
   1. Are they supportive?
   2. Are they critical?
   3. Do they attempt to take over and control the situation?
   4. Is the husband jealous of the baby's drain on the mother's time and energy?
D. What kind of support, other than family, is the mother receiving?
E. Are there sibling rivalry problems? Does she think there will be any? How does she plan to handle them? Or does she deny that a new baby will change existing family relationships?
F. Is the mother bothered by the baby's crying?
   1. How does it make her feel? Angry? Inadequate? Like crying herself?
G. Feedings
   1. Does the mother view the baby as too demanding in his needs to eat?
   2. Does she ignore the demands?
   3. Is she repulsed by his messiness, i.e., spitting up?
   4. Is she repulsed by his sucking noises?
H. How does the mother view changing diapers?
   1. Is she repulsed by the messiness, smells, etc.?
I. Are the expectations of the child developmentally far beyond his or her capabilities?
J. Mother's control or lack of control over the situation
   1. Does she get involved and take control over baby's needs and what's going to happen (waiting room and during exam interaction)
   2. Does she relinquish control to the doctor, nurse, etc. (undressing, holding, allowing child to express fears, etc.?)
K. Can the mother express that she is having fun with the baby?
   1. Can she view him as a separate individual?
   2. Can attention be focused on him and she see something positive in that for herself?
L. Can she establish and maintain eye-to-eye, direct contact, en face position, with the baby?
M. How does she talk with the baby?

N. Are her verbalizations about the child usually negative?

O. When the child cries, does she, or can she, comfort him?

P. Does she have complaints about the child that cannot be verified?

   1. Multiple emergency calls for very minor complaints, not major issues.

   2. Calling all the time for small problems, things that to you seem unimportant, but could be very major for her.

   3. The baby does things 'on purpose' just to aggravate the parents.

   4. In your presence the mother describes a characteristic you can't verify — e.g., baby cries continually.

   5. Tells you essentially unbelievable stories about the baby—e.g., has not breathed, is turning colours for the past 30 minutes and now seems fine.

Q. Manipulation of those working with the family: pitting nurse against lay therapist, doctor against social worker, through complaints and stories. Miscommunicating information, etc.

Prevention. Several attempts have been made to prevent child abuse. There is a statistical problem in evaluating the effectiveness of intervention programmes because of the low number of children who are actually physically harmed, but there are some encouraging results. In Chapter 7, a study concerned with the effects of extended contact at birth between mother and child was discussed: the incidence of injuries requiring hospitalization was lower in the extended-contact families than in the routine-contact ones. In some hospitals all parents who may have difficulty in forming attachment bonds because of the baby's need for special care are seen by a social worker and given the opportunity to discuss practical and social problems[38]. In another study, three groups of mothers were followed-up after the birth of their child. One group consisted of mothers not considered at risk on the basis of labour-room and post-partum observations. A second group of *at risk* mothers was given comprehensive paediatric follow-up by a physician and a health visitor, and a third group, similar to the second, was given no such assistance. In this latter group of 50 families, 5 children were later hospitalized for treatment of serious injuries whereas, by contrast, none of the high-risk intervention group nor the low-risk group required such hospitalization[37].

The behavioural approach may also have much to offer. It will be remembered from Chapter 3 that some psychologists consider behaviour to be the result of rewards and punishments. By analysing the patterns of stimulus and response, the contingencies that lead to abuse and neglect may be discovered. Abuse might be triggered by loud crying in the infant, for example, so that a parent could be given systematic desensitization treatment to increase toleration of loud noises. Perhaps parents who abuse their children see punishment as the main means of control. They might be briefed in the basics of the operant model and encouraged to achieve control with rewards instead of punishments[39]. This is a form of family therapy, which forms the subject of the final section of this chapter.

Prediction and prevention of violence between adults may be more difficult to achieve, partly because of the greater reticence to interfere with marital relationships and partly because of practical considerations — it may be very difficult to elicit the co-operation of both. Recent attempts to prevent the re-occurence of marital violence include the establishment of battered women's refuges. Such refuges seem to provide a much-needed service for women: several studies have indicated that many women return to a violent home because they have 'nowhere else to go'. Insofar as experience of violence in the home predisposes children to later violence as adults, such refuges for mothers and their children may reduce the probability of long-term negative consequences.

9.5 Family Therapy

Helping people with their psychological difficulties can take many forms. Some of these were discussed in Chapters 2 and 3: there, the emphasis was on treating the individual independently from his or her family group. Although the patient's relationships within the family might be discussed, parents or spouses would not usually be invited into the consulting room. A somewhat different approach is used by Masters and Johnson in their sex therapy (Chapter 8). They consider a sexual difficulty to reside not within one individual, but within the couple. For them, the couple's relationship is the patient and in order to treat the problem both partners are seen together.

A basic tenet of family therapy is that an individual's difficulties cannot be considered or treated adequately unless the nuclear family (and sometimes a larger network of relatives) is seen in therapy. This is analogous to medical treatment in many ways: it would be inappropriate to perform an operation on the heart without taking the patient's general state of health into consideration. Therapists who take this position contend that there are several advantages to such a treatment strategy. First, it provides an opportunity to observe how members of a family actually relate to one another. Rather than relying on one individual's view of what happens in the family, the therapist is able actually to see the patterns of interaction. The therapist's perceptions may be less clouded by personal needs. Second, the therapist is able to act as a kind of referee, encouraging the family members to consider how they are relating to each other and pointing out their conflicts. By acting in this way, the therapist may be able to help one member explain himself more clearly. Having someone present who is not punitive and who will provide support if necessary, may make it easier for a child to articulate his point of view, for example. Third, the therapist might choose to role play occasionally, indicating possible ways of reacting to comments other than those used by the family. In conjoint therapy, where there are two therapists, their relationship can act as a model for open and honest inter-action between adults. A fourth advantage over individual therapy, concerns the problem of generalization. Many therapists consider psychological difficulties to be evidence of trouble in relationships. In the therapeutic relation-ship, the patient is given the opportunity to discover the problems inherent in his or her usual ways of relating to people. However, if this person is then required to return to a family in which difficulties remain, it may be harder to put into practice what has been learnt. By considering the whole family, this problem is lessened. Of course, family therapy may not always be possible. One member may refuse or be unavailable for some other reason.

Bell[40] provides an example of family therapy. In his work with children (from 8 to 16 years of age), he asks both the child and the parents to attend. The initial interviews are designed to set the ground rules for therapy, especially to provide the child with the feeling that he or she is allowed to express emotions without fear of reprisal and that the therapist will be supportive. This is followed by a child-centred phase in which the youngster is encouraged to voice hostilities and to gain some control over the family's routines. The parents are asked to adjust their needs to the child's. If they agree, these demands are usually exhausted within a few weeks and the next phase, the parent-centred one, is begun. Here, the parents are given the opportunity to complain about the child, voicing their worries and irritations. This is a delicate phase and the child is allowed to defend himself. Bell provides an example of how these complaints can serve to open communication within the family. The parents were complaining about their son's seemingly irrational difficulties in going out in the car and being separated from the mother. The child then recalled two incidents, one in which he was misbehaving in the car and was told to walk the rest of the way home, and another when his parents threatened to put him out of the car in a strange city. After telling these stories and receiving a promise from his parents that they would not throw him out in the future, he travelled happily with them afterwards.

There is little direct evidence concerning the efficacy of family therapy compared with individual therapy, and there are some circumstances where it is inappropriate[41]. There is, however, considerable evidence about the importance of the family in the re-emergence of psychiatric difficulties. Brown *et al.*[42] were interested in factors associated with relapse in schizophrenic patients after they left hospital. They took several measures, including prior behavioural disturbance, impairment at work and the support the patients could be expected to receive once they were discharged from hospital. As a measure of support, they interviewed a key relative soon after the patient entered hospital, being especially interested in the number of critical and hostile comments made by this relative about the patient and the illness. When the relapse rates were later considered, this variable turned out to be the best single predictor: 58% of patients whose relative expressed several negative comments relapsed, but only 16% with relatives who expressed few negative comments. Indicators of previous behavioural disturbance had little predictive power. Similar results have been found for depressed patients[43]. Although these findings do not show that a supportive family is instrumental in actually preventing relapse, they are suggestive: perhaps if members of a patient's family were included in therapy, the prognosis would be considerably improved.

Another line of evidence that indicates that family therapy is important comes from studies of alcoholism and other kinds of drug dependence. These difficulties can be seen to lie solely within the individual, or they can be considered as instances of a family illness, the idea being that social as well as personality factors play a role in the aetiology and maintenance of drug abuse (see Chapter 11). If this position is taken, then assisting the alcoholic's or drug addict's family is critical. There is some evidence that a decrease in drug abuse occurs when family therapy is instituted, even when the abuse itself is not treated.

Marital Therapy

A particular example of family therapy concerns the relationship between spouses. Earlier in the chapter, the idea that all relationships — including the marital one — involve some kind of conflict was mentioned. This viewpoint is based on the premiss that it is most unlikely that two people will always have the same goals and requirements, thus making disagreement inevitable at times. For therapists who take this view, the aim of marital therapy is not to end conflict between partners, but rather to provide ways of resolving disagreements that would not rely on coercion or result in hostility. Several approaches have been taken in this field of therapy, some relying on verbal discussion of communication patterns, others using a more directive approach.

When considering the ways that partners communicate, the therapist (or physician, as this approach is well suited to the consulting room) might have two aims — to encourage sensitivity and to encourage expression of needs. Sensitivity involves looking behind what is being said. Many comments that pass between people can be interpreted on several levels. If, for example, a partner makes a complaint, this could be interpreted and reacted to simply as a statement of dissatisfaction. But on another level the complaint can often be seen to reflect an underlying need. Perhaps the complaint is that one partner is often out in the evening. The reaction to this might be a vigorous defense of rights. The therapist, again assuming the role of a referee, does not become involved in the action but reflects, with the couple, on their ways of reacting to one another. The therapist may note how the partners sit relative to each other, when and how they interrupt. He may suggest, for example, that the complaint about going out in the evenings expresses a need for companionship and indicates loneliness. A more active role may be taken, perhaps prescribing certain communicative exercises. In one kind of marital therapy, the partners are encouraged not to agree or disagree with what is being said but simply to attempt to understand it. This could be accomplished by asking one person to paraphrase what has been said as a first step and then to consider the underlying message as a second. For example, the comment:

I never see you in the evenings. I would like to see you.

could result in several responses. The reply could be

Complain, complain. If you were more pleasant, maybe I would stay home more often.

231

But if the listener considered the meaning behind these words, the reply could be:

> Are you saying that you're feeling lonely and that you'd like to see me more?

which is a much more sensitive response. By encouraging the partners first to attempt to understand what is being said, more effective communication may result.

Being able to express needs without attributing blame is also seen as important for resolving conflicts. Each partner would be encouraged to speak for her or himself. For example, a person might be discouraged from saying 'You never tell me I've done a good job'; rather, the emphasis is placed on personal perceptions — 'I never feel appreciated for what I do' might be a more effective comment[44, 45].

Another approach in marital therapy is known as contract therapy. Here, each partner is asked to state which changes in the other would contribute to their marital satisfaction. A list of very specific requirements would be drawn up; one partner might request that the other stay at home more, while in return being asked to stop spending so much money. At this point, a simple exchange might be arranged, in a *quid pro quo* arrangement: 'I will stay home x nights a week if you will spend only £y a week on clothes' for example. Alternatively, the partners might be encouraged to consider the underlying meanings behind these requests.

Some therapists consider marital distress in operant terms — that couples who are having difficulty in their relationships are less rewarding and more punishing than is conducive to a satisfying marriage. One group of researchers analysed conversations between distressed and non-distressed couples. They found a lower rate of rewarding statements and a higher rate of punishing comments in the distressed marriages. This result did not appear to be due to the personalities of the people involved, because when they were asked to converse with strangers, higher rates of rewarding comments were found[46]. In treating couples according to this model, contracting might be used: instead of threatening punishment in order to achieve goals, the partners would be encouraged to promise rewards. Other behavioural approaches of the social-skills-training kind could also be applied, such as modelling by the therapist, videotape feedback and role playing.

Jacobson[47] used several of these methods in marital therapy. His measures of distress included the ways that couples solved their problems and their scores on the Marital Adjustment Survey (a self-report questionnaire measuring the degree of marital satisfaction). The results of five couples who underwent his therapy were compared with five waiting-list control couples. For the treatment group, the incidence of positive problem-solving strategies increased, but no such effect was found for the comparison group. Similarly, the treatment group's scores on the MAS increased after therapy, a result impressively maintained 1 year after the end of therapy (see Fig. 9.5).

Some therapists have noted the need for divorce counselling as well. Divorce is typically a time of both lowered income and lowered self-esteem, and some

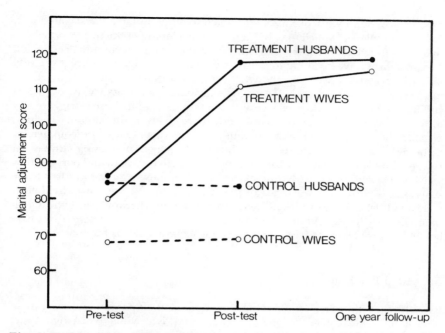

Fig. 9.5 Mean Marital Adjustment Scale scores for husbands and wives. The increased marital satisfaction reported by the treatment husbands and wives was maintained 1 year later. (Reproduced from Jacobson, *Journal of Consulting and Clinical Psychology*, 1977, 45, 92–100. © 1977 by the American Psychological Association. Reprinted by permission of the author.)

psychological assistance may be required. It is difficult not to make value judgements in this area, but it has been pointed out that divorce can have positive effects. Since most people who become divorced marry again afterwards, the act of divorce can be seen as an indication that the people involved are looking for a fuller and more satisfying relationship than they were experiencing previously.

Summary

The family plays an important role in transmitting the cultural beliefs and values that order our everyday lives. Because we are so steeped in these influences, it can be difficult to understand other cultural systems, yet awareness of the beliefs and values of other peoples can contribute to a fuller understanding of their behaviour. Culture affects the rights and obligations of members of a family and limits the choice of sexual or marital partners to some extent; in Western society it is likely that people will choose someone similar in many ways to themselves.

Studies on family discord have attempted to pinpoint factors associated with divorce or violence, which may be helpful in developing predictive or preventative measures. Differences in marital communication patterns and pre-marital circumstances have been found between distressed and happy couples. Family discord can result in violence, though the incidence of family violence is difficult to ascertain. Some workers believe that child abuse is associated with poor social conditions and environmental stresses; others suggest that abuse is triggered by difficult children. Premature babies are more likely to be abused, perhaps because they are harder to rear, because their mothers tend to be younger, or through failure of bonding soon after birth. One way of predicting families 'at risk' of child abuse relies on observations in the delivery room and post-partum ward and attempts at preventing abuse based on these signals have had some success. Since the re-occurrence of psychiatric difficulties in an individual is associated with the attitudes of the person's family, therapy that involves all members of a household may be an appropriate way of resolving various psychological problems. Marital therapy is one example of this approach.

Suggested Reading

The idea that children learn ways of behaving from their parents and carry these on to adulthood is considered in some detail by M. Rutter and N. Madge, *Cycles of disadvantage*, Heinemann Books, London, 1976.

T.M. Field (ed.), *High-risk infants and children*, Academic Press, London, 1980, includes papers on many aspects of parent – child relationships, including child abuse.

References

1. Gerson, M., The family in the Kibbutz *Journal of Child Psychology and Psychiatry*, 1974, **15**, 47 – 57.
2. Young, M. and Willmott, P., *Family and kinship in East London*, Penguin, Harmondsworth, 1957.
3. Geertz, C., *The religion of Java*, Free Press, New York, 1960.
4. Russell, J.K., Episiotomy, *British Medical Journal*, 1982, **284**, 220.
5. Udry, J.R., *The social context of marriage*, Lippincott, Philadelphia, 1971.
6. Segal, M.W., Alphabet and attraction: an unobstrusive measure of the effect of propinquity in a field setting, *Journal of Personality and Social Psychology*, 1974, **30**, 654 – 657.
7. Zajonc, R.B., Attitudinal effects of mere exposure, *Journal of Personality and Social Psychology*, 1968, Monograph **9**, 1 – 29.
8. Walster, E., Aronson, V., Abrahams, D. and Rottman, L., The importance of physical attractiveness in dating behaviour, *Journal of Personality and Social Psychology*, 1966, **4**, 508 – 516.
9. Murstein, B.I., *Who will marry who? Theories and research in marital choice*, Springer Books, New York, 1976.

11. Newcombe, T., *The acquaintance process*, Holt, Rinehart and Winston, New York, 1961.
12. Izard, C.E., Personality, similarity, positive affect and interpersonal attraction, *Journal of Abnormal and Social Psychology*, 1960, **61**, 484 – 485.
13. Hill, C.T., Zubin, Z. and Peplau, L.A., Break-up before marriage, *Journal of Social Issues*, 1976, **32**, 147 – 168.
14. Furstenberg, F.F., Premarital pregnancy and marital instability, *Journal of Social Issues*, 1976, **32**, 67 – 86.
15. Newson, J., and Newson, E., *Four years old in the urban community*, Penguin, Harmondsworth, 1968.
16. Berent, J., Relationship between family sizes of two successive generations, *Milbank Memorial Fund Quarterly*, 1953, **31**, 39 – 50.
17. Dominian, J., *Marital breakdown*, Pelican, Harmondsworth, 1976.
18. Langer, T.S. and Michael, S.T., *Life stress and mental health*, Collier-Macmillan, London, 1963.
19. Pope, H. and Mueller, C.W., The intergenerational transmission of marital stability: comparisons by race and sex, *Journal of Social Issues*, 1976, **32**, 49 – 66.
20. Bane, M.J., Marital disruption and the lives of children, *Journal of Social Issues*, 1976, **32**, 103 – 117.
21. Raschke, H.J. and Raschke, V.J., Family conflict and children's self-concepts: a comparison of intact and single-parent families, *Journal of Marriage and the Family*, 1979, **41**, 367 – 374.
22. Illeley, R. and Thompson, B., Women from broken homes, *Sociological Review*, 1961, **9**, 27 – 54.
23. Straus, M.A., Sexual inequality, cultural norms and wife-beating, *Victimology*, 1976, **1**, 54 – 70.
24. Gil, D.G., *Violence against children*, Harvard University Press, Cambridge, 1970.
25. Roberts, J. and Hawton, K., Child abuse and attempted suicide, *British Journal of Psychiatry*, 1980, **137**, 319 – 323.
26. Lynch, M.A., Ill health and child abuse, *Lancet*, 1975, **2**, 317 – 319.
27. Kinard, E.M., The psychological consequences of abuse for the child, *Journal of Social Issues*, 1979, **35**, 82 – 110.
28. Smith, S.M., *The battered child syndrome*, Butterworth, London 1975.
29. Gelles, R.J., Abused wives: why do they stay?, *Journal of Marriage and the Family*, 1976, **38**, 659 – 668.
30. Roy, M., *Battered women*, Van Nostrand Reinhold, New York, 1977.
31. Korsch, B.M., Christian, J.B., Gozzi, E.K. and Carlson, P.V., Infant care and punishment *American Journal of Public Health*, 1965, **55**, 1880 – 1868.
32. Straus, M.A., The social antecedents of physical punishment, *Journal of Marriage and the Family*, 1971, **33**, 658 – 663.
33. Gelles, R.J., *The Violent home*, Russell Sage, Beverley Hills, 1974.
34. Owens, D.J. and Straus, M.A., The social structure of violence in childhood and approval of violence as an adult, *Aggressive Behaviour*, 1975, **1**, 193 – 211.
35. Steinmetz, S.K., The use of force for resolving family conflict: the training ground for abuse, *Family Co-ordinator*, 1977, **26**, 19 – 26.
36. Vogt, I., Mother – child interaction and patterns of drug consumption, *In* Madden, J.S., Walker, R. and Kenyon, W.H., *Aspects of alcohol and drug dependence*, Pitman Medical, London, 1980.
37. Gray, J., Cutler, C., Dean, J. and Kempe, C.H., Perinatal assessment of mother – baby interaction, *In* Helfer, R.E. and Kempe, C.H., *Child abuse and neglect*, Ballinger, Cambridge, 1976.

235

38. Lynch, M.A., Roberts, J. and Gordon, M., Child abuse: early warning in the maternity hospital, *Developmental Medicine and Child Neurology*, 1976, **18**, 759 – 766.
39. Hutchings, J., The behavioural approach to child abuse: a review of the literature, *In* Frude, N., *The understanding and prevention of child abuse: psychological approaches*, Batsford, London, 1980.
40. Bell, J.E., Family group therapy — a new treatment method for children, *Family Processes*, 1967, **6**, 254 – 263.
41. Waldron-Skinner, S., Indications and contra-indications for the use of family therapy, *Journal of Child Psychology and Psychiatry*, 1978, **19**, 57 – 62.
42. Brown, G.W., Birley, J.L.T. and Wing, J.K., Influence of family life on the course of schizophrenic disorders, *British Journal of Psychiatry*, 1972, **121**, 241 – 258.
43. Vaughan, C.E. and Leff, J.P., The influence of family and social factors on the course of psychiatric illness, *British Journal of Psychiatry*, 1976, **129**, 125 – 134.
44. Bissonette, R. and Tapp, J., Premarital and marital counselling, *In* Taylor, R.B. (ed.), *Family medicine*, Springer-Verlag, New York, 1978.
45. Clements, W.M. and Wilson, J.L., Marriage and family counselling within the context of family practice, *In* Rakel, R.E. and Conn, H.F. (eds.), *Family practice* (2nd edn.), W.B. Saunders, London, 1978.
46. Birchler, G.R., Weiss, R.L. and Vincent, J.P. A multimethod analysis of social reinforcement exchange between maritally distressed and non-distressed spouse and stranger dyads, *Journal of Personality and Social Psychology*, 1975, **31**, 349 – 360.
47. Jacobson, R., Problem solving and contingency contracting in the treatment of marital discord, *Journal of Consulting and Clinical Psychology*, 1977, **45**, 92 – 100.

10
Adjustment to Life Changes

10.1   Introduction

This second part of the book is concerned with the ways that people develop throughout their lives. An important aspect of this process is predictability: as an individual develops, he or she learns how to predict the daily events of life, becoming more predictable to others and they to him. When circumstances change, however, a person must make adjustments in order to gain the ability to understand this novel situation and learn new ways of behaving within it. Adjustments are particularly evident when important events occur, such as marriage or the birth of a child, but even minor, everyday events ensure that life is a constant process of adaptation.

The adjustments required by the changes can be said to place the person under *stress*, a concept that has been used in several different ways. Selye[1] has concentrated on the way the organism adapts to events. His viewpoint is primarily physiological, arguing that it is the person's autonomic response to events that is the source of stress rather than the events themselves. This stress response is believed to be a non-specific and automatic response to all stressors. According to his model, the organism is weakened by prolonged or recurrent stresses since, over time, there is a decreasing ability to adapt. As the person is constantly knocked out of a homeostatic balance, the adjustments become progressively more difficult to make.

Although this 'response' model skirts the problem of what a stressor is, another approach to stress has concentrated on the events themselves, the stimuli, rather than the organism's responses to them. Some events are considered to be intrinsically more stressful than others, so that an understanding of adjustment could be gained through the consideration of these alone. This approach also has some inherent plausibility. The rate of psychological and somatic distress following natural disasters and severe accidents is very high, and it would seldom make sense to equate the loss of a spouse with, say, a change in residence. Support for this environmental view comes from several experimental studies, such as those on noise levels[2], where exposure to high decibel levels has been shown to affect performance on a wide range of tasks. However the same stressors may produce quite different reactions in different people.

Although both approaches provide insights into the process of adjustment, neither, on its own, can provide a full account. Both fail to take the *meaning* of events into consideration, a cognitive factor that previous chapters have shown is often important. It is difficult to see, for example, how either approach could adequately account for the results of the experiments on preparing patients for hospitalization and surgery discussed in Chapter 1. The events are the same for both prepared and unprepared patients, yet the responses differ. A more attractive approach to stress would not only take environmental and response factors into account but also provide an indication of how cognitive variables affect stress.

A Transactional Model of Stress

Cox[3] agrees that both the organism's responses and environmental demands are important in understanding stress, but, he argues, these are mediated by cognitive factors. These three aspects, stimulus, cognitions and response, are considered in some detail by Cox, along with a fourth influence, evaluating the consequences of the chosen response.

First, the demands an individual might experience are examined. These might be due to external environmental events or internal events due to psychological or physiological needs. A person may find that this environment has changed (e.g. losing a job) or that his physiological needs have not been met (e.g. being hungry), and both kinds of demands require adjustment of some kind. It seems that too few demands can be just as stressful as too many, as has been shown experimentally. In one study, subjects were assigned to one of three conditions. In the understimulating condition, they were asked to perform a

238

monotonous and unstimulating task (judging the intensity of a light in a sound-proof room for 3 hours). In the overstimulating condition, they were required to monitor several lights and sounds for 3 hours. Both of these tasks placed considerable demands on the subjects. As compared to a control condition group (who read magazines), the understimulated group showed increased nor-adrenaline secretion and the overstimulated group higher adrenaline and nor-adrenaline secretion[4].

The second aspect of Cox's analysis involves cognition: the person's perception of the demand is crucial for the understanding of stress. There may, for example, be the external demand of an exam in psychology, but if the student does not perceive the demand as being important, or feels well prepared, there will be little stress. Hunger may become stressful if there is no food about and it seems difficult to obtain, but not if a simple trip to the refrigerator will relieve it. Stress is said to occur when there is an *imbalance* between perceived demand and the perception of capability to cope with it. It follows from this that if the way people perceive events or the way they perceive their resources can be changed, then their reactions to the events should also change. A study in support of this view[5] involved showing an explicit film of circumcision procedures performed as part of the initiation rites of an Australian aboriginal tribe. The subjects' appraisal of the operation was manipulated through the use of three soundtracks. One emphasized the pain, the mutilation and the danger of disease; the second soundtrack emphasized the positive aspects of the procedure, indicating that the boys looked forward to it happily as a ritual that gave them manhood in the eyes of the tribe. Pain, danger and disease were denied. The third soundtrack provided the viewers with an opportunity to be detached from the operation, a scientific and objective view being taken. The researchers took several measures of the stress response, and found that the subjects showed significantly greater reactions to the first condition than to either of the latter.

The third aspect of Cox's model involves the psychological, behavioural and physiological responses to the stressful events. Responses can be described as involving direct action or as being palliative. *Direct action* can take many forms. If the stressful event can be anticipated, the person may take steps to reduce harm. Studying for the psychology exam or asking about the effects of an operation would be examples of such preparation. Alternatively, the person might become aggressive, attacking (physically or verbally) the perceived sources of the difficulty. Another response would be to attempt to avoid or escape from the source, which may be possible in physically stressful situations but more difficult in psychologically disturbing ones.

Although direct-action strategies involve attempts at mastery over stressful demands, *palliative* strategies involve moderating the distress evoked by the events. These measures could be intra-psychic — some of the defence mechanisms suggested by Freud, such as denial and rationalization, might be used — or symptom directed — alcohol and tranquillizers could be used to control the somatic response. In some instances, it may be that the person does not consciously perceive the nature of either the demands or his somatic response, as might be the case for Type A personalities (Chapter 2). Psychologists disagree about the appropriateness of these palliative measures. Although some psychotherapists who believe that the cause of distress and the individual's reaction to it may need to be altered question the appropriateness of strategies such as denial or tranquillizers, others have argued that their use is effective, at least in the short run. They may be more appropriate for short-term difficulties (such as surgical operations[6, 7]) than longer-term stresses.

Related to palliative strategies are measures designed to give a degree of control over emotions. Lief and Fox[8] describe how the setting for medical autopsies is made clinical, encouraging detachment in students who witness them for the first time. The autopsy room is brightly lit, certain parts of the body such as the face and genitals are covered and once the vital organs are removed the body is taken from the room, thus bringing the autopsy to the level of tissue alone. Similar efforts are sometimes made for students about to learn dissection: at first the bodies are face downwards, and the aspects of the person most related to life (the face and the hands) are left until the last.

Cox's final considerations involve consequences and feedback. A response may occur and be found to be adequate. If so, the individual may use the same response again at a later time. A student may find that studying for a psychology exam results in a pass mark — the demand has been met successfully. The next time an exam is set, the same response may be tried. If the action is found to be inadequate, however, the student may try another approach. The nature of psychology exams may be re-appraised — perhaps they aren't so easy to pass after all, so that more study seems to be necessary. In other words, the consequences of a response feed back and influence the appraisal of demands. Similarly, a patient's initial response to a poor prognosis might be denial but if increasing pain makes this response untenable (i.e. if it provides inadequate adjustment), the patient may come to use another coping strategy. A not uncommon one is for patients in such circumstances to become angry and disappointed with medical and nursing staff. Cox's model also accounts for the circularity of some stress reactions. A response may itself serve as a further source of stress. For example, a common response to widowhood is difficulty with sleeping; the lack of sleep may be felt to compound the problem so that a further response might be to consult with a physician in order to request a sedative.

This chapter explores some aspects of the process of adjustment. Research on various life events is considered, including the effects of old age and bereavement, reflecting as they do times of considerable demand coupled with a lowered capacity to change. Some researchers have emphasized the importance of environmental demands, others the role of response capability and yet others have taken a transactional view. Stress has been implicated in both physical and psychiatric illness, and much of the research discussed here can be characterized as *psychosomatic* research, which involves exploring the relationship between physiological and psychological mechanisms involved in illness. Frequently, investigators have taken the direction of casuality to be from the psychological to the physiological. Although there is little doubt of an association between the two (i.e. they often occur together), the direction of the effect is not always clear.

240

Psychosomatic medicine is a relatively new area of research, and there are many areas of controversy. The chapter concludes with a short review of some of the factors that seem to protect people against the effects of stressful events.

10.2 Life Events

Many events could be expected to require adjustment, including several minor ones. This section of the chapter discusses research that has related the demands caused by these events to illness. Psychosomatic medicine has not yet reached the point where there are measuring techniques available that can be taken as standard. Various research methods and dependent measures have been used, so that it is often difficult to compare the results of one study with those of another. Some researchers have concentrated on physical illness, others on psychiatric illness, and yet others have sought to understand how such events as social change, hospitalization and occupational stress affect the individual.

Physical Illness

One way of studying life events that has gained considerable popularity is based on the idea that adjustment is proportional to both the number and severity of experienced changes. Originally, Holmes and Rahe[9] chose 43 events that they considered to be relatively common and which would require a degree of adjustment. These events are shown in Table 10.1. Organized into a questionnaire format — called the Schedule of Recent Experiences — the list provided a means whereby subjects could check off events they had experienced over the previous 6 months or year. Holmes and Rahe had a sample of people rate each event for the degree of adjustment they felt would be required. By assigning each event a value, their relative importance could be ascertained. Some events, such as the death of a spouse or divorce were rated highly, whereas others, such as a vacation or minor violations of the law, were given low values. The ratings, which are also shown in Table 10.1, are called Life Change Units (LCUs). The death of a spouse was considered to be twice as stressful as marriage, which in turn was seen to be twice as stressful as a change in living conditions. This has been termed the Social Readjustment Rating Scale (SRRS).

The questionnaire has been used in several studies. For example, the incidence of such events in physicians' lives has been examined. The doctors were asked to fill out the questionnaire for the previous 18 months and were divided into three groups according to the number of LCUs they reported: high, moderate or low. Nine months later, the physicians were contacted again and asked about their illnesses since they filled out the questionnaire. LCU and significant health problems were, indeed, related to each other, in that 49% of the high LCU group reported illnesses, 25% of the moderate group but only 9% of the low LCU group. One might also expect that not only the incidence of illness, but also its seriousness would be related to the number and severity of life events. In order to test this hypothesis, Wyler *et al.*[10] asked 232 surgical,

241

Table 10.1 The Social Readjustment Rating Scale

(Reproduced from T.H. Holmes and R.H. Rahe, *Journal of Psychosomatic Research*, 1967, **11**, 213 – 218, by permission.)

Rank	Life event	Mean value
1	Death of spouse	100
2	Divorce	73
3	Marital separation	65
4	Jail term	63
5	Death of close family member	63
6	Personal injury or illness	53
7	Marriage	50
8	Fired at work	47
9	Marital reconciliation	45
10	Retirement	45
11	Change in health of family member	44
12	Pregnancy	40
13	Sex difficulties	39
14	Gain of new family member	39
15	Business readjustment	39
16	Change in financial state	38
17	Death of close friend	37
18	Change to different line of work	36
19	Change in number of arguments with spouse	35
20	Mortgage over $10 000	31
21	Foreclosure of mortgage or loan	30
22	Change in responsibilities at work	29
23	Son or daughter leaving home	29
24	Trouble with in-laws	29
25	Outstanding personal achievement	28
26	Wife begins or stop work	26
27	Begin or end school	26
28	Change in living conditions	25
29	Revision of personal habits	24
30	Trouble with boss	23
31	Change in work hours or conditions	20
32	Change in residence	20
33	Change in schools	20
34	Change in recreation	19
35	Change in church activities	19
36	Change in social activities	18
37	Mortgage or loan less than $10 000	17

Rank	Life event	Mean value
38	Change in sleeping habits	16
39	Change in number of family get-togethers	15
40	Change in eating habits	15
41	Vacation	13
42	Christmas	12
43	Minor violations of the law	11

psychiatric and gynaecological patients to check off life events that had occurred during the previous year. Each patient's diagnosis was coded for seriousness, so that the researchers could test the strength of the relationship between seriousness and LCUs experienced. They did in fact find a correlation between these variables for chronic diseases, such as diabetes and hypertension, but not for acute illnesses.

There are many studies similar to these, some of which have shown strong effects. The questionnaire has been modified for use with children, studies showing that, for example, hospitalized children have higher LCU scores than the non-hospitalized. However, caution is required in several respects. First, many of the studies have been retrospective, relying on memory for the incidence of events and sometimes for the incidence of illness. As shown in the chapter on memory, retrospective data is not reliable and the possibility that patients look for reasons for their illness in life events cannot be overlooked. Perhaps people who are likely to remember life events are also those who remember illnesses, so that the correlations may simply reflect differences in recall. This problem could be overcome to a large extent if prospective studies were undertaken and if medical records could be consulted. Perhaps the investigator could give the questionnaire to a group of people and then return later to collect evidence of physical illness. This research method was used by Rahe[11] in a study of enlisted navy men. They were asked to indicate their recent life events before 6 months deployment on a ship. On board, nearly identical environmental conditions existed for all the men and medical records were kept by the ship's doctor. At the completion of the trip, those who had high LCU scores before the cruise had a higher incidence of illness during it.

Even so, there are still problems with the interpretation of this kind of result, particularly in attributing causality. Many of the life events sampled (losing a job, divorce) could be the result of unrecognized illness, which only became apparent later. Inspection of Table 10.1 indicates that some of the events actually concern physical illness, thus confounding the picture. Another reason why attributing causality is problematic has to do with the distinction between disease and illness behaviour. In Chapter 6 it was pointed out that the incidence of symptoms in the general population is actually very high, with most people having some sign of disease much of the time. There is some evidence that life events make people more aware of their health status and more likely to consult their doctor[12]. Many of the events could be expected to have a demoralizing effect on people, making them less able to cope with their symptoms and more prone to seek medical help. In seeking this assistance, undiagnosed conditions may become more visible. These significant difficulties with life events research have led some to argue that the causal link between experience and disease has yet to be substantiated[13]. A further point is that the rating scale does not distinguish between positive and negative life events. The idea is that stress results whether events are welcome or unwelcome, since all require adjustment. According to the transactional model of stress, however, the person's appraisal of environmental demands is seen as being crucial, so one might expect that negative experiences would have more severe effects than positive ones. This viewpoint has been receiving greater support in recent years as the evidence mounts that only experience of negative life events are associated with subsequent illness[14, 15].

Psychiatric Illness

Similar criticisms have been levelled at research on the relationship between life events and psychiatric illness, but many workers in this area have been sensitive to such arguments and have taken care to make their studies as methodologically sound as possible. Some of the more important studies have been conducted by Brown and his colleagues. Rather than giving questionnaires, they conducted extended personal interviews with each person, being careful to date events and verifying the events through relatives. In their research, the degree of adjustment that an event entailed depended on both the particular circumstances and the interviewers' judgements of the threat such an event would pose for the average person. Objective data (e.g. police records) were consulted whenever possible. Some of the difficulties associated with memory can be reduced in these ways. Following other researchers, Brown has compared samples of 'healthy' 'normal' subjects who were randomly chosen from the population (to serve as control group) with groups of psychiatric patients. His noteworthy contributions have involved studies of depressed women and people with schizophrenia.

In the study of depressed women[16], 73 in-patients and 41 out-patients were interviewed, and their reports of life events were compared with a community sample of 250 women. The researchers inquired about a wide range of life experiences, but they found that most of the women had experienced some kind of event recently. It was only those experiences that implied a long-term threat of some kind, such as the loss of a friend or spouse, learning that a husband was seriously ill or the necessity of making an important decision, which distinguished between the two groups of women. Some 59% of the patients had experienced such a severe life event within the 9 months preceding the onset of depression, whereas only 26% of the community sample (some of whom were considered to be clinically depressed although they had not sought assistance) gave comparable reports. This indicated that severe events were associated with depression.

Brown argued that these events were causally related to depression, in that they often preceded the time when patients were beginning to feel a need for psychiatric help. He did not rule out the possibility that physical and biochemical factors might at times have been largely responsible for depression, but Brown contended that the cognitive component — the appraisal of the state of one's world — was primary. It might be that biochemical changes were associated with depression, but they might have post-dated the condition. Until research takes account of biochemical processes before the onset of depressive symptoms, he argued, physical changes cannot be said to have aetiological relevance.

But this is only one aspect of his contribution. Unlike investigators who have been content to find variables that distinguish between two populations, Brown wanted to provide an explanation of why some of the women who underwent stressful life events did not become depressed. (He has, however, paid less attention to the other side of the coin — why people who have not apparently undergone change do become depressed.) Brown's theory of depression is primarily a cognitive one. Like Beck (Chapter 2) he argued that it is changes in one's beliefs about the world that translate life events into depression. It is the meaning of the events that is important and not the events themselves. The idea is that some people are more vulnerable to the consequences of stressful life events than others, perhaps because of low self-esteem.

By re-analysing his data, Brown was able to find several variables that were relevant. Loss of the mother before the age of 11, lack of intimacy with a husband or boyfriend, having three children at home under the age of 14 or lack of paid employment were found to make the women vulnerable to the provoking effects of life events. In one or more of these circumstances, the individual may be less likely to believe that she will be able to cope with life's problems or to be able to resolve the present difficulties.

Thus, the argument is that experiencing severe life events is not in itself sufficient to bring on depression. Nor is vulnerability by itself enough: a person may not have a close confidant, but this would not result in depression if no severe life event was experienced. Rather, it is the combination of provoking events and vulnerability factors that is significant. Table 10.2 illustrates some of his data, giving in percentages the proportion of women who were depressed in the presence or absence of life events. For example, 32% of the women who experienced a severe event without an intimate relationship became depressed, but only 10% of those who had such a tie.

In his studies of acute schizophrenia, a slightly different causal mechanism was suggested. Here, Brown argued that life events trigger the onset of symptoms in those people already likely to suffer, rather than being responsible for the formation of the condition. The illness is said to be 'brought forward' in time due to these events (which could be quite minor). Interviews with schizophrenic patients and their relatives indicated a higher incidence of events in the 3 weeks before onset than in a sample of people chosen from the general population. Although the schizophrenic episodes seem to have been triggered by the events, the events themselves were not considered to be sufficient cause:

245

Table 10.2   Percentage of Women who were Depressed and who had a Severe Life Event and either Lack of Intimacy or Three Children at Home under the age of 14.

(Reproduced from G.W. Brown and T. Harris, Social origins of depression, *Psychological Medicine*, 1978, **8**, 577 – 588, by Permission of Cambridge University Press.)

Severe event or major difficulty	Lack of intimacy with husband/boyfriend		At least 3 children aged under 14 years	
	Yes	No	Yes	No
Yes	32%	10%	43%	17%
No	3%	1%	0%	2%

long-term tension in the home appeared to be associated with the probability that people would become disturbed after such changes.

Further support for Brown's conclusions on psychiatric illness has been provided by other workers using somewhat different research designs. But stressful life events occur fairly commonly and only a small proportion of people become clinically depressed, so it appears that other factors are important in the aetiology of psychiatric illness. Brown seems to have identified some of these, the vulnerability factors. Additionally, genetic influences are likely to be relevant. Cultural and familial factors also affect a person's decision to ask for assistance and to take on the sick role. It is likely that prospective studies will provide a better estimate of the significance of the link between life events and psychiatric illness than is currently available. Events interact with various background factors, so that the appropriate model is probably one of multifactorial causation[17].

Social Change

Urbanization and migration are two kinds of social change that have been given considerable attention. It could be expected that when a culture is changing rapidly, or when a person emigrates, the individual would be under pressure to adjust. One way of testing the hypothesis that change leads to illness, then, is to compare populations of people who have migrated or who live in an area of rapid social change with people whose environment is more constant. Many of the studies in these areas are epidemiological, in that health records for different populations are usually consulted.

Several studies that have used this approach indicate that migrants have a higher incidence of physical and psychiatric illness than those who do not change culture. In order to say that it is the change that *caused* the illness, however, it is necessary to show that migrants are similar to non-migrants, otherwise the higher incidence of illness may be due to factors only indirectly related to immigration. For example, those people who are recent immigrants have been found to be more likely to have cardiovascular disease than those who stayed in their original country: is this difference due to migration itself, or are people who are more prone to this disease more likely to emigrate? Perhaps they tend to have Type A personalities, for example (Chapter 2). With the present state of research in this area, it is not possible to conclude that there is a direct relationship between emigration and disease[18].

Somewhat less problematic is the research on urbanization, a term meaning the change of small towns into bustling cities. In such places, the environment is altering rapidly. One way of studying this topic is to compare the incidence of illness in cities where there is rapid growth with cities where growth has stabilized. Fig. 10.1 illustrates such a finding, with rates of hypertension mortality plotted against annual increase in size of the city[19]. Clearly, as the rate of expansion increases, so too does mortality. However, within this sample of cities, there may be many differences besides rate of expansion. Perhaps those cities where change is rapid also have poorer housing and sewage treatment or less satisfactory medical care, for example. More convincing support for the hypothesis that rapid social change increases the risk of morbidity would be given if a smaller area, with a more homogeneous sample, was studied. Tryola and Cassel[20] compared residents in fast-changing parts of North Carolina State with those living in slow-changing ones. Taking their data from the Public Health Records, they found that the mortality rates from coronary heart disease were greater in fast-changing parts of the state. They argue that this result is not due to differences in coroners' reports or selective migration. It may be that the residents in the fast-changing areas experience some incongruity between their old and new cultures, resulting in difficulties in adjustment. This interpretation is supported by studies that indicate that it is the children of immigrants who often have more difficulty in adjusting to a new culture: although their parents are supported in their previous customs by fellow migrants, the children live in two cultures — which may be in conflict with each other — simultaneously.

Stressful Effects of Illness

The interaction between life events and illness is well illustrated by the research examining the effects of disease and hospitalization described in Chapter 6. It became clear during the discussion of the sick role that the effects of disease are not purely biological — when someone becomes ill, the whole person is affected, including his or her social and psychological aspects. Any one of a large number of studies could be used to illustrate that the effects of disease are compounded by social factors. Depression is a common reaction to renal failure and viral infections, for example. Devlin *et al.*[21] found that 25% of patients who underwent surgery for anorectal cancer had psychiatric difficulties, mainly of depression. Patients reported that their personal relationships had been affected,

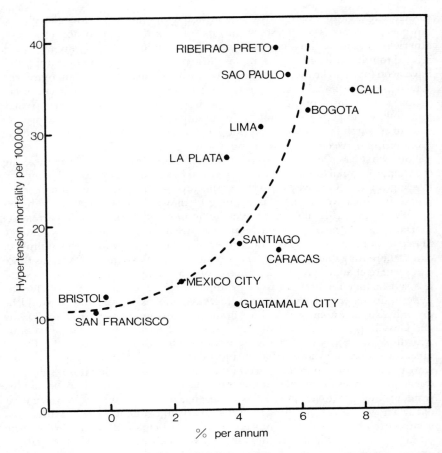

Fig. 10.1 The rate of growth of cities related to the incidence of hypertension mortality in the general population. (Reproduced from J.P. Henry and J.C. Cassel, *American Journal of Epidemiology*, 1969, 90, 171–200, by permission.)

particularly sexual ones due to embarrassment and fear of spillage. There was a high incidence of impotence in their sample, with less than 50% enjoying an active sex life. When one member of a family is ill it therefore affects the other members as well. Klein *et al.*[22] found that most spouses reported an increase in symptomatic levels during patients' illness, particularly nervousness and fatigue. Disease can involve loss and change, sometimes loss through death (see below), but often change in social role or self-image. A hysterectomy in a young woman is often followed by depression, for example, and the loss of a limb through amputation has been compared to the loss of a friend or spouse

248

through death[23]. Both involve a process of grieving.

Breast cancer provides an example of a particularly stressful disease that has implications for women's sexual identity and self-confidence as well as their physical health. Common responses include anxiety, depression, anger, guilt and fear. Women having mastectomies are twice as likely to seek psychiatric help than those having biopsy alone. Although most women do adjust to the operation, adjustment is associated with increased use of alcohol and tranquilizers[24, 25]. These studies illustrate the circularity of stress and disease: the illness may be due in part to stress and the illness, in turn, results in the need for further adjustment.

Part of the stress involved in illness can be related to factors of uncertainty and unpredictability in medical care. The research on preparation for surgery discussed in Chapter 1 is relevant, but there are other events occurring in hospital besides the operation and the associated pain. The transfer from a familiar environment to a novel one involved in admission to hospital[26] or change from one ward to another can be stressful (see the section on old age later in this chapter). Observing the illnesses and deaths of other patients could also be expected to have adverse effects on the individual. Bruyn et al.[27] examined patients' reactions to death and emergencies in a coronary care unit. Of the 29 patients studied, 17 witnessed such an event, and their blood pressure and anxiety levels were compared with those of the remaining 12 patients who did not. Thirteen of the 17 patients showed abnormal physiological responses, and over half became more anxious, compared to only one of the 12 patient comparison group. This study reflects the problem of iatrogenic illness — illness caused by the process of medical care itself — which is a topic considered in the final chapter.

Occupational Stress

Stress at work has been implicated in both mental and physical health. One way of isolating the effects of a specific variable, such as occupation, is by taking groups who differ on the variable (e.g. have different kinds of jobs) and looking for differences between the groups that can be attributed to that variable. Groups studied in this way have included the employed and unemployed, redundant and non-redundant and those in different types of occupation. Similarly, people have looked for systematic differences in the type of work undertaken by those who suffer coronaries and those who do not.

The focus of an early study on occupational stress concerned the incidence of coronary difficulties. A comparison between young coronary patients (24 – 40 years of age) and a matched group of healthy subjects showed significant differences in work patterns. In 91 % of the coronary cases prolonged job responsibility preceded the attack, whereas such responsibility was reported by only 20 % of the control group. 25 % of the coronary patients held two jobs, and 46 % worked 60 or more hours per week. Although heredity and diet differences were also found between the groups, the researchers considered occupational stress to be more significant in the aetiology of coronaries than these factors[28].

Psychologists have also been interested in the effects of unemployment on physical and mental health. Employment has several functions besides the purely financial, including social contact, a means of structuring time, and providing a sense of identity and personal status. It would be expected, then, that unemployment would have far reaching psychological effects on the individual and his or her family. Suicide rates and the incidence of psychiatric referral have been found to be higher among the unemployed. Another measure of mental health is the General Health Questionnaire (GHQ), which is designed for the detection of non-psychotic psychiatric disorders: the unemployed show higher scores than the employed. Further, GHQ scores have been shown to vary with employment status, with those who gain a job showing improvement in mental health, and those who lose one showing some deterioration[29].

Some of the studies of job loss and concomitant physiological change are retrospective or cross-sectional. Another approach is to follow a group of people about to become redundant and compare them with people whose jobs remain secure. Kasl and Cobb[30] approached the management and unions of two companies who had just heard that the companies were to close. They took blood pressure measures at this initial point, then at termination of the jobs and again at 6, 12 and 24 months afterwards. Compared to the control group (who showed no changes over the 2-year period), the blood pressure of the redundant workers was highest just before and just after their jobs were lost, and fell when a new position was found[31].

There is evidence that doctoring might be a particularly stressful occupation, with physicians showing a higher incidence of drug abuse, alcoholism and divorce than the general population. A study that has examined stress in doctors has been reported by Vaillant et al.[32]. In the late 1930s, a large group of male students were selected for intensive study by a university health service. Forty-seven of these attended medical school and they were compared with 79 fellow students who followed other occupations. There were no differences between the groups in socio-economic status or intellectual aptitude at the time of their entrance to university. All were followed by questionnaire and occasional interview over the next 30 years, and contact was lost with less than 5% of the sample. Information on three areas was collected: each individual's marital history was examined, not only through their own reports but also through their wives' reports; they were asked about their drinking and drug use histories in an attempt to gain some idea of the incidence of abuse; they were asked if they had consulted a psychiatrist for personal help, particularly if 10 or more visits had been made. Difficulties in these areas were considered to be symptoms of stress. On all these measures, the group of students who became physicians showed greater indications of stress, as shown in Table 10.3.

Other studies have shown that, within medicine, some specialities are more stressful than others. A comparison was made of the incidence of coronary heart disease in highly stressful medical specialities (general practice and anaesthetics) with that in low stress ones (pathology and dermatology). Questionnaires were sent to 1000 physicians in each group, and a respectable response rate of 65% was achieved. Coronary disease was some three times

250

Table 10.3   Relative Incidence of Difficulties in Physicians and Control Group

All comparisons were statistically significant. (Reproduced from G.E. Vaillant, N.C. Sobowale and C. McArthur, *New England Journal of Medicine*, 1972, **287**, 372 – 375, by permission.)

Difficulty	Physicians(%)	Controls(%)
Poor marriage or divorce	47	32
High drug use	36	22
10 or more visits to a psychiatrist	34	19
2 or more of the above difficulties	36	18

more prevalent in general practitioners and anaesthetists than in dermatologists and pathologists.

Attributing these results to occupational stress alone ignores the possibility of self-selection. Perhaps certain kinds of people are likely to choose medicine rather than another profession, or general practice rather than dermatology. Here, Vaillant's longitudinal study is helpful. When the students arrived at university, their childhood was evaluated by a psychiatrist over several interviews and by a home visit with the parents. These included a discussion of the students' early development, so that an indication of their life adjustment before they entered university could be gathered. When the medical and other students' results were pooled, as in Table 10.4, childhood experiences provided a good predictor of how well they were coping in later years. Amongst those with good childhood adjustment, only 15% experienced 2 or 3 of the symptoms under consideration, whereas almost half of those with relatively poor childhoods experienced 2 or more symptoms. Other analyses of the data indicated

Table 10.4   Percentages of Adults with High or Low Childhood Adjustment who showed Symptoms of Difficulty

(Reproduced from G.E. Vaillant, N.C. Sobowale and C. McArthur, *New England Journal of Medicine*, 1972, **287**, 372 – 375, by permission.)

Number of symptoms	Childhood adjustment	
	Good	Poor
0 – 1	85	53
2 – 3	15	47

that it was primarily those physicians whose early adjustment was poor who were most prone to symptoms in adulthood. These doctors were more likely to take up specialities that required primary responsibility for patient care, such as psychiatry, obstetrics and paediatrics. It appeared, at least for this sample of doctors, that self-selection into a speciality could account for the higher incidence of divorce, drug abuse and visits to a psychiatrist, rather than the profession itself. Vaillant speculated that some physicians may elect to assume direct care of patients in order to give others the care that they did not receive in their own childhoods, an idea that has gained some currency in other caring professions.

10.3 Old Age

Defining Old Age

Although chronological age is usually the way we decide whether a person is elderly, many of the important features of old age are masked by this measure. The range of the physical and social capabilities of elderly people is wide, so that chronological age does not provide a good criterion for predicting how a person will behave. Although many cognitive and physical differences can be found between the old and the young, these differences are due in part to other factors besides age itself. Different generations have had very different life experiences, for instance, a problem inherent in cross-sectional research. Younger people could be expected to have more practice and experience in many of the tasks used by psychologists, such as IQ tests for example, thus overall lower scores of older people could be attributed to less experience with the type of test rather than to lowered intelligence. When differences are found between two groups of people, it is important to consider the range of scores within each group as well. A previous example of this point was given in Chapter 8 during the discussion of sex differences (Fig. 8.1): sex actually explains very little of the variation in scores on creativity, so that knowing the sex of a subject increases predictability only slightly. Similar results have been found in studies comparing the old and the young. One task that has been commonly used is reaction times, in which subjects are asked to press a button as soon as they can manage after seeing a light or hearing a tone. Although response times increase with chronological age, age itself accounts for only 5 % of the range in scores. The young are more likely to engage in tasks that give them practice in reaction times, such as driving a car, and when the elderly are given considerable practice in such tasks they approach the young in speed. Similarly, age-related differences have been found between healthy men 68 – 86 years of age and athletic males aged 19 – 22, but not between the older subjects and non-athletic young men. Correlations between chronological age and various psychological, social and physiological measures have generally been low[33]. When defining old age it is necessary to specify the relevant variables and to note with whom the elderly are being compared[34, 35].

Much emphasis has been placed on psychological and environmental factors here because views of the ageing process can have significant effects on how the elderly are treated. A doctor or nurse who considers ageing to be due primarily to physiological deterioration may be less likely to recommend training programmes for the elderly. Yet such problems as incontinence respond well to techniques of behaviour therapy[36]. Caregivers with such a physiological view might be less likely to allow elderly patients to take responsibility for their decisions or to encourage independence. Barton *et al.*[37] observed residents and staff in a nursing home, paying particular attention to how the staff reacted to indications of independence in the residents. Residents who attempted to look after themselves were likely to receive responses that discouraged self-reliance, and praise was given if the residents accepted assistance.

Such practices may have important consequences for the welfare of patients, dissuading them from relying on and practising their own skills and abilities. In another study, nursing-home residents were divided into two groups. Some were told that many of the features of their living conditions were their own responsibility and this notion was reinforced by some small reminders. They were each given a plant to care for, they were encouraged to review how the home was run and to comment upon the complaints procedure, for example. The other residents were not encouraged to look after themselves to any degree, being told that the staff were responsible for their care. They, too, were each given a plant, but were informed that the staff would water it, and so on. After 3 weeks, self-report questionnaires indicated that the first group were more active and were happier than the second group, and these reports were supported by nurses' observations of the residents' general behaviour. At an interview, the responsible group seemed more alert. Strikingly, 71% of the group who were told that they would be given almost complete care showed some deterioration over the period of the study, whereas 93% of the self-reliant group showed improvement. The researchers argued that the debilitated condition of elderly people living in institutions is due in part to the environment in which they live. Without the opportunity and encouragement to make decisions about their lives, deterioration may result[38].

Problems of the elderly

Bearing in mind the wide variation in these processes of ageing, it is nevertheless worthwhile to consider many of the difficulties that older people encounter as a group. In modern Western society, youth is associated with promise and worth, whereas the elderly are considered less positively. (This is in contrast to some other cultures, where old age represents wisdom and leadership.) The old are often considered to be less competent than the young, so that failure may be attributed to lack of ability in the elderly, but lack of effort on the part of the young[39]. The increase in introversion and decrease in confidence associated with increasing chronological age may be due to such cultural stereotypes of the elderly.

Adjustment to retirement is a life event specifically associated with ageing, and there is evidence that life satisfaction decreases shortly afterwards. Chatfield[40] sent questionnaires to workers who were about to retire, to those who left work less than one year previously and to those who had been retired more than one year. Scores on the questionnaires indicated that the recently retired group were, indeed, less happy with their life, but that this decrease was no longer significant after 1 year. Possibly, adjustment takes about 12 months to achieve. In general, the contention that retirement is particularly stressful has not been supported by most evidence, although individual differences are again important. Financial and social support have been shown to be relevant to adjustment. Income loss is significant, in that those who feel secure financially have less difficulty in adjusting. Past employment history is also relevant — those who have had several job losses during their lifetime tend to view the prospect of retirement with anxiety. This may be due to an association between not working and financial difficulty, or perhaps those who have changed job often do not have adequate pensions. Where social support is concerned, the important factor in predicting how well someone will adjust to retirement is not the number of people an individual knows, nor the frequency of contact, but the quality of social relationships[41].

As a group, the elderly show a diminished ability to adjust to change. Particular care is therefore needed when adjustments are required, such as a change of residence. Several studies have indicated that the mortality rate is excessively high when the elderly are rehoused or transferred from one hospital ward to another. Some of these studies have not controlled for their health (sometimes they are moved because of deteriorating health) but even where this factor has been taken into account the findings are generally consistent. In one study, elderly patients who were moved from one hospital to another were compared with those who remained. The patients were matched on several relevant variables, including age, sex, length of hospitalization and organic and functional illness. When their mortality rates were compared for the first 4 months after transfer, the group of patients who had been moved showed an incidence of death four times higher than those who had stayed[42].

Part of the difficulty with relocation seems to be due to the relative lack of control the elderly have over events. Old age is a period of diminished power, both financial and social. As suggested by the study mentioned above on encouraging nursing-home residents to take responsibility for their care[38], a lack of control may have adverse effects on health. An experimental study has been performed to test the importance of relocation, friendship patterns and personal control on mortality rates in the elderly. People living in the community were randomly assigned to one of three conditions — minimal, moderate or maximum care. Minimal care involved giving information about existing services and encouraging the elderly and their families to use them if they chose. By contrast, maximum care involved direct intensive aid, often resulting in a change from home to institution. After 6 months, the maximum-care group showed the highest mortality rate, whereas those in the minimum-care group showed the lowest. Those who were uprooted were deprived of the greater degree of family support they had enjoyed and placed in an unfamiliar

254

environment, taxing their capacity to adjust[43]. The increasing emphasis on community (rather than hospital) care is, in part, a response to findings such as these.

Dying

Much has been written about the ways that people cope with their own death. Most of this work has come from doctors and nurses who are intimately involved with the dying, relying on their own feelings and observations of patients and their relatives. Kubler-Ross[44] has made a considerable impact with her contention that the dying work through five stages. The first reaction is often *denial*, a refusal to believe that death is imminent. This stage is characterized by statements such as 'No, not me, it can't be true' and may be coupled with isolation from others. Isolation may take the form of withdrawal or artificial, inauthentic relationships. Denial often recurs throughout the coping process. The second stage is characterized by *anger*, envy and resentment. Anger is often directed towards both staff and relatives, which may make it difficult for them to cope if it is taken personally. When anger does not prove effective, the third stage is entered. *Bargaining* is seen as an attempt to postpone death by looking for a reward for good behaviour. In the hope that doctors will take better care, offers to leave the body to science may be given. Fourth, and when death seems inevitable, *depression* is commonly experienced. Death involves more than the loss of one's own life — it also involves the loss of family, friends and plans for the future. This period is characterized by sadness and crying, and Kubler-Ross stresses the importance of allowing patients to work through this stage, rather than giving encouragement and reassurance that they will recover. Patients may need assistance in talking over their feelings. Finally, she believes that, given time and help, people come to the stage of *acceptance*, when they realize that the struggle is over and that it is time to die. This stage is characterized by silence and an increasing wish to be detached from others.

Other writers have taken issue with Kubler-Ross, contending that the terminally ill do not go through these stages in any set order, but may show all these reactions at any time. Some have found that few patients withdraw, for example, at the end of their lives. It seems from their observations that denial, anger, bargaining, depression and acceptance are not stages but reactions that occur and re-occur throughout the illness.

There is agreement, however, on the importance of considering not only the patient but also his or her family. On the one hand, their reactions are important for the patient. The spouse's ability to cope with financial and personal affairs may make it easier or more difficult for the patient to accept death. Kubler-Ross also points out that the reactions of friends and family may not be compatible with those of the patient: if they continue to deny death, it would be difficult for the patient to talk with them. On the other hand, the patient's family have needs in their own right and they, too, often cope in similar ways to the ill themselves. It is not uncommon for them to have feelings of anger and resentment towards the patient because of 'desertion' and feelings of guilt for not noticing the illness sooner. The family is sometimes angry at medical staff since they can be seen as somehow responsible, coupled with envy because they are able to care for the patient. It seems that the family often withdraws from the patient, leaving him or her isolated. Occasionally, the interests of friends and relatives are more important than those of the patient, especially if he is irretrievably unconscious.

It may be difficult for nursing and medical staff to cope with the complexity of emotions shown by patients and their families, and it has been argued that the difficulties are sometimes compounded by the staff's own feelings about death. Some writers contend that an important reason for entering the medical profession is to cure people, and that an inability to do so is a sign of failure for many, failures for which there is 'nothing else which can be done'. There is some evidence that, indeed, the terminally ill receive poorer care than those who are recovering. Leshan[45] measured the delay between the time that nurses received a bedside call from their patients and their reply. They took longer to answer the calls from the terminally ill than from those less seriously ill. The nurses were unaware of this difference in their responses. Another study indicated that those patients who had declined the most were moved the greatest distance from the nursing station[46].

The decision to tell or not to tell patients and their relatives about a terminal prognosis is one of the most anxiety-provoking responsibilities of medical and paramedical staff. There are some helpful articles written by doctors and nurses (e.g. see Refs. 47 and 48). Many writers have pointed out that action cannot be avoided: skirting mention of the terminal illness has consequences as much as open discussion, although the consequences may be different. Support from practising physicians can be found for both courses of action.

First, there is the research on the incidence of informing. Generally, the more recent the study the greater the proportion of caregivers who favour informing patients and relatives. In the early 1960s, 60 – 90% of doctors were found to be against it, whereas more recent studies have indicated that most are now in favour of giving this information. The decision seems to be influenced by several factors. One possibility is a general reluctance to transmit bad news: a series of experiments have indicated a reticence in people to give this kind of information, particularly if the news is to be given personally[49]. Another factor involves the patient's personality. 'Calm' patients are more likely to be told than 'emotional' ones, and there is some evidence that the MMPI personality questionnaire can be used to distinguish those who will show high emotional disturbance to knowledge about serious illness (see Chapter 2). On the whole however, there is little evidence that personality patterns can be used to predict the individual's response to terminal illness with any consistency. Hinton[50] took several measures, including personality tests and assessments of marital patterns, and related these to patients' reactions based on interviews with the spouse, on observations by nurses on the ward and on reports by the patients themselves. Although some correlations were significant, they were never very high. Few differences were found in the reactions of those judged emotional and those judged stable before the illness, which is interesting because this is one dimension that doctors report influences their decision.

A third factor concerns the patient's family circumstances. Although 67% of the physicians in one study said that the patient should be told, 37% reported that when their wishes were in conflict with the family's, the spouse's wish should be honoured. The patient's age and the way questions are asked also seem important. Cartwright and her colleagues[51] asked a sample of doctors what they would do in different situations, and some of their results are shown in Table 10.5. Most reported that they would tell a 55-year-old businessman who asks, but only 2% a young mother who seemed unaware.

Table 10.5   Telling Patients about a Terminal Prognosis

Responses of 323 doctors to hypothetical situations. (Reproduced from A. Cartwright, L. Hockey and J.L. Anderson, *Life before Death*, 1973, by permission of Routledge & Kegan Paul, London.)

What the doctor would probably do in these situations	People with cancer who will almost certainly die within 6 weeks (%)		
	Businessman of 55 who asks 'Is this going to kill me doctor?'	Young mother of 35 with young children who does not raise subject and seems unaware	Elderly widower who asks 'This won't kill me doctor, will it?'
Tell person the truth	65	2	13
Tell their spouse the truth	—	97	—
Say he does not know	10	—	—
Deny that he will die	12	—	39
Pass it off as a joke, change subject	4	—	34
Qualified answer	9	1	14

In the caring professions it seems most vital to minimize the number of instances where a problem is missed. An example of this was given in the previous chapter where child abuse was discussed: it is felt less of a mistake to remove a child from a home in which violence may well not occur than to leave a child in potentially dangerous circumstances. In medicine, a similar rule of thumb is often employed. When examining X-rays, for example, physicians make many more false positive errors than false negatives, perhaps 30 times as many[52]. Perhaps, too, this provides one reason why general practitioners explore organic problems exhaustively before considering psychological ones: it may be seen as much more important not to miss a physical problem than to recognize a psychiatric one. When this tendency is applied to informing patients of a terminal prognosis, it is easy to see one reason for the reluctance. Since some patients may lose all hope after being given the information and since it is difficult to know which patients really want to be told, the safe course of action is to inform very few. Just as it may seem better to judge a well person sick than a sick person well, perhaps physicians find it preferable not to tell a patient who does want to know than to tell a patient who doesn't[53, 54].

Another approach to research in this area has been to ask patients themselves whether they would wish to be informed of a terminal prognosis. Several studies have indicated that among patients who are not terminally ill, most would wish to be told. The problem with research of this kind is that the decision is largely hypothetical, with patients being asked to imagine how they would react under the circumstances. Since people are not particularly adept at predicting how they would respond in unfamiliar situations, as the research in Chapter 6 has suggested, these studies form a poor basis for indicating whether or not dying patients want to be told. One study has examined this point in more detail. Cappon[55] interviewed a range of people, some who were healthy, others who were ill and yet others who were terminally ill. To the question 'If you were very sick, would you want to know you were going to die?', there was a gradation of responses with, for example, 91% of the healthy wishing to know but only 67% of the dying. Although it seems that most terminally ill patients want to have this information, this is not always the case.

Given the confusing results of survey studies and the ethical problems with experimental designs, the issue might be considered as one primarily dependent on values and personal experience. Some have argued that keeping the information from patients can mean that staff have to guard against disclosure (distancing them from their patients) and that this can result in suspicion and mutual pretence. Behind the decision not to inform lies the assumption that patients will not be able to discern the deception, an assumption that may not be warranted: patients seem very sensitive to the non-verbal cues given by staff[56]. Open awareness, on the other hand, can be seen to facilitate communication, giving the patient an opportunity to die as he or she would like, to reconcile long-standing misunderstandings with friends and family and to help make plans for the bereaved[57]. It may be that the question is not 'What do you tell your patients?' but rather 'what do you allow your patients to tell you?'[58]. Listening to the terminally ill and observing the extent to which each individual attempts to gain information may provide the surest clues as to appropriate action. The attitudes that the caregiving staff have towards death are therefore critical, in that patients may not be able to discuss the possibility of death with those who are uncomfortable and avoid the topic.

If the decision to inform is taken, there are some additional problems to be considered. One is the importance of keeping records. There are indications that even when a prognosis is communicated to the patient, this action is not always made known to all staff members, so that some continue to avoid the subject. A second difficulty is that patients may not remember much of what they have been told. Perhaps because of repression (Chapter 2) or perhaps because of the shock involved (Chapter 4), some patients may not recall their prognosis or related information. Simply because the patient has been informed does not necessarily mean that this will be remembered.

The care of the dying has changed in recent years. An increasing awareness of their difficulties has helped define the responsibilities of the caregivers. The idea of 'safe conduct' has been suggested as the caregivers' role, requiring commitment to not only control pain, but also to approach the patient with acceptance, candour, compassion and mutual accessibility. Psychotherapy with the terminally ill, providing them with an opportunity to express their physical and emotional concerns, has been suggested. An important development is the hospice, an environment in which openness about death is encouraged. Many of the constraints found in hospitals are not present. Children and pets are welcome, staff members are encouraged to touch the patients, and drugs such as heroin and alcohol are available. The needs of the whole family are considered and not just those of the patient[59].

Bereavement

Not only the terminally ill are affected by the process of dying — the adjustment required of the bereaved is considerable, and research has provided indications of the severity of the change. In one survey, 2.9% of the admissions to a psychiatric hospital had lost a parent, a spouse, sibling or child in the 6 months before the onset of the illness, compared to a rate of 0.5% which would be expected by chance[60]. The number of consultations with general practitioners increases sharply with bereavement, one study showing a 7-fold increase in prescriptions for sedatives[61]. Many of the widowed report that their children show behaviour problems, and these difficulties have been found to be associated with poor adjustment in the parent[62]. Suicide among the widowed is high in the first few years after bereavement[63]. An increase in physical symptomatology has also been found by several researchers, with something like a 40% increase in mortality rates in the first 6 months following a spouse's death[64].

Several explanations for these findings could be suggested. The higher incidence of mortality could be due to homogamy (e.g. a tendency for the fit to marry the fit), mutual infection, a joint unfavourable environment or the loss of care that one spouse gives to the other. Although these factors are probably of importance, many researchers have argued that the most important is the 'broken heart' suffered by the survivor. The loss of companionship is thought to have serious detrimental effects[65].

The bereaved frequently show periods of somatic distress (loss of appetite and initiative) and preoccupation with images of the deceased. These reactions are considered to be part of normal grief and to be signs of deeper difficulties only when they are not resolved. Again, psychotherapy and organizations for the bereaved are thought to be of considerable assistance. In an attempt to determine factors that are associated with poor outcome after bereavement, Parkes[62] interviewed the surviving spouse 3 weeks, 6 weeks and 13 months after the death. The following factors were identified: low economic status, multiple life crises, severe distress, yearning anger and self-reproach, and short terminal illness with little warning of the death. The significance of this last factor has been given further support in another study that indicated that the risk of mortality in the bereaved was twice as high if the death occurred suddenly without the opportunity to prepare for it[66]. This result suggests that grieving begins before the death of a relative and that the shock may be lessened if relatives are given an opportunity to begin to adjust before the death.

10.4 Stress Buffering

The theme of this chapter is adjustment to change — the learning of new ways of coping with new situations. It is important to remember that adjustment is continuous, in that novel events occur throughout life. Any number of examples could be given — the birth of child, retirement, bereavement — to illustrate that being able to cope with change is an important aspect of living. If the stresses involved in such changes can be moderated or buffered in some way, then the negative psychological and physiological responses involved in adjustment may be reduced to some extent. Drugs are often used by the medical profession to help their patients and by the general population itself to cope with their anxieties. There are some 20 million prescriptions issued each year in the United Kingdom for benzodiazepines (tranquillizers) and 10% of the women and 5% of the men in this country can be considered to be dependent on them. Three areas of research that point to alternative psychological approaches to stress buffering are considered in this part of the chapter.

Cognitive Restructuring

The model of stress outlined earlier in the chapter indicated that stress involves not only demands from the environment but also individuals' appraisal of those demands. The way people react depends in part on their beliefs, values and attitudes about the event. Although it is true to say that some events are inherently stressful for humans (e.g. prolonged lack of sleep), many researchers have argued that in most everyday situations the 'cause' of the stressful response lies within the perceptions of the individual. This is not to say that these perceptions are wrong, but that they reflect belief systems. The implication is that if these beliefs can be altered the events will result in less stress.

Some researchers have noted that defence mechanisms can be effective. The study that examined subjects' responses to a film on circumcision procedures described earlier in the chapter provides a typical example of an experiment on cognitive defences. Denial is a common initial response to the possibility of one's own or a relative's death and may assist people in eventually coming to terms with the fact. Evidence that denial can be effective in reducing stress responses is given by a study of patients whose children were dying of leukemia. Parents who denied the fatal significance of the disease showed lower levels of cortical stress hormones than those parents who recognized the implications[67]. It will be remembered from Chapter 1 that although it was generally beneficial to inform patients explicitly of the procedures and consequences of surgery, certain patients showed somewhat worse outcomes. It seemed that these patients were using the mechanism of denial in order to cope, and that this mechanism was over-ridden by the information.

A procedure for providing alternative ways of coping with stress is called 'stress innoculation'. This approach is based on the possibility that people have difficulty in coping with change because they do not have adequate strategies available. Rather than encouraging denial of stressful events, attempts are made to provide new skills. The importance of self-instruction in dealing with novel situations was discussed in Chapter 3. Briefly, the suggestion is that in learning new skills — whether the skill is riding a bicycle or taking an exam — people often give themselves silent instructions about how to act. Stress innoculation training involves attempts to encourage adaptive rather than maladaptive self-instructions through three phases: education, rehearsal and application. The educational phase is designed to give the individual a framework for understanding the nature of responses to stressful events. The ways that interpretations of a situation can serve to increase physiological arousal and exacerbate the situation are discussed. To take an example of this approach, Novaco[68] described a programme with patients who commonly reacted with anger to frustrating events. When provoked, these patients would say to themselves things like: 'Who the hell does he think he is: he can't do that to me' or 'He wants to play it that way, okay, I'll show him'. By discussing these self-instructions, the patients were led to see the possibility that their emotional reactions to the situations were influenced by their cognitive appraisals.

The second phase — rehearsal — involves the exploration of alternative self-statements. Instead of maladaptive ones, adaptive responses are encouraged. In Novaco's study, this stage included training in relaxation similar to that used in systematic desensitization, i.e. muscles were alternately tensed and relaxed. Concurrently the patients were asked to analyse the situations in which they found themselves uncontrollably angry, looking for the events that triggered the anger and reflecting on alternative self-instructions they could have used. Instead of 'He thinks I'm a pushover; I'll get even', the patients were encouraged to instruct themselves to 'Stay calm. Just continue to relax', 'Don't assume the worst or jump to conclusions' and 'Time to take a deep breath'. In both imagination and role plays, the patients were asked to congratulate themselves when they successfully coped with their anger. An important point about this programme was not that it sought to inhibit anger itself but to give the patients a greater repertoire in their coping reactions and to encourage more socially acceptable ways of expressing themselves.

The third phase involves application of these new self-instructions. By asking the patients to keep diaries of their experiences outside the training sessions, Novaco was able to show that the programme was successful in real life. Encouraging an awareness of the importance of interpretations and providing alternative strategies for coping with situations enabled the patients to adjust to events more effectively. A similar programme has been applied to surgical patients and the pain they suffer, a study discussed in the next chapter.

Predictability and Control

There have been only a few experimental studies on loss of control in clinical populations. The research mentioned above on the elderly who were randomly assigned to minimal, moderate and maximum care is one example: the incidence of mortality was highest in the group of patients over whom considerable control was exercised. However, several studies in psychological laboratories have indicated that having a measure of control over events lessens their stressful effects. A typical study could involve giving electric shocks to subjects and taking psychological and physiological measures of distress. The experimental manipulation would involve giving one group of subjects a degree of control over the timing of the shocks whereas another group would not be given any control. For example, Hokanson et al.[69] gave the subjects in one condition the opportunity to call for a rest from shocks, whereas those in the second condition were dependent on others for their rests. In this particular study the measure was of systolic blood pressure: the pressure in the second group was higher than that of the first. Control has been hypothesized as being significant in the onset of depression. In a series of studies, Seligman has provided support for the idea that feelings of depression are the result of the perception that life events are unavoidable and uncontrollable[70].

Even when people are unable to control an outcome, there seems to be a need to know when it will occur. The frequency with which patients ask for information in hospital wards can be seen as an indication of the strength of their need for understanding, and the experiments on preparing patients for surgery show the significance of prediction. In one study, 14 patients who were transferred from coronary-care units to ordinary wards were randomly assigned to one of two groups. Seven were given a routine transfer, and the other seven were given preparation (when the transfer would occur, what the new ward would be like) and a member of the coronary-care staff visited the patients in the new setting. The researchers measured the incidence of complications in these two groups: five of the first group, but only one of the second group, had complications in the novel setting[71].

A scale similar to the Holmes and Rahe SRRS has been developed to assess the degree of adjustment involved in various aspects of hospitalization, shown in Table 10.6[72]. This was developed by asking patients to rank events they had experienced when in hospital from most stressful to least stressful. These events fell into several categories, such as unfamiliarity of surroundings and loss of independence. Most interestingly, many of the most stressful events were concerned with the incidental aspects of entering hospital — having strangers

Table 10.6   Hospital Stress Factors

(Reproduced from B.J. Volicer, M.A. Isenberg and M.W. Burns, *Journal of Human Stress*, 1977, **3**, 3 – 13, by permission.)

Factor	Stress scale events	Assigned rank	Mean rank score
1. Unfamiliarity of surroundings	Having strangers sleep in the same room with you	01	13.9
	Having to sleep in a strange bed	03	15.9
	Having strange machines around	05	16.8
	Being awakened in the night by the nurse	06	16.9
	Being aware of unusual smells around you	11	19.4
	Being in a room that is too cold or too hot	16	21.7
	Having to eat cold or tasteless food	21	23.2
	Being cared for by an unfamiliar doctor	23	23.4
2. Loss of independence	Having to eat at different times than you usually do	02	15.4
	Having to wear a hospital gown	04	16.0
	Having to be assisted with bathing	07	17.0
	Not being able to get newspapers, radio or TV when you want them	08	17.7
	Having a roommate who has too many visitors	09	18.1
	Having to stay in bed or the same room all day	10	19.1
	Having to be assisted with a bedpan	13	21.5
	Not having your call light answered	35	27.3
	Being fed through tubes	39	29.2

Factor	Stress scale events	Assigned rank	Mean rank score
	Thinking you may lose your sight	49	40.6
3. Separation from spouse	Worrying about your spouse being away from you	20	22.7
4. Financial problems	Thinking about losing income because of your illness	27	25.9
	Not having enough insurance to pay for your hospitalization	36	27.4
5. Isolation from other people	Having a roommate who is seriously ill or cannot talk with you	12	21.2
	Having a roommate who is unfriendly	14	21.6
	Not having friends visit you	15	21.7
	Not being able to call family or friends on the phone	22	23.3
	Having the staff be in too much of a hurry	26	24.5
	Thinking you might lose you hearing	45	34.5
6. Lack of information	Thinking you might have pain because of surgery or test procedures	19	22.4
	Not knowing when to expect things will be done to you	25	24.2
	Having nurses or doctors talk too fast or use words you can't understand	29	26.4
	Not having your questions answered by the staff	37	27.6

Factor	Stress scale events	Assigned rank	Mean rank score
	Not knowing the results or reasons for your treatments	41	31.9
	Not knowing for sure what illnesses you have	43	34.0
	Not being told what your diagnosis is	44	34.1
7. Threat of severe illness	Thinking your appearance might be changed after your hospitalization	17	22.1
	Being put in the hospital because of an accident	24	26.9
	Knowing you have to have an operation	32	26.9
	Having a sudden hospitalization you weren't planning to have	34	27.2
	Knowing you have a serious illness	46	34.6
	Thinking you might lose a kidney or some other organ	47	35.6
	Thinking you might have cancer	48	39.2
8. Separation from family	Being in the hospital during holidays or special family occasions	18	22.3
	Not having family visit you	31	26.5
	Being hospitalized far away from home	33	27.1
9. Problems with medications	Having medications cause you discomfort	28	26.0
	Feeling you are getting dependent on medications	30	26.4
	Not getting relief from pain medications	40	31.2
	Not getting pain medication when you need it	42	32.4

sleep in the same room and having to eat at different times from usual. By contrast, being put in a hospital because of an accident was ranked 24th, and knowing about a serious illness 46th. These results were not due to the order in which the events were given to the patients, since each event was placed on a card and the cards were shuffled before each presentation. It seems that the greatest adjustment has to do with the experience of hospitalization rather than the disease associated with the experience. This scale has been given some validation by a later study: those patients who reported that they had experienced many of the events on the scale were observed to show the largest changes on cardiovascular measures[73].

Social Support

The notion that fulfilling and intimate relationships with others assists in coping with changes has a long history. In this century, Durkheim — often considered the father of modern sociology — noted that suicide rates among the married were much lower than those among the divorced or never-married. He attributed this difference to a protective effect engendered by close relationships: life may not seem so stressful if there is at least one close relationship. Brown's findings (mentioned earlier in this chapter) concerning the lower incidence of depression in women with a confidant is also relevant. To take another example, Nuckalls *et al.*[74] reviewed the records of mothers for the incidence of complications during pregnancy and delivery (e.g. high blood pressure, prolonged labour), the extent to which they experienced life changes, and the degree of psycho-social support felt by the women (as measured by their marital happiness, friendships and confidence in the support they would be given by their families). For mothers who had high life-change scores both before and during pregnancy, those with low social support were some three times more likely to have one or more complications than those with high social support (91% versus 33%). In the absence of stressful events, no relationship between support and complications was found. Cobb[75] provides a review of research in this area.

The problem with studies of this kind concerns casuality again: being unmarried, divorced or unsupported implies more than just lack of a spouse. Although myocardial infarction patients are found to be more likely to be divorced than an age-matched comparison group, they are also more likely to have feelings of loneliness, a decreased sense of enjoyment and to be nervous[76]. In other words, much of the evidence for the moderating effect of social support is correlational and based on retrospective studies. However, this does not mean that the idea is misplaced and there is considerable descriptive and clinical evidence testifying to the importance of support. There is some research that at least meets the criticisms about retrospective analyses. In one longitudinal study, over 4700 adults were interviewed in 1965. They were asked about several aspects of their lives, including socioeconomic status, social contacts and the number of preventative measures they took to safe-guard their health. Nine years later, the investigators managed to follow up 96% of the sample. Those adults who reported close contact with others in 1965 were much less likely to have died by 1974 by a factor of 2.3 in the case of men, 2.8 for women[77]. This association held even when such variables as socioeconomic status, smoking habits, obesity, alcohol intake and physical activity 9 years earlier were taken into account. Preliminary results of a similar study concerning psychiatric illness have been reported recently. Henderson[78] examined a cross-section of the population in Canberra. 177 residents were interviewed a total of four times over a 1-year period. All were considered to be psychologically healthy at the time of the first interview. At each interview, measures of social support, life events and psychiatric disorder were taken. In keeping with the increasing evidence that only adverse life changes (rather than change *per se*) provide the important predictors of stress, the subjects were asked to indicate their negative experiences for the 4 months before the interviews. Henderson found support for his hypothesis that lack of adequate social relationships was associated with the onset of neurosis, but only in the presence of adverse life changes. As Brown's work indicated, it is the combination that is significant, and not one or the other independently.

Summary

To cope with events such as the birth of a child, bereavement or an illness, a person must make adjustments. These can impose stress. The term stress has been used to refer to both physiological reaction to the event and to the event itself, but a more adequate definition also takes the person's perception of the event into account.

Many studies have shown that the amount of change recently experienced by an individual — particularly adverse change — is related to the reported incidence of physical illness. Such changes may be associated with psychiatric illnesses in certain individuals who are 'vulnerable'. Illness itself causes stress, compounding the problem. The effects of stress may be lessened by the presence of social support, by altering an individual's perceptions of events, and by giving people more control over events.

Both redundancy and retirement have been shown to have stressful effects, adjustment to the latter being aided by adequate financial and social support. Elderly people as a group show a diminished ability to adjust to changes, such as a change in residence or a move between hospital wards. Whether or not patients are informed about a terminal prognosis, the process of dying requires considerable adjustment on the part of both patient and family. Specific stages in this adjustment process have been identified, and caregivers can assist in helping the family through the array of emotions expressed.

Suggested Reading

Different illnesses seem to have different psychological consequences — J.G.

Howells (ed.), *Modern perspectives in the psychiatric aspects of surgery*, Macmillan Press, London, 1976, and R.H. Moos, *Coping with physical illness*, Plenum Medical Books, London, 1977, consider the difficulties in coping with many conditions.

Some of Bowlby's early work on the importance of attachment was discussed in Chapter 7. A more recent extension of his thinking concerning bereavement and mourning can be found in J. Bowlby, *Attachment and loss* Vol. 3 Loss, Hogarth Press, London, 1980.

References

1. Selye, H., *The stress of life*, McGraw-Hill, New York, 1956.
2. Glass, D. and Singer, J., *Urban stress experiments in noise and social stressors*, Academic Press, New York, 1972.
3. Cox, T., *Stress*, Macmillan Press, London, 1978.
4. Frankenhaeuser, M., Nordheden, B., Myrsten, A.L. and Post, B., Psychophysiological reactions to understimulation and overstimulation, *Acta Psychologica*, 1971, **35**, 298 – 308.
5. Speisman, J.C., Lazarus, R.S., Mordkoff, A.M. and Davidson, L.A., The experimental reduction of stress based on ego-defense theory, *Journal of Abnormal and Social Psychology*, 1964, **68**, 367 – 380.
6. Cohen, F. and Lazarus, R.S., Coping with the stresses of illness, *In* Stone, G.C., Cohen, F. and Adler, N.E. (eds.), *Health psychology*, Jossey-Bass, London, 1979.
7. Cohen, F. and Lazarus, R.S., Active coping processes, coping dispositions and recovery from surgery, *Psychosomatic Medicine*, 1973, **35**, 375 – 389.
8. Leif, H.I. and Fox, R.C., Training for 'detached concern' in medical students, *In* Leif, H.I., Liet, V.F. and Leif, N.R. (eds.), *The psychological bases of medical practice*, Harper and Row, New York, 1963.
9. Holmes, T.H. and Rahe, R.H., The social readjustment rating scale, *Journal of Psychosomatic Research*, 1967, **11**, 213 — 218.
10. Wyler, A.R., Masuda, M. and Holmes, T.M., Magnitude of life events and seriousness of illness, *Psychosomatic Medicine*, 1971, **33**, 115 – 122.
11. Rahe, R.H., Life change and subsequent illness reports, *In* Gunderson, K.E. and Rahe, R.H. (eds.), *Life stress and illness*, Thomas and Co., Springfield, 1974.
12. Rundall, T.G., Life change and recovery from surgery, *Journal of Health and Social Behaviour*, 1978, **19**, 418 – 427.
13. Andrews, G., and Tennant, C., Being upset and becoming ill: an appraisal of the relation between life events and physical illness, *Medical Journal of Australia*, 1978, **1**, 324 – 327.
14. Dohrenwend, B.S. and Dohrenwend, B.P., Some issues in research in stressful life events, *Journal of Nervous and Mental Disease*, 1978, **166**, 7 – 15.
15. McFarlane, A.H., Norman, G.R. and Streiner, D., A longitudinal study of the psychosocial environment on health status, *Journal of Health and Social Behaviour*, 1980, **21** 124 – 133.
16. Brown, G.W. and Harris, T., *Social origins of depression*, Tavistock Publications, London, 1978.
17. Paykel, E.S., Contribution of life events to causation of psychiatric illness, *Psychological Medicine*, 1978, **8**, 245 – 253.

18. Hull, D., Migration, adaptation and illness: a review, *Social Science and Medicine*, 1979, **13A**, 25 – 36.
19. Henry, J.P. and Cassel, J.C., Psychosocial factors in essential hypertension *American Journal of Epidemiology*, 1969, **90**, 171 – 200.
20. Tyrola, H.A. and Cassel, J.T., Health consequences of cultural change: the effect of urbanization on coronary heart mortality in rural residents, *Journal of Chronic Diseases*, 1964, **17**, 167 – 177.
21. Devlin, B.H., Plant, J.A. and Griffin, M., Aftermath of surgery for anorectal cancer, *British Medical Journal*, 1971, **3**, 413 – 418.
22. Klein, R.F., Dean, A. and Bogdonoff, M.D., The impact of illness upon the spouse, *Journal of Chronic Diseases*, 1967, **20**, 241 – 248.
23. Parkes, C.M., Psychosocial transitions: comparison between reactions to loss of a limb and loss of a spouse, *British Journal of Psychiatry*, 1975, **127**, 204 – 210.
24. Jamison, K.R., Wellisch, D.K. and Pasnau, R.O., Psychosocial aspects of mastectomy: 1. The woman's perspective, *American Journal of Psychiatry*, 1978, **135**, 432 – 436.
25. Lewis, F.M. and Bloom, J.R., Psychosocial adjustment to breast cancer: a review of selected literature, *International Journal of Psychiatry in Medicine*, 1979, **9**, 1 – 17.
26. Tolson, W.W., Mason, J.W., Sachar, E.J., Hamburg, D.A., Hanlow, J.H. and Fishman, J.R., Urinary catecholamine responses associated with hospital admission in normal subjects, *Journal of Psychosomatic Research*, 1965, **8**, 365 – 372.
27. Bruyn, J.G., Thurman, A.E., Chandler, B.C., and Bruce, T.A., Patients' reactions to death in a coronary care unit, *Journal of Psychosomatic Research*, 1970, **14**, 65 – 70.
28. Russek, H.I. and Zohman, B.L., Relative significance of hereditary, diet and occupational stress in CHD of young adults, *American Journal of Medical Science*, 1958, **235**, 266 – 275.
29. Jackson, P.R. and Stafford, E.M., Work involvement and employment status as influences on mental health, Paper presented at the BPS Social Psychology Section Conference, 1980.
30. Kasl, S.V. and Cobb, S., Blood pressure changes in men undergoing job loss, *Psychosomatic Medicine*, 1970, **32**, 19 – 38.
31. Cobb, S., Physiologic changes in men whose jobs were abolished, *Journal of Psychosomatic Research*, 1974, **18**, 245 – 258.
32. Vaillant, G.E., Sobowale, N.C. and McArthur, C., Some psychologic vulnerabilities of physicians, *New England Journal of Medicine*, 1972, **287**, 372 – 375.
33. Fozard, J.L. and Thomas, J.C., Psychology of ageing, *In* Howells, J.G. (ed.), *Modern perspective in the psychiatry of old age*, Brunner/Mazel, New York, 1975.
34. Heron, A. and Chown, S.M., *Age and function*, Churchill Livingstone, London, 1967.
35. Rosen, S., Plester, D., Elmofty, E. and Rosen, H.V, High speed audiometry in presbycusis: a comparative study of the Mabaans in the Sudan with urban populations, *Archives of Otolaryngology*, 1964, **79**, 18 – 32.
36. Mandelstam, D., *Incontinence and its management*, Croom Helm, London, 1980.
37. Barton, E.M., Baltes, M.M. and Orzech, M.J., Etiology of dependence in older nursing home residents during morning care: the role of staff behaviour, *Journal of Personality and Social Psychology*, 1980, **38**, 423 – 431.
38. Langer, E.J. and Rodin, J., The effects of choice and enhanced personal responsibility for the aged, *Journal of Pesonality and Social Psychology*, 1976, **34**, 191 – 198.
39. Reno, R., Attribution for success and failure as a function of perceived age, *Journal of Gerontology*, 1979, **34**, 709 – 715.

40. Chatfield, W.F, Economic and sociological factors influencing life satisfaction of the aged, *Journal of Gerontology*, 1977, **32**, 593 – 599.
41. Conner, K.A., Powers, E.A. and Bultena, G.L., Social interaction and life satisfaction: an empirical assessment of late-life patterns, *Journal of Gerontology*, 1979, **34**, 116 – 121.
42. Killian, E.C., Effects of geriatric transfers on mortality rates, *Social Work*, 1970, **15**, 19 – 26.
43. Blenkner, M., Environmental change and the ageing individual, *Gerontologist*, 1967, **7**, 101 – 105.
44. Kubler-Ross, E., *On death and dying*, Tavistock Publications, London, 1970.
45. Leshan, L., *In* Bowers, M., Jackson, E., Knoght, J. and Leshan, L. (eds.), *Counselling the dying*, Thomas Nelson, New York, 1964.
46. Watson, W.H., The ageing sick and the near dead; a study of some distinguishing characteristics and social effects, *Omega*, 1976, **7**, 115 – 123.
47. Souhami, R.L., Teaching what to say about cancer, *Lancet*, 1978, **2**, 935 – 936.
48. Bloch, S., Instruction on death and dying for the medical student, *Medical Education*, 1976, **10**, 269 – 273.
49. Tesser, A. and Rosen, S., The reluctance to transmit bad news, *In* Berkowitz, L. (ed.), *Advances in experimental social psychology*, Academic Press, London, 1975.
50. Hinton, J., The influence of previous personality on reactions to having terminal cancer, *Omega*, 1975, **6**, 95 – 111.
51. Cartwright, A., Hockey, L. and Anderson, J.L., *Life before death*, Routledge & Kegan Paul, London, 1973.
52. Garland, L.H., Studies in the accuracy of diagnosic procedures, *American Journal of Roentgenology* 1959, **82**, 25 – 38.
53. Scheff, T.J., Decision rules, types of errors and their consequences in medical diagnosis, *Behavioural Science*, 1963, **8**, 97 – 107.
54. McIntosh, J., The routine management of uncertainty in communication with cancer patients, *In* Davis, A. (ed.), *Relationships between doctors and patients*, Teakfield, Westmead, 1978.
55. Cappon, D., Attitudes of and towards the dying, *Canadian Medical Association Journal*, 1962, **87**, 693 – 700.
56. Shands, H.C., Psychological mechanisms in patients with cancer, *Cancer*, 1951, **4**, 1159 – 1170.
57. Glaser, B.G. and Strauss, A.L., *Awareness of dying*, Weidenfeld and Nicolson, London, 1966.
58. Saunders, C.M.S., The moment of truth: care of the dying person, *In* Pearson, L. (ed.), *Death and dying*, Case Western Reserve University Press, Cleveland, 1969.
59. Saunders, C., A therapeutic community, St. Christopher's hospice, *In* Schoenberg, B., Carr, A.C., Peretz, D. and Kutscher, A.H. (eds.), *Psychological aspects of terminal care*, Columbia University Press, New York, 1972.
60. Parkes, C.M., Recent bereavement as a cause of mental illness, *British Journal of Psychiatry*, 1964, **110**, 198 – 204.
61. Parkes, C.M., Bereavement, *British Medical Journal*, 1967, **3**, 232 – 233.
62. Parkes, C.M., Determinants of outcome following bereavement, *Omega*, 1975, **6**, 303 – 324.
63. MacMahon, B. and Pugh, T.F., Suicide in the widowed, *American Journal of Epidemiology*, 1965, **81**, 23 – 31.
64. Parkes, C.M., Benjamin, B. and Fitzgerald, R.G., Broken heart: a statistical study of increased mortality among widowers, *British Medical Journal*, 1969, **1**, 740 – 743.

65. Lynch, J.J., *The broken heart*, Basic Books, New York, 1977.
66. Rees, W.D. and Lutkins, S.C., Mortality of bereavement, *British Medical Journal*, 1967, **4**, 13 – 16.
67. Wolff, C.T., Hofer, M.A. and Mason, J.W., Relationship between psychological defenses and mean urinary 17-hydroxy corticosteroid excretion rates *Psychosomatic Medicine*, 1964, **26**, 576 – 591.
68. Novaco, R., *Anger control: the development and evaluation of an experimental treatment*, Heath and Co., Lexington, 1975.
69. Hokanson, J.E., DeGood, D.E., Forrest, M.S. and Brittain, T.M., Availability of avoidance behaviours in modulating vascular stress responses, *Journal of Personality and Social Psychology*, 1971, **19**, 60 – 68.
70. Seligman, M.E.P., *Helplessness*, W.H. Freeman, San Francisco, 1975.
71. Klein, R.F., Kliner, V.A., Zipes, D.P., Troyer, W.C. and Wallace, A.G., Transfer from a coronary care unit: some adverse responses, *Archives of Internal Medicine*, 1968, **122**, 104 – 108.
72. Volicer, B.J., Isenberg, M.A. and Burns, M.W., Medical-surgical differences in hospital stress factors, *Journal of Human Stress*, 1977, **3**, 3 – 13.
73. Volicer, B.J. and Volicer, L., Cardiovascular changes associated with stress during hospitalisation, *Journal of Psychosomatic Research*, 1978, **22**, 159 – 168.
74. Nuckalls, C.B., Cassel, J. and Kaplan, B.H. Psychosocial assets, life crises and the prognosis of pregnancy, *American Journal of Epidemiology*, 1972, **95**, 431 – 444.
75. Cobb, S., Presidential address 1976: Social support as a moderator of life stress, *Psychosomatic Medicine*, 1976, **38**, 300 – 314.
76. Theil, H.G., Parker, D. and Bruce, T.A., Stress factors and the risk of myocardial infarction, *Journal of Psychosomatic Research*, 1973, **17**, 43 – 57.
77. Berkmal, L.F. and Syme, S.L., Social networks, host resistance and mortality *American Journal of Epidemiology*, 1979, **109**, 186 – 204.
78. Henderson, S. Social relationships, adversity and neurosis *British Journal of Psychiatry*, 1981, **138**, 391 – 398.

PART 3
Doctor – Patient
Communication

11
Pain, Placebos and Drug Dependence

11.1   Introduction

The first section of this book provided an outline of important topics in psychology, including perception, learning and intelligence. Their interdependence was emphasized: for example, it was not possible to explain the principles of learning (Chapter 3) without recourse to the processes involved in interpretation (Chapter 1). The second section of the text explored human development, with particular emphasis on the family as a socializing influence. Questions of early infant – adult interaction, sexual identity and adjustment to life events all contribute to a better understanding of the individual, and the family plays an important role in these respects. It has become increasingly clear that one aspect of an individual's make-up cannot be separated from other aspects; this is essentially what is meant by 'whole person' medicine.

This third section of the text considers fields of study that are of direct relevance to medicine, including pain, the doctor – patient consultation and the influence of the doctor's attitudes, beliefs and training on medical care. Many of the topics covered in the first two sections of the text assist in the understanding of these areas.

In many respects, the present chapter is an extension of the previous one. In Chapter 10 the relationship between change and illness was considered. Not only the extent of change but also the meanings that individuals give to these changes were shown to be associated with the onset of physical and psychiatric illness. Some researchers have argued that there is a causal link between the two, with stressful events increasing the risk of illness. In this chapter, pain, placebos and drug dependence are considered, with emphasis on the importance of interpretation and evaluation of these experiences. That pain can have important social and psychological consequences as well as physiological ones was shown through the discussion of the sick role (Chapter 6) and receives more attention here. One example of how cognitive factors may affect the experience of pain is given by the second topic, placebo effects. Although the strength and importance of placebo effects can be exaggerated, this part of the chapter illustrates the complexity of the research. An important part of the difficulty in placebo research has been the lack of good experimental design. Finally, the area of drug dependence is considered, general findings being examined from addiction research rather than consideration of specific conditions such as opiate or alcohol dependence. The pharmacological properties of a drug do not seem to be as significant in dependence and relapse as is commonly supposed: psychological and social aspects appear to be equally important. For these three aspects of medical care then – pain, placebos and drug dependence — the distinction made between psychological and physiological processes is far from clear.

11.2   Pain

The Experience of Pain

In medical textbooks, the topic of pain is usually considered in terms of pain receptors and neural pathways. An understanding of the anatomical structures and physiological processes involved in pain is important, but there are some assumptions underlying this emphasis that are not altogether valid[1]. Consideration of only the sensory pathways involved in the experience of pain suggests that a good, perhaps even a one-to-one, relationship between the magnitude of tissue damage and the person's experiences could be found. Although this is sometimes the case, there is strong evidence that this is not always so, and these exceptions to the rule need to be taken into account when understanding pain. For instance, studies show that the amount of pain experienced by patients (as measured by the amount of analgesia required) can be modified by giving information about what to expect during their stay in hospital and the sensations that could be expected after surgery (Chapter 1).

276

This could not be accounted for using a purely physiological approach.

Much of the impetus for research into the experience of pain has been provided by Beecher, an anaesthetist. While treating soldiers in the Second World War, he was struck by the lack of correspondence between their reports of pain from injuries sustained on the battlefield and reports from civilians having less traumatic injuries and operations during peacetime. Many of the soldiers did not request pain relief for severe wounds — about 60% reported either slight or no pain. Beecher at first considered the possibility that there were some inhibitions about reporting pain even if they felt it, but this was not an adequate explanation because the soldiers were willing to voice their complaints about the relatively slight pain involved in injections. He concluded that it was not necessarily the magnitude of an injury that was significant in the experience of pain but, rather, the circumstances in which it occurred[2]. Childbirth provides another example. Although there are large individual differences during childbirth, it would be expected from the magnitude rule that there would be some correlation between obstetric measures and women's self-reports about how painful labour had been. However, neither amount of bleeding, labour time nor the weight, head circumference and presentation of the foetus have been found to be associated with how women describe their delivery[3].

The puzzle of these observations is complicated further by another assumption underlying a purely sensory model of pain — that pain and injury co-occur. Like the magnitude rule, this is often the case, but not always. There are reports of quite severe injuries being suffered with little pain, as in some religious ceremonies in India where large steel hooks inserted in the back muscles can be tolerated with no apparent pain[4]. Conversely, there is evidence for the experience of pain without injury, as in the couvade. In some cultures, couvade customs have to do with the father staying in bed with his wife and child for several days after birth. For the Trobrianders of the Pacific, however, the custom is much more dramatic: men appear to experience labour pains as their women give birth. While he seems to suffer pain, she gives birth with apparently little discomfort and returns to work immediately afterwards[5]. Equally startling are reports of phantom limb pain. Patients who have a limb amputated sometimes complain of pain in the leg or arm that has been removed, pain that is persistent, long-term and difficult to relieve. In general, phantom limb pain occurs where there is the sudden loss of the limb and not following gradual deterioration, such as in leprosy. The person may feel the pain involved in the injury that led to the amputation rather than the amputation itself[6].

Observations such as these render purely sensory explanations of pain unsatisfactory, and several theories have been put forward to account for them. Some researchers have approached the problem from the point of view of personality. A distinction can be made between the degree of pain experienced and willingness to report it. Those who feel much pain in clinical settings score higher on the neuroticism scale of the Eysenck Personality Inventory (see Chapter 2), but this may be due to their feelings of pain at the time when the questionnaire is given rather than their 'neuroticism' — when the pain subsides the scores on such questionnaires become less extreme. Those who are more likely to *express* complaints about their pain score higher on the extraversion scale of the EPI, suggesting that the reporting of pain is related to learning and cultural expectations. In this context, it has been noted that people coming from Northern and Western countries tend to express their pain less readily than those from Latin countries. It is unclear whether these findings are due to actual differences in sensitivity or simply due to cultural taboos about expressing feelings.

Reactions to painful stimuli may 'run in families'. This could be due to genetic factors, but there is some evidence that observational learning is also important. Craig and Prkachin[7] persuaded the subjects in their study to undergo several electric shocks. They were asked to rate the intensity of the shocks on a scale of 1 to 100, which served as a measure of increasing discomfort. Half the subjects were given the shocks along with a confederate who was instructed to give ratings about 25% below theirs'. The confederate thus acted as a model whose apparent discomfort was less than the subjects'. The other half of the subjects were given the shocks with the confederate acting only as an observer. The important distinction between the two conditions was that the first group was exposed to another person who reported considerable tolerance to each of the shocks. There were two main findings of interest. First, the verbal ratings of the subjects exposed to the tolerant model were lower than those not so exposed: the first group reported less discomfort than the second one. This result could have been due to conformity alone, i.e. that the modelled group simply reported less pain because it seemed to be socially desirable to do so. In order to test for the possibility that modelling had an effect on actual sensitivity, the researchers analysed the subjects' verbal reports for indications of how well they could discriminate between various levels of shock. The argument was that if the model-exposed subjects did not discriminate as well as the others, this would indicate less actual sensitivity. They found that those in the model condition did not discriminate as finely as those in the control condition, supporting the hypothesis that social modelling not only affects *reports* of personal distress but also affects *sensitivity* to shock intensity.

The differences between the groups were not outstandingly strong and the physiological measures that the researchers took showed no significant differences. However, if such a short exposure to a tolerant model can affect sensitivity even slightly, then prolonged observation in the real world could be expected to have a strong effect. Perhaps the cultural and familial differences in pain reports found by other researchers have their basis in observational learning. For example, Apley[8] studied children for whom no organic cause for their complaints of abdominal pain could be discovered. He compared these children with a control group who did not make such complaints. He found several differences between these groups, but the most striking was their family background. The incidence of similar pains was some six times higher in the families of the complaint group. Apley also noted that the children's complaints of pains were often associated with stressful events, such as beginning school or the birth of a sibling. He argued that this difference between the groups was due to a combination of heredity and environment: children coming from families in which one or both parents continually suffer from recurrent pains are likely to grow up learning that pain is one way of coping with anxiety.

Further evidence that feelings of pain are associated with stress comes from a study of appendicectomy patients. After the operation, they were asked about their life events in the 38 weeks before the onset of pain. Some 59% had experienced an event that was considered to be threatening to them, as compared to 31% in a non-patient community sample. This finding is consistent with the work discussed in the previous chapter that stressful events can lead to illness. However, an additional analysis was performed in this study. In some appendicectomy operations the appendix is found not to be acutely inflamed, although the symptoms mimic those of appendicitis. In many cases, this may be due to the irritable bowel syndrome but a particular kind of life event was found to distinguish between those patients whose appendix was found to be acutely inflamed and those whose appendix was normal or only mildly inflamed. These life events were ones that implied a long-term and severe threat to the patients (similar to those associated with the onset of depression, as described in the previous chapter). Only 25% of the acutely inflamed patients had experienced such an event, compared to 59% of the not acutely inflamed patients. In most cases, the event had occurred within 9 weeks of the operation[9]. For these patients, the pre-operative pain may have been a response to the life events rather than to organic damage.

Several theories have been put forward to account for such observations as well as those on phantom limb phenomena, the couvade and the toleration of pain in religious ceremonies. Perhaps the best known is Melzack and Wall's 'gate theory'. Briefly, they suggest pain involves not only physical sensations but also emotional and evaluative reactions to these sensations. They argue that signals from an injured site run to the dorsal horn of the spinal cord, which acts like a gate between peripheral fibres and the brain. The gate is opened (i.e. the dorsal horn cells are excited) by small fibres running from the site of stimulation and is closed by other larger fibres from the same site. But the gate is also affected by fibres from the reticular system of the brain, which can serve to inhibit or excite the dorsal horn cells. They use this basically neurological model to account for many of the observations about the experience of pain. They suggest, for example, that sudden loss of a limb removes not only the excitatory fibres but also inhibitory ones, so that the gate remains permanently open and the cells in the dorsal horn continue to fire. Minimal tissue damage could cause severe pain if the fibres from the brain open the gate wider than usual, whereas considerable damage would not be noticed if the gate were closed, as, perhaps, in the case of the World War II soldiers mentioned above[10, 11].

The important point about their model is that, as well as receiving neurological information from the injured site, the emotional and evaluative properties of an injury also affect the perception of the pain through the descending influence of the brain. The ways in which such personal meanings are translated into, and interact with, physiological events remains unclear, but their theory represents a real advance in the attempt to integrate physiological and psychological processes in the experience of pain.

Two important considerations in pain-control research must be mentioned before methods for relieving suffering are outlined. The first problem concerns measurement, the second concerns the context in which research is performed. Of these, the more intractable is measurement. Physiological measures, such as the level of corticosteroids in the blood, heart rate or respiration rate are useful, but there is often little relationship between measures, in that corticosteroid level is not always related to heart rate, for example[12]. Another measure that could be taken is the amount of analgesia requested by patients: as mentioned above, however, this is open to cultural and personality influences. A third possibility is the amount of analgesia given by staff, but this, too, is affected by social and psychological factors. Bond and Pilowski[13] took measures of subjective pain (see below), patients' requests for analgesia and responses of the nursing staff. Their study indicated that the perception of pain did not always result in a request for medication, requests when made did not always lead to administration by staff and the strength of medications administered were not proportional to pain levels. The sex of the patient seemed particularly relevant. Nursing staff were much more likely to take the initiative with female patients in administering analgesia and more likely to refuse requests from male patients (Table 11.1)[14].

Table 11.1 Pattern of Administration of Analgesic Drugs to Men and Women in Radiotherapy Wards

Drugs requested and given during 1 week. (Reproduced from M.R. Bond, *Pain*, 1979, by permission of Churchill Livingstone.)

	Men	Women
Number of patients	15	12
Number of occasions drugs given at patient's request	23	28
Number of occasions drugs given on initiative of nurses	1	22
Number of occasions on which nurses refused patient's request for drugs	18	0

Given these problems with the above measures, several techniques designed to measure the degree of subjective pain have been developed. In the Bond and Pilowski study mentioned above, the patients were asked to indicate their experience of pain by placing a mark on a 10-cm line between the extremes of 'I have no pain at all' and 'My pain is as bad as it possibly could be':

I have no pain at all ＿＿＿＿＿My pain is as bad as it possibly could be

Researchers who have used this visual analogue scale have worked on the assumption that, because the scale is marked privately, it provides an accurate indication of patients' feelings, being relatively unaffected by what they believe should be expressed to others. Another method of measuring subjective pain is by asking patients to match their discomfort with tourniquet-induced pain[15]. The patient is asked to report when the induced pain reaches the level that is equal in intensity to his usual clinical pain. A third alternative measure of subjective pain is the McGill Pain Questionnaire[16], which provides a way of separating out the various components of the pain experience. Pain is considered to have three dimensions — sensory, emotional and evaluative. The sensory component involves the detection and intensity of input. It is considered to be purely informational, providing the person with knowledge about the extent of tissue damage. The emotional component involves the aversive qualities of pain and the fear generated by pain, whereas the evaluative component involves cognitive and judgemental processes. The words that patients use to describe their pain are analysed, giving measures on all three scales, so that each can be considered independently. Unfortunately, comparisons between these various pain-rating scales have shown that they do not correlate particularly well, indicating that they are measuring different aspects of the pain experience[17] or that it cannot be reliably measured.

These difficulties with the measurement of pain compound the complexity of pain-control research. A second problem concerns the use of laboratory versus 'real life' situations. Experiments under the controlled conditions of the laboratory have their advantages, but induced pain may have different effects on subjects than clinical pain for several reasons. Whereas the former is short-lived and can be stopped by the subject, clinical pain is often persistent, beyond the patient's control and accompanied by high levels of anxiety[16]. In the laboratory, pain is induced by stimuli that are novel to the subject (e.g. electric shock, the application of a tourniquet or immersion of a hand into ice-cold water for long periods), whereas patients often have prior experience with clinical pains, either personally or through observation of others. Given the importance of interpersonal factors in the experience of pain, findings in the laboratory may not be applicable to clinical settings, where the expectations are quite different. The important point for the present purpose is this: given that the meaning of painful stimuli could be expected to be very different in the two situations, results found in the laboratory may not always be relevant for clinical populations. Certainly, laboratory tests do not predict post-operative need for analgesia[18].

Alleviation of Pain

In order to understand the pain-control techniques below, it is important to consider two points. The first is that pain can be measured along more than one dimension. The sensory component involves the intensity of information coming from the injured site, and the emotional and evaluative components involve the person's reactions to this information. Although these components interact, there is the implication that the emotional and evaluative components are learned, and if the interpretation of the information can be changed, then the experience of pain can be modified. This has been shown experimentally. In one study, subjects were asked to report the amount of distress they experienced while a hand was immersed in very cold water (2 °C), being told about the sensations the immersion would give (i.e. coldness, tightness of the skin, numbness). One group of subjects was told that the experience would be painful, whereas the other group did not receive the pain warning. Thus, the subjects' emotional and evaluative interpretations of the ice water were manipulated. The results indicated that the subjects given no pain warning were less distressed and actually showed higher hand temperatures, differences showing up during the latter half of the 6-min experiment. Although both groups had similar expectations about sensations, the way this information was processed was different, having both physiological and psychological effects on their ability to tolerate the experience[19].

These observations should not be taken to mean that there is reason for making light of distress once it is experienced or is likely to be experienced. It may be that this experiment showed differences because the subjects had little prior experience with the particular situation — i.e. placing a hand in ice-cold water for 6 min. In this sense the experiment is artificial and makes only a theoretical point. There may appear to be some inconsistency with the research discussed in Chapter 1, where giving patients realistic information about hospital procedures and the sensations they would experience reduced anxiety and the need for analgesia. However, those researchers concentrated on providing information about purely sensory aspects of operations, without interpreting them as painful or otherwise. Although some psychologists have advocated clear and authoritative warnings about the likely pain, it remains to be shown conclusively whether this is always appropriate.

The second point concerns the functions of pain. When pain is experienced, the feelings serve as a signal that attention is required. Since pain is a subjective symptom, some way of convincing others of the experience is required. If the individual can display tissue damage, assistance can usually be acquired. But if no organic problem can be found, the person may well have difficulty in gaining help. The caregiver has several options to take. On the one hand, he or she might consider the possibility that the examining procedures and technology available to the medical profession are not adequate to discover the source of the discomfort. On the other hand, the caregiver could speculate on the possible reasons why this complaint is being presented. Malingering is a possibility: the dismissal of a report of pain might be appropriate if the patient is faking, although it could be argued that faking is an indication of some psychological need. Alternatively, the caregiver could conclude that the patient is seeking attention and then dismiss the complaint. However, the question arises as to whether the use of pain complaints for attention-seeking is unreasonable. Several practising physicians have noted that pain can serve as a 'ticket' for entry into the consulting room: by presenting a complaint, the patient may be hoping for the opportunity to discuss personal affairs, an opportunity that might otherwise not be available. The concern of such physicians would be to discover the underlying reasons behind the request for assistance. In such circumstances the patient may not be aware of how complaints are being used and may feel pain just as real as any other, as in the case of the patients given an appendicectomy mentioned above.

Five techniques for alleviating pain and helping people to cope with the pain they feel are discussed here. Surgical techniques are beyond the scope of this book, but it is likely that they, too, involve a degree of reinterpretation of sensory information. Nor is acupuncture considered, although this technique is receiving increasing attention and acceptance, and may be effective because it involves the release of endorphins[20]. Biofeedback is mentioned in the section on operant learning procedures (Chapter 3).

Pharmacological techniques. Perhaps the most obvious method of pain relief involves the blocking of neural transmission. Cocaine, for example, is an

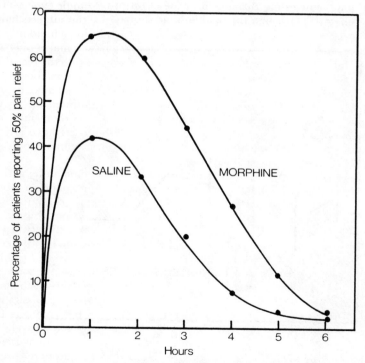

Fig. 11.1   Percentage of patients reporting 50% pain relief over a 6-hour period from 10 mg morphine sulphate or sterile saline. (Reproduced from R.W. Houde, S.L. Wallerstein and A. Rogers, *Clinical Pharmacology and Therapeutics***, 1960, 1, 163–174, by permission.)**

effective analgesic because it blocks nerve conduction from the injured site. The operation of the opiates such as morphine, is much harder to specify. It is difficult to state precisely what sites are responsible for analgesic properties, although sites appear to exist in the midbrain and spinal cord[21]. The distinction between the physical sensation an injury causes and the reaction to that sensation is usually used to explain the effects of morphine — i.e. that it operates on the systems responsible for emotional and evaluative reactions. It seems that morphine acts not by blocking sensations but by changing the patient's consciousness of the sensory input. For instance, the percentage of cancer patients who reported at least 50 % pain relief from morphine or saline solution is shown in Fig. 11.1. All patients had chronic pain due to their disease, the majority from bone metastases. The evaluations of effectiveness were conducted 'double blind' (i.e. neither the person who administered the drug nor the person who evaluated its effectiveness knew which patients were receiving morphine or saline solution) and measures were taken at hourly intervals. There was also a substantial response to saline solution and the time-effect curve mimicked that of morphine, suggesting that much of the effect of morphine may be due to placebo effects[22]. Although the double-blind design of the study precludes the

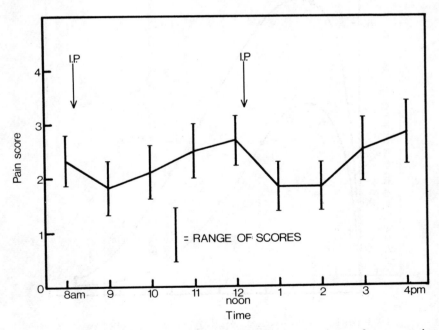

Fig. 11.2   Post-operative pain relief following injections of pentazocine (1P) in patients with lumber disc disease. (Reproduced from M.R. Bond, J.P. Glynn and D.G. Thomas, *Journal of Psychosomatic Research*, 1976, 20, 369–381, by permission.)

possibility that the effect is due to experimenter expectancy effects, it is unfortunately not possible to show from studies of this kind whether the patients are actually feeling less pain. Perhaps they felt obliged in some way to report a drop in discomfort and the obligation may not have been equal in the two conditions. The placebo effect is discussed in more detail in the next part of this chapter.

Personality factors have been shown to be related to patients' reports of the alleviation of pain. Fig. 11.2 illustrates a typical course of pain relief from an analgesic (in this instance pentazocine given to patients with lumber disc disease). Shortly after administration, pain scores (as measured by the visual analogue scale) fall and then rise again. However such a picture does not take individual differences in pain relief into account, as shown by Fig. 11.3. Those

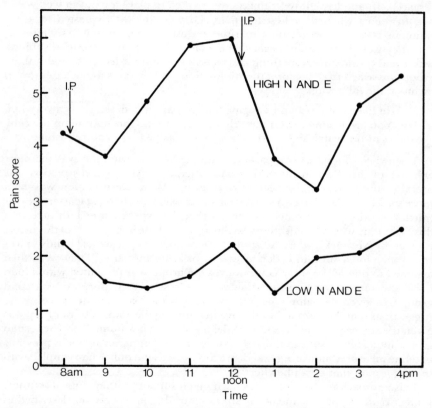

Fig. 11.3   Pain relief following injection of pentazocine in patients with high neuroticism and extraversion (N and E) scores (upper curve) and those with low scores (lower curve). (Reproduced from M.R. Bond, J.P. Glynn and D.G. Thomas, *Journal of Psychosomatic Research*, 1976, 20, 369–381, by permission.)

who scored high on the Neuroticism and Extraversion scales of the EPI gave consistently higher reports of pain and were strongly affected by the analgesic, whereas medication seemed to have less effect on those patients who scored low on both scales[23].

Cognitive techniques.   The notion that a person's beliefs about himself and his environment are crucial for understanding his behaviour and experience has been emphasized throughout the book. Cognitive techniques for alleviating pain focus on interpretations, encouraging the individual to modify his evaluations of the sensory information. The study described above, in which one group of subjects were told that the ice-cold water would be painful, whereas the other group was not so informed, is a typical example of this kind of research. In another study[24] subjects were asked to place a hand in iced water and to report when they first felt pain. One group was requested to use a rationalization procedure, the experimenter asking them to say to themselves that they were in the study because they had to be. Another group of subjects was asked to imagine something distracting (being in a lecture), and a third group was asked to reinterpret the stimulation. Instructions to the latter group included the following:

> . . . I'd like you to try and imagine that you are in a desert. It is a very hot day. You are feeling uncomfortably hot and tired. Concentrate on the cool aspects of the water and try to interpret this as pleasant and refreshing.

As has been found in comparable studies, this last condition was the most effective of the three in increasing pain tolerance. Although distraction was useful (group 2 was more tolerant than group 1), reinterpretation was even more so. There may also be a suggestion effect operating here, at least in the distraction condition. It seemed important that the experimenter indicated that this technique would be effective. An illustration of the importance of this factor is given by Melzack *et al.*[25]. All subjects were asked to place their hands in ice-cold water for a time in order to gain a baseline measure. They were then assigned to one of the three conditions. One group was presented with a loud noise and music, but no suggestion was made as to their purpose. A second group was given the same noise and music, but the experimenter gave strong suggestions that they would be effective in reducing the pain. A third group was given the suggestion, but in this case the noise was a low hum. Only the second group indicated a substantial decrease in pain compared to their previous baseline measure, indicating that distraction was useful only when coupled with the suggestion that it can be effective.

This approach to pain relief has been given support within clinical settings. Langer *et al.*[26] applied some of the stress-innoculation techniques described in the previous chapter to surgical patients. They were assigned to one of two groups: one group of patients was given examples of how attention to and perceptions of a noxious event has an influence on how that event is experienced. They were taught to use selective attention, being encouraged to focus on the positive aspects (e.g. the improvement in health) that the treatment would bring. Compared to patients who were not given such instructions, the experimental group had fewer requests for sedatives, spent less time in hospital (an average 5.6 days compared to 7.6 days in the comparison-group patients) and showed less anxiety and greater ability to cope as evaluated by nurses. No physiological differences between the groups were found. It seems that cognitive techniques are effective in real-life situations as well as in the laboratory.

Hypnosis. Hypnosis is an area of research that has only recently gained a measure of acceptance among psychologists, partly because of the difficulty in ascertaining what a hypnotic state might be. Although hypnotists characterize it as a 'trance state' — a unique form of consciousness — it is difficult to distinguish hypnotized subjects from those who have been coached. Experienced hypnotists cannot always tell the difference. Psychologists interested in hypnosis debate whether it is a unique state or an example of other, more established forms of behaviour, such as role playing. Such a basic problem has made it difficult to carry out controlled experimental studies.

A more profitable line of research has investigated susceptibility, defined as the degree to which a person is 'able to enter into hypnosis and become involved in its characteristic behaviour' (Ref. 27, p. 175). Several scales have been developed to test for susceptibility, such as the Stanford Hypnotic Susceptibility Scale[28]. Several short tests are used, such as the willingness of the subjects to fall backwards into the hypnotist's arms. Hypnosis can only be used confidently for highly susceptible subjects, as shown by Fig. 11.4[29]. There is evidence that the hypnotized subject actually registers the pain, but there seems to be some barrier to it becoming openly conscious.

Although most research has been performed in the laboratory, there are several case studies that indicate that hypnosis can lead to pain reduction in clinical populations. The method has been used in helping cancer patients[30] and in childbirth, for example, not only in cases of normal births but also for caesarian sections, as the following case illustrates:

A patient who presented an obstetrical emergency illustrates the advantages of having available someone familiar with hypnotic procedures. A woman expecting a baby had been poorly handled on the ward of the hospital. She had been there for hours with an impacted breech before . . . the ward consultant became aware of her. At that time she had a high fever, a systolic blood pressure of over 200, and a heart rate of more than 150 beats per minute. She evidently needed a caesarean operation, but the anesthetist refused to give any general chemoanesthesia, and the operation under local anesthesia was not judged feasible. Hence [the consultant], who was to do the surgery, determined to use hypnosis. Although he had not seen her before and she was completely naive to hypnosis, he hypnotized her during the ten to fifteen minutes in which he was scrubbing and preparing her abdomen. The record obtained by the anesthetist during the course of the operation showed that the vital signs steadily returned to normal despite the progress of the surgery. A normal infant was delivered, and the mother's recovery was uneventful. The record was later reviewed by a senior obstetrician who described it as remarkable. (Ref. 31, p. 22).

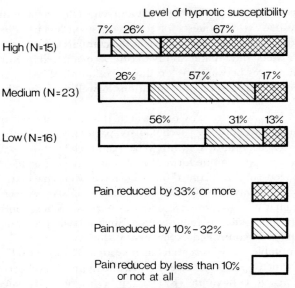

Level of hypnotic susceptibility

High (N=15)   7% 26%   67%

Medium (N=23)   26%   57%   17%

Low (N=16)   56%   31%   13%

Pain reduced by 33% or more

Pain reduced by 10% - 32%

Pain reduced by less than 10%
or not at all

Fig. 11.4 People with low susceptibility to hypnosis experience less pain relief than people with high susceptibility. (Reproduced from E.R. Hillgard, *Pain,* **1975 1, 213–231, by permission.)**

Behavioural approaches.   Operant approaches to medical care have been considered in Chapter 3 (e.g. providing rewards to reduce smoking) and Chapter 6 (providing rewards to increase patients' activity). The idea behind the use of reinforcement for pain relief is that pain responses, like other kinds of behaviour, are shaped and maintained by rewards as well as by the pain itself. Complaints of pain can, in other words, be used as an interpersonal device to gain attention and sympathy as well as analgesia. From a learning theory point of view, such behaviour is no different from any other: the individual has simply learned that complaints of pain can be used in order to gain rewards. Bonica and Fordyce[32] have reported a study in which 36 patients who had difficulty with chronic pain were no longer given reinforcements for their 'pain behaviour'. Instead of receiving analgesia when they asked for it, the patients were given medication at fixed time intervals. Rewards were given for increases in activity and exercise. Although activity levels increased, medication intake and subjective reports of pain decreased. When asked, the patients rated their pain as being less intense and as causing less interference with daily activities. Further, these results were maintained some 22 months later. Although there was no control group in this study and there was considerable screening of patients, the lack of previous success with more traditional treatments makes the results encouraging. This applicability of behavioural treatments to pain relief illustrates the multifactorial nature of pain and the interdependence of behavioural and physiological variables.

Psychotherapeutic approaches.   One psychotherapeutic perspective on pain relief involves a consideration of the social life events that may contribute to the aetiology and severity of an illness. Psychosomatic illness is discussed in the previous chapter. Another perspective concentrates on the way that pain and illness are used to deal with unpleasant situations, i.e. hypochondriasis. Taking on the sick role and complaining of pains are ways of coping and seeking attention and help. It is often the case that individuals are unaware of how they are using pain, and even if careful investigation does not show evidence of physical abnormality, the pain is real to the patient.

It is likely that the behavioural treatment outlined above was effective because the patients were given rewards not for their 'pain behaviour' but rather for indications that they were learning to cope with their difficulties. The psychotherapeutic approach also holds that pain and illness are sometimes used by the patient in order to gain care and sympathy and agrees that attention-seeking behaviour requires examination. The difference is that pain complaints are seen as an indication of an underlying conflict, suggesting that this conflict should be explored. An extract from a case report illustrates this point of view. The woman involved had a history of cancer:

> The present hospitalization was prompted when the woman came into the surgery outpatient clinic complaining of a severe and constant pain in her left side. No apparent cause for this pain could be ascertained by physical examination in the clinic, but a coincident finding was the presence of another enlarged submandibular lymph node. She was admitted for an excision biopsy of this node.
>
> When interviewed, she appeared to be in considerable discomfort and was preoccupied with what she described as a severe and sharp pain in her left side. Signs of depression were immediately noted, including psychomotor retardation, poor eye contact, low-pitched and monotonous voice and expressions of fatigue and despair. Early in the interview it was learned that she was well aware of her diagnosis of reticulum cell sarcoma and the eventual possibility of death as a consequence of that disease.
>
> However, she talked almost exclusively about the pain in her side, which had been the only reason for her seeking help at this time. She stated that the pain had been constant and severe over the last three months and prevented her from being more active around the house and socially. The pain concerned her much more than did the enlarged node in her neck, which she dismissed by stating that the surgeons would simply 'cut it out' in the same fashion as they had two years earlier, and there would be no further consequences. The pain in her side was a different story altogether, for it had never occurred before and she was afraid that it represented a new direction of spread or growth of her tumor. Further exploration of this notion revealed concern that this meant death was imminent. The woman confessed that in recent months she had been spending more and more of her time preoccupied with thoughts about her death.
>
> She was encouraged to elaborate some of her thoughts concerning death, and the balance of the interview was focused on this topic. Among her greatest fears was leaving behind her 11-year-old son in the care of his untrustworthy father. She also expressed the fear that death would be painful and that in the end her doctors would abandon her. The patient received support from the interviewer for her fears and concerns. She cried spontaneously throughout this part of the discussion.

289

As the interview ended, all observers noted that the woman's affective state had improved dramatically: she had become more animated, and her eye contact with the interviewer had increased.

One day later, during routine rounds, the woman was seen again. She enthusiastically summoned the interviewer to her bedside and somewhat sheepishly reported that the pain in her side had disappeared immediately following the interview on the previous day and had not returned. It was the first time in three months that she had been without pain in that area. Owing to complications in the subsequent biopsy procedure, she remained in the hopsital a total of six weeks, with no recurrence of pain. (Ref. 33, pp. 494 – 5).

For this patient, simply listening to her concerns and taking them seriously resulted in disappearance of the symptom of pain. Apley[8] in his work with children with abdominal pains, reported similar findings. Many of the children, once they had been reassured that their abdomens were normal and had been given some attention, had no recurrence of pain. In these cases only minimal psychotherapy was required in order to alleviate the pain.

11.3   Placebo Effects

Placebo effects are generally defined as those effects of a treatment that are not attributable to the mechanics of the treatment itself, but rather to the circumstances surrounding it. For example, in Fig. 11.1 just over 40% of the patients who received saline solution reported substantial pain relief 1 hour after its administration, compared to just over 60% who received morphine. When a new drug is tested it is therefore necessary to compare it with placebos, lest any demonstrated effect be due to non-specific factors. Similar precautions are taken in psychological experiments. One of the purposes of control groups is to guard against the possibility that the real reason for a change is some aspect of the situation that the experimenter is not intending to manipulate. When studying the effects of biofeedback, for example, it would be important to have a control group hooked up to the equipment but not given contingent feedback, in case simply being attached to the apparatus leads to some improvement. In this sense, placebo effects are something of a nuisance because they make evaluations of treatments more difficult than they might otherwise be.

In another sense, they are a fascinating subject of study in their own right. That saline solutions can affect patients' reports of their pain is very surprising, and this phenomenon may provide much information about the psychology of medical care. There are many studies that suggest that these non-specific aspects of treatment are significant. Placebo effects have been shown in dentistry, in surgery, to be addictive, to mimic the effects of active drugs, to reverse the effects of potent drugs and to have an effect on bodily organs. The placebo effect is considered in some detail here because unwarranted conclusions are often drawn from data such as those shown in Fig. 11.1, and it is important to examine the methods of many of the studies that have been frequently cited.

One of the better known of the placebo studies was conducted by Park and Covi in 1965[34]. They set out to test the hypothesis that placebos work because patients have a belief in the active potency of the drugs that their doctors prescribe. If this is the case, they reasoned, then when patients are told that the medication is inert the effect should be lost. Park and Covi did this with 15 newly admitted patients believed to have neurotic disorders. They told their patients:

> Many people with your kind of condition have been helped by what are sometimes called 'sugar pills', and we feel that a so-called sugar pill may help you, too . . . A sugar pill is a pill with no medicine in it at all. I think this pill will help you as it has helped so many others . . . (Ref. 34, p. 337).

and one week later interviewed them again. Of the 14 patients who agreed to the course of treatment, 13 showed improvement, often substantial improvement.

This result has been termed remarkable and in many ways it is, but a closer look at the researchers' behaviour makes the findings much more understandable. Psychiatric patients — particularly neurotic patients — often improve after an initial interview. Perhaps some of the factors discussed in Chapter 3 are operative, in that the patient is given hope, sympathy and warmth during the interview. This is relevant because Park and Covi did conduct such an interview with all their patients: an hour in the first instance and then a further 15 – 30 min when the placebo was offered. This adds up to a considerable amount of time with each person. It is possible that a large proportion of the improvement was due to these inter-personal factors: a control group, offered equivalent interview attention but no placebo, is required before such a possibility could be ruled out. Further, only eight of the patients actually believed that the pills they were given were inert, the rest being either unsure, or certain that active drugs were involved. Simply because the researchers told their patients the pills were only sugar did not mean that they were believed.

Individual Differences

Although the results portrayed in Fig. 11.1 are not unusual for placebo-controlled studies, they are often misinterpreted, apparently suggesting to some that most patients could be given pain relief from placebos alone. This is not the case. On average, only about 35% of patients obtain relief, but the range is probably from 0 to 100% depending on the treatment in question, the disease and situational factors such as the patients' and physicians' belief in the efficacy of the treatment.

People who respond to placebos are called reactors (as opposed to non-reactors) and this difference has stimulated much research on personality variables. A trait for reactivity has been sought after, researchers predicting that an individual would have the same reactivity in different situations. However, this viewpoint has found little support and is now largely abandoned. There is little evidence that a stable personality trait is operative. Demographic characteristics, such as age and sex are not consistently related, nor is IQ. It is not yet possible to predict with any certainty which people will react to placebos.

Part of the difficulty may be due to the design of many studies on placebo reactors. To take one example, Lasagna et al.[35] describe how they gave 93 patients placebos and morphine in alternate dosages. Twenty-seven reacted consistently to placebos, 11 being always relieved of pain, 16 rarely or never relieved. This smaller group of 27 was studied extensively, but no differences could be found between the reactors and non-reactors in terms of type of surgery, anaesthesia, IQ or observations by ward personnel. The only difference they could discover was that all the reactors were very positive and enthusiastic about their hospital care, whereas only 4 of the 16 non-reactors felt this way. Although this result could be taken as evidence for personality differences, such a conclusion is not justified since the assessments were taken after the placebos were given. Since the non-reactors had suffered more pain during their stay, they could therefore be expected to be less enthusiastic about their care.

On the other hand, there is evidence that certain conditions are more conducive to placebo reactions than others, notably emotionality, depression and anxiety. Some of the highest rates of placebo reactors have been found in psychiatric populations[36]. Indeed, it has been argued that the success of many forms of psychological therapy is really due to placebo effects; i.e. it is not necessarily what the therapist believes he is doing that is important, for instance behavioural therapy or verbal psychotherapy, but rather the care, hope and explanations the therapist gives to his or her patients (see Chapter 3, and Ref. 37).

How do Placebos Work?

Accordingly, research on placebos has changed from interest in reactors and non-reactors to the mechanisms of the effect. For those who are relieved of pain, what processes are involved?

One theory relies on the idea of classical conditioning, and is based on observations of Pavlov's dogs. In some of the studies, the dogs were given morphine and, as in the case of food and salivation, some of the animals came to show a response to morphine before they were given the injection. The suggestion is that, in humans, the placebo effect works similarly: patients feel better because this is a conditioned response to taking medication. The classical conditioning position would predict that as the number of occasions on which placebos are administered increases, the percentage of patients reporting relief would decrease. This is, in fact, what occurs.

Another possibility is based on the notion of cognitive consistency. It was pointed out in Chapter 1 that people seek consistency in their interpretations of the environment, in order to make the environment predictable and meaningful. When consistency is difficult to discover, special efforts are made to fit events into an individual's theories about the way the world works. This notion can be applied to placebo effects with some success. A patient who takes a (placebo) medication has several perceptions. These include a belief in a physician who has recommended the medication and interpretations of his bodily state. According to the cognitive approach, these two perceptions should be consistent; i.e. if the person feels no different after taking the medication he could change his beliefs about the doctor (he could come to doubt the doctor's competence), his beliefs about his illness (that it must be worse than originally thought) or his interpretations of his bodily state. Placebo effects could be present in those patients who make the third change, if they became more aware of the times when they did, in fact, feel better and paid less attention to the times when they feel unwell. They may also come to interpret their sensations as less painful following their doctor's reassurance.

A third possibility is that placebos do not affect the experience of pain at all, but only bias patients' responses. They may report that they feel better, when in fact just as much discomfort is felt. Perhaps some patients (those who are reactors) feel in some way obliged to report that they are better when a physician has taken time to treat them. This is a difficult hypothesis to test, but there is evidence that placebos do not affect the sensory component of pain. In a laboratory study, Feather et al.[38] exposed their subjects to painful radiant heat, half of whom were given a placebo, the other half nothing. As expected, those given placebos were less willing to label the heat as painful. But was this difference due to changes in sensitivity? They tested this possibility by asking subjects to discriminate between slightly different levels of heat. If the placebo group was less sensitive, they should not have been able to make such fine discriminations as the no-placebo group. In fact, there were no differences in sensitivity, suggesting to the researchers that placebo effects are simply due to response bias. If this is the correct explanation for the placebo effect, there are important implications. The high rate of placebo prescribing is misplaced and may even be counterproductive if patients come to mistrust their caregivers and only tell them what it is believed they wish to hear. However, response bias may not provide a full explanation for the placebo effect because Feather et al. do not consider that pain consists of more than the sensory component. Two people may have the same sensations, but owing to the emotional and evaluative components experience different degrees of pain. Their research design took only the sensations into account.

There are some clues to the physiological action of placebos. In the cases of both placebos and narcotics, there is a tendency to increase the dosage over time, with repeated dosages over long periods both become less effective and there are withdrawal difficulties. These similarities have led some researchers to suggest that placebos work by releasing endorphins (endogenous morphine-like substances) into the body. This suggestion could be tested through the injection of naloxone, an opiate antagonist that blocks the opiate receptor sites. If, when naloxone is given the placebo effect is no longer found, this would provide strong evidence for a link between placebos and endorphins.

Levine et al.[39] studied patients whose impacted wisdom teeth were to be removed. Two hours after surgery, all patients were given a placebo and then, after a further hour, either placebo or naloxone. The first prediction the researchers made concerned the effect of naloxone versus placebo, and the

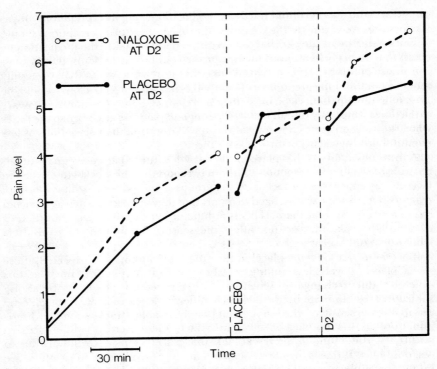

Fig. 11.5 The effect of naloxone on pain. Both patient groups were given a placebo as their first drug. There was no difference in the pain levels before D2, when one group was given naloxone, the other a placebo. 1 hour after D2, the naloxone group reported higher pain levels. (Reproduced from J.D. Levine, J.C. Gordon and H.L. Fields, *Lancet*, 1978, 2, 654–657, by permission.)

results are shown in Figure 11.5. As expected, those patients who were given naloxone reported greater pain 1 hour after administration than did those given placebos. This is represented by the data points on the far right of Fig. 11.5 (after D2). Differences between these groups were not significant previously. It would seem then, that the naloxone enhanced the pain relative to placebos.

These researchers also distinguished between placebo reactors and non-reactors, reasoning that if placebo effects are produced by endorphins, they should be reversed by naloxone. The differences between these groups should be diminished after naloxone administration. In fact, this was found to be the case, providing evidence that placebo effects are naloxone-reversible. Further, after naloxone, the increase in pain levels for placebo reactors were greater than for non-reactors, bringing them to the same level of pain experience. Finally, the researchers observed that naloxone had no obvious effect on placebo non-reactors.

Thus, this study suggests that the analgesic effect of placebos is real (i.e. not simply due to response biases) and is based on the action of endorphins. Like morphine, placebos seem to operate on the emotional and evaluative components of pain and not the sensory components. This study does not indicate, however, how the message 'Take this, it will be good for you' from a trusted physician is translated into the release of endorphins. Although the psychological explanation is incomplete, these results indicate that placebos cannot be used to distinguish functional from organic illnesses. That saline solution can relieve pain does not mean that the pain is psychogenic: it simply means that there are methods of dealing with pain other than by pharmacological agents.

Side-Effects of Placebos

Part of the 'magic' of placebos is their apparent ability to induce side-effects. Often, the type of side-effect is related to the type of medication under study: nausea with antispasmodic placebos or drowsiness with tranquillizer placebos, for instance. This seems very odd indeed and is sometimes used as an indicator of the strength of placebo reactions. However as in the case of the Park and Covi study mentioned above, the emphasis on placebo side-effects may be due to the lack of adequate control groups. Studies reporting side-effects have only a small proportion of their patients presenting complaints. Although some of the complaints are dramatic — e.g. visible skin rashes — these are in the minority. It may be that researchers, now alert to the possibility, are eager to find them. Where do patients get the idea that nausea is sometimes produced by antispasmodic placebos? Presumably from questions from the investigators.

The most likely explanation for the reporting of side-effects is a greater awareness of bodily reactions during illness and clinical trials than usual. If clinical trials included a control group of healthy subjects, a better estimate of the incidence of minor illness could be uncovered. In a survey of healthy subjects not taking medication, 25% of the subjects reported an inability to concentrate in the 3 days before the survey, 23% reported excessive sleepiness and 40% fatigue. Had these subjects been taking medication or placebos, these difficulties might have been attributed to the drugs, and called side-effects[40]. The inclusion of control groups in this area of research is vital, but often neglected.

11.4 Drug Dependence

The theme of this chapter is the interdependence between psychological and physiological states. Research on pain and placebos indicates that the distinction that is often made between the mind and the body is a false one, since in both cases the person's psychological and physiological states need to be taken into account in order to understand the phenomena. Drug dependence (or addiction) provides another example. An analysis of dependence that takes only pharmacological action into account soon runs into theoretical difficulties. Although agents can be ranked according to their addictive properties (opiates more than barbiturates and alcohol), these properties in themselves are not sufficient to explain why some people come to be dependent and others do not. Once again, personality characteristics were suggested as having some explanatory power, but the search for a pre-addictive personality has now been largely abandoned. As an indication of this, the 1980 edition of the American Psychiatric Association's diagnostic manual no longer includes alcoholism and drug abuse as indications of personality disorder. There is, however, evidence that addicts themselves are very dependent people, relying on people and institutions for their well-being to an excessive degree[41]. There may also be a genetic component in some dependencies, such as alcoholism[42].

The assumption is often made that once someone becomes physically dependent, it is very difficult to end this dependency. Although most rehabilitation programmes have had limited success, physical dependence is not usually the problem. Theories of dependence have been shaken by observations of American servicemen who returned from Vietnam. About 40% of the enlisted men in Vietnam were considered to have used heroin regularly[43], raising fears of widespread use on their return home. But very few continued to use heroin after discharge. Only 7% of those detected as users (by urine tests) were addicted 9 – 12 months after their return[44]. This result, found with a drug that is considered to be highly addictive, has forced a fundamental reconsideration of social and psychological factors in addiction. Nor is this result unusual, since French and British soldiers were also able to adjust after their return home from earlier conflicts in the area. These findings provide good evidence of recovery from heroin use on a large scale without specific interventions.

It seems that the environment has much to do with dependence on drugs. Availability is an important factor. The higher than would be expected proportion of medical profession addicts (doctors, pharmacists, nurses) may be explained in terms of easy access to drugs rather than vulnerable personalities[45]. The high rate of alcoholism among merchant seamen and journalists, where alcohol is part of the subculture, provides further evidence for sociogenic factors[46]. Sociologists, in particular, stress that it is not possible to generalize about drug usage without consideration of its familial and cultural context[47].

Increasingly, those concerned with addictions are considering the similarities between the various kinds of dependence, be it dependence on eating, alcohol, gambling or drugs. There appear to be many similarities in both aetiology and treatment. Emphasis is placed on a person's total environment, which includes his personality, his social context and the drug itself. Once drug administration is established it becomes more than simply reinforcing, it becomes part of the person's life-style. Smokers given cigarettes with no nicotine will continue to puff at them for days[48]. Those using heroin often become addicted to the ceremony of inserting the needle. Dependence fills time, structures life, provides a reassuring ritual and offers an identity[41]. In fact, it is this aspect of dependence, rather than the pharmacological properties of drugs, that makes it

296

so difficult to treat. It is popularly assumed that physical dependence is more dangerous than psychological dependence, but from the viewpoint of relapse and rehabilitation, psychological dependence is the more important. This suggestion is supported by the observation that cravings for drugs are not marked in institutions after the first weeks (and it seems that the trauma of 'cold turkey' has been over-emphasized), but become significant to the individual once he has been discharged and returns to his old way of life. This has led Wikler[49], a leading proponent of the learning theory approach, to stress the importance of stimulus control. Some programmes for smokers include, for example, asking the person not to smoke in his or her usual location, but in an unfamiliar and unconducive location, such as the garage.

There are several problems in assessing the effectiveness of treatment programmes. An important difficulty is with definition: should the criterion of success be complete abstinence, or simply some improvement? Few researchers have examined any changes in interpersonal difficulties, a criterion that may well be equally significant for the individual and the family. Nor do many studies include waiting-list control groups in their design, so that it is not possible to rule out the effects of spontaneous remission. Drug use declines with age, for example, and this may account for many of the reported treatment effects. Further, the samples of addicts involved in treatment programmes may be atypical, usually being those whose problem has come to the attention of the police or who attend because of family pressures. Since motivation is likely to be important, those who attend under duress would be expected to have a lower chance of rehabilitation. Those who drop out of programmes may also be quite different from those who stay, so their data need to be considered: they should be included in the 'failure' rate, but this is rarely done[50].

Notwithstanding these difficulties in assessing the effectiveness of treatment, the general rule is short-term recovery with quick relapse. Whatever the treatment approach and the condition, only about 30% of patients are dependence-free a year after treatment ends. A wide variety of techniques have been used in rehabilitation, including behavioural (e.g. operant and classical conditioning, social skills training), psychotherapeutic and substitute (e.g. methadone for heroin addicts, nicotine gum for smokers) approaches. The similarities in success rates for different treatments is reminiscent of the controversy between psychotherapists and behaviour therapists discussed in Chapter 3. Specific effects might be operative (some people may remain dependent for personality reasons, others for occupational ones yet others because of pharmacological effects), or all treatment programmes may have something in common that is responsible for change (such as peer or family support).

An example of the difficulties experienced when only one aspect of the individual's problem is considered is given by Whitehead[51]. He observed that about 80% of his patients experienced opiate withdrawal symptoms while being maintained on methadone. These symptoms included complaints of cramps, longing for drugs and severe subjective distress. This is paradoxical, in that such observations would not be expected from a purely pharmacological stand-point. Whitehead noted that these difficulties coincided with changes in life-style, often emotional changes to do with increased autonomy and responsibility. In several patients there was a close relationship between the onset and remission of both symptoms and life stresses, as illustrated by the following case:

> L.H. is a 30-year-old Mexican American addict of 15 years duration. Mr. H. was maintained on 120 mg/day of methadone. He was promised he would receive three take-home doses of methadone a week if he could maintain heroin-free urine during the next month. As the month deadline approached, the patient complained of 'icky' sick feelings, chills, and postmicturition nausea. He was observed to have coryza and to be diaphoretic. He requested more methadone and suggested we were experimenting on him by secretly decreasing his dose. Five days before the deadline he reported he had used heroin and that his symptoms were gone. Heroin was confirmed by urinalysis and the increase in responsibility was deferred.
>
> Approximately six months later the same patient was offered a job. In the following two days, continuing daily methadone, the patient began to feel 'icky' and to sweat profusely. He suffered from headaches, nausea, and occasional vomitting. The next day when he began work the symptoms continued and were augmented by headache and a mild exacerbation of chronic asthma. He believed this methadone dose had been decreased, that he was having 'withdrawals', or that he was 'coming down with something'. Medical examination was negative. Five days later the patient's employment was terminated. All symptoms remitted completely. (Ref. 51, pp. 189 – 190).

Summary

An understanding of the three topics covered in this chapter — pain, placebos and drug dependence — relies on an appreciation of the interdependence of physiological and psychological factors (mind and body).

The magnitude of an injury is not always predictive of the amount of pain experienced and, indeed, pain may be experienced when no injury is apparent. Pain involves not only physical sensations from the injured site, but also emotional and evaluative reactions to these sensations. Responses are affected by many factors including personality, cultural variables and family background. Measurement is difficult. Objective physiological measures show little correlation with one another, and the amount of analgesia requested by a sufferer or provided by a caregiver is open to social and psychological influences. Subjective measures, such as rating scales, provide other possible techniques of measurement.

Five different methods of pain relief are considered. First, relief of pain through pharmacological techniques appears to work in different ways with different drugs. For example, cocaine seem to block nerve conduction from the injured site, unlike morphine which does not appear to stop input but rather changes the patient's consciousness of this sensation. Second, cognitive techniques are successful in relieving pain. Instructions to re-interpret the painful stimulation are more effective than simply distraction from the sensation, although this has some benefits. Third, hypnosis can provide relief to 'susceptible' individuals, although the mechanism is not clear. Fourth, behavioural analysis and suitable alteration of the rewards that shape and maintain an individual's reactions to pain reduces the need for analgesia. Fifth, psychotherapeutic techniques consider how to meet the needs underlying pain expression, resulting in a reduction not only of expressed pain, but also of experienced pain.

In certain cases, individuals can show improvement after a treatment when given a non-active drug — placebo effects. Around a third of people react to placebos, and reactivity seems highest in psychiatric populations, although few predictive personality variables have been identified. Placebos may work because, after taking medication, 'feeling better' is a conditioned response; alternatively, people may re-interpret their bodily sensations. Another possibility is that reactors may simply *say* they feel better when in fact they are experiencing the same sensations. There is some evidence that placebos operate by releasing endorphins in the body; i.e. they have a physiological action.

Physical dependence on drugs is not, as commonly believed, usually the major problem to overcome in drug dependence. The many other factors involved, including availability of the drug, the individual's personality, family background and general life style, make it difficult to treat successfully. Relapse may occur if the person returns to the situation in which drug abuse originated.

Suggested Reading

R.A. Sternbach (ed.), *The psychology of pain*, Raven Press, New York, 1978, gives a good introduction to pain research. M. Jospe, *The placebo effect in healing*, Lexington Books, Lexington, Mass., 1978, reviews studies on the placebo effect and considers many possible explanations for it.

Many of the issues in addiction research are discussed in W.R. Miller (ed.), *The addictive behaviours*, Pergamon Press, Oxford, 1980.

References

1. Leventhal, H. and Everhart, D., Emotion, pain and physical illness, *In* Izard, C.E. (ed.), *Emotion and psychopathology*, Plenum Press, New York, 1979.
2. Beecher, H.K., Pain in men wounded in battle, *Annals of surgery*, 1946, **123**, 96 – 105.
3. Uddenberg, N., Childbirth pain, *In* Oborne D.J., Gruneberg, M.M. and Eiser, J.R. (eds.), *Research in psychology and medicine* (vol. 1), Academic press, London, 1979.
4. Kosambi, D.D., Living prehistory in India, *Scientific American*, 1967, **216**, 105 – 114.
5. Malinowski, B., *Sex and repression in savage society*, Kegan Paul, Trench, Trubner, London, 1927.
6. Simmel, M.L., The reality of phantom sensations, *Social Research*, 1962, **29**, 337 – 356.
7. Craig, K.D. and Prkachin, K.M., Social modelling influences on sensory decision theory and psychophysiological indexes of pain, *Journal of Personality and Social Psychology*, 1978, **36**, 805 – 815.

8. Apley, J., *The child with abdominal pains*, Blackwell, London, 1975.
9. Creed, F., Life events and appendicectomy, *Lancet*, 1981, **1**, 1381 – 1385.
10. Melzack, R., *The puzzle of pain*, Penguin, Harmondsworth, 1973.
11. Wall, P.D., The gate control theory of pain mechanisms, *Brain*, 1978, **101**, 1 – 18.
12. Leiderman, P.H. and Shapiro, D., *Psychobiological approaches to social behaviour*, Tavistock Publications, London, 1965.
13. Bond, M.R. and Pilowski, I., Subjective assessment of pain and its relationship to the administration of analgesics in patients with advanced cancer, *Journal of Psychosomatic Research*, 1966, **10**, 203 – 208.
14. Bond, M.R., *Pain, its nature, analysis and treatment*, Churchill Livingstone, Edinburgh, 1978.
15. Sternbach, R.A., *Pain patients: traits and treatments*, Academic Press, London, 1974.
16. Melzack, R., The McGill pain questionnaire, *Pain*, 1975, **1**, 279 – 299.
17. Reading, A.E., A comparison of pain rating scales, *Journal of Psychosomatic Research*, 1980, **24**, 119 – 124.
18. Parbrook, G.D., Steel, D.F. and Dalrymple, D.G., Factors predisposing to postoperative pain and pulmonary complications, *British Journal of Anaesthesia*, 1973, **45**, 21 – 33.
19. Leventhal, H., Brown, D. Shacham, S. and Engquist, G., Effects of preparatory information about sensations, threat of pain and attention on cold pressor distress, *Journal of Personality and Social Psychology*, 1979, **37**, 689 – 714.
20. Sjolund, B., Terenius, L. and Erickson, M., Increased cerebrospinal fluid levels of endorphines after electroacupuncture, *Acta Physiologica Scandinavia*, 1977, **100**, 382 – 384.
21. Goldstein, A., Opoid peptides (endorphines) in pituitary and brain, *Science*, 1976, **193**, 1081 – 1086.
22. Houde, R.W., Wallerstein, S.L. and Rogers, M., Clinical pharmacology of analgesics, *Clinical pharmacology and therapeutics*, 1960, **1**, 163 – 174.
23. Bond, M.R., Glynn, J.P. and Thomas, D.G., The relation between pain and personality in patients receiving pentazocine (Fortral) after surgery, *Journal of Psychosomatic Research*, 1976, **20**, 369 – 381.
24. Jaremko, M.E., Cognitive strategies in the control of pain tolerance, *Journal of Behaviour Therapy and Experimental Psychiatry*, 1978, **9**, 239 – 244.
25. Melzack, R., Weisz, A.Z. and Sprague, L.T., Strategies for controlling pain, *Experimental Neurology*, 1963, **8**, 239 – 247.
26. Langer, E., Janis, I. and Wolper, J., Reduction of psychological stress in surgical patients, *Journal of Experimental Social Psychology*, 1975, **11**, 155 – 165.
27. Engstrom, D.R., Hypnotic susceptibility, EEG-Alpha and self regulation, *In* Schwartz, G.E. and Shapiro, D. (eds.), *Consciousness and self-regulation*, Plenum Press, London, 1976.
28. Weitzenhoffer, A.M. and Hilgard, E.R., *Stanford Hypnotic Susceptibility Scale*, Consulting Psychologists Press, Palo Alto, 1959.
29. Hilgard, E.R., The alleviation of pain by hypnosis, *Pain*, 1975, **1**, 213 – 231.
30. Finer, B., Hypnotherapy in pain of advanced cancer, *In* Bonica, J.J. and Ventafridda, V., *Advances in pain research and therapy* (vol. 2), Raven Press, New York, 1979.
31. Hilgard, E.R., Hypnosis and pain, *In* Sternbach, R.A., *The psychology of pain* Raven Press, New York, 1978.
32. Bonica, J.J. and Fordyce, W.E., Operant conditioning for chronic pain, *In* Bonica, J.J., Procacci, P. and Pagni, C.A. (eds.), *Recent advances on pain* Charles C.Thomas, Springfield, 1974.

33. Kuhn, C.C. and Bradnan, W.A., Pain as a substitute for the fear of death, *Psychosomatics*, 1979, **20**, 494 – 495.

34. Park, L.C. and Covil, Non-blind placebo trial, *Archives of General Psychiatry*, 1963, **12**, 336 – 345, copyright 1963, American Medical Association.

35. Lasagna, L., Mostelle, R.F., von Felsinger, J.M. and Beecher, H.K., A study of the placebo response, *American Journal of Medicine*, 1954, **16**, 770 – 779.

36. Lowinger, P. and Dobie, S., What makes placebos work?, *Archives of General Psychiatry*, 1969, **20**, 84 – 88.

37. Shapiro, A.K. and Morris, L.A., The placebo effect in medical and psychological therapies, *In* Garfield, S. and Bergin, A.E., *Handbook of psychotherapy and behaviour change* (2nd edn.), Wiley, Chichester, 1978.

38. Feather, B.W., Chapman, C.R. and Fisher, S.B., The effect of a placebo on the perception of painful radiant heat stimuli, *Psychosomatic Medicine*, 1972, **34**, 290 – 294.

39. Levine, J.D., Gordon, J.C. and Fields, H.L., The mechanism of placebo analgesia *Lancet*, 1978, **2**, 654 – 657.

40. Reidenberg, M. and Lowenthal, D., Adverse nondrug reactions, *New England Journal of Medicine*, 1968, **279**, 678 – 679.

41. Hafen, B.Q. and Peterson, B., *Medicine and drugs* (2nd edn.), Lea and Febiger, Philadelphia, 1978.

42. Goodwin, D.W., Genetics of alcoholism, *In* Pickens, R.W. and Heston, L.L. (eds.), *Psychiatric factors in drug abuse*, Grune and Stratton, London, 1974.

43. Brill, H., Introductory thoughts regarding treatment and rehabilitation, *In* Schecter, A. and Mule, S.J., *Rehabilitation aspects of drug dependence* CRC Press, Cleveland, 1977.

44. Lukoff, I.F. and Kleinman, P.H., The addict life cycle and problems in treatment evaluation, *In* Schecter, A. and Mule, S.J, *Rehabilitation aspects of drug dependence*, CRC Press, Cleveland, 1979.

45. Murray, R.M., An epidemiological and clinical study of alcoholism in the medical profession, *In* Madden, J.S., Walker, R. and Kenyon, W.H., *Aspects of alcohol and drug dependence*, Pitman Medical, London, 1980.

46. Glatt, M.M., *A guide to addiction and its treatment*, Medical and Technical Publishing, Lancaster, 1974.

47. Chein, I., The use of narcotics as a personal and social problem, *In* Wilner, D.M. and Kassenbaum, G.G. (eds.), *Narcotics*, McGraw-Hill, New York, 1965.

48. Goldfarb, T.L., Jarvik, M.E. and Glick, S.D., Cigarette nicotine content as a determinant of human smoking behaviour, *Psychopharmacologica*, 1970, **17**, 89 – 93.

49. Wikler, A., Dynamics of drug dependence, *Archives of General Psychiatry*, 1973, **28**, 611 – 616.

50. Gearing, F.R., Evaluation of treatment programmes, *In* Schecter, A. and Mule, S.J., *Rehabilitation aspects of drug dependence*, CRC Press, Cleveland, 1977.

51. Whitehead, G.C., Methadone pseudowithdrawal syndrome, *Psychosomatic Medicine* 1974, **36**, 189 – 198.

12
The Consultation

12.1   Introduction

The research discussed in previous chapters has shown that a better under-standing of people can be obtained by taking several aspects of their lives into account. No one viewpoint is adequate for all purposes. Just as knowledge about a person's anatomy will be helpful in some circumstances but less applicable in others, personality characteristics provide useful information in some cases, whereas in others the environment is more relevant. In schizophrenia, for example, although vulnerability may have a hereditary component, the environment seems to play a significant role in the precipitation of and recovery from this condition. Similarly, it is not possible to predict whether someone will experience abdominal pains on the basis of physiology alone: the occurrence of appendicitis-like pains is related to the occurrence of stressful life events.

The way a doctor interviews a patient determines to a large extent the kinds of information that will be discovered. A physician who concentrates solely on organic difficulties is unlikely to become aware of how health problems are influenced by other people or how the condition will affect the other aspects of a patient's life. The doctor may not discover, for example, that a recommen-dation of bed rest could not be followed because the patient is responsible for the care of an elderly relative. In the first part of this chapter, some of the research on interviewing is presented. This work provides several suggestions on how to take case histories, but many of the points apply equally well to longer-term relationships with patients.

The majority of the research discussed in this book has been concerned with patients — the ways they see their illnesses and the psychological components of their care. Comparatively little attention has been given to the psychology of caregiving — the ways that a physician's viewpoint can affect care. However, there have been several indications that this is important. For instance, the personal feelings of doctors towards sexual matters are related to patients' willingness to discuss them (and thus to gain help), and the childhood background of physicians is related to personal use of drugs and alcohol (and thus affects the doctor's ability to give help). These results indicate that the type of care given depends not only on the patient and the condition but also on the attitudes and perceptions of the doctor. The second part of the chapter covers some of the research on these factors. One related area that is not covered here concerns the stressful effects of doctoring on doctors themselves[1]. There is a growing literature on the problems that medical and nursing staff encounter in their work. Much research indicates that the strains of, for instance, telling patients and relatives about a terminal prognosis, or working long hours under pressure, is associated with psychological problems such as drug abuse and marital conflict. Whether such signs of difficulty are due to the job itself or to such factors as the relative ease with which doctors can obtain addictive drugs or to self-selection into the profession is hard to say. Partly because such problems have consequences for the care of patients, and partly because there is an increased awareness that physicians, as well as patients, have the right to emotional support, the idea that doctors should be able to request assistance is becoming more acceptable. This is in line with thinking in other professions, such as social work and nursing, where care for the caregivers is seen as an important facet of practice.

12.2   Interviewing

There are several reasons why skill in interviewing is important for the practising doctor. As mentioned above, consideration of the patient's obligations and perceptions of the illness are significant. Insofar as these are related to outcome, an understanding of these factors is an important aspect of medical care. There is a more general reason for competent interviewing, however, having to do with the satisfaction that a patient feels about the consultation. Roughly speaking, satisfaction with care has cognitive and emotional components, although they are often related to each other. Cognitive satisfaction appears to be associated with the doctor's verbal behaviour. In general practice consultations, the opportunity to ask questions and to gain information about illness and treatment is predictive of patients' satisfaction with interviews. Emotional satisfaction, on the other hand, seems to be related more closely to the doctor's non-verbal behaviour. The ability to show care and concern by tone of voice, body movements and body posture is significant in this respect[2]. Both verbal and non-verbal aspects of interviewing are discussed below.

Verbal Behaviour

That there is room for improvement in doctor's interviewing skills has been shown in studies by Peter Maguire. As discussed in Chapter 1, it seems that physicians often have the expectation that patients have *either* a social/psychological difficulty *or* an organic complaint. Physical illness is often missed in psychiatric patients, and surgeons and general practitioners often do not inquire about personal difficulties associated with physical diseases. Although much of the work on interviewing skills has involved medical students (rather than practising physicians) there is little evidence that length of training or experience are in themselves related to interviewing ability. For example, Helfer[3] compared the interviewing skills of senior medical students with those of students just entering the medical course. He found that senior students fared worse at eliciting important problems besides those presented by the patients themselves. They obtained less information about personal difficulties than did the new students, suggesting that medical training actually had a detrimental effect on some interviewing skills. Further, the senior students often inhibited the patient's communication by the use of medical jargon.

Maguire and Rutter[4] have outlined the deficiencies in interviewing skills commonly encountered in this research. It should be noted that their concern was with history taking, a situation in which emphasis is placed on the collection of information. The same emphasis may not be appropriate to consultations in which the doctor and patient have met several times before, although many of these points are relevant. In this research, the students were allowed about 15 min for an interview with a psychiatric patient. They were asked to concentrate on current problems and to write up the history afterwards. The students were close to their final examinations. Seven of the common deficiencies were:

1. Insufficient information obtained. The students obtained only one-quarter of the information an independent judge considered important and easily obtainable. One-third of the students failed to elicit the patients' main illnesses or problems, and relevant psychological and social aspects were most commonly neglected. The students were unaware of the paucity of information they obtained, seriously overestimating the amount of useful information they had recorded. In another study[5], 80% of the students avoided personal aspects of the patients' problems, particularly sexual or marital problems. When these topics were raised by the patients, the students avoided any further inquiry, perhaps because they were concerned not to appear intrusive or perhaps because these topics were personally embarrassing.
2. Failure to control the interview. The students often allowed the patients to

talk at length about matters apparently unconnected to the problem at hand. Realizing that the patients' communications seemed inappropriate, the students felt unable to either re-direct the interview or to examine the reasons why they were being given this information. Although Maguire suggests that the patient should be encouraged to be relevant, it can also be argued that re-direction of the interview is not always suitable when the purpose is not primarily history-taking. Stiles *et al.*[2] note that patients' emotional satisfaction with general practice consultations is associated with the opportunity to tell their own story in their own words.

3. Lack of systematic procedure. The interviews were conducted in a rather haphazard way, with little obvious connection between consecutive topics. This lack of procedure often resulted in important gaps in the history, and patients were sometimes left confused about the purpose of the interview.

4. Premature focus on problems. The students often assumed that the problem first presented was the only relevant one and focused the interview prematurely. Usually, this focus took either a social or organic direction. In Maguire's study, the students tended to assume that the patients would have only one problem and concentrated on this to the exclusion of related problems or unconnected but equally important difficulties.

5. Lack of clarification. Students were reluctant to ask for clarification on vague or contradictory information. In a similar study[5], only 22% of the students attempted to clarify what patients meant by such vague phrases as 'feeling run-down' or 'tense'. Given that most people are unable to specify the position of many of their internal organs or to understand the meaning of many common medical terms such as constipation or palpitation, the need to clarify what each patient means by such statements is important. Students were also unlikely to establish the medications currently used by the patients or to encourage accurate dating of symptoms, even though the patients often possessed the necessary information.

6. Deficiencies in style. Two main deficiencies in the way students asked questions were found. One concerned the use of leading questions (questions that make an assumption about the patient). The use of leading questions may be helpful in inquiring about topics that the patient may find too embarrassing to volunteer. For example, renal dialysis often has considerable effect on patients' sexual relations. In such an instance it may be more appropriate to ask 'In what ways has dialysis affected your sexual relationship?' (which assumes that it has) than 'Has dialysis affected your sexual relationship?' (which may be too embarrassing to acknowledge). On the other hand, leading questions can restrict the information gathered: the above question may provide information on sexual matters, but perhaps not on feelings of dependency on the dialysis machine, another common anxiety. Asking too many leading questions can easily bias the interview towards what the doctor feels is important, and not what the patient wants to say.

   A related deficiency involved the use of several questions at once, without waiting for an answer to each one. For example one student inquiring about feelings of depression asked 'You were losing weight? . . . and what about sleeping? . . . waking early? . . . I mean, how did all this affect you?' The patient responded to one question, but the student did not follow up on other aspects.

7. Failure to prepare the patient. After the interviews, patients often reported that they wished the students had made some effort to explain the kinds of information they required and the time they had available. Most of the students began immediately by asking questions about the patients' main complaints. Maguire *et al.*[5] reported that only 8% of the students explained the pupose of the interview and only 4% mentioned the time available. Only 10% of the students ended the interview within the time specified: perhaps more co-operation between the participants could have been gained if patients understood the restrictions and the intentions of the interviewer.

These findings suggest that doctor – patient communication could be improved by providing students with a model for conducting an interview. This protocol could point out many of the deficiencies listed above and suggest remedies. Maguire has conducted a series of studies examining such a model. He has shown that students are able to increase the amount of information they acquire by seeing and hearing themselves interview a patient and by following a systematic procedure during the interview. In one typical study, students were divided into two groups. Those in the experimental group were first videotaped while interviewing a patient. They were then presented with a handout explaining the model, and the course tutor asked the students to consider the problems the consultation presented while referring to the model and to the videotaped interview. Students in the control group also interviewed a patient, but were not given a handout or any other feedback.

When the students in both groups interviewed a second patient a week later, those in the experimental group obtained three times as much relevant and accurate information as those in the control group. Further, the patients of the experimental group rated their student interviewers somewhat more favourably than did patients of the control group, suggesting that the patients benefited as well.

In his model, Maguire makes a distinction between content (what information should be collected) and technique (how it might best be gathered). Students hearing themselves on audiotape learn the skills related to content adequately, but in order to develop a good interviewing technique, videotape seems to be particularly helpful. A synopsis of his model is presented below, and a fuller description can be found in Ref. 4. Similar training programmes have been found to be helpful in improving the interviewing skills of practising physicians[6].

Content. (i) Details of the main problems. The interviewer should be particularly aware that a patient may have several problems and that these may

306

be physical, social and psychological in nature. After establishing the primary difficulty, the interviewer should ask whether there are any problems the patient would like to mention: in fact, the interviewer should assume these problems exist. For the problems that there is time to explore, the date of onset, the subsequent development of the problem, precipitating or relieving factors, the help given to date and the availability of support should be discussed.

(ii) Impact of the problem on patient and family. It is unlikely that physical complaints have no social and psychological consequences. The patient's ability to do his job, his ability to pursue leisure activities and the quality of his relationship with the family are all relevant here.

(iii) Patient's view of his problems. As was shown in Chapter 6, the patient's beliefs about his illness and treatment are often better predictors of his behaviour than medical views. By obtaining a clear understanding of these beliefs, the physician is in a better position to provide effective reassurance and to correct misconceptions. Maguire provides an example of a patient who had been admitted to hospital with myocardial infarction. Having been led to believe by a staff member that it was of a minor nature, he was unwilling to follow his doctor's advice to restrict his activities. The doctor failed to realize the reason for the lack of compliance because he did not understand the patient's view of the illness.

(iv) Predisposition to develop similar problems. The patient's background is significant here, both psychologically and organically. Details of the family of origin, occupation, the patient's early development and childhood, sexual development, interpersonal relationships and previous health may be noted.

(v) Screening questions. Finally, the content of the interview should include an exploration of areas not yet covered. If the consultation has been primarily concerned with physical complaints, then it is appropriate to inquire about social and psychological difficulties; if the interview has been biased toward personal problems, then the physical well-being of the patient should be considered.

Technique. (i) Beginning the interview. The interviewer should take particular care to greet the patient both verbally, using the correct name and title, and non-verbally (e.g. by shaking hands, moving toward him). The interviewer should also indicate clearly where the patient is to sit and to introduce himself if they have not met before.

(ii) Discussing the procedure of the interview. As aids to understanding and remembering, a short explanation of the time available and the procedure to be used is in order. For example, if the interviewer plans to take notes, this should be mentioned and the patient's feelings about it should be elicited. Although note-taking may improve the accuracy of the doctor's memory, it may also inhibit the patient. If the interview is to be conducted in public (e.g. a hospital ward), the patient should be given the opportunity to voice hesitations about talking of personal matters and to move somewhere with more privacy. The theme of this aspect of the consultation is that doctors should make every attempt to put the patient at ease. In the section on non-verbal behaviour (below), other ways in which the doctor can contribute to feelings of comfort in his patient are discussed.

(iii) Obtaining the relevant information. After the opening of the interview, the patient should be encouraged to outline his important difficulties. Perhaps an open-ended question such as 'Can you begin by telling me what problems brought you here today?' could be used. The doctor could encourage the patient to continue by saying 'Go on' or 'Can you tell me more about that?' One technique, termed reflection, involves simply repeating, with a flat non-evaluative voice, a few words spoken by the patient. The repeated words appear to direct the patient's attention towards his feelings about a topic.

Most commonly, questions will be used to gain information. As mentioned above, asking several questions at once is not conducive to good communication. Nor are questions that restrict the range of possible answers always appropriate. To ask 'Was it because you walked too quickly or ate too much?' forces the patient to choose between two alternatives: perhaps both or neither seem correct to him. A distinction can also be made between open and closed questions. Open questions (e.g. 'How do you feel about your mother coming to stay?') allow the patient considerable latitude in his reply, whereas closed questions (e.g. 'Will there be enough room?') narrow the possibilities considerably. Frequent use of closed questions will elicit answers to the questions asked, but suffers from the problem that the doctor may not ask the most appropriate questions. This is particularly likely when social and psychological information is being sought.

Listening is another important skill in interviewing. Rather than determining the direction of the interview entirely, it is often important to allow the patient to say what he wants in his own way. Silence is often needed by patients (and doctors) to consider what has gone on before, or to formulate questions.

(iv) Terminating the interview. Students report that ending an interview is often difficult. Two or three minutes should be left at the end to review the information given, to ask if any important information has not been transmitted and to provide the patient with an opportunity to ask questions.

Non-verbal Behaviour

Although verbal behaviour is important in the consultation, the understanding of the relationship between doctor and patient requires consideration of non-verbal behaviour as well — 'While we speak with our vocal organs, we converse with our whole body.' (Ref. 7, p. 55). The gestures and bodily movements that surround a verbal statement modify its meaning. For instance, the comment 'Come in, Mr Smith' can give very different impressions depending on the speaker's non-verbal behaviour. If the speaker looks at his visitor, rises to greet him and perhaps shakes his hand, friendliness is indicated, but if he continues to look at his desk and issues the invitation in a routine manner, indifference is the likely impression. Several experimental studies support the notion that non-verbal aspects of conversation are mainly responsible for the emotional quality of the relationship between two people, whereas verbal communication is more relevant to their shared cognitive tasks and problems. For example, non-verbal signals have a greater impact than verbal ones on assertiveness and friendship[8]. Much of the work on social skills training described in Chapter 3 is based on the idea that inadequate non-verbal behaviour is responsible for many of the difficulties that various groups of patients encounter. The aim of this section of the chapter is to explore the importance of non-verbal behaviour in doctor – patient communication.

Broadly speaking, researchers in this area have taken one of two positions. One group of workers has maintained that every expression or bodily movement is part of a larger context that will influence its meaning to a large extent. For example, eye gaze can have two distinct and almost incompatible meanings, depending on the circumstances. When two people know each other well and the circumstances are friendly, long periods of looking at each other suggests intimacy, but when issues of status are at hand, gaze may indicate aggression[9]. Similarly, depending on the relationship between the participants, touching may indicate caring or dominance[10]. In adopting this position, the behaviour of both participants must be taken into account, since they both contribute to the context.

A second group of researchers has suggested that many expressions bear a close relationship to emotional state. They are concerned with the relationship between behaviour and emotional feelings — that looking downwards is a sign of embarrassment, for example. This approach is often associated with either psychoanalytic or evolutionary traditions. One of the lines of evidence that Freud gave for his contention that emotions are often repressed and find expression in ways that the ego does not monitor (Chapter 2) comes from his observations of patients in analysis:

> When I set myself the task of bringing to light what human beings keep hidden within them, not by the compelling power of hypnosis, but by observing what they say and what they show, I thought the task was a harder one than it really is. He that has eyes to see and ears to hear may convince himself that no mortal can keep a secret. If the lips are silent, he chatters with his finger tips . . . (Ref. 11).

It may be inappropriate to ask which of these approaches is the correct one. As in many areas of psychology, one model does not account for all observations, and in this case both provide insights into the reasons why people behave as they do. In the outline of research given in this section, both approaches are used and their implications for doctor – patient communication considered.

Vision.   One way to explore the importance of various non-verbal cues is by experimenting with various combinations and testing for general principles. For example, the amount two people look at each other and the distance between them appear to be inversely related. Argyle and Ingram[12] reported that people look at their fellow conversationalists more frequently when they are separated by a large distance than when they are close together. They suggest that eye gaze and distance can substitute for each other as signs of intimacy, so that in order to keep a constant level of intimacy people will look at each other less often and for shorter periods of time as they come closer together. An example of a similar situation to this experiment can be found in crowded buses — everyone is standing close together and studiously looking out of the window or at the advertisements.

Eye gaze is not necessary for person-to-person interaction (talking over the telephone is possible, for instance), but it does play an important role. When a person is speaking, he will tend to look at his partner infrequently and for short periods of time, presumably because he is concerned with formulating what he is going to say. Attention is mainly focused on thinking. However, speakers do look at their partners occasionally, apparently to gain information as to whether they are being understood. Observation of conversations indicates that it is during these times that listeners provide feedback, nodding their heads and murmuring agreement. (When conversationalists cannot see each other, the pause between the time when one speaker stops and the other begins is longer and there are fewer interruptions[13]). When a person is listening, he will spend most of his time looking at the speaker, showing attention to what is being said. Listeners who do not look and who do not nod their heads are often judged to be unfriendly and uninterested in the speaker. Whether speaking or listening, the amount of gaze a person gives appears to affect others' perceptions of friendliness and warmth[14].

A patient who is visually ignored by his doctor may well feel that the physician is not especially warm or caring towards him. Maguire and Rutter[4] place considerable emphasis on non-verbal communication in their interviewing model, particularly stressing the importance of looking at the patient while he is talking. Several examples of the practical importance of these considerations are given by Byrne and Heath[15]. They videotaped consultations and related the physicians' behaviour to the patients' reactions. In several cases, patients hesitated or fell silent when their doctors began to read or write on the medical records. In the following example, the patient stopped talking about her problem at line 3, just when the doctor began writing. Only at line 4, when the doctor looked up, did the patient begin again:

1. Patient:	No, well, even the training centres for the unemployment . . . unemployed . . . they don't like them after a certain age to return there 'cos they say it's . . . they're too old . . . you see.
2. Doctor:	I see.
3. Patient:	So . . .
	(3.5 s)
4. Patient:	So I don't think there's . . . (Ref. 15, p. 330)

It seemed that the shift of eye gaze and attention away from the patient and towards the records effectively suspended the consultation.

It is also important that both interactants have an equal opportunity to see the other's face and eyes during conversation. Argyle *et al.*[13] compared conversations in which both participants could see (or not see) each other equally well with those in which one participant could see the other better than he could be seen. This latter condition resulted in more feelings of discomfort and difficulty in the person who was seen but who could not see the other. The person with more visual information tended to dominate the encounter and felt more comfortable.

This result provides another pointer for doctor – patient communication. It is usual for a doctor to place his desk near a window, because of the light it throws. Yet a disadvantage of this position is that the doctor often sits between the window and the patient, with the light behind. This seating arrangement can result in the doctor's face being cast in shadow while the patient's face is well lit, a situation similar to that of the experiment described above. In such circumstances, the patient may be unable to see the doctor's face clearly, and therefore may be unsure of facial expressions and the direction of gaze.

Posture and gestures. The posture assumed by interactants is important for conversation. A slight forward lean has been shown to be associated with perceptions of warmth[16]. Although closed arm positions appear to indicate coldness, rejection and inaccessibility, moderately open arm positions convey warmth and acceptance[17]. Changes in posture can convey a wealth of information. They often accompany a change in topic and can be used to signal the end of a conversation. If people are seated while talking, for instance, when one participant stands up the aim is often to finish the exchange. A conversationalist may serve notice that he wants to say something important by changing position or becoming restless. It is important that physicians recognize the significance of movements not only in their patients but also in themselves. A doctor who finds himself changing position constantly and keeping his arms closed around his body might reflect on his feelings toward the patient. Movement is also used to emphasize a point or to demonstrate an idea. The representation of size with the hands is a common occurrence: people often hold them far apart when describing a large object, close together when describing something small.

Facial movements comprise perhaps the most expressive non-verbal signals. Many appear to be common to all cultures, since people of very different upbringings smile, laugh and cry in similar ways. That the congenetally blind show these expressions to some extent suggests there may be an innate basis. Paul Ekman is an important researcher in this field, taking as his starting point Darwin's observations about the cross-cultural nature of many facial expressions. Ekman presented photographs of models portraying various expressions to people from very different cultures. There was considerable agreement in identifying the nature of emotions shown (happiness, surprise, anger and so forth)[18].

This is not to say that everyone uses these expressions to the same extent, even within cultures. Women are generally more expressive than men, and part of the reason why some people seem to be warmer than others is due to their expressiveness. Counsellors who smile frequently and who show interest by nodding their heads frequently are often rated as being more facilitative than counsellors who show little emotional involvement[19].

Proximity. One way of describing the distance between people is in terms of 'personal space' — a kind of bubble of territory that surrounds people. In order to find out the size of this space, several strategies can be used. One method is to simply observe conversationalists and measure the distance between them. When standing or talking casually, interactants usually keep about 2 - 2½ feet between them. A way of testing the validity of this observation is, simply, to walk closer to someone and measure the distance at which he or she begins to move backwards. The point at which this occurs is the edge of the bubble. It seems, from experiments of this type, that the bubble is not round: people will tolerate more proximity at their sides than at the front or back.

The boundaries of personal space vary according to several situational factors as well. Intimacy of topic is one variable, as is the relationship between the participants (e.g. friends or strangers) and cultural background (e.g. Mediterranean peoples generally stand closer together than Anglo-Saxons). Hall[20] categorized proximity into four zones: Intimate (0 - 18 inches), Personal (18 inches - 4 feet), Social (4 - 12 feet) and Public (greater than 12 feet). The topic of conversation and the relationship between the participants using these different zones varies. For example, two people standing or sitting between 4 and 12 feet apart are more likely to be speaking socially than personally or intimately.

Status is also related to proximity. Those with high status are observed to have more territory than those with low status[21]. Not only will a director of a company have a larger office than those working for him, he will also have a larger desk that will serve to maintain a large space around him. The way in which a person enters another's office is a good example of how non-verbal behaviour can indicate relative status. Burns[22] reports a study in which subjects were asked to fill out questionnaires indicating which of the people in various situations was superior to the other in status. Three of these situations are represented in Fig. 12.1.

To some extent, a patient entering a doctor's office is entering territory that 'belongs' to the physician. The way in which the patient acts may provide a good indication of how comfortable or uncomfortable he feels in the doctor's presence. Conversely, the way the patient is greeted may give him an indication of the doctor's concern with status. If the doctor stays seated and waits for the patient to come to the desk, the patient may consider the doctor to be asserting higher status. Although many other variables (e.g. clothing, tone of voice) are important in the real-life consultation, this example of the role of non-verbal behaviour provides an indication of how the participants' behaviour at the beginning of the consultation can have an effect on the whole interview. Another feature associated with status is height, in that those of higher status often have higher and more comfortable chairs. Ley and Spelman[23] suggest that one reason why patients do not follow doctors' advice is because they do not understand it and are diffident about asking questions. It may be that any feature of the consultation that emphasizes a difference in status may not be conducive to good communication.

Associated with proximity are studies on touching. Just as the distance between interactants depends on their cultural background, touching is

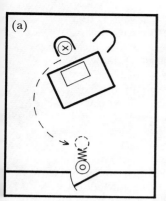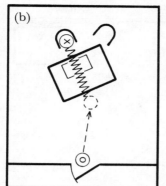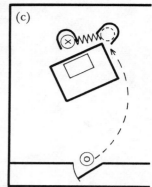

Fig. 12.1 Three examples of the way one person could enter another's office. In (a), person O steps into the office while person X rises and greets him: O was considered to have higher status than X. In (b), O moves towards X, who remains seated: O was seen as being of lower status than X. (c) illustrates one situation in which both were considered to be of equal status: O moves towards X and sits beside him without hesitation. (Reproduced from T. Burns, *Discovery*, 1964, 25, 30–37.)

associated with culture. Jourard observed the frequency of touching between couples in restaurants in various countries. In France, it was 110 contacts per hour, in the United States 2, and in England none. The nature of the relationship between two people is also relevant to touching. Jourard[24] asked his subjects to indicate who touched them (e.g. mother, father, same-sexed friend) and how frequently they were touched on various parts of their bodies. As would be expected, only the hands were touched by everyone and the trunk of the body and the genitals were touched infrequently. The relevance of this study to doctor – patient communication is that touching and intimacy seem to be closely related to each other, such that if touch occurs the relationship is interpreted as a close one. Johnson[25] reported that nurses often find their patients begin disclosing very personal information during intimate forms of touching. Conversely, patients may feel violated when being physically examined by a doctor who has not taken time to establish some rapport.

Arrangement of furniture in the surgery. The research discussed above indicates that the non-verbal behaviour of conversationalists has considerable effect on their relationship. The environment in which an interaction takes place also has an influence on the encounter (see also Chapter 6). Although there is little research specifically concerned with the arrangement of furniture in the consulting room, it is possible to suggest a setting that is conducive to good communication and not at odds with it. Fig. 12.2 illustrates one possibility. Since people become uncomfortable if they are unable to see the face of a fellow

313

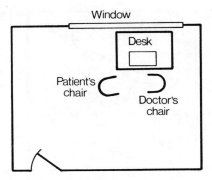

Fig. 12.2 A suggested office design consistent with research in social psychology. The window is at the side of the doctor and patient, rather than behind the doctor. Both participants are seated on the same side of the desk, so that the distance between them can be varied and so that the situation is likely to be considered co-operative rather than competitive. The chairs are of similar height and comfort.

conversationalist yet can themselves be seen, the desk in this room is sited beside the light source, so that the doctor's face is not lost in the window's glare. Both doctor and patient are seated on the same side of the desk for two reasons. First, the distance between them can be varied to suit the requirements of the situation. It may be that the common practice of placing a desk between the doctor and the patient restricts the degree of intimacy between them, keeping them always about 4 feet apart and outside the personal zone. Typically, conversationalists move between zones as their relationship and topics of conversation change: greater proximity may be needed in times of distress than the intervening desk may easily allow. Secondly, there is some evidence that the positions people take up around a desk reflect the nature of their encounter. Sommer[26] reported that individuals who are asked to interact casually prefer corner seating, cooperating individuals prefer to sit on the same side of the desk and competing individuals choose to sit opposite one another. It may be that people are more likely to regard the situation as competitive if they are asked to sit opposite one another, an expectation inappropriate to the consultation. Finally, in order to minimize differences in status — perhaps encouraging patients to be less diffident and ask more questions when they do not understand a doctor's recommendations — chairs are similar in height and comfort[27].

Sensitivity. Probably the most important of the non-verbal factors is the physician's sensitivity to the behaviour and feelings of the patient. Part of this sensitivity involves an awareness of patients' non-verbal behaviour, such as hesitations, restlessness and signs of embarrassment. It is not possible, as yet, to specify the 'best' way to communicate with all patients, particularly about a poor prognosis. Psychology has been able to provide some guidelines — it is

314

important not to assume that once a patient has been informed the information has been understood or that further information is unnecessary — but studies in this area do not indicate that all patients should be treated in the same way. What might be appropriate for one person may be hurtful or shocking for another. In many of the studies on preparing patients for hospitalization and surgery mentioned elsewhere in the book, providing information about procedures and sensations they are likely to experience has been useful for most patients, but not all. Perhaps because people under the care of doctors are given the same label — patients — there is a tendency to consider this heterogeneous group as being very similar to each other.

An example of a difficult communication is telling parents that their child is handicapped. Parents of Down's Syndrome children have complained that they were not told together (one spouse being left to inform the other), that they were not told soon enough, that they were told in front of a large group of people rather than in private and that they were not given enough information[28]. Svarstad and Lipton[29] reported a significant relationship between parental acceptance of mental handicap in their child and the nature of professional communication to them about the condition. Parents who received specific, clear and frank communication were more likely to accept the diagnosis than those who received vague and hurried information. Coming to terms with the disability was not related to any measured characteristics of the child (age, sex and IQ) the parents (social class) or the professional who informed them (age, sex and level of experience).

These findings do not, however, indicate that all parents could be informed in the same way. Although 60 – 80% of parents would have liked to have been told together, there remains the 20 – 40% who would not have wished this. Although some were glad that they had been told about the mental handicap straight away, others report that they would 'prefer to wait until the diagnosis is confirmed' or 'glad they waited a week — we might have rejected him' (Ref. 30, p. 24).

Another aspect of sensitivity is a recognition that the physician's own behaviour will be studied and interpreted by patients particularly when they are unsure about diagnosis and treatment. To take Down's Syndrome as an example again, Cunningham[28] describes how it was the changes in hospital routine and reactions of the staff that had made some parents concerned about their children:

I knew something was wrong as soon as he was . . . born. They all looked at each other and went very quiet. Some other people then came in . . . but when I asked was he all right, they said he was fine and not to worry . . . but I knew they knew all the time, so why didn't they say something instead of keeping me wondering and worrying all that time?

and:

I guessed she wasn't all right. She was always the last baby brought up from the nursery after feeding and people — doctors, students and nurses and all that — kept popping in to see us but never seemed to want anything. (Ref. 28, p. 314)

315

There has been considerable emphasis on the concept of 'accurate empathy', particularly in the literature on psychotherapy. It has been defined as 'the ability to be sensitive to another's current feelings and the verbal facility to communicate this understanding in a language attuned to the patient's present feelings'. Thus, empathy requires an ability not only to understand feelings but to *express* this understanding as well. There is recent evidence of its importance in doctor — patient communication. DiMatteo and Taranta[31] focused on patients' perceptions of the rapport they had with their doctors and on the characteristics of physicians that contributed to this rapport. They found that the ability of physicians to understand the emotions of others and the ability to communicate this understanding was associated with patient satisfaction. There is also evidence that medical training does little to encourage empathy, in that final-year students have no greater skill than first-year students, and the level of empathy remains low throughout[32]. Attempts to increase sensitivity have been described by DiMatteo and Taranta[31] and Kent *et al.*[33]. Teaching programmes often include an opportunity for trainees to role-play a consultation and then the patients (who are sometimes actors and actresses and sometimes patients living nearby) provide information on how they felt about the interview. Although assessment of such training is difficult, some studies (e.g. Poole and Sanson-Fisher[32]) have shown that sensitivity can be improved through these kinds of experiences.

12.3 Deciding on Treatment

In Chapter 6 the notion that patients do not consult their doctor on the basis of symptoms alone was discussed. It became apparent that going to see the doctor was influenced by social and personal factors as well as physiological ones. It seems that people often consult their physician only when their difficulties become physically or socially incapacitating. Similarly, there has been research conducted into the factors that influence how physicians decide to treat patients. Here, too, behaviour cannot be explained simply by examining patients' conditions. There is a wide variation, for example, in the number and type of prescriptions given by doctors, with some giving up to 6 times as many as others. Part of this variation might be due to patient selection: in group practices, patients could choose one doctor when they have a complaint that requires medication but another doctor when they would prefer a sympathetic ear. However, it seems unlikely that all the variation could be due to this kind of self-selection and several other factors have been found to be associated with prescribing patterns. The doctor's training, use of advice from colleagues and the advertising of pharmaceutical companies seem important[34]. General attitudes towards prescribing are also relevant, with physicians who have favourable attitudes towards tranquillizing drugs, for example, prescribing them for a higher proportion of patients than those with less favourable attitudes[35].

Besides the number of prescriptions written, the quality of prescribing is also important. In one study, an indication of physicians' dissatisfaction with their job was related to incautious prescribing. A group of doctors were asked to indicate their degree of agreement or disagreement with a number of statements, such as:

'Assuming that pay and conditions were similar, I would just as soon do non-medical work'.
'My work still interests me as much as it ever did'.

Those doctors who disagreed with items like the first one and who agreed with items like the second were said to have high job satisfaction. Prescribing records were then reviewed, particularly those prescriptions for drugs that current pharmacological research had suggested were contraindicated in some way. The results showed that the more-satisfied doctors were less likely to prescribe these medications than the less-satisfied ones. They were also less likely to sign prescriptions without first seeing the patient and so were perhaps in a better position to observe signs which could lead to adverse reactions[36].

In another similar project, physicians' attitudes towards emotional disturbance in their patients was found to be related to prescribing patterns. Those who agreed with such statements as:

'The distress shown by many neurotic patients is due more to a lack of control than real suffering'.
'Until the advent of more effective methods of treatment, there is little to be done for psychiatric patients',

were more likely to issue repeat prescriptions for tranquillizers and to ask ancilliary workers to fill out the forms. Agreements with such statements was also related to low job satisfaction and low general morale[37].

There is some evidence to suggest that more stingent prescribing would not work to the detriment of patients. Marsh, a general practitioner, reports that he avoids prescribing when social, psychological or interpersonal needs seem more relevant than pharmacological ones. He has also attempted to reduce the number of drugs he uses, claiming that by using a limited range of medications he understands their effects well and can monitor their side-effects. When asked, only 1% of his patients felt that they were not given a prescription often enough[38]. Indeed, since nearly 20% of patients do not cash their prescriptions[39], it can be argued that the doctor and patient fail to agree about appropriate action in about one-fifth of consultations where a prescription is given.

The enthusiasm of a physician for a particular drug may alter its effectiveness. Although much of the evidence for this notion is correlational (so that other factors may be relevant as well, e.g. perhaps enthusiastic doctors prescribe more appropriate drugs or dosages), there is some experimental evidence which provides further support. Haefner et al.[40] first divided their sample of physicians into two groups: those whose attitudes were favourable towards the use of tranquillizers and those whose attitudes were less positive. Then 111 newly admitted patients to the hospital (diagnosed as schizophrenic) were randomly assigned to the physicians. For the first 4 weeks of the patients' stay, all doctors were asked to give the same dosage of medication. Measures of patient improvement were also taken: these were based on interviews (where the assessors did not know which doctor the patient had seen) and on observations of behaviour on the wards. The results showed a relationship between physician attitudes and patient improvement. Patients who were under the care of doctors with more favourable attitudes towards chemotherapy showed greater improvement than did patients under doctors with less favourable attitudes, despite the fact that they were given the same dosages of the same medications. Such studies support the suggestion that the doctor is 'one of the most potent drugs available' to his or her patients.

Personal characteristics of the physician are also relevant to patient care in hospitals. One study[41] examined the effects of the sensitivity of junior doctors on patients with chronic asthma. The doctor's supervisors rated their sensitivity according to the following instructions:

> Please rate each physician according to the degree to which each treated his patients as real, whole persons with feelings rather than a representative case of pulmonary pathology.

In making their ratings, the supervisors felt that concerns about the general welfare of the patient (i.e. concerns about non-asthma and non-medical problems) and willingness to respond to the patients' demands were two important features of a sensitive physician. The researchers then took several measures of how the doctors cared for their patients, particularly their prescribing patterns. Those doctors who were rated high in sensitivity were found to prescribe differently from those of low sensitivity, in that they were less likely to give medications that had adverse side effects. They were more likely to treat different kinds of patients in different ways, adjusting their prescribing practice to suit each patient. There was also evidence that they took the patients' general welfare into account in their prescribing, giving aid to difficulties other than asthma more frequently.

It seems, then, that prescribing patterns are not altogether rational and scientific or based solely on the appropriateness of a particular drug. A similar point can be made about surgical procedures. Like prescribing, there is evidence that the decision to operate depends on the physician's expectations and the resources available. The classic study on surgical procedures was conducted in the 1930s. At that time, most children had their tonsils removed, a procedure that is currently practised much less frequently. At first, 1000 children, 11 years of age, were examined. Some 61% of these had had their tonsils removed previously. The remaining 39% were then examined by a group of physicians who selected 45% of these for tonsillectomy and passed the rest as fit. Those said to be healthy by this group of doctors were then re-examined by a second group of physicians, who recommended that 46% be given a tonsillectomy. When the remaining 116 children were seen again by a third group of doctors, 51 were advised to have the operation. After three examinations, only 65 children remained. These were not examined further because the supply of doctors ran out. There seemed to be no correlation

318

between the recommendation of one physician and that of another regarding the advisability of the operation, so that the probability of a child being given a tonsillectomy depended principally on the physician rather than on the child's health[42].

Even today there is a wide variation in the use of surgical interventions. Here again it is unlikely that this is due only to medical factors. Part of the variation seems to be related to the supply of surgeons: it has been estimated that a 10% increase in the surgeon: population ratio results in about a 3% increase in the per capita utilization of their services. An increase in the number of surgeons living in an area does not appear to be the result of increased demand; rather, demand seems to follow supply to some extent[43]. In one study, the surgical rates in Ontario, Canada, were examined. Considerable variation in the proportion of patients who underwent operations was found for different areas of the province: 7-fold differences for colectomies, 5-fold for appendicectomies. This is surprising since the colectomy operation, in particular, is usually considered to be non-discretionary. The factors that could explain most of the variation in these rates were the availability of hospital beds and the number of physicians living in the areas. The more resources available, the larger the number of operations that were performed[44].

Even within one hospital there is variation in the number of operations performed, with some surgeons taking a more 'radical' approach than others. Howie[45] studied 5 surgical units that worked in strict rotation on emergency admissions. Three of the units took a cautious or conservative approach to appendicectomies, preferring not to operate if the patient seemed to have a reasonable chance of recovery. The surgeons in the other units were more radical, believing that it would be proper to operate in most instances and only refraining if there was good reason not to intervene. Over a period of 9 months, the radical surgeons removed an average of 72 acutely inflamed appendices per unit, whereas the conservative surgeons removed only 46 per unit.

Thus, it seems that the decision on how to treat a patient is not determined solely by the condition. In part, this is because diagnosis is often problematic. One study indicated that almost half of the diagnoses for patients with abdominal pain were changed during their stay in hospital. Although controversial, there is increasing interest in computer-assisted diagnosis, with some research indicating that computers are more accurate at diagnosis than senior clinicians for some conditions[46]. Besides diagnostic differences, however, there are the biases and expectations of individual doctors to consider. Some seem to place more emphasis on avoiding 'false negatives' than others who might be more concerned with 'false positives'. Each physician has his or her own personal experience that will influence decisions.

Summary

Studies on history taking indicate that medical students do not learn interviewing skills adequately through observation and experience alone. They

319

tend, for example, to gather too little information, to focus prematurely on problems and to accept patients' ambiguous statements without seeking clarification. Many of these difficulties can be remedied by following the interviewing model outlined in this chapter. The model provides several pointers, including a summary of how information could be gathered (e.g. the kinds of questions that might be used, how an interview could be ended) as well as what information might be relevant (e.g. the social and psychological consequences of illness, the support a patient's family might be able to provide). The amount of information obtained can be increased after training in the use of this model.

The non-verbal behaviour of both doctor and patient is also important for the consultation. The interest an interviewer shows by the use of eye contact and facial expression determines the impression given more effectively than does verbal behaviour, indicating that physicians should be aware of the way they present themselves to patients. A busy hospital ward may not be the most conducive environment for talking of personal matters, and the organization of furniture in the consulting room may have consequences for the self-assurance and comfort of the patient.

There is a wide variation in the kinds of prescribing patterns and rates of surgical interventions that patients encounter. This seems to result from differences in physicians' beliefs and expectations rather than differences in patients' conditions.

Suggested Reading

A short guide to doctor – patient communication, with many useful references, is *Talking with patients* Nuffield Provincial Hospitals Trust, London, 1980. Bennett's book (see Ref. 4) includes several papers on various aspects of the doctor – patient relationship.

There are many books on non-verbal communication, such as S. Weitz (ed.), *Nonverbal communication* (2nd edn.), Oxford University Press, New York, 1979. A recent one, R, Rosenthal (ed.), *Skill in nonverbal communication*, Oelgeschlager, Gunn and Hain, Cambridge, Mass., 1980, contains papers on how people might improve their non-verbal abilities, including a chapter on doctor – patient communication.

References

1. Cartwright, L.K., Sources and effects of stress in health careers, *In* Stone, G.C., Cohen, F. and Adler, N.E., *Health psychology*, Jossey-Bass, London, 1979.
2. Stiles, W.B., Putnam, S.M., Wolf, M.H. and James, S.A., Interaction exchange structure and patient satisfaction with medical interviews, *Medical Care*, 1979, **17**, 667 – 681.
3. Helfer, R.E., An objective comparison of the paediatric interviewing skills of freshmen and senior medical students, *Paediatrics*, 1970, **45**, 623 – 627.

4. Maguire, P. and Rutter, D., Training medical students to communicate, *In* Bennett, A.E. (ed.), *Communication between doctors and patients*, Oxford University Press, Oxford, 1976.

5. Maguire, P. *et al.*, The value of feedback in teaching interviewing skills to medical students, *Psychological Medicine*, 1978, **8**, 695 – 704.

6. Verby, J.E., Peer review of consultations in primary care, *British Medical Journal*, 1979, **1**, 1686 – 1688.

7. Abercrombie, K., Paralanguage, *British Journal of Disorders of Communication*, 1968, **3**, 55 – 59.

8. Argyle, M., Alkema, F. and Gilmour, R., The communication of friendly and hostile attitudes by verbal and non-verbal signals, *European Journal of Social Psychology*, 1972, **1**, 385 – 402.

9. Exline, R.V., Visual interaction: the glances of power and preference, *In* Cole, J.K. (ed.), *Nebraska Symposium on Motivation*, University of Nebraska Press, Lincoln, 1972.

10. Whitcher, S.J. and Fisher, J.D., Multidimensional reactions to therapeutic touch in a hospital setting, *Journal of Personality and Social Psychology*, 1979, **37**, 87 – 96.

11. Freud, S., Fragments of an analysis of a case of hysteria. *The standard edition of the complete works of Sigmund Freud* (Vol. 7), Hogarth Press, London, 1973; also from *The Collected Papers of Sigmund Freud*, Vol. 3, edited by Ernest Jones, MD. Authorized translation by Alix and James Strachey. Published by Basic Books, Inc., by arrangement with The Hogarth Press Ltd. and The Institute of Psycho-Analysis, London. By permission of Basic Books, Inc., Publishers, New York.

12. Argyle, M. and Ingram, R., Gaze, mutual gaze and proximity, *Semiotica*, 1972, **6**, 32 – 49.

13. Argyle, M., Lalljee, M. and Cook, M., The effects of visibility on interaction in a dyad, *Human Relations*, 1968, **21**, 3 – 17.

14. Exline, R.V. and Winters, L.C., Affective relations and mutual gaze in dyads, *In* Tomkins, S. and Izard, C. (eds.), *Affect, cognition and personality*, Springer, New York, 1965.

15. Byrne, P.S. and Heath, C.C., Practitioners' use of non-verbal behaviour in real consultations, *Journal of the Royal College of General Practitioners*, 1980, **30**, 327 – 331.

16. LaCrosse, M.B., Nonverbal behaviour and perceived counsellor attractiveness and persuasiveness, *Journal of Counselling Psychology*, 1975, **22**, 563 – 566.

17. Smith-Hanen, S., Effects of nonverbal behaviour on judged levels of counsellor warmth and empathy, *Journal of Counselling Psychology*, 1977, **24**, 87 – 91.

18. Ekman, P., *Darwin and facial expression*, Academic Press, London, 1973.

19. Tepper, D.T. and Haase, R.F., Verbal and non-verbal communication of facilitative conditions, *Journal of Counselling Psychology*, 1978, **25**, 35 – 44.

20. Hall, E.T., *The hidden dimension*, Bodley Head, London, 1969.

21. Argyle, M., *Social interaction*, Methuen, London, 1969.

22. Burns, T., Non-verbal communications, *Discovery*, 1964, **25**, 30 – 37.

23. Ley, P. and Spelman, S., *Communicating with the patient*, Staples Press, London, 1967.

24. Jourard, S.M., An exploratory study of body accessibility, *British Journal of Social and Clinical Psychology*, 1966, **5**, 221 – 231.

25. Johnson, B.S., The meaning of touch in nursing, *Nursing Outlook*, 1965, **13**, 59 – 60.

26. Sommer, R., Further studies of small group ecology, *Sociometry*, 1965, **28**, 337 – 348.

27. Editorial, Non-verbal communication in general practice, *Journal of the Royal College of General Practitioners*, 1980, **30**, 323 – 324.

28. Cunningham, C., Parent counselling, *In* Craft, M., *Tredgold's mental retardation* (12th edn.), Baillière-Tindall, London, 1979.

29. Svarstad, B.L. and Lipton, H.L., Informing parents about mental retardation, *Social Science and Medicine*, 1977, **11**, 645 – 651.
30. Armstrong, G., Jones, G., Race, D. and Ruddock, J., *Mentally handicapped under five*, Evaluation Research Group Report 8, University of Sheffield, 1980.
31. DiMatteo, M.R. and Taranta, A., Non-verbal communication and physician – patient rapport, *Professional Psychology*, 1979, 540 – 547.
32. Poole, A.D. and Sanson-Fisher, R.W., Understanding the patient, *Social Science and Medicine*, 1979, **13A**, 37 – 43.
33. Kent, G., Clarke, P. and Dalrymple-Smith, D., The patient is the expert, *Medical Education*, 1981, **15**, 38 – 42.

13
Compliance

13.1   Introduction

Like the previous one, this chapter is concerned with doctor – patient communication. Here, the emphasis is on compliance — the extent to which patients do or do not follow their doctors' advice, and the factors that affect this. Some of the work in this area has been concerned with doctors' beliefs about patients' adherence to their recommendations. Davis[1] reported that many of the physicians in his sample believed that when they prescribed a drug, most or all of their patients complied promptly, but empirical investigations of adherence suggest that this expectation is an unrealistic over-estimation. Further, doctors do not seem able to distinguish between patients who comply and those who do not[2].

Non-compliance can be said to occur if a patient makes an error in dosage or timing or takes other medications that interact dangerously. Studies on this problem have given various indications of the degree of non-compliance, ranging from about 4% to 92%, with a median of about 45%. To take one example, children on a 10-day course of penicillin due to streptococcal infection were studied. Parents were responsible for the medication, and although most of them correctly identified the child's diagnosis, knew the name of the medication and how to obtain it, few of them ensured the completion of the programme. Although the medication was free, their physicians were aware of the study and the families were given advance notification that they would be visited, by the third day 59% of the children were not receiving penicillin and by the sixth day only 29% were continuing treatment.

The wide range of reported findings may be due to various factors, such as design and measurement. Some researchers have taken 90% compliance as satisfactory, but others have insisted on 100%. If patients are simply asked about their adherence, the rate often appears reassuring, but if objective tests are taken (e.g. urine or stool analysis) the rate of adherence often appears much lower. Thus simply asking a patient if he or she has followed advice does not seem to be a valid way of measuring compliance[3].

The emphasis placed here on compliance is not intended to suggest that it is necessarily important that patients always follow advice. It has been noted by several writers (e.g. Stimson[4]) that there is an implicit assumption behind much of the work in this area. The assumption is that patients should obey their doctors' instructions, and failure to do so indicates some kind of deficiency within the patient. The terms used (by some researchers) — obedience, refusal, failure to co-operate, indeed the words 'patient' and 'compliance' themselves — suggest that some blame lies with a person who does not take prescribed medication or does not follow advice. Such a view can be justified only if the doctor – patient relationship is seen as an authoritarian one, with the physician being the expert who knows what is best. However, this view has been strongly challenged in recent years, with many preferring to consider the relationship as one in which both parties *negotiate* a course of action. Seen in this way, it may not be appropriate for patients to always adhere to their doctors' advice. Indeed, it has been argued that this is unimportant for many conditions[5] and that in some circumstances non-compliance can be the only rational course of action open to a patient. As considered here, compliance is used as an example of how doctor – patient communication can succeed or fail, depending on the care physicians take in understanding the needs and circumstances of their patients. In this first section of the chapter, compliance is more appropriately seen as a dependent measure of communicative success, rather than an end in itself. The section does, however, include many suggestions about how adherence to doctors' advice can be improved (and see Chapter 3).

In another respect, compliance can be detrimental to health. The second section of this chapter gives a brief outline of some of the research in iatrogenic illness — those conditions that are the result of medical care. In part, such conditions are a result of a medical system that includes large hospitals, where the risk of infections is high, and a reliance on drugs that may have unexpected side effects. Because of such risks, the patients may come to believe that the disadvantages of medical care outweigh the advantages. Further, medical staff themselves can also detract from good health, as in the case of incautious prescribing patterns.

13.2 Factors Affecting Compliance

Several suggestions have been put forward to account for the low rates of compliance mentioned above. Many researchers describe their results in terms of 'predictive power' — the extent to which any one factor can distinguish between groups of compliers and non-compliers. The eventual aim is to identify relevant factors and then take steps to minimize their influence. There is evidence that this approach is effective. Inui et al.[6] randomly assigned hospital doctors responsible for hypertensive patients to one of two groups. One group received a 1 - 2 hour tutorial on compliance, and the other group served as a control. The experimental group was encouraged to be sceptical about compliance, and many of the factors outlined below were discussed. A 40% increase in the number of patients taking most of their pills was reported, and at the end of the study hypertension was considered to be adequately controlled in 67% of the patients of this tutored group, but only in 36% of the patients of the untutored group. The patients of the tutored doctors were also found to be more knowledgeable about their drug regime and dietary requirements, and had more accurate views of the seriousness of the disease, the efficacy of the drugs and the consequences of not taking them. These results indicate that, with greater awareness on the part of physicians, non-compliance can be reduced. Although Davis[1] reported that two-thirds of the doctors in his sample attributed non-compliance to patients' unco-operative personalities, few associations between compliance and personality have been found. Other aspects of the problem have been investigated as described below.

Situational Factors

An individual's unique circumstances influence his decision to comply or not comply with medical advice. Many of the factors explored in relation to the sick role (Chapter 6) are relevant here. As in the case of acceptance of the sick role, family support is important. For example, mothers who report that they have difficulty in caring for their children tend to be non-compliant[7]. The example set by others in the family is also significant. Osterweis et al.[8] looked at the strength of the association between use of medication in the individual and his family. They found that use by other family members was a good predictor, a better one than severity of the illness.

Often, the patient is not the person responsible for compliance. Children, for example, depend on parental advice. The presence of family members living with the patient seems to be related to compliance in adults too. In one study[9] patients living with a spouse or relatives were found to be twice as likely to take their medication as those living in isolation. There is also evidence that the degree of medical supervision is relevant. Hare and Wilcox[10] reported that non-compliance was found in only 19% of in-patients, 37% of day patients and 49% of out-patients. Results such as these have led to the suggestion that teaching self-medication while in hospital may increase out-patient compliance.

It should also be pointed out that compliance with medical advice is often considered in broader terms than simply pill-taking. Francis et al.[11] asked mothers why they missed appointments made for their children. Some of the most frequent replies were lack of transport and the presence of other family problems. It seems that the decision to make and keep appointments is not as closely related to the severity of the illness as to its relative urgency. Gabrielson et al.[12] examined factors that affected parents' decision to make an appointment with a doctor when a school nurse indicated one was needed. Although further help was sought by most of the parents, almost all of these perceived the illness as being more urgent and important than other problems in the family at the time. Less than 10% of the parents who saw the condition as more urgent than other family problems failed to comply, whereas 50% of the parents who felt it was not as urgent ignored the advice. As in accepting the sick role, compliance appears to be related to the costs and benefits to the individual, and these will be determined to some extent by his or her unique circumstances.

The Treatment Regime

The treatment regime influences the degree of compliance in several ways. One reason for the variation in reported compliance rates may be due to the possibility that patients are likely to adopt the portion of the prescribed regime that requires least adjustment in habits or disruption of family routines. For example, more compliance in weight-reduction programmes could be expected when oral medication designed to suppress appetite is recommended rather than changes in diet[13]. (This is not to say that pill-taking should be the treatment of choice in such a situation.) The complexity of the regime has also been shown to be important, in that as the number of drugs or their frequency is increased, the likelihood of compliance is decreased. Hulka et al.[14], who examined the compliance rates of patients with diabetes or congestive heart failure, found fewer than 15% errors when only one drug was prescribed, 25% when there were two or three, and 35% errors when more than five drugs were used to control these conditions. Similarly, the frequency with which pills should be taken is associated with compliance. One report[15] indicated a doubling in the number of patients not complying when the frequency was increased from one to four tablets per day.

A third way in which a treatment regime may affect compliance concerns unpleasant side-effects. Adherence could be expected to decrease if the treatment feels more painful than the illness. However, the relative contribution of this aspect of treatment may be smaller than imagined: only 7% of patients treated for hypertension mentioned this as a reason for stopping treatment. Possibly the degree to which side-effects lower compliance is related to patients' preparation for them. Research has shown that poor preparation for surgery (Chapter 1) and bereavement (Chapter 10) has adverse effects on people's ability to cope, suggesting that being able to anticipate unpleasant side-effects might reduce non-compliance.

Nor would side-effects necessarily have to be actually experienced. Elling et al.[16] reported that one reason why inadequate dosages of penicillin were given by mothers to their children with rheumatic fever was their concern over the long-term effects of such a medication. One mother gave her child only some of the medication because she believed strong drugs should be given sparingly. Thus, the anticipation of long-term negative effects seems to be important.

This last point is related to another factor: patients' beliefs about the efficacy of a particular treatment. On the one hand, there is the question of diagnosis. A patient could not be expected to follow a physician's advice if he or she did not believe that the doctor had the condition correctly identified. Becker *et al.*[7] measured both the degree to which mothers agreed with the physician's diagnosis and mothers' opinions of how sure the doctor was of the diagnosis for their children. They combined these measures to give a 'degree of certainty' score and found that this measure was predictive of compliance. The higher the certainty score the more closely were the doctor's recommendations followed.

Even if both doctor and patient agree on the diagnosis, however, there is agreement about the treatment to be considered. Doubts about the recommended procedure have been identified as a reason for not following advice. A patient is more likely to take his medication if the physician believes in its efficacy and importance[17]. Presumably, these beliefs are communicated to the patient. It may also be necessary for the patient's beliefs about the causes of the illness to be similar to the doctor's. For example, many people believe that the 'cause' of ulcers is emotional (e.g anger), whereas few see the stomach's acidity as relevant[18]. If a patient believes that emotions alone are responsible, then the necessity for acid neutralization would not be apparent and the point of small meals and drugs less sensible. Two further examples illustrate this point. In attempting to reduce the incidence of cervical cancer, screening procedures have been advised and efforts have been made to discover why some women attend these clinics whereas others do not. Compared to non-attenders, women who followed the advice for screening were more likely to believe that (i) the test could detect the cancer, (ii) the test could detect the cancer before the women themselves could notice it and (iii) that early detection leads to a more favourable prognosis[19]. The non-attenders apparently saw little reason to come since they did not believe in the efficacy of the screening. Similarly, Gabrielson *et al.*[12] found a relationship between parents' faith in the effectiveness of professional care and their decision to take up the school nurse's advice to seek further help. Thus, the patient's beliefs about his illness and treatment are of clear relevance to compliance.

Nature of the Illness

The severity of the illness could be expected to affect the degree of compliance. However, this is not strictly the case, since it seems that it is the patient's perceptions of severity that are significant. Researchers have found little relationship between doctors' views of seriousness of condition and compliance[20], but the way in which a patient views the illness does have some predictive value. In the research mentioned above by Gabrielson *et al.*[12] parental belief that the child's condition was sufficiently serious to affect his school work was associated with help-seeking. The importance of this factor is discussed in more detail in Chapter 6.

Related to perceived seriousness is perceived susceptibility. Continued use of penicillin prophylaxis in patients with a history of rheumatic fever was related to their subjective estimate of the likelihood of having another attack as well as their view of the seriousness of the attack[21]. Similarly, mothers' views of their children's susceptibility have been found to be important. Mothers who felt that their children contacted illness easily and often and who perceived illness as a serious threat to children in general, were more likely to give medication and to keep follow-up appointments than mothers who did not hold these views[22]. Although it is not always possible to test the validity of these perceptions, the findings are similar to those concerning young adolescents' use of contraceptives: girls who feel more susceptible to pregnancy are more likely to use contraceptives conscientiously.

Other indications that perceived seriousness is important for compliance comes from work concerning patients' decisions to end treatment. If how the person feels is a significant factor, then it would be expected that as symptoms are reduced, compliance would decrease. This view is supported by several studies. For example, Caldwell *et al.*[23] asked patients why they had discontinued therapy: the most frequent reason, mentioned by 39%, was that they now felt well. Again, compliance seems to be related to the sick role: if someone no longer feels ill, then some of the expectations surrounding the sick-role — which include co-operation with the doctor — no longer appear to be relevant.

A third feature of illness is its duration. A good example of an illness that requires long-term control is diabetes. Charney[24] examined the adherence rates in diabetics who had been diagnosed either 1 – 5 years or more than 20 years before the study. Although non-compliance was 30% in the new group, longer-term patients showed an 80% non-compliance rate. Other studies have indicated that as illness passes the acute stage patients seem less likely to adhere to the treatment regime.

Understanding

Even if patients felt able to cope with situational factors, had confidence in their treatment and believed that non-compliance could have serious consequences, they would nevertheless be unable to adhere to their physician's recommendations if they did not understand them. The extent of misunderstanding can be surprising. For example, Boyd *et al.*[25] found that about 60% of patients misunderstood their doctors' verbal directions about the method for taking medication. This is not an unusual result. The lack of understanding may be due to factors such as doctors' belief that patients are not concerned with understanding their treatment (and therefore do not take care to explain it) or because patients do not ask questions when they are unclear about recommendations. Doctors may also overestimate the knowledge that patients possess. Boyle[26] found a high proportion of people had incorrect beliefs about the location of their internal organs. 80% wrongly located their stomachs and 58% their hearts. Another possibility is that material given to patients is too difficult for many to understand. There are ways of estimating the percentage of the population who could be expected to understand a given piece of writing. In one study, these techniques were applied to leaflets explaining X-rays: for some of

Table 13.1   Interpretations Given to Some Labels on Medicine Bottles

(Reproduced from J.M. Mazzulo, L. Lasagna and P.F. Griner, *Journal of the American Medical Association*, 1974, **227**, 929–931, copyright 1974, American Medical Association, by permission.)

Medication and instructions	Interpretation	Percentage of subjects giving interpretation.
1. Thioridazine		
'3 times a day'	With meals	80.5
	Every 8 hours	13.4
	10 a.m., 2 p.m., 6 p.m.	4.4
2. Penicillin G		
'3 times a day and at bedtime'	After meals and at bedtime	89.5
	10 a.m., 2 p.m., 6 p.m., 10 p.m.	4.5
	Other	5.0
3. Nitrofurantoin		
'With meals'	Before	53.7
	With	32.8
	After	13.4

these leaflets, only 40% of the target population could be expected to understand them[27].

Studies concerning the interpretation of labels on medicine bottles indicate that here, too, lack of understanding is prevalent. Often, this is due to ambiguity in the instructions. In one project, the researchers asked their subjects to specify when they would take the medication given the instructions on the bottles. Some of the results from this study are shown in Table 13.1. Taking thioridazine first, only 13.4% of the subjects interpreted the instructions correctly — three dosages spread throughout the 24 hours. Apparently, many considered the day to mean only the waking day, some 18 hours. In the case of penicillin G, 89.5% would take the drug after meals, whereas it ought to be taken on an empty stomach. Conversely, Nitrofurantoin should be taken on a full stomach, but 53.7% said they would take it before eating. These results can be compared with interpretations when the instructions are more specific and less ambiguous, as shown in Table 13.2. Here a much smaller proportion of the subjects made mistakes[28].

Remembering

Yet another factor to be considered is memory. A patient would need to

Table 13.2 Percentages of Subjects who gave Correct and Incorrect Interpretations to Instructions on Medicine Bottles when the Instructions were made Less Ambiguous

(Reproduced from J.M. Mazzulo, L. Lasagna and P.F. Griner, *Journal of the American Medical Association*, 1974, **227**, 929–931, copyright 1974, American Medical Association, by permission.)

Medication and instructions	Interpretation	Percentage
1. Penicillin G		
'30 minutes before	Correct	91.0
meals and at bedtime'	Incorrect	9.0
2. Nitrofurantoin		
'To be taken imme-	Correct	85.1
diately after meals,		
4 times a day'	Incorrect	14.9

remember the recommendations if he is to take medication without error. Svarstad[29] reported that more than 50% of the patients he interviewed made at least one error in describing their doctors' recommendations one week after the consultation. As might be expected, those patients who remembered more accurately adhered more completely. Other evidence indicates that many of the doctor's statements are forgotten much more quickly than within one week. Different studies have found that patients had forgotten about 40% within 80 min, 50% within 5 min and over 50% immediately after the consultation. It also seems that the number of statements forgotten increases with the number given, such that a patient could be expected to remember three out of four statements, but only four out of eight[30]. Perhaps the high rate of forgetting found in these studies is due to a tendency by doctors to give too many directions at one time.

Some solutions to the difficulties that memory poses to doctor – patient communication have been suggested. One possibility is to reduce the number of instructions to a minimum. Another suggestion comes from experimental work in the psychology of memory — the 'primacy effect' discussed in Chapter 4. People remember the first item they hear better than subsequent items. That is, people recall best what they hear first. Ley[31] reports that when advice in a consultation was given first, as compared to when it was usually given, recall increased from 44% to 75%. In the same study, he also asked physicians to stress the significance of advice that they considered crucial, on the assumption that patients would tend to forget statements that they subjectively believed to be unimportant. Ley's hypothesis that these subjective beliefs could be modified and that this would have an effect on memory was supported: in this condition recall increased from 44% to 64%. A third possibility concerns the specificity with which advice is given. Bradshaw *et al.*[32] provide evidence that recall of instructions about dieting increases if the advice given is specific (e.g. 'You must lose 7 pounds in weight') rather than general (e.g. 'You must lose weight'). Patients who were given specific instructions recalled 49% of the advice, whereas patients given general recommendations remembered only 19%. It was shown above that precise instructions are understood more readily than vague ones: it also appears that precise advice can be recalled more readily as well.

One final study deserves mention under this heading. Patients leaving hospital were given detailed information concerning their diagnosis, the name, dosage and purpose of the drugs prescribed, and some general advice about diet, etc. All were given this material verbally but, in addition, about half were also provided with the information in written form, which they could take away with them. When they returned for follow-up, both groups were asked about their recollections of the information; significantly more material was remembered by those patients who had been given both verbal and written material[33].

Ley[30] reports the results of an attempt to improve the communication between doctors and patients based on some of the findings considered above. Patients' recall of information was monitored before and after the doctors in the study read a manual outlining the importance of such factors as stressing important advice, giving specific recommendations rather than general rules and giving instructions before other information. As shown in Table 13.3, the proportion of statements recalled by patients increased for all four doctors in the study after they had put the manual's recommendations into practice.

It can also be noted from Table 13.3 that the order of effectiveness of the different doctors remained the same before and after reading the manual, which

Table 13.3   Patients' Recall of Information Before and After the Doctors had Read the Manual Provided

(Reproduced from P. Ley, *British Journal of Social and Clinical Psychology*, 1979, **18**, 245–255, by permission.)

Doctor	Mean proportion recalled by patients	
	Before	After
A	0.52	0.61
B	0.56	0.71
C	0.57	0.73
D	0.59	0.80

suggests that certain doctors may be better at putting over information and that characteristics of the physician are significant.

The Doctor – Patient Relationship

The quality of this relationship (often measured by patients' satisfaction with their care) is also relevant to compliance. Ben-Sira[34] points out that patients often have little knowledge of the principles of diagnosis and treatment, being unable to judge the technical competence of their doctor accurately. Also, since medical treatment usually does not give immediate relief from physical disturbance, the quality of the relationship is the main source of information available to the patient about the doctor's skill. Using correlational methods (i.e. those that do not, in themselves, enable causality to be established), Ben-Sira found support for the hypothesis that patients' satisfaction was closely related to their doctors' show of concern and interest. In addition, patients were more likely to turn elsewhere when they felt dissatisfied with the personal aspects of their care than with the technical aspects, a result replicated in several other studies (e.g. DiMatteo et al.[35]). In other words, the way the doctor cared for the patients seemed more important to them than the treatments used.

This raises an interesting question about physician style. Should doctors be informal and friendly or should they be distant and authoritarian? The evidence is mixed. Some studies have indicated that an authoritarian approach is conducive to compliance, but others have found the opposite[36]. It is likely that the correct approach depends on the individual patient and the specific condition, so that accurate generalizations are not possible as yet. Intimacy does seem important, however: patients who did not keep appointments in one study tended to be those who felt they could not talk easily and intimately with their doctor[37]. Similarly, patients who described their physicians as 'personal' adhered to instructions better than those who described them as 'business-like'[38]. Some continuity of care may be significant: seeing the same doctor on subsequent visits increases the probability of compliance and appointment-keeping[22].

Some of these aspects of doctor – patient communication are often out of an individual doctor's control or awareness, but many of the factors discussed above (taking care that patients are able to remember recommendations, using time to understand the patient's beliefs about his or her illness and taking the patient's unique circumstances into account when giving advice) can all be expected to improve the quality of the relationship. Other research has shown that ensuring adequate understanding of information given to patients in hospital increases their satisfaction with care. Certainly, inability to find out what they want to know about their condition, their treatment and the hospital routine have been found to be among the most frequently expressed complaints by hospitalised patients[39].

One difficulty with some of these studies is that the researchers simply asked patients about their understanding, compliance and satisfaction. The relation-ships discovered between these variables could therefore simply be due to patient characteristics: i.e. that the same people who report they were satisfied would also report that they understood and would adhere to their physician's advice. Other patients may report that they are unhappy with their care regardless of the behaviour of the physician. An alternative method could be to measure what a patient knows about the treatment, and compare this with what the doctor said the patient was told. If these two measures correspond, the communication could be said to be successful. This procedure, used with patients with diabetes mellitus, has indicated that there is an association between these two measures: patients who receive the message that the doctor intends to give tend to be satisfied with their care[40].

An alternative strategy would be to observe examples of doctor – patient communication, measure behaviour that could be important, and then see if these measures relate to feelings of satisfaction and evidence of compliance. Using this method, failure to co-operate with advice has been related to certain kinds of doctors' behaviour: these include collecting information but ignoring patients' requests for feedback, and concentrating on their patients' medical situation but ignoring their psychological and social circumstances[41]. Some important work has been conducted on communications between paediatricians and mothers who had brought their children to emergency casualty clinics. Medical interviews were tape-recorded, the patients' charts reviewed and follow-up interviews were conducted. In this research, mothers' satisfaction with their care was related to the friendliness of the doctors involved and their show of understanding and concern for the children. The use of medical jargon was inversely related to satisfaction, and mothers often complained about the lack of introduction to the doctors on duty[42]. In another study using the same research methods, a significant positive correlation was found between doctors' warmth and patients' compliance[43]. Interestingly, there was little association between the duration of the consultation and mothers' satisfaction or mothers' knowledge of the diagnosis[44], a result also found in studies of general practice. Patients report that they are satisfied with the length of the consultation if they are given the opportunity to say what they want to say. These findings indicate that the way in which the time is used is more important than the actual length of the consultation[35]. Using recorded consultations, the type of verbal behaviour that made the largest single contribution to patient satisfaction was found to be the giving of objective information about illness and treatment by the physician[45]. Many of the verbal and non-verbal aspects of interviewing discussed in the previous chapter are important for the quality of the doctor – patient relationship. Table 13.4 presents a summary of the variables found to be important for patient compliance and patient satisfaction with care.

13.3 Iatrogenic Illness

Behind the research on compliance lies the assumption that it is always in patients' best interests to follow their physicians' advice. Not all writers agree

Table 13.4   A Summary of the Findings Related to Patient Compliance

These Variables are Important for Successful Doctor – Patient Communication.

Factor	Consideration
Situational factors	The support given by the patient's family and the difficulties the family presents are relevant. Complying with a physician's advice involves costs as well as benefits.
Treatment regime	The frequency and number of drugs prescribed have an effect, as do the patient's views of the side effects and efficacy of treatment.
Nature of the illness	The patient's perceptions of the severity of the illness and of the consequences of non-compliance (rather than medical views) are significant. Compliance decreases with length of illness and with the improvement of the patient's health.
Understanding	Patients cannot be expected to adhere to a doctor's recommendations if they do not understand them. The difficulty and ambiguity of material given to patients is often under-estimated.
Remembering	Many patients do not comply simply because they cannot remember the doctor's instructions. Some solutions to this problem include giving important instructions first and reducing the number of instructions to a minimum.
The doctor – patient relationship	The quality of the relationship is associated with compliance, in that patients who are satisfied with the interpersonal aspects of their care are more likely to follow advice.

with this assumption. Some have contended that the way medicine is organized in Western societies sometimes works to the detriment of patients. A leading proponent of this position is Illich[46] who discusses iatrogenic illness (*iatros*, Greek for physician; *genesis*, meaning origin).

Clinical iatrogenic illness refers to the ways in which medications, physicians and hospitals can be pathogens or 'sickening agents'. As an example of how medications can produce ill-health, the side effects of drugs could be mentioned. The use of amphetamines in the 1960s as appetite suppressants to aid slimming resulted in some people becoming addicted. The prescribing of thalidomide to help women during pregnancy is another instance that is often cited. Barraclough *et al.*[47] argue that many suicides could be prevented if barbiturate prescribing was more careful, and in 1975 about half of those who died by overdose had received a prescription for the drug used within the previous week[48]. In Chapter 10, some of the stressful effects of hospitalization were noted, and this experience may have severe consequences for some patients. In one project, all the patients who entered a hospital over a 1-year period were studied. One patient in 12 had some major adverse reaction to their care, particularly to the drugs they were given. About one-quarter of the deaths in the hospital during that time were considered to be due to adverse drug reaction[49, 50]. In a recent survey of British hospitals, some 19% of the patients were diagnosed as having an infection — about half of these were acquired while they were in hospital[51]. It may be that even in many cases of severe and acute illness, hospital care may not be necessary. Some studies of the effectiveness of coronary units have suggested that their popularity is not commensurate with their clinical effectiveness. Mather et al.[52] randomly assigned coronary patients to home care with the support of family doctors or to intensive care in hospitals: they found no differences in mortality.

Perhaps the strongest criticism of medical care has come from those concerned with childbirth. They argue that women who are giving birth are not 'patients' but people performing a natural act. They cite evidence that women who have babies at home run a lesser risk for themselves or their children than those who enter hospital[53]. One criticism of this evidence is that women who are more 'at risk' are more likely to be hospitalized than those not at risk, thus artificially inflating the incidence of complications in hospitals. However, there are indications that this biased sampling does not account for all of the difference, and that for most women home confinements are not more (and may be less) dangerous than hospital confinements[54]. It may be that part of the problem is the way women are confined to bed soon after they arrive. Flinn et al.[55] asked mothers-to-be if they would be willing to walk about during the first stage of labour (when the cervix is dilating) rather than be kept in bed. Of those women who expressed an interest, half were nursed in bed with traditional procedures. The other half were allowed to walk about, visiting the television room to be with friends and relatives or making a drink in the kitchen. So that the foetal heart beat could be recorded, they wore a compact monitoring device. All women were nursed in bed during the second and third stages of labour. When the birth records of these two groups of women were compared, the ambulant mothers had shorter first stages (on average 2 hours shorter), were more likely to have a normal delivery and required less analgesia. Their foetal heart rate pattern was also more satisfactory during the birth. The researchers took Apgar scores of the infants, which gave an indication of their general health and responsiveness at birth: the scores of the ambulant group were significantly better.

Results such as these argue against routine medical interference at birth. Since the health of pregnant women has been improving over the last several decades, the need for obstetric interference could be expected to have decreased. That the opposite is the case suggests to some that much of this interference is unnecessary. Induction of labour has received the strongest criticism. Richards[56] argues that the implications of induction have not been adequately assessed and that its widespread use is not based on clinical advantage but rather on the belief that the birth process should be under the control of obstetricians.

This relates to another of Illich's criticisms of the medical system — the social aspect. Although it is difficult to gather empirical evidence that would support or refute many of his contentions, he argues that the individual has lost control over his health to the medical profession. Increasingly, when someone has a problem the doctor is called upon to relieve it. Although this has many advantages, there are also some distinct disadvantages. The proportion of the national wealth devoted to curative medicine has been increasing more quickly than virtually any other sector of the economy. Since many diseases could be prevented at a much lower cost, perhaps a greater proportion of resources should be aimed at providing a better diet and improved housing and at educating people to take more care of themselves. It has been estimated, for instance, that all the medical improvements made since World War II have been cancelled out by the increase in smoking. The emphasis on cures in the profession may lead people to believe that their health problems can be solved when the time comes, making them less likely to take preventative measures in the short-term. When the medical system takes responsibility for health, it is argued, the individual is not encouraged to look after himself.

As an example of this latter point, the prescribing of psychotropic drugs can be used. They are prescribed more often than any other group of medications. In one study, 87% of doctors agreed that 15 mg of Librium daily would be a reasonable recommendation for a middle-aged housewife who was having marital problems[57]. The argument against such a recommendation is twofold. First, it treats only the symptom and not the cause of the difficulty. Although a tranquillizer may give palliative relief, the individual may become dependent on continuing dosages. Second, when a doctor prescribes a drug for the control of a personal or interpersonal problem, he or she may also be providing the patient with a model for dealing with it. By using a biochemical solution, the physician may imply that the problem is biochemical in origin and the patient's responsibility to examine and seek to alter relationships is reduced. The doctor may be prescribing a way of life as well as a drug[58].

This brief discussion of iatrogenic illness should not be taken to mean that physicians or the medical system generally are solely responsible for these difficulties. Medical care in any culture reflects that society's values and beliefs, so that the emphasis on intervention and high technology is consistent with prevailing cultural views. There is also, of course, the problem in balancing the illnesses caused by medical care with the illnesses relieved. A medical procedure such as vaccination may prove detrimental to some people but this must be considered in relation to the lowered incidence of disease in the general population.

Attempts to balance the positive and negative effects of medical care come up against the difficulty in knowing what a 'cure' might be. As in the case of psychiatric illness, it is not always possible to say that a patient has recovered completely from a physical illness. No one measure is adequate to give a complete picture of recovery[59]. Patients' self-reports of health do not necessarily correspond to the medical view, so that a physician might consider an individual well but this might not be that person's perception. A patient may recover from a myocardial infarction from a physiological point of view, but never return to work. Renal dialysis may prolong a life but create feelings of dependency. When a painful or embarrassing test is conducted, there is the assumption that the results will be more important than the distress experienced by the patient. An example of how doctors and patients can use different criteria for deciding between different courses of treatment is provided by some work in oncology. As a measure of clinical effectiveness, a 5-year survival rate is generally used: using this criterion, surgical procedures are preferable to radiotherapy. The operation provides a better chance of prolonged life at the risk of an early death, whereas radiotherapy provides a smaller chance of prolonged survival but with little risk of an early death. However, this criterion may not be the most suitable from the patient's point of view. McNeil[60] found that for elderly patients at least, the longer-term gain offered by surgery was not so important as its short-term threat. Many patients preferred radiotherapy. Here, the 5-year survival rate criterion was not the optimum one from the patients' standpoint.

In other words, the measures used to assess outcome may not give results that are consistent with each other. The weighting given to one kind of measure (e.g. organic) over another kind (e.g. psychological) is largely a value judgement, rather than a scientific one. There is the need to choose treatments and assess their outcomes on the basis of several criteria, including the beliefs and attitudes of patients themselves.

Summary

Some understanding of why so many patients do not adhere to their doctor's recommendations can be given by examining how they perceive their treatment. Several factors have been shown to be important in this respect, many similar to those involved in the decision to consult the doctor in the first place. These include situational variables such as family support and the patient's own views about the illness. Two often-neglected factors concern the difficulties patients can have in remembering and understanding advice. All these aspects affect the general quality of the doctor – patient relationship.

Medical care involves risks as well as benefits: these include side-effects, such as adverse reactions to drugs or hospitalization. These risks could affect patients' compliance. The medical system may also influence how people view illness, relieving them of some of the responsibility for their own health. This has implications for the treatment of personal problems and the adoption of preventative measures.

337

Suggested Reading

More detail about research on compliance can be found in D.L. Sackett, and R.B. Haynes (eds.), *Compliance with therapeutic regimes*, Johns Hopkins University Press, London, 1976.

A reply to Illich's[46] contention that the medical system is causing more harm than good is provided by D.F. Horrobin, *Medical hubris*, Churchill Livingstone, London, 1978.

References

1. Davis, M.S., Variations in patients' compliance with doctors' orders, *Journal of Medical Education*, 1966, **41**, 1037 – 1048.
2. Kasl, S.V., Issues in patient adherence to health care regimes, *Journal of Human Stress*, 1975, **1**, 5 – 18.
3. Norell, S.E., Accuracy of patient interviews and estimates by clinical staff in determining medication compliance, *Social Science and Medicine*, 1981, **15E**, 57 – 61.
4. Stimson, G.V., Obeying doctor's orders : a view from the other side, *Social Science and Medicine*, 1974, **8**, 97 – 104.
5. Leading Article, Non-compliance: does it really matter?, *British Medical Journal*, 1979, **2**, 1168.
6. Inui, J.F., Yourtee, E.L. and Williamson, J.W., Improved outcomes in hypertension after physician tutorials, *Annals of Internal Medicine*, 1976, **84**, 646 – 651.
7. Becker, M.H., Drachman, R.H. and Kirscht, J.P., Predicting mothers' compliance with pediatric medical regimes, *Journal of Pediatrics*, 1972, **81**, 843 – 854.
8. Osterweis, M., Bush, P.J. and Zuckerman, A.E., Family context as a predictor of individual medicine use, *Social Science and Medicine*, 1979, **13A**, 287 – 291.
9. Parkes, C.H., Brown, G.W. and Monck, E.M., The general practitioner and the schizophrenic patient, *British Medical Journal*, 1962, **1**, 972 – 976.
10. Hare, E.H. and Wilcox, D.R.C., Do psychiatric in-patients take their pills?, *British Journal of Psychiatry*, 1967, **113**, 1435 – 1439.
11. Francis, V., Korsch, B. and Morris, R., Gaps in doctor – patient communication, *New England Medical Journal*, 1969, **280**, 535 – 540.
12. Gabrielson, I.W., Levin, L.S. and Ellison, M.D., Factors affecting school health follow-up, *American Journal of Public Health*, 1967, **57**, 48 – 59.
13. Davis, M.S. and Eichhorn, R.L., Compliance with medical regimes, *Journal of Health and Human Behaviour*, 1963, **4**, 240 – 249.
14. Hulka, B.S., Cassel, J.C., Kupper, L.L. and Burdette, J.A., Communication, compliance and concordance between physicians and patients with prescribed medications, *American Journal of Public Health*, 1976, **66**, 847 – 853.
15. Gatley, M.S., To be taken as directed, *Journal of the Royal College of General Practitioners*, 1968, **16**, 39 – 44.
16. Elling, R., Whittemore, R. and Green, M., Patient participation in a pediatric program, *Journal of Health and Human Behaviour*, 1960, **1**, 183 – 191.
17. Rickels, K. and Briscoe, E., Assessment of dosage deviation in out-patient drug research, *Journal of Clinical Pharmacology*, 1970, **10**, 153 – 160.
18. Roth, H.P., Patients' beliefs about peptic ulcer and its treatment, *Annals of Internal Medicine*, 1962, **56**, 72 – 80.
19. Kegeles, S.S., A field experiment attempt to change beliefs and behaviour of

women in an urban ghetto, *Journal of Health and Social Behaviour*, 1969, **10**, 115.

20. Bonnar, J., Goldberg, A. and Smith, J.A., Do pregnant women take their iron?, *Lancet*, 1969, **1**, 457 – 458.

21. Heinzelmann, F., Factors in prophylaxis behaviour in treating rheumatic fever, *Journal of Health and Human Behaviour*, 1962, **3**, 73.

22. Becker, M.H., Drachman, R.H. and Kirscht, J.P., A new approach to explaining sick-role behaviour in low-income populations, *American Journal of Public Health*, 1974, **64**, 205 – 218.

23. Caldwell, J.R., Cobb, S., Dowling, M.D. and deJongh, D., The dropout problem in hypertensive therapy, *Journal of Chronic Diseases*, 1970, **22**, 579 – 592.

24. Charney, E., Patient – doctor communication: implications for the clinician, *Pediatric Clinics of North America*, 1972, **19**, 263 – 279.

25. Boyd, J.R., Covington, T.R., Stanaszek, W.F. and Coussons, R.T., Drug defaulting, *American Journal of Hospital Pharmacy*, 1974, **31**, 485 – 491.

26. Boyle, C.M., Differences between patients' and doctors' interpretation of some common medical terms, *British Medical Journal*, 1970, **2**, 286 – 289.

27. Ley, P., The measurement of comprehensibility, *Journal of the Institute of Health Education*, 1973, **11**, 17 – 20.

28. Mazzulo, J.M., Lasagna, L. and Griner, P.F., Variation in interpretation of prescription instructions, *Journal of the American Medical Association*, 1974, **227**, 929 – 931.

29. Svarstad, B., Physician – patient communication and patient conformity with medical advice, *In* Mechanic, D., *The growth of bureaucratic medicine*, Wiley, New York, 1976.

30. Ley, P., Memory for medical information, *British Journal of Social and Clinical Psychology*, 1979, **18**, 245 – 255.

31. Ley, P., Towards better doctor – patient communications, *In* Bennett, A.E. (ed.), *Communication between doctors and patients*, Oxford University Press, Oxford 1976.

32. Bradshaw, P.W., Ley, P., Kincey, J.A. and Bradshaw, J., Recall of medical advice, *British Journal of Social and Clinical Psychology*, 1975, **14**, 55 – 62.

33. Ellis, D.A., Hopkin, J.M., Leitch, A.G. and Crofton, J. 'Doctors' orders': controlled trial of supplementary written information for patients, *British Medical Journal*, 1979, **1**, 456.

34. Ben-Sira, Z., The function of the professional's affective behaviour in client satisfaction, *Journal of Health and Social Behaviour*, 1976, **17**, 3 – 11.

35. DiMatteo, M.R., Prince, L.M. and Taranta, A., Patients' perceptions of physicians' behaviour: determinants of patients' commitment to the therapeutic relationship, *Journal of Community Health*, 1979, **4**, 280 – 290.

36. DiMatteo, M.R., Non-verbal skill and the physician – patient relationship, *In* Rosenthal, R. (ed.), *Skill in non-verbal communication*, Oelgeschlager, Gunn and Hain, Cambridge, Mass., 1979.

37. Alpert, J.J., Broken appointments, *Pediatrics*, 1964, **34**, 127 – 132.

38. Geersten, H.R., Gray, R.M. and Ward, J.R., Patient non-compliance within the context of seeking medical care for arthritis, *Journal of Chronic Diseases*, 1973, **26**, 689 – 698.

39. Cartwright, A., *Human relations and hospital care*, Routledge Kegan Paul, London, 1964.

40. Romm, F.J. and Hulka, B.S., Care process and patient outcome in diabetes, *Medical Care*, 1979, **17**, 748 – 757.

41. Davis, M.S., Variations in patients' compliance with doctors' advice, *American Journal of Public Health*, 1968, **58**, 274 – 288.

339

42. Korsch, B.M., Gozzi, E.K. and Francis, V., Gaps in doctor – patient communication, *Pediatrics*, 1968, **42**, 855 – 870.

43. Freemon, B., Negrete, V.F., Davis, M. and Korsch, B.M., Gaps in doctor – patient communication, *Pediatric Research*, 1971, **5**, 298 – 311.

44. Korsch, B. and Negrete, V.F., Doctor – patient communication, *Scientific American*, 1972, **227**, 66 – 74.

45. Stiles, W.B., Putnam, S.M., Wolf, M.H. and James, S.A., Interaction exchange structure and patient satisfaction with medical interviews, *Medical Care*, 1979, **17**, 667 – 681.

46. Illich, I., *Limits to medicine*, Pelican, Harmondsworth, 1977.

47. Barraclough, B.M., Nelson, B., Bunch, J. and Sainsbury, P., Suicide and barbiturate prescribing, *Journal of the Royal College of General Practitioners*, 1971, **21**, 645 – 653.

48. Murphy, G.E., The physician's responsibility for suicide, *Annals of Internal Medicine*, 1975, **82**, 301 – 304.

49. Ogilvie, R.I. and Ruedy, J., Adverse reactions during hospitalisation, *Canadian Medical Association Journal*, 1967, **97**, 1445 – 1450.

50. Ogilvie, R.I. and Ruedy, J., Adverse drug reactions during hospitalisation, *Canadian Medical Association Journal*, 1967, **97**, 1450 – 1457.

51. Meers, P.D., Infection in hospitals, *British Medical Journal*, 1981, **1**, 1246.

52. Mather, H.G. *et al.*, Acute myocardial infarction: home and hospital treatment *British Medical Journal*, 1971, **3**, 334 – 338.

53. Barry, C.N., Home versus hospital confinement, *Journal of the Royal College of General Practitioners*, 1980, **30**, 102 – 107.

54. Tew, M., The safest place of birth, *Lancet*, 1979, **1**, 1388 – 1390.

55. Flinn, A.M., Kelly, J., Hollins, G. and Lynch, P.F., Ambulation in labour, *British Medical Journal*, 1978, **2**, 591 – 593.

56. Richards, M.P.M., Innovation in medical practice: Obstetrics and the induction of labour in Britain, *Social Science and Medicine*, 1975, **9**, 595 – 602.

57. Linn, L.S., Physician characteristics and attitudes towards legitimate use of psychotropic drugs, *Journal of Health and Social Behaviour*, 1971, **12**, 132 – 140.

58. Lader, M., Benzodiazepines — the opium of the nurses?, *Neuroscience*, 1978, **3**, 159 – 165.

59. Sechrest, L. and Cohen, R.Y., Evaluating outcomes in health care, *In* Stone, G.C., Cohen, F. and Adler, N.E., *Health psychology*, Jossey-Bass, London, 1979.

60. McNeil, B., Fallacy of the five-year survival in lung cancer, *New England Journal of Medicine*, 1978, **299**, 1397 – 1401.

Appendix
Using The Library

The contents of this book are, necessarily, selective. Perhaps the biggest problem facing someone who wishes to study topics falling outside this book or who wishes to follow up areas in greater detail, is in knowing where to start. The purpose of this appendix is to give a brief guide to some library resources.

In order to gain a general overview of an area, books and review articles are often useful. Research papers may be concerned with a small problem, which might be too specific for your interests.

The library catalogue of books is the key to finding a book on the shelf on the subject in which you are interested. The author catalogue will enable you to find a book by a given author or editor or institution. The subject catalogue can take two forms. There is the subject catalogue arranged alphabetically by the names of subjects. A book should be found under the most specific term used in the catalogue that describes the subject of the book. Cross-references guide you to related headings under which you may find books of interest. The second type of subject catalogue is the classified catalogue. In this catalogue the arrangement corresponds to the arrangement of books on the shelves, that is, the entries are grouped by the classification symbols. This should mean that all aspects of a subject are brought together by the classification system that the library is using.

Although books will usually give a wide view, they are sometimes rather out of date. Journal articles provide up to date information — but how do you find an article on your subject out of the thousands printed in the hundreds of different scientific journals? To help with this, there are indexes, which are publications that list articles found in other journals: that is, they give the minimum information necessary to look up the original article. Abstracts are similar publications, but they also give a brief summary of the original article.

The most important medical index is *Index Medicus*, which since 1960 has been produced monthly. Each month articles are listed in a subject section and also in an author section. Every year the entries in all twelve monthly issues are cumulated so that you only need to look up under one heading to find articles on that subject published during the year. A most important third section in each monthly issue and in each *Cumulated Index Medicus* is the *Bibliography of Medical Reviews*. This small section lists recently published review articles and thus provides articles giving a more up to date account of a subject than that found in books, and yet still provides a wider view of a subject than the narrow special aspects dealt with in other articles. The review article also provides a good starting point to locate relevant articles elsewhere through its normally extensive bibliography given at the end of the article.

The subject headings used in *Index Medicus* are listed in *Medical Subject Headings* which is published annually and should be consulted to obtain alternative terms and broader or more specific headings under which relevant material will be found.

All entries in *Index Medicus* give full details to enable you to look up the article elsewhere. For example under the heading SLEEP DEPRIVATION in the monthly issue of *Index Medicus* for August 1981 there are several references, one of which is:

Cumulative effects of sleep restrictions on daytime sleepiness.
Carskadon, M.A. et al. **Psychophysiology** 1981 Mar;
18(2): 107 – 13.

which means that on pages 107 to 113 in the March 1981 issue of the journal *Psychophysiology* there is an article by Carskadon on sleep restriction. The 18(2) means that this issue is part 2 of the 18th volume of the journal, which is another way of identifying the journal issue.

Note that all references in the scientific literature more or less follow the above style of citation and that you should be able to work out from the above what any reference that you have means. A point to bear in mind is that the library will not take all the journals referred to in *Index Medicus*, but the article should be available from the library Inter-Library Loans section. A further point is that *Index Medicus* gives the English translation of all articles cited even when the original article is in another language. In these cases, the whole reference is given in brackets with an indication of the language of the original.

Another most useful index is *Science Citation Index*. There are thousands of scientific journals, but only a fraction publish the bulk of the really significant literature, and it is this literature that the Science Citation Index aims to cover. This index appears bi-monthly and has an annual cumulation.

The essential idea of the index is this. All scientific papers refer to other articles as support for what the author has written, and therefore these other articles must be related to the subject of the article in which they are cited. The *Science Citation Index* allows you to start with an author who you know has written on a subject and to find out who has cited their work. The *Science Citation Index* also allows a direct subject approach. Using the *Permuterm Subject Index* section you can find names of authors who have used the subject in which you are interested in the titles of their articles. If you then go to the Citation or Source Index you can proceed to discover further relevant articles using the author name once again as the key.

Two other publications of direct interest are *Psychological Abstracts* and *Sociological Abstracts*, which not only give the necessary details to enable you to look up original articles on psychological and sociological topics, respectively, but also give a synopsis of the articles in question.

In addition to these printed sources, another guide to the literature is the librarian who should be able to explain the catalogue, indexes and abstracts, locate relevant material on the shelf and obtain documents required from other libraries if they are not available in your own library.

Index

bis after a reference number indicates that the topic is separately mentioned on the same page of the text, and *ter* three times: *passim* indicates that the references are scattered throughout the pages mentioned.

Bandura, A., 77–83
Beck, A., 52–54, 195, 245
Beecher, H., 21, 277
Behavioural medicine (*see also* Behaviour modification), 66
Behaviourism, 67, 70, 72, 81–83
Behaviour modification (*see also* Cognitive learning; Instrumental conditioning; Observational learning; Respondent conditioning)
  and child abuse, 228
  and compliance, 76, 86–87
  and drug dependence, 297
  and exercise, 155, 288
  and incontinence, 253
  and marital therapy, 232–233
  and pain, 155, 288
  and sexuality, 188
  assessment of, 87–90
  behaviourism, 67
  functional analysis, 75
  in the classroom, 75
  target behaviour, 75
  versus psychotherapy, 64–66, 87, 88–90
Behaviour therapy, *see* Behaviour modification
Behavioural style, *see* Temperament
Bem sex role inventory, 196
Bereavement (*see also* Death), 109, 240, 248–249, 256–260
Biochemistry, v, 47–245, 336
Biofeedback, 77
Binet, A., 113, 114, 117
Birth, *see* Childbirth
Blindness, 152, 168, 311
Blood pressure (*see also* Hypertension), 77, 249, 250, 262, 266
Bond, M., 280, 284–285
Bonding (*see also* Attachment; Parent–child relationship)
  and brain damage, 167
  and child abuse, 173–174, 223, 226–227
  and childbirth, 173–174, 180, 223, 277
  and multiple caregiving, 179–180
Bowlby, J., 165, 171–182*passim*
Brain damage (*see also* Neural connections), 95, 108–109, 112, 118, 167, 223–224
Breast cancer, *see* Mastectomy; Cancer

Breast-feeding, 180, 216
Brown, G., 141, 230, 244–246, 266
Bystander intervention, 134–137

Cancer (*see also* Mastectomy)
  and depression, 247, 249
  and pain, 284–285, 287–288
  patients' views of, 337
  predicting patients' reaction to, 57
  screening for, 327
Cerebral hemispheres, 190
Chemotherapy, *see* Drugs
Child abuse (*see also* Violence), 173–174, 181, 222–229
Child development (*see also* Parent–child relationship)
  cognitive, 113–114, 125–127, 171, 172, 179, 181–182, 188–193, 278
  maturation, 125–126, 190–191
  social 161–182, 189–193, 251–252, 278
Childbirth (*see also* Attachment; Bonding; Prematurity; Pregnancy)
  and child abuse, 173–174, 226
  and iatrogenic illness, 335
  and siblings, 161, 163
  anoxia during, 122, 181
  labour, 215, 266, 277, 335
  mortality, 164–165
  pain during, 18, 174, 277, 287–288
  preparation for, 18–19, 163–164
  separation at, 161, 173–174, 277
  staff reactions, 315
  stress and, 163–164, 266
Children (*see also* Attachment; Bonding; Child development; Parent–child relationship; Family)
  and illness, 127, 259*bis*
  in hospital, 31–32, 127, 161, 172, 175, 243
  preparation for hospitalisation, 31–32, 79, 175, 176–177
  therapy with, 181–182, 230
Class, *see* Social class
Classical conditioning, *see* Respondent conditioning
Cognition (*see also* Information Processing; Cognitive learning)
  personality, 49–54
  pain, 276–279, 281–283

and non-verbal behaviour, 311, 312, 314
and prescribing, 316–318
Down's syndrome, *see* Mental handicap
Dream analysis, 40
Drugs (*see also* Compliance; Drug dependence; Placebo effect; Prescribing; Side effects)
  administration of, 280, 316–318, 336
  analgesia, 28, 174, 227, 280, 283–287, 335
  and advertising, 195, 316
  and hyperactivity, 84
  during childbirth, 174
  iatrogenic illness, 260, 317, 334–336
  in coping with stress, 239–340, 249, 250, 259, 286–287, 336
  in different cultures, 215
  in psychiatric illness, 37, 54, 317–318
Drug abuse, *see* Drug dependence
Drug dependence (*see also* Smoking)
  aetiology, 260, 296, 334
  alcoholism, 122, 147–148, 231, 296
  and iatrogenic illness, 260, 316–318, 334–336
  and personality, 47, 231, 296*bis*
  and placebos, 290, 293
  in doctors, 250–252, 296
  maintenance, 296–298
  on tranquilizers, 260
Durkheim, E., 266
Dying, *see* Death; Bereavement

Ebbinghaus, H., 95, 96, 101
Education
  and intelligence tests, 112–114, 121, 123
  and pregnancy, 199
  in sex therapy, 188, 205
  of children, 20, 75, 121, 123
Egbert, L., 27
Ego, 39–41, 309
Ekman, P., 311
Elderly (*see also* Ageing; Death), 124–125, 149, 253, 337
Emotion
  and experience of pain, 279–285*passim*
  and terminal illness, 255–257
  control over, 240
  cross-cultural comparisons, 311

effect on foetus, 163, 164
embarassment, 202–203, 304, 309, 337
frustration, 261–262
Empathy, *see* Sensitivity
Employment (*see also* Occupation)
  after myocardial infarction, 152–153
  importance of, 164, 195, 245, 250, 298
  mother's, 172, 173, 180, 245
Endorphins, 283, 293–294
Environment (*see also* Behaviour modification; Culture; Hospitals)
  and compliance, 76, 313–314
  and drug dependence, 296–297
  and gender identity, 188–189
  and genetics, 37, 47, 118–121
  and health, 144–145
  and intelligence, 118–125, 126–127
  and motor development, 125
  and pain, 276–279, 288
  and schizophrenia, 47*ter*
  of doctor–patient interview, 313–314
  physical, 140–145
  social, 134–140, 145–155
Epidemiology, 246
Episiotomy, 215
Erickson, E., 42
Errors, Types of, 257–258, 319
Ethics
  and informed consent in children, 127
  of aversion therapy, 68
  of experimentation, 10, 25, 65, 68, 162, 179
  of medical training, 315
Ethnocentrism, 215
Ethology, 171–172
Experimental design, *see* Research methods
Expectations
  and context, 8–9
  and diagnosis, 9, 11–12, 19, 195, 304
  and experimentation, 19–21
  and personality, 19–20, 200
  and physical appearance, 11
  and placebos, 21, 292–293, 295
  and socialisation, 147
  and surgery, 21
  in society, 132–134, 146–148
  of ill people, 147–148
  of pain, 281, 282
  of sex roles, 187, 189–193